The Unthinkable Revolution in Iran

THE UNTHINKABLE REVOLUTION IN IRAN

CHARLES KURZMAN

HARVARD UNIVERSITY PRESS
Cambridge, Massachusetts, and London, England

First Harvard University Press paperback edition, 2005

Library of Congress Cataloging-in-Publication Data

Kurzman, Charles.
The unthinkable revolution in Iran / Charles Kurzman.
   p. cm.
Includes bibliographical references (p.) and index.
ISBN 0-674-01328-X (cloth)
ISBN 0-674-01843-5 (pbk.)
1. Iran—History—Revolution, 1979.
2. Protest movements—Iran.   I. Title.
DS318.8.K87 2004
955.05′42—dc22   2003056907

Designed by Gwen Nefsky Frankfeldt

Contents

Preface

Iran first entered my consciousness, as it did many Americans', when U.S. diplomats were taken hostage in 1979. A quarter-century has passed, and I still recall my outrage. I remember participating in an anti-Iran rally with some of my high school classmates. In rush-hour traffic outside a mosque, we waved placards that read, "Honk if you hate the Ayatollah." Lots of drivers honked. They probably did not realize—I know we didn't—that the mosque was Saudi affiliated, that almost all Saudis and Iranians were of different sects within Islam (Sunni and Shiʿi), and that the Islamic governments of Saudi Arabia and Iran were mutually hostile. I was quite embarrassed when a teacher later pointed this out to me. As I started to learn about Iranian history, I realized how misguided our reference to "the Ayatollah" had been, given that there are many ayatollahs, and that Ruhollah Khomeini—our target—no longer carried this title in Iran. In 1978, during the revolution, he came to be referred to as "Imam," a unique title that set him apart from other high-ranking Shiʿi Muslim religious scholars. Continued reference to "the Ayatollah" in the West was a sign of ignorance or hostility.

Since that time I have studied the Persian language, visited Iran, and met and worked with untold numbers of Iranians. Although I have shed some of my ignorance, I still see the Iranian Revolution as a "deviant" case. It imposed the first Islamic republic in recent times, and it remains the only instance of a mass Islamic revolt. Indeed, the Iranian Revolution was one of the most popular upheavals in world history:

10 percent or more of the Iranian population participated in the demonstrations and general strike that toppled Shah Mohammad Reza Pahlavi. By comparison, less than 2 percent of the population participated in the French Revolution, and less than 1 percent participated in the overthrow of Soviet communism.

The Iranian Revolution is deviant in an academic sense as well. According to social-scientific explanations for revolution, it shouldn't have happened when it did, or at all. These theories lead us to expect sullen quiescence in the face of the monarchy's armed forces, or scattered protest in light of the radicals' lack of resources, or various other scenarios. The more we learn about the details of the revolution, the more evidence we find that resists existing explanations.

In particular, we discover an atmosphere of overwhelming confusion. As protest mounted against the shah, Iranians had no idea what was going to happen. Would the shah's regime fall? Would protest be suppressed, or peter out? Iranians polled friends and strangers ceaselessly to find answers to these questions, yet the answers careened unpredictably. In such momentous times, Iranians could not even predict their own actions, much less those of their compatriots.

This book examines the experience of confusion that was so widespread during the Iranian Revolution. The analysis is limited to the period up to February 11, 1979, when the shah's regime was overthrown. But the implications of this study may reach beyond that date, and beyond the uniquely deviant circumstances of the Iranian Revolution. If my analysis is correct, then mass protest is truly unpredictable, not just in advance but also retroactively. The vale of confusion that accompanies such phenomena washes out all attempts to link preconditions with outcomes.

On its twenty-fifth birthday, is the Islamic Republic of Iran about to face a revolution of its own? Will other regimes in the Middle East, or elsewhere, undergo mass upheaval? Does the overwhelming military might of the United States government inoculate it against protest, either in its overseas occupations or in the homeland? These questions would remain unanswerable, even if we had perfect information about the attitudes and intentions of everyone involved, which of course we do not. We can only guess at the future. We cannot know how people will act in a situation of confusion until it is upon them. Massive change cannot be known in advance, but only as it is happening. Widespread knowledge of change is part of the change itself. People sense that something big is occurring, and their responses help shape the event.

This conclusion may sound abstract, but it has real political consequences. If we want to change the world—and who doesn't?—then we are marching boldly toward a situation of confusion, the moment when old patterns begin to be disrupted and new ones take their place. For change as significant as a revolution, we cannot know in advance who will cling to the old ways and who will embrace the new. All that remains is to pursue the goal for its own sake, because we consider it the right thing to do. All we can do is try to make the unthinkable thinkable. That is what Khomeini did. Whether or not we agree with his goals, we can learn from his pursuit of them.

The Unthinkable Revolution in Iran

CHAPTER 1

Introduction

In just one hundred days, protests would bring down the Iranian monarchy. Demonstrations would multiply into the millions. Strikes would spread and shut down the economy, including the oil industry that propped up the regime. Shah Mohammad Reza Pahlavi, on the throne for thirty-seven years, would flee Iran, only to be replaced by a caretaker government that would last just thirty-seven days before it, too, was chased into exile. A revolutionary regime would come to power, headed by Imam—known in the West by his earlier title, Ayatollah—Ruhollah Khomeini.

But in October 1978, this drama was hard to foresee. A seemingly stable regime, led by a monarch with decades of experience, buoyed by billions of dollars in oil exports, girded with a fearsome security apparatus and the largest military in the region, and favored by the support of the world's most powerful countries—how could such a regime fall?

The U.S. Central Intelligence Agency, whose business it was to know such things, reported innocuously on October 27 that "the political situation is unlikely to be clarified at least until late next year when the Shah, the Cabinet, and the new parliament that is scheduled to be elected in June begin to interact on the political scene." During the previous month, the U.S. Department of State had suggested that the shah would weather the current storm of protest, though without "the same position of unquestioned authority he formerly enjoyed." The Defense

Intelligence Agency offered its prognosis that the shah "is expected to remain actively in power over the next ten years."[1]

At the end of October, the U.S. embassy in Tehran—despite standing orders to "emphasize the factual rather than the analytical"—began to wonder aloud whether this episode might unfurl differently. On October 30, the political officer John D. Stempel drafted a report to Washington stating, "for the first time in two decades, serious coffee-house thought is being given to other possibilities" besides the shah's rule. Some of the shah's supporters, he concluded, are "'thinking the unthinkable' for the first time." On November 9, Ambassador William H. Sullivan adopted the phrase "thinking the unthinkable" as the title for a memorandum that nearly cost him his job: "it is probably healthy," he wrote, "to examine some options which we have never before considered relevant."[2]

The U.S. government was receiving similar information from a variety of channels. In August, the Iranian ambassador in Washington surprised the U.S. national security adviser by suggesting that the shah was in trouble. In October, State Department officials were startled to hear two longtime academic specialists on Iran debate whether "political events in Iran could be likened more to an avalanche ([Marvin] Zonis) or to a raging forest fire ([James] Bill)." In early November, a U.S. consul reported major disaffection among Iranian military officers in Tabriz, an important provincial capital, and was reprimanded by the U.S. ambassador for "rumor-mongering."[3]

As it turned out, the White House did not like to think the unthinkable. President Jimmy Carter, whose human rights campaign did not extend to Iran, was shocked by Sullivan's report and canceled his appointments for the day. Soon he concluded that Sullivan was overly pessimistic and therefore not to be trusted with the mission of saving the shah's regime. Carter wanted to fire the ambassador, and was only dissuaded by the secretary of state's insistence "that it would be a mistake to put a new man in the country in the midst of the succession of crises that we probably [face]."[4]

Unlike the U.S. government, the Iranian oppositionist Mehdi Bazargan had no desire to see the shah maintain his power and cannot be accused of wishful thinking. He had struggled against the dictatorship for decades, always peacefully, and had suffered repeated imprisonment as a result. In April his house had been damaged by a bomb, presumably planted by the shah's security police, near which was found a note: "This is your first warning from the Underground Organization for Vengeance."[5] Yet Bazargan too considered the revolution "unthinkable."

On October 22, Bazargan met with Khomeini in a villa outside Paris, where Khomeini had just moved after fourteen years' exile in Iraq. They discussed the strategy of the revolution. Bazargan's goal was to convince Khomeini that the opposition should take up the shah's offer of free and fair parliamentary elections the following summer. With this legal basis and public tribune, Bazargan argued, the movement could then turn methodically to capturing executive power. He called this his "step-by-step" plan.[6]

Khomeini would hear none of it. The revolution will succeed completely, and soon, he insisted. But the Americans will not allow this, Bazargan protested. Khomeini responded: "America will not oppose us, because we speak the truth." Bazargan tried to lecture Khomeini on the ways of the world:

> The world of politics and the international environment are not like the clerical circle of Najaf and Qom, where logic and truth may be sufficient. We face a thousand difficulties and problems, and they will crush [our] schemes and plans. They won't surrender just because we speak the truth.

Bazargan saw that he was getting nowhere. Khomeini "considered the case closed and rejected. He said, 'When the shah has gone and I have returned to Iran, the people will elect parliamentary representatives, and then a government.'" Bazargan was flabbergasted. Khomeini's "indifference to and heedlessness of the obvious problems of politics and administration grieved me." At the same time, he recalled, "I marveled at and admired his seeing things so simply, his quiet certitude that success was near."[7]

Bazargan ceded to Khomeini's leadership. He returned to Tehran and gave up on his step-by-step plan—even turning down the prime ministership when the shah's officials offered it to him in mid-November, in jail. "It's too late," he told them. But it was only a few weeks too late.

Before his meeting with Khomeini, he might have jumped at the opportunity.[8]

In the next one hundred days, the U.S. government tried and failed to organize a military coup on the shah's behalf, over Ambassador Sullivan's objections of futility. Khomeini came to power, appointing Bazargan as his first provisional prime minister. The revolution that seemed so unlikely only a few months before came to pass.

What do people do when they are surprised? According to the sociologist Harold Garfinkel, they seek to reduce their anxiety about a world that seems out of control by assiduously generating explanations that make the world make sense again. Breaches in the fabric of routine need to be sewn up.[9] After the Iranian Revolution, those who had considered the upheaval unthinkable became preoccupied with understanding how they could have been so mistaken. Mehdi Bazargan concluded that he had misjudged U.S. support for the shah. Quoting Jimmy Carter's American critics, he argued that the United States had abandoned the shah and allowed the revolution to occur. The U.S. government also engaged in a self-critique. The Central Intelligence Agency commissioned a still-classified review of its performance even before the shah fell. Over the next few months, a congressional subcommittee faulted intelligence gatherers and policy-makers for not heeding warning signs; an internal State Department analysis argued, "we were unprepared for the collapse of the Pahlavi regime because we did not want to know the truth"; and a partisan debate emerged over who "lost" Iran.[10]

The social sciences make a profession of this sort of second-guessing. They take unexpected events and try to make them less unexpected after the fact. Explanation is a matter of *retroactive prediction:* had we known A, B, and C ahead of time, we could have seen the event coming. Notice that this is different from actual prediction: A, B, and C are frequently not known ahead of time, but only after the fact. And this is not to say that history is the sort of apparatus in which causes lead automatically to outcomes. Human action always retains a healthy streak of unpredictability. Nonetheless, explanations are evaluated by how well they reduce this residual element: a successful explanation leaves little to chance and free will; a less successful explanation leaves more. Social scientists may never achieve retroactive prediction, but they aspire to it.[11]

The more unexpected the event, the greater the effort needed to make sense of it. Protest movements pose particular difficulties because they intentionally challenge the expectations of routine social behavior. Predicting these movements retroactively is thus one of the greatest quests in social science: to discover the regularities underlying irregularity—the rules underlying behavior that flouts the rules. Among the most dramatic rule-flouting events are those massive protest movements that manage to take over the state and earn the title of "revolution," the greatest of which are able to defy explanation for generations. Indeed, this may be a measure of their greatness. The French Revolution of 1789, the quintessential revolution, has attracted academic attention like a hypnotic Rorschach test for more than two hundred years. Each generation returns to it and projects new meaning upon it, expresses dissatisfaction with older explanations and devises new ones.

The Iranian Revolution of 1979 may also prove, by this criterion, to be great. Despite a language barrier and evidentiary difficulties that limit Western scholarship, the Iranian Revolution has already, in less than one generation, offered observers at least half a dozen faces. Each chapter of this book will address one of these explanations and examine its application to a particular phase of the revolutionary movement.

The problem with these explanations is that they leave a residual of evidence that just doesn't fit. For example, the shelfful of documentary collections recently published by the current government in Iran—though no doubt intended to solidify the regime's own, cultural explanation of the revolution—chronicles a host of events that don't fit the framework. Rather than attribute this deficiency to the incomprehensibility of Iranians, or postpone it for consideration by the proverbial "future research," I'd like to incorporate unpredictability into an "anti-explanation."

Anti-explanation is an attempt to understand the experience of the revolution in all its anomalous diversity and confusion, and to abandon the mirage of retroactive predictability. Anti-explanation begins by comparing the lived experience of the event with the main explanations offered by studies of revolution:

Political (Chapter 2): Revolutions occur when a regime relaxes its pressure and offers opportunities for successful mobilization. In Iran, the monarchy's repression relaxed somewhat in 1977. But the Islamists in Iran began their mobilization only after the shah rescinded his liberalization late in the year.

Organizational (Chapter 3): Revolutions occur when oppositional groups are able to mobilize sufficient resources to contest the regime's hold on the population. In Iran, the Islamists mobilized the nationwide "mosque network" against the regime. But the mosque network was not a preexisting resource for the Islamists and had to be constructed and commandeered during the course of the mobilization.

Cultural (Chapter 4): Revolutions occur when a movement can draw upon oppositional norms, ideologies, beliefs, and rituals in a society. In Iran, the revolutionary movement drew upon Shi'i Islamic themes and practices. But it modified these cultural elements, sometimes drastically, to make them conducive to protest.

Economic (Chapter 5): Revolutions occur when economic problems worsen, especially after a period of relative prosperity. In Iran, the oil boom of the mid-1970s gave way to a troubling recession in 1977. But this recession was no more severe than previous ones, and the groups that suffered the most were not the most revolutionary.

Military (Chapter 6): Revolutions occur when the state's repressive capacity breaks down and is unable to suppress protest. In Iran, the shah did not use the military to crack down definitively. But the military did not break down; it continued to repress protests actively up to the last moments of the revolution.

These snippets are, of course, simplifications, and this is not an exhaustive list—nor could it be, since the demand for academic novelty makes social scientists infinitely creative in devising new explanations. I've lent my hand, too, in a minor way, to this enterprise. But I've come to share the discontent of certain historical researchers who wonder aloud about "chaos theory," "not-so-inevitable revolutions," and the anti-explanatory implications of "revolutionary process."[12] I can't help thinking about the evidence that doesn't fit the explanations, especially the individual stories that can't be reduced easily to sweeping statements about entire populations.

Mahmud, for example—not his real name—was a thirty-year-old car mechanic living near Tehran during the revolution. He went to many of the large demonstrations. As one demonstration was dispersing, people whispered to one another about a follow-up protest: "Hey, buddy, tomorrow at 8 A.M., Such-and-Such Square." As it happened, Mahmud was planning to take his children into the hills near town for a picnic and some exercise, so he disobeyed the call. "I was religious, but not blindly religious," he explained. That picnic saved his life. The demonstration he missed was fired upon by security forces as protesters staged a peaceful sit-in in Zhaleh Square. The event came to be known as "Black Friday." Almost a hundred people were massacred. When I interviewed Mahmud eleven years later, he recalled his near-martyrdom with a touch of awe, tinged with guilt. "It was just luck," he said.[13]

By contrast, Hossein Akbari, a young engineer in Tehran, came home one afternoon at the end of the revolution and told his wife that Khomeini had ordered everyone into the streets. The military was still attempting to resist the revolution, and hundreds of people had already died that day. "I tried to stop him from going," his wife recalled. "He said, 'I'm no different from the others, am I? My blood's no redder than theirs, is it? You should be proud if martyrdom is my destiny.' He comforted me and left." After a long night of building roadblocks, Akbari was shot and killed.[14]

Shaykh Morteza Ha'eri, a prominent religious scholar in the seminary city of Qom, so feared state retaliation that he tried to usher protesters out of his mosque. He told them he sympathized with their grievances against the regime, but not with their method of expressing grievances publicly. "I know that steps must be taken, and I am taking them," he told the protesters. "But this sort of thing—my view is that it must be peaceful, not in such a way that they will do in the ʿAzam Mosque, too, like the Fayziyeh Seminary" (see Chapter 3).

None of the usual explanations for revolution can account for all these incidents. Mahmud's attitude is at odds with cultural explanations that emphasize obedience to religious leaders in Shiʿi Islam, the predominant branch of Islam in Iran. Akbari's insistence on risking his life conforms to cultural explanations, but it runs counter to political explanations that stress the weakening of the state and the opening of opportunities for protest. Haʾeri's nervousness adheres to a political-opportunity explanation but doesn't fit organizational arguments that attribute the revolution to a cohesive and oppositional mosque network. The more I learned about the Iranian Revolution, the more theoretical anomalies I discovered.

Men and women found themselves caught up in circumstances they recognized as historic, facing moral and political choices they knew they would replay in their minds for the rest of their lives. "One day of revolution equals twenty years of normal life," one interview respondent told me, citing John Reed's famous book on the Russian Revolution, *Ten Days That Shook the World*.[15] The choices made on these days—to prefer a picnic to a protest, to risk martyrdom, to protect one's mosque from state attack—were improvisations thrown together in situations nobody thought possible.

The unthinkability of revolution extends to this individual level. Even hard-core revolutionaries, firm believers in their movement's ultimate success, were surprised at the "unexpected speed" with which the movement was progressing. Other Iranians were all the more shocked by the sudden historicity of their lives. "A year before," a leading feminist recalled, "I heard news about demonstrations, but I didn't feel that it was something very important. That is, I thought, well, something is happening, but I didn't think that it would bring about a basic change in my country. Later, in September 1978, at the start of school, when we began classes, everything had changed. All of a sudden, the feeling arose that things weren't that way anymore."[16]

Things weren't that way anymore—this is the essence of the revolutionary experience, and the confusion of such moments differs from the ordinary uncertainty that characterizes huge portions of our lives. Arguably, each section of the daily newspaper is dedicated to one aspect of institutionalized uncertainty, that is, an arena in which we expect not to know what will happen tomorrow: news, sports, business, style. We're used to dealing with this sort of uncertainty. We know what it means to bet on sports or stocks or to "keep up" with the latest news and styles. To the extent that the rules of the game stay relatively constant, we expect the unexpected. But when we sense that the rules of the game are suddenly changed, and we no longer know what to expect, that is confusion. To attempt a more formal definition: confusion is the recognition of deinstitutionalization, that is, the breach of routine social patterns.

Before this breach, people cannot predict how they will respond to situations that they are hard-pressed to imagine. Risks that seemed gallant in the abstract come to appear less attractive. Unlikely heroes rise to the occasion. In Iran, self-described "fanatics" who had pledged to give their lives for the cause told me they turned and ran when security forces arrived. Bystanders who had not been particularly engaged in politics suddenly became enraged upon "hearing about or participating in events in which government forces treated people with violence and injustice" and resolved not to rest "until the Shah and the government that did such inhuman things to their fellow Iranians no longer existed."[17]

This changeability contradicts one of the dominant premises of contemporary social science, namely, the stability of preferences. If people maintain relatively unchanging patterns of likes and dislikes, they will learn about themselves over time and therefore be able to estimate their behavior in any hypothetical situation. This may be the case for routine situations, but not for revolutions. During the course of the Iranian Revolution, preferences changed radically and quickly. One reason for these changes, a reason that gets mentioned over and over in the testimony of protesters, is the emergence of options that were previously dismissed as unthinkable. "A friend has told me how a group of professors at the University of Tehran decided to form a society for freedom of speech in November 1978," the sociologist Said Amir Arjomand reported. "Within two weeks they realized they were so overtaken by events that they changed the formal purpose of their society to the abolition of the monarchy and establishment of a republic."[18]

When new options emerge and get taken seriously, protesters testify, it's almost always someone else's doing. That is to say, people were constantly guessing at the likelihood that other people would take to the streets, or go on strike, or demand the overthrow of the regime. The willingness of other people to engage in protest shaped the context in which people decided to participate themselves. "Everyone was there," a student from Tehran recalled, explaining his own participation in the revolutionary movement. "There were so many people. If it was just a small demonstration, I didn't go. But those huge demonstrations—fear had no meaning then."[19]

This may sound circular: protest movements attract participants through increased participation. But participants don't know ahead of time exactly what is going to happen. At the moment they decide to protest, or not to protest, they can't be sure how many other people are going to join in. The decision is made in a context of hearsay, rumor, conflicting predictions, and the intense conversations that surround breaks from routine behavior. These conversations help to assure people who are considering doing something strange and dangerous that other folks will go along.[20]

Much of the experience of revolution, then, seems to focus on the question of viability: does the opposition movement appear to have a chance of unseating the regime? When Iranians answered "yes," they joined the movement in huge numbers. Only then did they begin to consider the monarchy illegitimate. Only then did they testify to the power of Islam. Even Khomeini, in exile in autumn 1977, ordered his followers to mobilize only when he considered the movement to be viable, basing his judgment on reports—mistaken, as it happens—of large demonstrations mourning the recent death of his son. A few thousand Khomeini supporters agreed that the people were "ready" and began to look for pretexts for protest. But most Iranians didn't consider Khomeini's movement to be viable until the following autumn, and they ignored his calls for mass uprising until then.

Revolution may seem—retroactively—inevitable. Yet we must remember that observers and participants don't know this at the time. As one Iranian newspaper columnist noted in the final days of the revolution: "In Tehran, conversations are limited to this: how will the revolution, which has gone half-way, deal with the fundamental power of the government? Will [the government] resign? Will there be a fight? And how far would fighting go?"

Recapturing this experience of confusion is the essence of the anti-explanation of revolution presented here. Ultimately, I don't believe social scientists will ever be able to predict revolutions, since the revolutionaries themselves don't know what is going to happen, and their behaviors are responses to this confusion. All that is left to social scientists, after the fact, is to examine the mindset of the moment. But this is nothing to sneer at. It is a challenging endeavor to sift through the evidence and try to understand what was going through people's minds in a particular place, in a particular context, in dramatic historic times.

CHAPTER 2

The Emergence of Protest: Political Explanations

1977

In 1976, Jimmy Carter campaigned for the presidency of the United States on a platform that emphasized the promotion of human rights. Carter, a religious man, felt that the United States had a moral duty to protect rights around the world, even in countries fighting against Communism. Addressing the Democratic Party convention, he spoke of the "unique role" of the United States in the world and called for an "unceasing effort to preserve human rights": "To all people I say that after two hundred years America still remains confident and youthful in its commitment to freedom and equality, and we always will be."[1]

The shah of Iran, a Cold War ally of the United States, was concerned about Carter's rights campaign. The shah made it a point to monitor U.S. politics, had known five U.S. presidents during his long reign, and prided himself on his savvy navigation of Washington's political currents. If Carter's concern for human rights were directed at Iran, it might jeopardize the warm and supportive alliance the shah had built with Carter's predecessors. The shah's rule, by his own admission, was based on the idea that Iranians were not ready for rights and needed strong and capable tutelage for the foreseeable future. "There is a limit to the speed with which men and nations can develop in freedom," the shah wrote in 1960, especially in Iran, where "the majority of our people are still illiterate" and "the Western concepts of parliamentary democracy and political parties remain new to us." The opposition's demands for political rights, he wrote from exile in 1980, "were in reality nothing more than demagoguery that would result in a caricature of democracy such as has been seen so often in discredited multi-party systems."[2]

If Iranians gained the right to free speech, they might criticize the fabulous wealth that the shah and his family were embezzling from the country's oil revenues. Billions of dollars flowed into the Pahlavi Foundation and other privately controlled shells. If Iranians gained the right to a fair trial, judges might decide that peaceful opposition to the shah's policies was not grounds for arrest, torture, and execution.[3] If Iranians gained the right to fair elections, they might select a parliament that challenged the absolute power of the shah.

When Carter won the Democratic nomination for president, the shah grumbled privately that "the USA is controlled by the Jews," and that Carter's concern for the rights of Iranians was due to "this same influence." After the revolution, the shah and his supporters blamed Carter for arranging his ouster. "Liberalization with a gun pointed at one's head," the shah wrote, instigated a "heedless, pell mell rush toward anarchy." The director-general of the French intelligence service was convinced that Carter "decided to replace" the shah. The United States "took the Shah by the tail, and threw him into exile like a dead rat," according to one of the shah's generals. A survey of Iranian expatriates in Southern California found the leading explanation for the revolution to be foreign plots, as did a recent survey in Isfahan. Iranians hostile to the revolution appeared to feel more comfortable blaming outside forces than their own compatriots.[4]

Conspiracy theories such as this have a long history in Iran. Since the beginning of the twentieth century, many Iranians have attributed their country's fate to the machinations of the Great Powers. "The educated Nationalists seemed to feel," British reporters observed in 1910, "that the issue of the struggle depended neither upon the efforts of the Shah nor upon those of his enemies, but upon the actions of the British and the Russian Governments. Wherever one went brilliant talk reigned upon the subtler points of British and Russian diplomacy." Not all conspiracy theories are misguided: the Russians and British *did* support the Iranian coup d'état of 1911; the British *did* support the Iranian coup d'état of 1921; and the United States *did* support the Iranian coup d'état of 1953. There is documentary evidence of this.[5]

Still, it is a strange thing to have participants and longtime *supporters* of a revolution claim that they did not witness history in the making. One such denial came from Ahmad—not his real name—an Iranian man I interviewed in Istanbul, Turkey. Ahmad had long been active in the religious opposition to the shah. By day he worked in an office building in the center of Tehran. By night he and four childhood friends clandestinely copied and distributed open letters and cassettes from Khomeini. They couldn't operate in mosques, because most clerics were opposed to such dangerous activism. The only reason the revolution succeeded, Ahmad said, was that Carter came to office. According to Ahmad, the shah spent $4 billion opposing Carter's election—an outrageous exaggeration—and Carter never forgave him. Sure, Carter and the shah traded state visits and mouthed pleasantries for the record. Everybody remembers Carter's famous toast to the shah on the eve of 1978: "Iran, because of the great leadership of the Shah, is an island of stability in one of the more troubled areas of the world. This is a great tribute to you, Your Majesty, and to your leadership and to the respect and the admiration and love which your people give to you." Carter was lying, Ahmad told me. Carter wanted the shah thrown out, and he brought Khomeini in to do the job—not realizing that Khomeini was righteous and divinely inspired and would turn out to be so powerful.[6]

Ahmad's analysis puzzled me. The academic in me demands the presentation of plausible evidence, and Ahmad had none. Moreover, I wondered why Ahmad, and others like him who still felt warmly toward the revolution, would attribute its success to Jimmy Carter. Perhaps they did not think of themselves as history-makers. When applying for jobs, Iranians don't present themselves in the tidy terms of a résumé; in literature, they don't have a long tradition of autobiographical testimony; in political discussions, many believe the conspiracy-theory dictum that history always happens elsewhere. Visible events such as demonstrations and strikes, in this view, are merely symptoms or distractions. History gets made "behind the curtain," in the Persian phrase.

But if Ahmad and other Iranians were conspiracy-minded, then that should have shaped their decision to participate in protest. If they suspected that Carter hated the shah, they may have tried to take advantage of the opportunity. If they believed that the U.S. human rights campaign was tying the Iranian government's hands in its dealings with oppositionists, they may have felt freer to protest. I asked Ahmad, "So did you feel safe as a result of Carter and human rights?"

He answered: "No." With this one word, Ahmad rejected one of the most important theories of revolution in contemporary social science.

––––––––––

In the late 1970s, as revolution grew in Iran, prospects for revolution faded in the West. The protest movements of the 1960s, which some feared and others cheered as precursors to revolutionary transformation, had splintered and dissipated. The decline of Western social activism in the 1970s led to serious soul-searching on the left. One movement veteran has speculated, "perhaps what had scarred us even more than the Sixties themselves was their failure . . . their disappearance into thin air." The collapse of these movements "left not only political wreckage but a spiritual and psychological crisis," another former activist has written. "Those who had banked on a political revolution that turned out not to be imminent wanted relief from the imperious superego that beat at them saying, It is you yourselves—your will, your commitment, your politics—who failed."[7]

One way to relieve the imperious superego was to argue that failure was the fault not of the activists but of unconducive conditions. This form of explanation epitomized the new turn in the study of revolution and protest movements, which was taken over by a generation of academics who had themselves participated in and supported the activism of the 1960s. The student movement, for example, did not fail because of its "inefficiency and bungling," one sympathetic sociologist wrote in the late 1970s; "it was inefficient and bungling almost from the start, but that made no difference." Movements, he concluded, "succeed or fail for reasons other than the ability of their leaders, their federated or centralized structure, their use or rejection of violence."[8]

A leading candidate for unconduciveness was the state. Protest movements and revolutions succeed, according to this perspective, only when the state has been weakened somehow—usually by international pressure. This hypothesis formed part of an academic movement that came to be known as "bringing the state back in," and its major pioneer was a Harvard sociologist named Theda Skocpol. Her doctoral dissertation, published in 1979, examined three great revolutions—France in 1789, Russia in 1917, and China in 1949—and asked why they succeeded while others had failed. Skocpol began by dismissing the importance of revolutionaries in the study of revolutions: "In the first place, an adequate understanding of social revolutions requires that the analyst take a nonvoluntarist, structural perspective on their causes and processes." Instead, she argued, international pressures caused certain states to collapse, creating crises that were then exploited by revolutionaries. "The doors were swung open for the expression of popular discontents," Skocpol wrote of the French Revolution. "It was the breakdown of the concerted repressive capacity of a previously unified and centralized state that finally created conditions directly or ultimately favorable to *widespread* and *irreversible* peasant revolts against landlords." This approach drew implicitly on the precedent of the nineteenth-century French intellectual Alexis de Tocqueville, whose analysis of the French Revolution also focused on the state's lifting of restraints, among other factors: "When a people which has put up with an oppressive rule over a long period without protest suddenly finds the government relaxing its pressure, it takes up arms against it."[9]

In the 1980s, Tocquevillean analyses became the norm in the study of revolutions and protest movements. For revolutions, Skocpol's focus on state breakdown was central. For other social movements, the concept of "political opportunity structure" played an analogous role. The sociologist Doug McAdam's influential book on the U.S. civil rights movement, first published in 1982, brought this term into widespread usage: "The opportunities for a challenger to engage in successful collective action," McAdam argued, "vary greatly over time." These variations are "related to the ebb and flow of movement activity"; the "crucial point," he stressed, is that the political system can be more open or less open to challenge at different times.[10]

Numerous academic observers of the Iranian Revolution aligned themselves with this approach. Indeed, the popularity of structural analysis survived even Skocpol's defection. This episode reversed the usual relations between theory-builders and area specialists in social science. Typically, area specialists criticize theory-builders for not knowing enough about a particular region: the theory may explain things elsewhere, but it doesn't work in *our* area of expertise. Three years after publishing her book on the French, Russian, and Chinese Revolutions, Theda Skocpol tried to preempt such criticism by admitting that her analysis didn't work well for the Iranian Revolution. The Iranian state was *not* weakened, she wrote; it was under *little* international pressure; and it broke down only *after*, not before, widespread protest emerged. Many area specialists, however, rejected these modifications and continued to apply her theory, on the grounds that the Iranian Revolution "fits more than she acknowledged, the patterns Skocpol identified in her book." The political scientist Hossein Bashiriyeh, for example, quoting Tocqueville, argued that liberalization under international pressure "was a major and immediate factor in the regime's disintegration of power." The economist Jahangir Amuzegar, also quoting Tocqueville, argued: "Contrary to the belief that revolutions do not occur in a vacuum, it was precisely the political vacuum created by the regime that attracted the opposition like a powerful magnet."[11]

These explanations imply that the Iranian opposition took heart from Carter's human rights pressure and the shah's limited liberalization, and responded with increasing activism. Did it?

The liberal opposition in Iran was little more than a supper club. It had once held power briefly, in the early 1950s under the nationalist prime minister Mohammad Mossadeq, but the movement had sputtered into virtual dissolution after a coup ousted Mossadeq in 1953. By the early 1970s, the movement consisted of a handful of writers and lawyers with no organization and no desire to build one. At a meeting in March 1977, on the occasion of Mossadeq's birthday, a writer thanked the host: "I hope this will continue forever, and next year will be just like this." "Of course," replied the host. "In any case, this is the result of your pen's work." The company then exchanged similar compliments all around, apparently unaware of the irony of this small band congratulating itself on having met for a meal.[12]

In the context of repression so severe that a supper club could not consider itself immune, Carter's human rights campaign made a considerable stir. In January 1977, as Carter was taking office, the Iranian author 'Ali-Asghar Hajj-Seyyed-Javadi published a long open letter to the shah's court, criticizing the government and calling for reforms. A fellow liberal oppositionist recalls: "Some people were saying, 'Why haven't they seized and killed Hajj-Seyyed-Javadi?' . . . If he had written the letter five years earlier, they would have seized him and thrown him in prison. If they didn't kill him they would at least have thrown him in prison." In June 1977, three liberal oppositionists published a shorter open letter calling for the respect of constitutionalism and human rights. "If we had done this a year and a half ago," one of the signers commented at the time, "we would have been in Evin [Prison]." Later in June, another open letter marked the revival of the Writers Association. "The government wouldn't dare jail all of us in the present climate on human rights," said one of the forty signers. In October, liberal oppositionists formed an "Iranian Committee for the Defense of Human Rights." One of the founders "suggested it was the belief that torture is no longer practiced which explains the readiness of people such as himself to speak out and sign letters as they have over the past year."[13]

In summer 1977, liberal opposition groups began to organize semipublic protest meetings that the security forces treated relatively leniently. A small gathering outside the Tehran bazaar in August was dispersed without the use of force. A larger prayer meeting with oppositional overtones was allowed to proceed in September, and another in early October. Ten consecutive nights of sharply worded poetry readings in mid-October saw no government crackdown, drawing audiences in the thousands to the Iran-Germany Association in Tehran.[14]

The new leniency was also expressed in laws and royal edicts requiring indictment of suspects within twenty-four hours of arrest; allowing defendants in security tribunals to choose civilian counsel; opening trials to the public and international observers; and guaranteeing that defense attorneys would not be jailed for their efforts, among other things. The authorities began to send political prisoners, especially demonstrators, to civilian instead of military courts. Prison conditions were improved a bit.[15]

These reforms were limited in scope and not always applied in practice. Peaceful demonstrations, for instance, continued to be put down forcibly. In an incident that weighs heavily in leftist accounts of the revolution, shanty-dwellers in the south of Tehran, protesting the destruction of their homes in August 1977, were attacked and arrested. Relatives of political prisoners held a demonstration outside Tehran in early October and met a similar fate, as did protesters at several student demonstrations. Opposition figures continued to be arrested, including twenty-five religious scholars in mid-1977, the most prominent being Ayatollah Mahmud Taleqani, a senior religious leader and longtime liberal opponent of the regime, who was sentenced to ten years in prison in August 1977. Reports continued to emerge of the torture of political prisoners. The atmosphere of apprehension did not disappear overnight. A prominent oppositionist lawyer explains why he did not write an open letter in early 1977, though he would have liked to: "In 1977 . . . we believed that the authorities would not kill us for this sort of activism, but the risk of going to prison, the risk of problems being created at work, the risk of restrictions on my family—I took these to heart."[16]

These risks increased dramatically in November 1977, when the shah visited Jimmy Carter in Washington. Outside, the visit did not go smoothly. The police tear-gassed anti-shah demonstrators across the street from the White House, and the fumes wafted to the South Portico, where the shah and the president stood with their wives, crying from the chemicals.[17]

Inside, however, they dried their tears and got down to business: oil, the world economy, arms sales, the Cold War—but hardly rights. In the ten months since Carter had taken office, State Department officials had been at pains not to press the human rights theme too strictly on Iran. One official testified before Congress, for example, that human rights in Iran should be evaluated "in the light of local sociological, economic and historical considerations. Fortunately," he added, the shah's and "our basic political/strategic interests are very similar." Another official emphasized the "gratifying trend" of "significant and important developments in the field of human rights in Iran in the last year or so." When the shah came to visit in November 1977, Carter's signature theme was not on the agenda and only got raised in the president's brief remark in a private session: "You have heard my statements about human rights. A growing number of your own citizens are claiming that these rights are not always honored in Iran." The shah defended his record and Carter let the matter drop. The White House then released a statement indicating that the two men had reviewed the positive steps Iran was taking on the matter of human rights, and the shah recalled in his last autobiography, which was generally hostile to Carter, that the talks "had gone well."[18]

Even as the shah arrived in Washington, his regime's partial tolerance of oppositional activity was disappearing. Peaceable oppositional meetings were no longer immune from state repression. A poetry reading at Aryamehr Technical University in Tehran on November 15 was banned as the hall filled; the students already inside occupied the hall and refused to leave until they were assured of a safe exit. It took all night, but the head of the university finally received the assurances from the security forces. As the students left, they were attacked anyway. Several days later,

> more than 350 riot police wearing U.S.-made helmets and armed with wooden truncheons invaded Tehran University and battered students indiscriminately, according to witnesses. About 65 persons, including four professors, were injured and 100 students arrested. The attack came hours after the shah returned here from Paris, where he stopped after the U.S. visit.

The next week, a group of moderate oppositionists gathered in a private garden in Karaj, near Tehran. Busloads of "club-wielders" charged into the garden, breaking arms and fracturing crania. For good measure, they also smashed the cars parked outside. Four oppositional academics were arrested and beaten in late 1977, and the house of one was attacked.[19]

The opposition could not help noticing the chilling of the political atmosphere. "Following the shah's visit to Washington," the liberal critic Mehdi Bazargan told U.S. diplomats several months later, "repression again seemed the order of the day." "After returning from his visit to America," an opposition group agreed in a pamphlet in late 1977, the shah "threw himself into a new course intended to seek revenge against the insurgent people of Iran and freedom seekers." Even U.S.

diplomats noted the change. The embassy in Tehran reported that the Iranian government "clamped down rather severely in late November," and an internal State Department memorandum noted in December that "recent events in Tehran have made it clear to all of us that the Iranian Government is substantially increasing its use of force in dealing with political opposition."[20]

The liberal opposition responded prudently. It ceased all public protests, at least for the moment. Several liberal groups were founded during this period, but their activities were confined to the issuing of a handful of statements. Even such limited activism as this, one oppositionist noted at a press conference in January, was "very likely to bring about difficulties and restrictions for us." "Under present conditions," a liberal told his colleagues the same month, "we are keeping watch and keeping silent." The liberals do not appear to have been proud of their prudence. Some blamed other liberals for fearing a "severe response on the part of the government" and for worrying too much that "they'll arrest us all." After a particularly rancorous planning meeting in early 1978, one liberal oppositionist recalled, "this political movement was halted."[21]

Khomeini, in exile in Iraq, was aware of the shah's steps toward political liberalization. In a speech in September 1977, he noted that "a certain opportunity [for protest] has been found, and it is to be hoped, God willing, that good opportunities will arise." But Khomeini sounded almost despairing of the possibility of taking advantage of such opportunities. He began with an apology for having repeated himself in an earlier lecture: "When humans get old and senility overtakes them, all of their faculties grow weak. Just as their bodily powers grow weak, their mental powers, spiritual powers, the ability to pray, and the quality of prayer also grow weak." Khomeini appeared to recover his enthusiasm as he continued, but he hardly sounded like a man who expected to lead a revolution: "With all this prostitution [both literal and figurative], the good people of Iran are not saying anything. I don't know why they're not saying anything . . . When are they going to speak out and say something and protest?"[22]

Bolder elements within the liberal opposition were in fact speaking out and protesting, and in October there were several small Islamist demonstrations as well. Khomeini apparently became aware of the liberals' activity around this time. In a speech of November 1, 1977, he emerged from several days of seclusion, prayers, and tears following the sudden death of his eldest son. Khomeini seems to have taken heart from this oppositional activity:

> Today in Iran, an opportunity has appeared. Make the most of this opportunity . . . Now, [oppositional] party writers are stirring. They are making critiques. They are writing letters and signing them. You too should write letters. A hundred gentlemen of the clergy should sign them . . . Inform the world. You can't reach the world from inside Iran; send [your letters] outside the country for them to be published, or send them here somehow, and we'll get them published. Write critiques, write about the troubles, and give it to them [government officials], like the few people who we've seen stir and speak out at length and sign their names. No one's done anything to them . . .
>
> This is an opportunity that must not be lost, and I am afraid that this little man, the shah, is bringing his accounts into harmony with them [the Americans]. Even now they are busy settling accounts . . . God forbid that this should succeed, and that he [the shah] should consider his footing firm. This time is not like the previous times. This time will cause major damage to Islam.

Khomeini also struck a note of relative powerlessness: "While all the pens and all the activities and all the publicity are against us, our hands are tied. We have produced nothing. By this I mean that we have no publicity and no means of publicity, no radio to spread our words, no publications." Still, tracing the history of Islamic activism in Iran over the past century, Khomeini appeared to be optimistic about the limited opportunities generated by liberalization, and he encouraged the clerical opposition, following the liberal opposition's example, to write open letters to the government and to international organizations.[23]

For a brief interlude, if this speech is any indication, the Islamist opposition may have felt that international pressure could lead to a genuine liberalization. As Ayatollah Hossein Montazeri, one of Khomeini's top followers, later recalled, "We didn't expect Carter to defend the shah, for he is a religious man who has raised the slogan of defending human rights. How can Carter, the devout Christian, defend the shah?" Similarly, Ja'far Salehi—then an activist seminary student, now a *hojjat al-Islam* ("proof of Islam," a scholarly ranking just below ayatollah)—recalled that "the situation in 1977 was not as suffocating as before, and the country was living in what they [regime officials] called an open political atmosphere. On the order of then-President Carter of America, they had planned a safety valve for the feelings and beliefs of the people." Other clerical activists, however, have rejected the influence of Carter's human rights campaign. The prominent revolutionary Hojjat al-Islam Mohammad Javad Bahonar, for example, sounded a strident note in claiming that "nothing good for us could come from America. We never had any hopes or expectations that something positive could come from America." Hojjat al-Islam Hossein Vafi, a seminary student in the late 1970s, argued that "liberalization only opened the mouths of certain university and clerical individuals, but did not spur the [revolutionary] movement." At the time, a group of Islamist activists issued a pronouncement deriding the regime's "half-hearted political liberties" and noting that "in the last six months alone, more than thirty Iranian activists have been martyred in the streets at the hands of security hirelings."[24]

On November 12, 1977, Khomeini's third proclamation of this period sounded skeptical of the genuineness of the "opportunity" Khomeini had made much of on November 1:

I am compelled to warn the people against a great danger in order to save the nation from the deception and tricks of foreigners and their functionaries. This recent inattentiveness of the regime that gave a chance to the writers to write and to the speakers to talk is a big trick to vindicate the shah and to pretend an acclaimed freedom, and to attribute the crimes to the administration, which is nothing but a stooge. Writers also cannot, in this repressive and intimidating atmosphere, introduce the center of the crimes, i.e., the shah himself . . .

[The shah wants to] secure his position by meaningless and limited freedom, and thereby prepare the atmosphere for continuation of his rulership, and once again begin his savage attack with much more atrocity and disaster . . .

Now, it is the duty of all Muslims, especially that of the great *'olama'* [religious scholars] and intellectuals . . . to take advantage of the opportunity to tell and write everything that should be said to the international authorities and other human societies . . .

I emphasize that worthy and responsible individuals who hold the initiative avoid making themselves known, and learn from past experience.[25]

As before, Khomeini recommended writing to international authorities. Now, however, he called liberalization "a big trick" designed to divert criticism away from the monarchy. This diversion may have been working. Richard W. Cottam, an American professor close to the Iranian opposition, testified at the time that liberal oppositionists in Iran were less outspoken than dissidents in the Soviet Union; according to an Iranian leftist, the open-letter campaign had criticized only particular policies, rather than the regime itself, before November 1977. Khomeini's final cautionary remark, urging "worthy and responsible individuals" to "avoid making themselves known," suggests that Khomeini did not consider his followers to be safe from repression. Perhaps he feared a crackdown scenario like the Hundred Flowers in China, which were allowed to bloom briefly before the thaw froze over. Khomeini reiterated this position four days later in a message to supporters outside Iran, referring to the "temporary opportunity that has appeared" in Iran but calling the writings of the opposition "limited and hypocritical" and urging his supporters to "take the initiative with complete caution and clear-sightedness."[26]

Despite the increasing suspicion of political liberalization evident in this speech, it was at this moment that Khomeini's followers inside Iran began to mobilize. I have not yet seen a letter from Khomeini ordering a mobilization, though according to various sources such a letter was written in 1976, spring 1977, or December 1977. It seems odd that post-revolutionary collections do not include this document, but whether or not the smoking gun exists, Khomeini's followers clearly began to mobilize at the end of 1977. Several mid-level followers of Khomeini reactivated the Society of Qom Seminary Instructors, a group that had been dormant for a half-dozen years, and decided to meet every other week. The Society of Struggling Religious Scholars of Tehran started to issue pronouncements and organized itself into neighborhood committees.[27]

The open letters of early 1977, foundational events in liberal accounts of the Iranian Revolution, scarcely appear in the official accounts written by the Islamist movement that came to power in 1979.[28] In the same way that it suppressed liberal hopes for Iran's future, the Islamist government also suppressed liberal versions of the past. Suppression extended even to the name given to the past: the Islamic Republic of Iran refers to the "Islamic Revolution," specifically to exclude liberal participants and aspirations. But the Islamist account contains an element that the other accounts do not. In November 1977, as the shah ingratiated himself with Jimmy Carter, liberals were in retreat. Only the Islamist opposition chose this juncture to gear up its activism.

This mobilization did not move in the paths trod by the liberals and tolerated briefly and partially by the shah's reforms. Open letters to international organizations, for example, played only a small role in the Islamists' campaign. One letter was planned in late 1977, on the occasion of an upcoming visit to Iran by Kurt Waldheim, the secretary-general of the United Nations. Seyyed Hasan Taheri Khorramabadi, a mid-level seminary instructor in Qom, was responsible for rounding up signatures among religious scholars. "Not everyone was willing to put their name under just any pronouncement," he recalled. "In many instances, such an act had resulted in arrest and prosecution." Khorramabadi was able to gather a fair number of signatures, he said, but by the time Waldheim arrived in January, subsequent events had made the letter "moot," and it was never sent or publicized.[29] Rather, the Islamists engaged in the one form of mobilization that the shah had never allowed: street demonstrations. The regime consistently met these demonstrations with force.

The moment that triggered demonstrations was not good news from Washington but bad news from Iraq. On October 23, 1977, Mostafa Khomeini, Ruhollah's eldest son and chief aide, died suddenly in exile. He was in his mid-forties and in prime health, according to the Islamist account, and must have been assassinated by the shah's notorious security police, SAVAK.[30] Unsympathetic rumors have also suggested that the cause was a long-standing heart condition or some other, unspeakable illness.

As soon as the news reached Iran, devout Muslims organized mourning ceremonies in the major cities. Mostafa was a respected religious scholar—hojjat al-Islam, or even, according to Khomeini's supporters, an ayatollah—and his father was one of the five or six most senior ayatollahs in Shiʻi Islam. But the significance of the ceremonies went beyond the religious credentials of the family. The Khomeinis' political credentials, their long-standing opposition to the monarchy, and their exile gave the mourning for Mostafa a political cast. "Even mentioning the name of Imam Khomeini meant six months in prison," Khomeini's followers noted, perhaps with some exaggeration, in an anonymous pamphlet published several months later. Some supporters referred to Khomeini by his Persian initial, the letter "khe," a seminary student recalled. In Qom, mourners initially "refrained from mentioning the name of Imam Khomeini, and thus the martyr was not named explicitly." One speaker referred to "he whose name rhymes with Kuleini," a participant recalled. (Muhammad al-Kuleini was a Shiʻi theologian of the tenth century, still influential in the twentieth.) A seminary student, rejecting such caution, pulled his cloak over his head for anonymity and started a chant of "Hail to Khomeini." Part of the crowd took up the chant, and the service dissolved into disorder, according to a SAVAK report. After some time, the service continued. Now prayer leaders were emboldened to speak the name of the deceased. In Shiraz, too, the prayer leader failed to mention Mostafa's name until a midranking religious scholar in the audience—who happened to be the prayer leader's cousin—called out to him, "Tell the audience the reason for organizing this service."[31]

The security police in Yazd, in southern Iran, expected trouble at the memorial service for Mostafa. Officers warned the city government to take precautions to prevent the commemoration from turning into a political demonstration. Apparently they succeeded—five consecutive days of services were held, but there are no reports of protests. In other cities, mourners held ceremonies in defiance of official bans, though most avoided open political statements. In Mashhad, where the ceremony was held despite a ban, a speaker praised the Khomeinis, father and son, and was immediately arrested. Officers in Ahwaz stood by just in case, keeping watch and maintaining radio contact with headquarters. In Tehran, a speaker announced that "if, God help us, the shah goes to heaven, we don't want to!"[32]

In Shiraz and Tabriz, mourners broke further political taboos. They spilled out of the mosque into small demonstrations, led by devout students. "Death to the shah," they chanted—possibly the first moment in the revolution that this slogan was raised.[33] A SAVAK memorandum described the scene in Shiraz:

> [The speaker] declared, "Oh God, accept the sympathy of those present, who have gathered in this ceremony, for the passing of this descendant of the Great Messenger. Accept our condolences and sympathy for the Seyyed far from his homeland [a euphemism for Khomeini]." Everyone said, "Amen." Then he said, "Oh God, return the refugees far from their homeland to the homeland, and liberate the captives." At this point the ceremony came to an end. As the people began to leave, some shouted slogans in front of the door: "Hail to Khomeini! Upon Khomeini be peace!" At this point, the mosque door was shut by several city officials, led by Mr. Zu'lqadr. The crowd in the courtyard grew frightened. Some people were outside the mosque, the rest inside the courtyard. Outside the mosque they were shouting "Hail to Khomeini!" Inside the courtyard they took up the slogan again, "Hail to Khomeini!" A large number of women wearing black veils on their heads, who were leaving the Molla Mosque by the women's door, saw the officials in front of the mosque beating a few [protesters] and raised the slogan, "Death to the shah!" The slogan was taken up inside and outside the mosque.[34]

At commemorative services in the Arak Mosque in Tehran, a speaker not only named the deceased—huzzahs went up from the crowd—but also professed loyalty to the deceased's father. He did this in an unusual way, by referring to Khomeini as imam—an unprecedented and highly charged title alluding to the twelve imams, male descendants of the Messenger Muhammad, who are held by Shi'i Muslims to have been divinely selected for leadership of the Muslims. Twelver Shi'is—the dominant branch in Iran—believe that the Twelfth Imam, Abu'l-Qasim Muhammad, went into a state of "occultation," or hidden-ness, in the ninth century, and will return one day as a messiah to establish the reign of Islam under his just rulership. Calling Khomeini imam introduced connotations of messianic deliverance, though his followers did not go so far as to suggest that he was, in fact, the messiah. A handful of writings by Khomeini's adherents had begun to use the title imam, but this was probably the first time it had been spoken publicly.[35]

The novel title upended the traditional hierarchy of Shi'i religious authority. For the past several centuries, religious authority had followed from scholarship. A scholar gained titles and authority through recognition of his (rarely her) intellectual achievements—first by his teachers, who granted permission to teach; then by his peers, who granted a certain title (for example, in the twentieth century, ayatollah); then by his followers, who adopted him as a "source of imitation" *(marja'-e taqlid)* out of respect for his great erudition. Khomeini had passed through these phases by the mid-1970s. But the title imam placed him above the other sources of imitation, and it did so more for his political leadership than for his scholarship. The other sources of imitation resented this inversion of the hierarchy. Several of them in Qom refused to attend one series of mourning ceremonies, according to a SAVAK report, because "the religious speakers were going to call Ruhollah Khomeini the undisputed source [of imitation] for the Shi'i world and the abovementioned ayatollahs construed this as an insult to themselves, and refrained from attending the ceremonies." The following week, merchants at the Tehran bazaar commemorated Mostafa's death by striking, ignoring a recommendation by the elderly Ayatollah Seyyed Ahmad Khansari to open their shops.[36]

The shah's clampdown three weeks later did not deter Khomeini's followers. Rather, they became *more* politically active. On December 2, further mourning ceremonies were scheduled in Qom for the fortieth day after Mostafa's passing, and this time the Islamists were prepared. In the intervening weeks, they worked to raise consciousness among seminary students in Qom. Bazaar merchants began to hear rumors that the fortieth would be observed with strikes and protests. On the fortieth day, speakers stood at a microphone, not at the pulpit. They gave overtly political speeches, not simply eulogies—speeches that were taped, copied, and sold around the country. They presented a fourteen-point resolution to the mourners for approval by acclaim. The resolution called for the return of Khomeini from exile, the release of political prisoners (Ayatollahs Taleqani and Montazeri were mentioned by name), the re-opening of religious and university institutions shut for their oppositional activity, the protection of freedom of speech, the banning of pornography, the right of women to wear *hejab* (modest clothing, usually interpreted in Iran to mean headscarfs), attention to the plight of the poor, economic independence from international capitalists, the ending of relations with Israel, and the return of the Islamic calendar, abrogated in favor of an "imperial" calendar several years earlier. "That's right!" the mourners chanted as each demand was read out. These resolutions fell far short of demands for the replacement of the monarchy by an Islamic republic, but they represented the Islamists' first concerted entry into the political field in more than a decade.[37]

After the ceremony, a crowd led by young clerics started to march toward the Fayziyeh Seminary, which had been closed by state authorities in 1975 after student demonstrations. "Hail to Khomeini, Death to the shah," they chanted. Security forces beat the demonstrators and fired in the air, but the streets were so full that they were unable to disperse the crowd. In the early evening, after more services, another demonstration ensued, and again protesters chanted provocative slogans. They smashed eight bank windows and a police kiosk, and managed to climb the walls of the Fayziyeh Seminary, but security forces caught them and beat them with sticks and clubs. Twenty-eight were arrested. The leaders of the protest were exiled to remote towns. In mourning services the same day in Khomeini's hometown of Khomein, the speaker called Khomeini imam and was promptly barred from preaching.[38]

Three weeks later, on December 20 and 21, the Islamists organized demonstrations around the country, turning the annual religious processions of Tasu'a and 'Ashura into political demonstrations. In Tehran, thousands marching out of the grand bazaar waving banners with antiregime slogans were attacked and arrested by the authorities. In nearby Shahr-e Rey, the mosque area was surrounded by police, who watched as the ceremony continued. The participants stuck to the traditional proceedings, but during refrains shook their fists at the police and city officials. At the end of the year, Parviz Sabeti, the director of internal security for the monarchy's security police, reviewed the activities of "religious fanatics" and their allies in a lengthy memorandum that made clear he considered "clerical extremists" to be the most active and threatening wing of the opposition:

These activities appeared in the form of raising street demonstrations, shouting anti-national slogans, burning a number of liquor stores, breaking the windows of a number of cinemas and bank branches, distributing dangerous pronouncements, giving oppositional and inflammatory speeches, and carrying placards and banners with inflammatory slogans on the two above-mentioned days [Tasuʿa and ʿAshura], and similar seditious demonstrations in the country's higher-education environs over the past month.[39]

Islamist activists were ready for further mobilization. In December 1977, activists in Qom now shared an optimistic "spirit" and felt that "something could be done," one of their leaders recalled. According to a merchant activist, they asked one another: "What will be our next excuse to arouse the people against the regime?" An excuse would soon arrive.[40]

If revolutions were like pressure cookers, exploding when the lid is lifted, we would expect the steam to start coming out of the opening. Instead, the Islamists' aggressive demonstrations were directed at the part of the lid that *hadn't* been opened. But if the Islamists weren't obeying the constraints of liberalization, why *did* they mobilize in the fall of 1977? Their comments at this time suggest that they were paying more attention to public opinion than to state reforms.

Khomeini and his followers had long sought to overthrow the Iranian monarchy and to institute an Islamic republic, but even the most ardent revolutionaries did not think this would be feasible for decades. In the wake of the suppressed protests of 1962–1964, Khomeini and other religious radicals decided that the country was not yet ready for Islamic revolution. As Khomeini stressed in his 1970 lectures on Islamic government, the ground needed to be prepared:

> It is our duty to work toward the establishment of an Islamic government. The first activity we must undertake in this respect is the propagation of our cause; that is how we must begin . . . We must propagate our cause to the people, instruct them in it, and convince them of its validity. We must generate a wave of intellectual awakening, to emerge as a current throughout society, and gradually, to take shape as an organized Islamic movement made up of the awakened, committed, and religious masses who will rise up and establish an Islamic government.[41]

As part of this propagation movement, the Islamists founded schools, set up publishing houses, printed journals, and issued thousands of photocopied proclamations, all with the explicit intent of raising consciousness among the people. Khomeini did not believe in 1970 that this work would bear fruit immediately: "Ours is a goal that will take time to achieve . . . We must persevere in our efforts even though they may not yield their result until the next generation." For this reason, the Islamists devoted particular attention to proselytizing among youths.[42]

In November 1977, the Islamists decided that these efforts had succeeded. The protests accompanying the mourning for Mostafa Khomeini were viewed as a sign that the consciousness-raising of the previous decade and a half had borne fruit. Ruhollah Khomeini's message of November 12 inflated these protests into major events, despite the fact that out of a population of more than thirty million, twenty thousand Iranians at most may have participated:

> Such a great demonstration for this occasion was a verbal and active response to the many years of absurdities of this incompetent agent . . . [It was] an indication of hate towards the tyrannical regime [of the shah] and an actual referendum and a vote of no confidence against the treacherous regime . . . The nation—from clergy and academicians to the laborers and farmers, men and women—all are awakened.[43]

This speech was taped and distributed among Khomeini's followers in Iran. They apparently agreed with his assessment. An activist in Qom argued in the following months that "the Muslim nation of Iran has awakened, and no longer swallows the deceit of these songbirds." The younger generation targeted by the clerical revolutionaries had come of age with "unexpected speed," an Islamist leader in Yazd wrote in mid-1978. A historian of the Islamist movement, writing just after Mostafa's death in the fall of 1977, echoed this sentiment: "One must recognize that under present conditions, the Muslim masses have become increasingly conscious of the truths of Islam, and now understand that the Qur'an summons its followers to arm themselves, to be prepared militarily for an armed uprising."[44]

In January 1978, an Islamist leader in Qom commented similarly in a speech to activists: "Our awakened Muslim society, conscious society, [has turned] a hopeful eye to the path of the great leader, the esteemed *marjaʿ* [source of imitation], our *imam,* our *aqa,* his honor the fighting grand *ayatollah,* Khomeini."[45]

The narrative of mass awakening soon became the orthodox Islamist explanation for the outbreak of the Iranian Revolution. Yet it was almost surely inaccurate. Most Iranians were not sufficiently "awakened" at the end of 1977 to join revolutionary protests: until late summer 1978, such protests rarely attracted more than a few thousand participants. Even within the clerical establishment, as discussed in the next chapter, there was less than full-hearted support for revolution.

Accurate or not, the perception was important. The constant repetition of this theme suggests that Khomeini and his clerical followers believed a threshold had been achieved, a threshold that made it plausible to launch a revolutionary movement against an entrenched ruler. This perception of what I call "viability" did not flow from a breakdown of the state, or from political opportunities—indeed, the timing of the "awakening" coincided with the removal of what little political opening the shah had allowed.

CHAPTER 3

Mobilization of the Mosque Network:
Organizational Explanations

EARLY 1978

On January 7, 1978, an afternoon newspaper in Tehran published an insulting profile of Khomeini under a pseudonymous byline. "These days," the article began, "thoughts turn once again to the colonialism of the black and the red, that is to say, to old and new colonialism." The collusion of "the black and the red" was a standard phrase in the Pahlavi lexicon, used to refer to a putative alliance between feudal (black) and leftist (red) opponents of the monarchy's "modernization" project. This alliance went looking for a clerical mouthpiece two decades ago, the article continued, in order to dupe the devout. When the plot "proved unsuccessful with the country's high-ranking scholars, despite special enticements," there was only one man left for the job. "Ruhollah Khomeini was an appropriate agent for this purpose," the article said, a rare reference to Khomeini in the Iranian press since his exile in 1964. "It was said that he had spent time in India and was in contact there with institutions of English colonialism, and this is how he became known by the name 'Seyyed Hindi.'"

The article went on to suggest that Khomeini's opposition to the shah was prompted and paid for by British oil interests. Fortunately, the article concluded, this plot failed, and remained only as an object lesson: "Millions of Iranian Muslims will remember how the enemies of Iran collaborate with one another whenever their interests require them to do so, even in the sacred and respected garb of a cleric."[1]

The newspaper reached Qom, two hours south of Tehran, at dusk on

January 7 and immediately caused a stir. In the evening, seminary students gathered, passed the article around, and handwrote copies to be posted around town—they couldn't afford to buy copies of the paper on their spare student stipends, and photocopying was not safe for oppositionists in Qom. The students added the addendum: "Tomorrow morning, as a protest, meeting at the Khan Seminary." Independently, eight radical scholars, who had only recently re-activated the Society of Qom Seminary Instructors, gathered late in the evening to arrange a collective response to the slanderous article. "Something must be done," a thirty-year-old hojjat al-Islam told his colleagues. "I believe the author of the article wanted to see what the people's reaction would be, and if we don't mobilize, it will mean the regime wins." Two scholars at the meeting proposed that a few minutes in each seminary class be devoted to discussion of the offending article. They were outvoted by those who wanted classes to be cancelled for a day in protest. But these radical teachers controlled only a handful of classes; most seminaries were run by the half-dozen highest-ranking ayatollahs. It was too late at night to ask for their support, so the plotters divided up the task of visiting the ayatollahs early the following morning.[2]

The next morning, students gathering at the radicals' classes learned of the decision to strike. "On the advice of their instructors," one participant recalled, the students "said, 'Let's go and ask the *maraje'* [religious leaders], the theology teachers of the religious circles, what their view is on this article.'" This was a time-honored method in the repertoire of protest in Qom, where any seeker had the right to approach senior scholars and ask their opinion on a pressing issue of the day. But this day's query was no neutral appeal to the expertise of seniority. The radical students knew what response they wanted: they were hoping to pressure the senior scholars into publicly denouncing the offending article and expressing sympathy with Khomeini. Several hundred strong, the students marched from house to house, clashing along the way with police, beating two men accused of being government agents, and breaking some bank windows. The police used a tractor and batons to try to disperse the crowd, but they did not open fire that day, and there were no serious casualties among the protesters. When the students reached their destinations, they sat in the courtyard and waited for each ayatollah to come out and address them.[3]

The senior scholars were hesitant to support open protest. When representatives of the radical teachers came to the home of Shaykh Morteza Ha'eri early on January 8, requesting participation in the strike, he immediately telephoned his senior colleagues. They agreed to strike, but only for one day. When the students came around later in the day, Ha'eri expressed his fear of open protest. "Of course I am very angry about the insult to his honor the Ayatollah Khomeini, and I condemn it in all respects. I know that steps must be taken, and I am taking them. But this sort of thing—my view is that it must be peaceful, not in such a way that they will do in the 'Azam Mosque, too, like the Fayziyeh Seminary"—which had been ransacked and closed following student protests in 1975. Ayatollah Kazem Shari'at-Madari seems to have been similarly cautious. He kept the crowd waiting for more than an hour, then told them: "Before your arrival, I was busy working on this, and I am continuing to telephone, write, send messengers to Tehran, and so on. I continue to work on this. I hope that they [regime officials] will refrain from this sort of insult, and ones like it, but I can do no more than this."[4]

Ayatollah Mohammad-Reza Golpayegani, by contrast, sounded considerably more sympathetic to the protesters: "Maintain your unity and solidarity and continue your peaceful demonstration. You will undoubtedly find success." Some activists were disappointed, however, that Golpayegani also spoke about marginal issues that seemed to cast a trivial light on the offending article: according to one account, he sounded a plaintive note of impotence; "I telegraphed members of parliament [several years ago on another matter], but they didn't pay any attention." Only Ayatollah Shehabuddin Najafi-Mar'ashi, so moved that he cried during his speech, was an unqualified success with the student activists. He too said he had written to Tehran in protest and, pleading old age and heart trouble, asked to be excused from further efforts. But he stated his support for the demonstrators several times, in no uncertain terms, according to a transcribed recording of his speech: "I hope that, God willing, God . . . will add daily to your successes . . .

May God grant your wishes, which shall, God willing, strengthen Islam, strengthen the Qur'an, and strengthen religion, God willing." If these ayatollahs assumed that their comments were being monitored by the shah's security police, they were correct. The Qom branch of SAVAK sent summaries of their main points to Tehran the same day.[5]

The one-day student strike was extended to a second day because activists in the Qom bazaar had organized a shutdown for January 9. Some shopkeepers had closed already on January 8, according to SAVAK reports. One of their leaders approached Hossein Musavi-Tabrizi, a leader of the radical seminarians, and asked how the religious scholars could return to work when the bazaar was shutting down on their behalf. Musavi-Tabrizi later recalled that he wasn't sure the activists could pull off a closure of the bazaar, and it was too late in the evening to gather the seminary instructors group for a second meeting. So he told the bazaari to bring a crowd to his seminary class early the following morning—if enough merchants showed up, he would adjourn class and have his students lead the demonstration around to the other seminaries. The next morning went just as planned, and the news of the bazaar strike was enough to shame the high-ranking scholars into ending their classes abruptly.[6]

The students continued their rounds of the houses of religious leaders, joined by ever-larger crowds of local residents, several thousand early in the day to over ten thousand by late afternoon, according to estimates by both protesters and police officials. Unlike the previous day, the protesters apparently made an effort not to antagonize the security forces. They marched silently to the houses of religious leaders, rather than chanting confrontational slogans, admonishing those who shouted to "observe the silence."[7]

In the late afternoon, security forces set up a roadblock with two trucks outside a police station. When the marchers reached the roadblock, a police commander ordered them to clear the sidewalks. The demonstrators were starting to comply when somebody—the protesters claim it was provocateurs, police officials claim it was the protesters—threw stones through a nearby bank window, providing an excuse for security forces to attack the crowd with batons. At this point demonstrators began to shout slogans, break store windows, and resist the security forces with branches and stones. The officers fired shots in the air, scattering the protesters momentarily, but as the crowd regrouped the police began to level their weapons at the protesters. Clashes continued until 9 P.M.[8]

Five people died in the event, according to a list recently produced by the Center for Documents on the Islamic Revolution, a pro-revolutionary institute that had every interest in inflating the number of casualties. This figure is even lower than the monarchy's official toll of nine, or the estimates of U.S. diplomats, who first reported twenty to thirty dead, then fourteen. The Iranian opposition did not accept these figures. Rumors spread immediately that one hundred or more were killed, and opposition estimates ranged up to three hundred. A small survey in Tehran the following week found that more people believed the opposition's casualty figures than the government's. The opposition charged that large numbers of bodies were trucked away by the government; in addition, fearing arrest or kidnapping, a number of wounded and killed were said to have been kept from hospitals and morgues. This may have been the case, but the lack of documentation in recently published SAVAK files makes it unlikely. Moreover, as one former seminary student has reasoned, it seems implausible that the families of these martyrs would have kept silent about their loss after the rise of the Islamic Republic, which raised the massacre at Qom to the pedestal of iconic heroism.[9]

The tragedy was immediately taken up throughout Iran as an atrocity to be avenged. Within a week, according to U.S. diplomats in the capital, "major" demonstrations had emerged in at least eight cities, and general strikes had been launched, with partial success, in at least three. Opposition accounts spoke of far more widespread protests and typically identified the Qom massacre as a precipitating event—a "heartbreaking tragedy," according to the pronouncement of one group of strikers in Tehran, that served as an "example of the misdeeds of the oppressive regime."[10]

There were 9,015 mosques in Iran in the mid-1970s, according to a report by the Ministry of Endowments, which was responsible for supervising religious and charitable institutions.[11] These buildings constituted a massive institutional network, perhaps the largest civil organization in the country. The "mosque network," linked by religious leaders around Iran, reached into every neighborhood and village, providing spatially and culturally central locations for collective action. It would seem obvious, then, that the mosque network provided the infrastructure for the religiously inflected protest that emerged in early 1978.

Moreover, contemporary academic analyses of social movements urge observers to focus on just such institutional underpinnings of protest. Movements emerge not from rootless and isolated individuals, in the current view, but from institutions that provide the solidarity and resources needed to press collective claims. African-American churches are the classic example in the literature on North American social movements. Not only did these churches provide the civil rights movement with meeting spaces, solidarity, a powerful rhetoric, and fundraising experience, but they were autonomous from white America—the government and other white institutions had no say in who the parishioners selected as their preacher, and no grip on the churches' pursestrings.[12]

Iranian mosques arguably enjoyed a similar autonomy. Unlike the clerisy of Sunni Islam, which is organized hierarchically under the direct control of a state ministry in almost all Muslim-majority countries, religious scholars in Shiʿi Islam raised most of their funds independently, from the devout, and were incompletely incorporated into the institutions of the state. Ironically, the victory of the Iranian Revolution wound up subordinating the mosque network to the state, accomplishing what successive monarchs had failed to achieve. But in the 1970s, the Shiʿi mosque network was available for protest activity in a way that Sunni mosques were not.[13]

Some analyses take the autonomy argument further, contending that the Pahlavi state ignored or tolerated its religious opponents while repressing secular ones severely. In this view—sometimes promoted by secularists seeking to discredit or downplay the religious forces' role in the revolution—the mosque network was left intact while other oppositionist organizations were destroyed. For instance:

The security forces had focused mainly on the college community, civil and military servants, the large industrial organizations, and other middle-class people who were politically concerned. These new [religious] activists were not only unknown to the authorities, but there was additionally no way to cut their lines of communication. Their organization was, therefore, uncrushable.[14]

The single greatest piece of evidence for this position, cited several times in the literature on the Iranian Revolution, is a statement by Mehdi Bazargan, the liberal oppositionist appointed by Khomeini as interim prime minister in 1979: "In spite of the power of the security forces, the mosques and religious centers were sanctuaries where we met, talked, prepared, organized and grew."[15]

Bazargan's statement must be weighed, however, against a large body of evidence suggesting that mosques were considered dangerous places for oppositionists. A teenager from Tabriz, for instance, recalled that he and other protesters went to the mosque because "we could talk there." I asked if that meant there was no fear of the security forces inside the mosque. "Sure we were afraid. We only talked with people we knew. If someone was in the mosque who we didn't know, we didn't talk."[16] A factory worker near Isfahan was asked if he and other oppositionists met in their village mosque. He replied, "Yes, but generally if you wanted to talk [politics] it was in hiding, for the people themselves were against us; when a molla wanted to make a speech, the people opposed it; they were afraid that they [the agents of the regime] would come and burn everything, destroy everything."[17]

Similarly, a student leaving a mosque in Tehran lamented "that the mollas [religious leaders] can not afford to be too explicit in their references, for they would face imprisonment." A follower of Ayatollah Morteza Motahhari in Tehran didn't share oppositionist tracts with many of his friends because he wasn't sure he could trust them. A religious scholar in south Tehran recalled that "activist youths" were driven out of the mosques, "which fell into the hands of traditionally pious people who were either unaware of the movement issues or too fearful to step into the vanguard of the movement." A popular anecdote in Iran described a class of religious students with undercover agents in their midst. The cleric tells his students to untie their turbans and then to tie them up again. The agents are unable to re-tie their turbans and are thus identified.[18]

Religious scholars echoed these fears. One ayatollah in Tehran apparently requested that American embassy visitors park several blocks away, and that they not identify themselves over the phone, on the assumption that SAVAK—the security police—had him under surveillance. A religious scholar in Qom grew to fear a government trap and stopped going to women's houses for his "temporary marriages" (a legitimate contractual relationship in Shi'i Islam). Another religious scholar, in conversation with an anthropologist, "couched his voice in low, near inaudible tones, when he spoke of tyranny, for he was aware that he might be overheard."[19]

The fear and suspicion reflected in these anecdotes are substantiated by the state's harsh treatment of mosques and the religious opposition. Recently published SAVAK papers document the close attention that the government paid to the mosque network.[20] For example:

> The roving Monday evening Qur'anic study class met at 7:30 P.M. on October 26, 1974, in the house of Hajj Mohsen Rafiq-Dust, which is located in Khorasan Avenue at Ziba Avenue, across from the 'Attar Girls' School, with Dr. Seyyed Mohammad Beheshti present. Approximately one hundred people attended this session, most of them youths between twenty-five and thirty years old. After the evening prayer and supper, Dr. Beheshti translated and analyzed verses seventy to seventy-seven of Chapter 3 of the Qur'an. During his discussion, he explained in Qur'anic terms the characteristics of hypocrites and how to breach the opposing lines and break their spirit.[21]

Islamist activists, like their secular counterparts, were known to the authorities, arrested, exiled, tortured, and killed by the Pahlavi regime. In an article published several years ago, I compiled a partial listing of more than six hundred religious scholars who had received such treatment in the 1970s. In addition, during the last year of the monarchy, the government stormed, shelled, or otherwise attacked more than two dozen religious buildings.[22] In June 1978, for example, demonstrators in Shiraz found that a mosque was no protection against the security forces. One eyewitness recounted, "The soldiers poured into the mosque. They burned the motorcycles that were in the mosque courtyard. They dragged the people who were trying to escape outside. 'We didn't do anything,' they kept saying but the police put handcuffs on them and threw them into the trucks anyway. I saw this with my own eyes."[23]

State repression kept all but the most committed Islamists from daring to protest. Non-revolutionary religious scholars had cleansed the manuals of Islamic obligations of all hints of activism, according to one radical Islamist. Even the famous Qur'anic subject of "bidding good and forbidding evil," often used as the basis for clerical activism, had disappeared from the manuals and "came to be seen as quite superfluous . . . no longer worth discussing . . . [and] irrelevant to the times." Khomeini's son Ahmad complained after the revolution that most religious scholars had preferred to remain silent on political matters, hanging the shah's picture in their mosques and keeping their complaints to themselves. "They observed religion outwardly, and they were also devout," Ayatollah ʿAli-Akbar Hashemi-Rafsanjani recalled after the revolution, but "if we had been pious like these gentlemen, like those who declared struggle unlawful, today this very same university [of Tehran] would have remained . . . a filth-house, as well as the streets . . . radio, television, the government—all would have remained filthy."[24] Allameh Mohammad Taqi Jaʿfari-Tabrizi criticized such quietists in a private lecture in 1975, quoted in a SAVAK report:

> Among the pious, there are those who believe in the hidden, who pray, people who are always deep in thoughts of the hidden, who are consumed with a law that has no external [real-world] existence. [They say,] "We must not permit people who wish to apply these laws in the world, where they have no sovereign existence." . . . [But] the pioneers of history never rejected struggle. All of their efforts were for the existence [of the law in the world], and for them this was holy.[25]

Ayatollah Mohammad Beheshti attributed the failure of seminary student protest in 1975 to the lack of "enlightened leadership" in the religious establishment. In the 1960s, after Khomeini's exile, religious leaders told more junior scholars to keep quiet and not expose the seminaries to further repression, one activist later recalled. In an interview in the mid-1970s, an anthropologist writes, one leading religious scholar of Qom said "that he doesn't enter politics. In fact, he stressed that he allowed no political discussions in his schools, his classes, his mosques, and even among his followers."[26]

Repression was not the only problem for the Islamist radicals. Many of the leading clerics had theological as well as pragmatic reasons for refusing to challenge the regime. The replacement of the monarchy with an Islamic republic led by a single religious scholar—Khomeini's goal—was a novel view, not widely shared by other senior scholars, as discussed in the next chapter. Indeed, some senior scholars were willing to cooperate with the monarchy to develop religious-education materials that would teach obedience to the regime.[27]

This is not to say that non-revolutionary scholars were entirely pleased with the shah's regime. They had numerous grievances about secularization, foreign influence, state control of religious institutions, and "the entire trend of Iranian society," according to a social scientist who interviewed several religious scholars in 1974. Religious scholars "protested frequently against the un-Islamic actions of [successive] governments," though none of them demanded the ouster of the monarchy until Khomeini, according to a preacher who was barred from the pulpit for his outspokenness. In 1973–1974, an American anthropologist interviewed eighteen religious scholars and found "a definite posture" of opposition to the state's repressiveness and intrusions into the field of religion. In 1977, just a year before the revolution, the sociologist Said Amir Arjomand interviewed two dozen high-ranking religious scholars and found considerable grievances, expressed almost entirely in reformist terms. As late as December 1978, with the revolution in full swing, Ayatollah Kazem Shari'at-Madari—one of the most prominent religious leaders in Iran—told reporters that the overthrow of the Pahlavi dynasty was not necessary: "What we have in the [1906] constitution is enough, if it is implemented." The 1906 document set up a constitutional monarchy with veto-power oversight by a panel of religious scholars.[28]

As the Islamists stepped up their revolutionary mobilization, some religious scholars tried to distance themselves from clerical activism. One preacher, for example, told a SAVAK agent that the protests of December 1977 were the work of police provocateurs: "In my view, this is a political ploy. The government has a strategy in this game. One of the reasons demonstrations were held throughout the country may have been to show America that if we give freedom in this country, the result is that the stability and security of the country is shaken—to justify a crackdown and the lack of freedom."[29]

On several occasions, senior religious scholars all but ushered demonstrators out of their mosques. Shaykh Ha'eri in Qom tried to convince student protesters at the 'Azam Mosque not to demonstrate for fear of government retaliation. In March, Hojjat al-Islam Morteza Aba'i told those gathered for a mourning ceremony at the 'Azam Mosque:

> Considering that the mischief-making agents [of the government] are planning to take advantage of demonstrations [and] slogan-shouting, it is requested of the respected gentlemen that they give the enemy no excuse and refrain from any sort of demonstration, either during the ceremony or afterwards. Given this advice, anyone who takes such steps is not one of us.[30]

In July 1978, Ayatollah Hossein Khademi of Isfahan urged relatives of political prisoners to leave his house: "Dear respected sisters, I implore you to end your sit-in and hunger strike and return to your homes. Rest assured that if, God forbid, the aforementioned acceptance of your demands proves illusory, you can come back to me."[31]

Whereas politically cautious religious scholars were in charge of the mosque network, younger, revolutionary Islamists were not generally in positions of control as the revolution broke out. Khomeini was in exile, though he maintained a role in the Qom religious establishment, contributing to students' modest stipends. Many of the other senior activists were sidelined in other ways. Ayatollahs Mahmud Taleqani and Hossein Montazeri were in jail; Ayatollah Mohammad Beheshti had stopped teaching because of his repeated arrest. The majority of clerical revolutionaries were of middle-rank or lower. Among teenaged seminary students, the most active segment of the Islamist movement, only 40 percent were politically involved on the eve of the revolution, according to the estimate of a seminary activist.[32]

Moreover, each act of protest further shrank the ranks of the Islamists. As an anthropologist describes his interview with a religious scholar in Tehran in the mid-1970s, "It was his opinion that it was better to be vague in relationships between mosques because of the difficulty which existed between Islam and the government. The less organization there is, the more difficulty the government has in its coercive powers upon Shi'ites." After the protests of December 1977, for example, five of the most active mid-level scholars in Qom were exiled to small towns in distant provinces. The exiles were virtually lost to the movement—activists in Qom knew what cities they had been sent to but had no contact with them, and didn't even have their addresses, according to a seminary student who was sent from Qom to locate several exiles and get their signatures on a petition. When Islamists convened the Society of Qom Seminary Instructors in early January, in an attempt to mobilize the mosque network, they had only eight participants, and at least one of them—Nasser Makarem—"was a friend of Mr. Shari'at-Madari and could not be counted as an activist." At least thirty-seven more mid-level scholars were exiled from various cities in the first half of 1978, including Makarem.[33]

The mosque network, in other words, was not controlled by the Islamists at the outset of the revolutionary movement. It was controlled by more cautious senior scholars who had to be convinced to join forces with the radicals. "Everybody has got to strike," one militant religious scholar told another in Mashhad in February. "We can't just strike by ourselves."[34]

Revolutionary Islamists sought to commandeer the mosque network. They did so, beginning in late 1977 and early 1978, through three strategies, each of which was designed to convince their more cautious clerical colleagues that opposition to the revolution would be more costly—in moral, public-relations, and even physical terms—than support. These strategies convinced the moderates that the revolutionary movement was viable enough to be allowed into the mosques.

The primary tactic was to challenge senior scholars publicly, in effect embarrassing them into a more revolutionary position.[35] Khomeini spoke repeatedly on this theme. For instance, in 1971 he declared, "I consider it my duty to cry out with all the strength at my command

and to write and publish with whatever power my pen may have. Let my colleagues do the same—if they consider it proper, if they regard themselves as belonging to the nation of Islam, if they consider themselves to be Shi'a—let them give some thought to what needs to be done."[36]

The Qom protest of January 1978 was largely played out on this theme. One of the most contested aspects of the newspaper article that touched off the protest was the suggestion that Khomeini was alone among senior religious scholars in opposing the monarchy. Marching to the houses of senior scholars, radical students demanded to hear their views on this topic. The senior scholars apparently felt compelled to comply. Even non-revolutionary clerics such as Ayatollah Shari'at-Madari offered words of respect to Khomeini and sought to present themselves as active critics of the offending article. Ayatollah Golpayegani went even further: "They [regime officials] lie when they say we are in agreement with their actions. The religious scholars are all in opposition."[37]

After the killings on January 9, the non-revolutionary ayatollahs issued even more pointed statements. Still, however, they focused on the tragedy and not on the legitimacy of the state; they called for mourning ceremonies but not for political protests.[38] Khomeini responded from exile with a somewhat backhanded compliment:

> The great *maraje'* [sources of imitation] of Islam in Qom have expressed themselves courageously both in their speeches and in their [written] declarations, including the one they issued two or three days ago on the occasion of the fortieth day after the massacre and the general strike ordained for that day, and they have stated who is responsible for the crime—not explicitly, it is true, but by implication, which is more effective. May God keep them steadfast.[39]

This dynamic continued throughout the year of revolution: radical Islamists challenged reformists and pressured them with public invitations to join the revolutionary movement, with the reformists being pulled somewhat reluctantly along.

A second tactic of the revolutionaries was to expose themselves to state repression, thereby radicalizing the moderates. For example, almost all the senior religious scholars called for restraint in the fortieth-day mourning ceremonies for the January killings in Qom. As Ayatollah Shariʿat-Madari said in an open letter, "It is our expectation that the Muslim public will maintain complete dignity and calm in the observation of the aforementioned ceremonies."[40]

In the northwestern city of Tabriz, however, radical Islamists refused to remain calm. As mourners arrived for a memorial service at the central mosque, they found it locked and guarded by police. A crowd gathered, quickly turned hostile, and overran the police, then set about trashing banks, liquor stores, and government buildings. Many opposition sources admit that the crowd—more specifically, radicals within the crowd—initiated the violence. The first stone may have been cast by Mohammad Tajala, a twenty-two-year-old university student and follower of Khomeini, who was then shot and killed. Most university students in the city, it should be noted, were busy with separate protests of their own that day at the Tabriz University campus. The state reacted with a massive application of force, bringing in troops and tanks from nearby bases. As in Qom in January, official and opposition casualty counts differed widely: the government admitted to fewer than ten deaths, while the opposition claimed five hundred. Recent pro-revolutionary reviews of the event, however, have stated definitively that the total was thirteen dead.[41]

On the afternoon of the Tabriz riot, Shariʿat-Madari heard that his call for calm had been undermined, and he repeated his instructions for a stay-at-home strike: "no sort of convulsive expressions and destructive demonstrations are permissible." Yet as a result of this act of provocation and the ensuing repression, Shariʿat-Madari felt compelled to come out with a statement defending the radicals, whose methods he condemned: "When the government, itself, does not respect the law, and discriminates in its application, what can it expect of others?" This was not good enough for the radicals, who denounced and defrocked Shariʿat-Madari after the revolutionary movement came to power. Among the charges was his criticism of the heroic uprising in Tabriz as destructive.[42]

On several occasions, revolutionaries brought their point home directly, taking sanctuary at the houses of non-revolutionary senior scholars and counting on their protection. Relatives of political prisoners staged sit-ins at Ayatollah Hossein Khademi's house in Isfahan and at Ayatollah Najafi-Mar'ashi's house in Qom; in August, radical Islamists sat in at Khademi's house and Ayatollah 'Abdollah Shirazi's house in Mashhad. These ayatollahs remained somewhat aloof from the revolutionary movement, but they allowed their residences to be used for radical purposes. These sanctuaries were still not immune to state repression; the August sit-in at Isfahan was forcibly ended by security forces.[43]

The radicals' third tactic was to threaten moderate religious scholars with hardball lobbying, reminding them in terms that were sometimes less than respectful that a public image of acquiescence would do little for their popularity. Ayatollah Mohammad Saduqi, a close associate of Khomeini's from his days as a seminary student in Qom in the 1930s, specialized in this form of pressure. After the January massacre, Saduqi traveled to Qom from his home in Yazd to ask the senior scholars' permission to mobilize protest against the regime. They told him to wait for their say-so. In late March 1978, he apparently decided he had waited long enough, for he arranged protests in honor of the martyrs of the previous month. Security forces opened fire on the demonstrators who poured out of Saduqi's mosque, killing twenty-seven, by official count, or more than one hundred, according to the opposition.[44] Thereafter Saduqi was uncompromising. In a letter to Ayatollah Abu'l-Qassem Kho'i in Najaf, he wrote:

Not a single sentence has been heard from your direction expressing your disgust and hatred of these terrible actions [of the state]. Silence in the face of these inhuman acts might be a sign of approval of such treason.[45]

In a letter to Ayatollah Khademi of Isfahan:

People, especially the young, expect the clergy to lead, and the silence of the clergy in response to the people is contrary to their expectation. The recent silence of the clergy has been extremely costly to the clerical community.[46]

In a telegram to the three leading ayatollahs of Qom:

The cruelties of this oppressive regime are beyond what words can say and pens can write . . . The Muslim people of Iran have been awaiting the promulgation of the orders of the great religious leaders, and have been counting the days impatiently.[47]

Such messages may have had some effect. According to a SAVAK report in September, "middle-of-the-road religious scholars" were "expressing their solidarity with the radical religious scholars in order to protect their own position among the devout."[48]

The Iranian Revolution was remarkably non-violent compared with other movements, but verbal attacks sometimes shaded into threats and even physical attacks on non-revolutionary religious scholars. In May, radicals may have threatened Ayatollah Ahmad Khansari and other Tehran religious scholars who had opposed the revolutionary mobilization—though this information is suspect, as the source is a royal official who wished to discredit the opposition. In August, the security police in Mashhad reported that "pro-government religious scholars are opting not to take sides, out of fear of persecution by religious fanatics, or are being forced to participate in their [oppositional] meetings." In September, Ayatollah Shariʿat-Madari met with regime officials and tried to start a campaign for political moderation: "The negative reaction to Shariʿat-Madari's tentative first efforts was so great and so threatening that he has now lapsed into piqued and official silence." Months later, radicals attacked the homes of two pro-government religious scholars in Dezful, and a third was beaten in the streets of Tehran.[49]

By early 1979, when the Pahlavi dynasty fell, non-revolutionary Shiʿi leaders had been silenced or persuaded to join the revolutionary movement. Already in August 1978, the chief of SAVAK complained at a meeting of military commanders that "a complete solidarity has emerged among them. Even the *akhund*s [a disrespectful term for religious scholars] who worked and lived with the system have become oppositionists. The religious scholars who support the state have decided to keep completely silent, and this silence shows their solidarity with the others." In city after city, learned elderly scholars found themselves losing popularity to brasher young politicos: in Hamadan, Ayatollah Mohammad-Taqi ʿAlemi lost out to Ayatollah Asadollah Madani, a less learned but more revolutionary scholar. Ayatollahs ʿAbdollah Shirazi and Hasan Qomi in Mashhad found themselves under the influence of lower-ranking hojjat al-Islams. Ayatollah Kazem Shariʿat-Madari's considerable sway over Tabriz and the northwest of Iran was so weakened, according to a supporter of his, that people "follow anybody who raises the banner of Khomeini." Ayatollah Khademi, "once considered the leading opposition figure in Isfahan, now states that he believes only the Communists can benefit from all this disruption." Losing influence to Ayatollah Jalaluddin Taheri and other radicals, he sank into "despair," decided to "stop attempting to influence events," and "stopped attending [mosque] services." Khomeini's representative in Tehran, Ayatollah Mohammad Beheshti, told activists in Isfahan, "Use Khademi as a symbol, but organize a leadership office yourselves." As for the three senior ayatollahs of Qom, Beheshti bragged, "They are being cooperative. But nobody listens to them."[50] Virtually the entire mosque network was mobilized for revolution: for organizing demonstrations, coordinating general strikes, distributing scarce food, ensuring neighborhood security, and handing out arms in the two final days of the upheaval.

This is the image commonly associated with the mosque network, but it is the image of an end-point, not a starting-point. Indeed, according to the sociologist Mansour Moaddel, the revolution may have been "the first time in their history" that the clerics "unanimously turned against the state." Before the revolutionary movement, the mosque network was not a particularly valuable resource. It was a *potentially* valuable resource that had to be commandeered before it could be mobilized.[51]

CHAPTER 4

Shiʿi Appeals: Cultural Explanations

MID-1978

The fortieth day of mourning for the martyrs of Qom (January 9) was commemorated with public ceremonies that generated protests and further martyrs in Tabriz (February 18). The fortieth day of mourning for the martyrs of Tabriz was commemorated with ceremonies and protests in dozens of cities, generating further martyrs in Yazd and elsewhere (March 28–31). The fortieth day of mourning for the martyrs of Yazd was commemorated with ceremonies and protests in dozens of cities, generating further martyrs in Qom and elsewhere (May 6–11).[1]

This cycle of mobilization—"doing the forty-forty," as one activist flippantly called it—came to a halt on June 17, the fortieth day of mourning for the martyrs of early May. Mourning ceremonies were cancelled. Storekeepers and students around the country observed a one-day strike in honor of the fallen, but there were no public protests and no casualties. "The armed forces and police were stationed everywhere in advance," a liberal opposition newsletter declared two days later, "but the people were well aware of the police's destructive strategy of provocation. They give the dictatorial regime's agents no excuse to intervene."[2] The forty-day cycle ended half a year before the shah was overthrown.

Why did the cycle end? Khomeini's call for a day of mourning on June 17 sounded no less strident than his earlier pronouncements: "Once again we must sit in fortieth-day mourning of those killed in Qom and other cities," Khomeini said on June 10. "Now that the great nation of Iran has consciously risen up . . . let [its leaders] continue the struggle until this regime is overthrown." A few days earlier, Khomeini had commemorated the martyrs of June 5, 1963, with a blistering speech in Najaf, Iraq: "We are all duty-bound to rise up against this person [the shah]. An active uprising, a national uprising . . . I would be the first to take up arms, if I could."[3]

Less militant religious leaders repeated earlier calls for calm. Shari'at-Madari, Golpayegani, and Najafi-Mar'ashi—the three leading ayatollahs of Qom—issued a joint pronouncement specifically instructing mourners to stay in their homes on June 17 so as to prevent further casualties. "I didn't want bloodshed and insisted there be peace," Shari'at-Madari told a reporter, adding that he scheduled the strike for the thirty-eighth day, rather than the fortieth, so that it would not coincide with a religious holiday.[4]

Perhaps the Iranian opposition heeded the moderates' call for calm because moderates had been the best-known casualties of early May. Followers of Ayatollah Shari'at-Madari had been killed in his house in Qom when plainclothes officials burst in. Ayatollah Golpayegani was hospitalized with a heart attack when officials occupied his house and beat his students. Ayatollah Najafi-Mar'ashi was so upset by a similar episode on the same day that he went to London for medical treatment. Secret-police reports attributed some or all of these attacks to the Islamist opposition, but the moderate religious leaders blamed the regime.[5]

Perhaps this victimization gave the moderates' calls for a peaceful commemoration of the fortieth day of mourning a moral authority that their previous calls for calm had not enjoyed. In Ahwaz, for example, religious scholars specifically cited the moderates' appeal in their own plan to "remain in their houses on the aforementioned day and refrain from receiving visitors." A leading scholar in Mashhad used almost the same language, promising to "stay in my house and refrain from receiving the public."[6] Another religious activist also called on Iranians "to remain in their houses," explaining:

> While respect for the martyrs necessitates the holding of memorial services to commemorate and praise their pure souls, we have learned from experience the ways of the despotic and oppressive regime. Any gathering hands

the enemy an excuse so that opportunists may again murder the honorable population. Once again gathering places may be painted with the blood of the sinless and the oppressed.[7]

Even Khomeini's followers, who had little respect for the moderates' political position, called for calm in June. Their statements suggest a strategy of pragmatism. A group of mid-level religious scholars in Tehran, including some of Khomeini's most militant lieutenants, recommended non-confrontation on June 5, the anniversary of the 1963 tragedy: "The religious scholars of Tehran, following the great sources of imitation"—if this were singular, it would mean Khomeini; the plural refers to the more moderate senior clerics in Qom—"announce that, because present conditions in Iran show that the regime intends to produce another June 5 [tragedy], what better way to demonstrate the grandeur and greatness of the historic day this year than with passive resistance. Throughout Iran, people should not go out of their houses at all on Monday, June 5. They should refrain from any type of street demonstration. In the truth of the day's prayers, they will neuter the plans of the tyrannical regime."[8]

A group of Khomeini's most fervent followers—the evidence is in their use of the title "Imam" Khomeini, still in quotation marks because of its novelty—added a postscript to their call for mourning on June 5: "It is requested that order and calm be completely respected." Handwritten anonymous flyers, passing from hand to hand around the country, also called on Iranians to observe the June 5 commemoration by not leaving their houses until 5 P.M. Ayatollah Saduqi, the firebrand of Yazd, also accepted the non-confrontational approach of the senior scholars of Qom, offering this cryptic explanation for his uncharacteristic moderation: "We have received the request of our Muslim brothers that no excuse be handed to the enemy." Perhaps Saduqi and other militants felt that their followers agreed with a bearded street peddler in Qom who told a reporter on June 17, "we have had enough of violence and casualties." Perhaps they believed—despite official denial— that the shah had personally commanded troops to fire on demonstrators in May, and felt that this presaged a major crackdown. Perhaps they were intimidated, a SAVAK report suggested, by the latest round of arrests of religious scholars.[9]

Whatever their motivation, the Islamists came to regret their prudence. A pronouncement soon afterward warned that the regime "judged these nationwide strikes, [conducted] in splendid silence, [expressing] the public's hatred and revulsion [of the regime], as tribute to the dictator. It is announcing the end of the struggles of the Iranian nation, unaware that the nation thus showed that its sole purpose was to choose whatever form of mobilization it considered appropriate for reaching its goal."[10]

In short, pragmatism prevailed over religious duty in June 1978, even for radicals who believed that "respect for the martyrs necessitates the holding of memorial services" and agreed with Khomeini that "we must sit in fortieth-day mourning."

———————

Almost 90 percent of Iranians are Shi'i Muslims; no other country has nearly so high a proportion of Shi'is as Iran. This distinctiveness is frequently cited in cultural explanations of the Iranian Revolution, which suggest that the religion of Iran is conducive to a revolutionary mindset. Shi'ism came to be associated with revolutionary fervor, both by Soviet scholars ("among all the Muslim clergy the Shi'ite clergy is distinguished by its socio-political activism") and Western observers: "Shi'i Islam offered an ideological view of history that gave meaning and legitimation to an opposition movement. Shi'i Islam is a religion of protest with an ideology and symbolism well suited to protest and opposition."[11]

Fortieth-day mourning ceremonies—observed in many Sunni Muslim societies as well—are often cited as evidence that Shi'i Islam is "well suited" to protest movements.[12] As one sociologist has suggested:

[T]here came to be no need for revolutionary leaders to tell the public when and in what form they should demonstrate against the Shah. The cycles of these religious rituals set the exact dates and reasons to engage in protest activities, autonomously contributing to the mobilization of the people against the state. This cycle more or less continued until 1979.[13]

Other authors note:

Just as Hussein is mourned not only on the 10th day of Muharram but also forty days thereafter, it is customary for Shi'ites to mourn the deceased forty days after their death. Those killed in the riots [of January 1978] were mourned publicly forty days later by the multitudes in towns all over Iran. In Tabriz the riot police then fired on the mourners, creating new martyrs, and new cycles of remembrances forty days later. Four times this occurred, generating a chain reaction of mourning demonstrations and shootings, with more and more people participating every 40 days. That procession of events laid the ground for the final assault on the bastion of the Shah's regime.[14]

Clearly there is evidence to support this position. The forty-day cycles helped to broaden the revolutionary movement from its base in Qom to dozens of cities throughout Iran. They carried the movement through the first months of open protest. They provided a culturally resonant structure for mobilization that did not have to be invented from scratch.

But cultural explanations such as these also face evidence that *doesn't* fit. For one thing, they don't account for the *ending* of the forty-day cycle in June 1978, half a year before the shah was forced from his throne. The cancellation of the June mourning ceremonies forces us to question the "autonomous" effect of "customary" cultural practices. These practices, it turns out, weren't automatic. They operated only with the forbearance of cultural brokers—the conflicted community of religious leaders, in this case—who could turn them on or off like a faucet.

Moreover, the cultural brokers had only recently invented the practice of politicized fortieth-day mourning ceremonies. Historically, fortieth-day mourning in Iran was a non-political event in which families, friends, and well-wishers would gather to express their respect for the deceased. The Islamist movement changed the ritual by calling on all Muslims to honor the deceased; by organizing large-scale mourning ceremonies around the country; and by transforming grief recovery into grief-based mobilization. Mourning lost its otherworldly quietism and gained a this-worldly activism.

The first such use of fortieth-day mourning, so far as I can find, occurred in 1963. For a year, Khomeini and his followers had organized ever-increasing demonstrations against various policies of the monarchy, among them royal abuses of power, legal capitulations to the United States, and relations with Israel. The relative importance of these issues is a subject of debate. On June 5, 1963, the military opened fire on a massive demonstration in Qom, killing thousands, according to protesters.[15] An anonymous group calling itself the "Council of United Muslims" issued a short pronouncement that may have been the first public, political use of fortieth-day mourning in Iran:

> In support of the lofty goals of the religious scholars, particularly the great source of Shi'i imitation, his honor . . . Ruhollah Khomeini [a long series of honorifics is deleted]. In protest against the shah's dictatorship and the merciless killings and inhuman acts of the ruling circle. In sympathy with the survivors of the martyrs, the grieving fathers and mothers and the orphaned children: a general strike is announced. Nobody should go outside on this day, to prove to the world once again that the ruling circle is the only hooligan, looter, rioter, and reactionary, not the dignified nation of Iran. Please pass along [this statement] after reading.[16]

It is possible that the idea of a public fortieth-day mourning occurred to the Council of United Muslims because of a coincidence of the calendar. The June 5 tragedy took place just a few days before 'Ashura, the annual mourning for Imam Husayn—'Ashura, the nine days leading up to it, and the fortieth day after it (known as *arba'in*, or fortieth, in Arabic) are all commemorated traditionally with non-political processions. Planning for the *arba'in* observances most likely placed fortieth-day mourning in the front of devout Shi'i Muslims' minds that month.

The political use of fortieth-day mourning underwent further transformation in the fall of 1977, after the death of Mostafa Khomeini. In place of a general strike, Islamists in Qom and elsewhere organized public memorial ceremonies. In early 1978, such use came to be routine, so routine that even non-revolutionaries like Shari'at-Madari and his colleagues issued calls for fortieth-day-mourning-as-protest. The cancellation of these events in June 1978 resulted in a return to the 1963 precedent of a stay-at-home strike. In the post-revolutionary period, the regime further transformed the practice, institutionalizing public mourning to mobilize support for the regime.[17]

Today it may seem like the public observance of mourning rituals in Iran was always a political act. But the political implications of this cultural practice were an outcome of the protest movement's success, not a cause of it. The Islamists intentionally transformed the traditional practice on explicitly pragmatic grounds: to mobilize the masses.

When the transformed practice ceased to perform this function, they merely stopped using it, as was the case in June 1978. When they felt it would be useful, they could turn to it again, as they did in mid-January 1979, organizing huge marches in Tehran and other cities to commemorate the *arbaʿin* of Imam Husayn. A leading Islamist in Tehran testified to the pragmatism of the practice at the end of that day. He turned to a colleague and said, "Today went well, thank God, but we don't have a theme or excuse for renewed demonstrations on January 27. What is to be done?" His friend laughed and replied, "But God will provide something! We have to set our minds to it."[18]

––––––––––

Does culture shape us, or do we shape it? Surely the answer is "both." But in the study of social movements, there are two distinct uses of culture. One side emphasizes cultural continuity—the ways that culture shapes us. In this view, culture is a structure analogous to political-opportunity structures and organizational structures, which can, in some circumstances, be conducive to particular forms of protest mobilization. For example, the forty-day mourning cycle is a cultural resource that exists in Shiʿi Islam but does not exist in some other cultures. It is part of the cultural context out of which Iranian protest grows. In more strategic terms, it is part of the "tool kit," "repertoire," or "cultural reservoir" on which Iranian protest can draw.[19]

A second approach emphasizes cultural change, focusing on the ways in which we shape culture. In this view, protest movements construct new cultures as they go along. Not everything changes all at once, but even the elements carried over from earlier practices are recast with new meaning in the new context.[20] The forty-day mourning cycle in Iran, for example, had a quite different meaning before and after its adaptation for revolutionary purposes in late 1977.

Thoughtful observers have recommended that the two approaches be combined, but this may not be possible. The difficulty is illustrated in the concept of social-movement "framing." This concept, elaborated in the 1980s and 1990s by the sociologists David Snow, Robert Benford, and others, focuses on the appeals that movements make to potential recruits, bystanders, opponents, and other audiences. The concept combines a constructionist approach (movements construct novel frames) and a structural approach (a movement's frames succeed if they resonate with the preexisting culture).[21]

If we try to combine the two approaches, the constructionist view of culture undermines the structural view. Take the example of Iranian mourning rituals. The Islamist movement drew upon preexisting rituals, yet it also changed their meaning. Could we have said in early 1977 that because Iranian culture includes a forty-day mourning cycle, the country was more likely than other countries to undergo a revolution? I think not. Rather, a knowledgeable observer would probably have noted that this mourning cycle had been put to protest purposes only once in Iranian history, in 1963, and that movement had come to naught. It is only because the revolutionary movement later *changed* the meaning of the mourning cycle that we read history backward and call this culture element conducive to protest. Another way of saying this might be: "All cultures have mourning rituals. If any of these rituals gets used in a protest movement, should we emphasize the preexisting ritual, or should we emphasize the movement's adaptation of that ritual?"

What about a less ambitious structural argument, one that says, "Preexisting cultural traditions don't tell us *where* protest occurs, but they can tell us *how* protest occurs. That is, each culture shapes the movements that grow out of it." In early 1977, what would we have guessed that a future Islamist movement in Iran would look like? We probably would have emphasized the cultural expressions of previous Islamist movements in Iran: the tradition of boycotts, wielded against a foreign tobacco concession in the 1870s; the tradition of sit-ins at sanctuaries, used to great effect during the Constitutional Revolution of 1906; the tradition of assassination, adopted by Islamist militants in the 1940s and 1960s; and the mass demonstrations that brought Khomeini to national attention in 1963. One of the few scholars to study Islamist protest in Iran before the revolution noted several of these precedents and emphasized the continuity of Shi'i political expression in Iran.[22] Yet the Islamist movement of 1977–1979 broke from precedent. In addition to demonstrations, pioneered in 1963, it turned to novel forms: politicized mourning rituals, as well as politicized Ramadan observance and a new theory of religious authority. To the extent that the revolutionary movement constructed its own culture, it foils our attempts at retroactive prediction.

In the summer of 1978, the Iranian revolutionary movement looked as though it might stall. The stay-at-home strike of June 17 broke the movement's forty-day cycle, and it was not clear what event would spark the next major protest. Activists tried to generate their own turning points, with only partial success. In a number of cities, radicals burned down theaters that showed indecent films; in Isfahan and Tehran, restaurants catering to foreigners were bombed. But none of these protests gelled into a nationwide movement, despite government crackdowns that might have provided rallying points for coordinated protest. The shooting of protesters outside an oppositional religious ceremony in Rafsanjan on July 15, for example, did not occasion mourning or protests in other cities.[23]

During this period, the government made conciliatory overtures that threatened to split the opposition. Even as street protests continued to be met with force, the government publicized various liberalizing measures, culminating with the shah's announcement that he would hold free elections the following year: "In terms of political liberties, we will have as much liberty as democratic European nations. And, as in democratic countries, the limits of freedom will be specified . . . Sedition, defiance, and backsliding from the law are not tolerated by any country, especially the most democratic ones."[24]

Khomeini rejected talk of elections as a "trick," but the liberal opposition responded to various reforms with cautious optimism. Publicly, liberals said that "the holding of free elections is impossible in current conditions of repression." Privately, Mehdi Bazargan said he and his associates found certain reforms "interesting" and were "taking a step-by-step approach." "However," Bazargan added, "all Iranians remained deeply suspicious of the shah's intentions. How could a man who had ruled autocratically for 37 years suddenly be converted?" Other liberals became optimistic, even euphoric, about the possibility for meaningful reform, according to the historian Nikki Keddie, who conducted extensive interviews in Iran in June and July 1978. Liberals pushed for further concessions, testing the limits of the new liberalization: a speech in Gilan, a defense at a political trial in Mazandaran, a press conference and oppositional meeting in Tehran. This last event reached the limits: the meeting was broken up by security officials and the organizer arrested. Meanwhile, the liberal opposition took care to avoid confrontational protests that were sure to be repressed. One activist insisted to a U.S. diplomat that confrontational protests were "government provocations" designed to show the world that Iranians were not ready for democracy.[25]

To revive the movement, Islamists transformed a variety of religious ceremonies into political events. For example, the birthday of the Hidden Imam, on 15 Sha'ban—falling on July 21 in 1978—was normally a joyous occasion, comparable in some ways to the celebration of the birth of the Christian messiah, Christmas. In 1978, however, Khomeini called for the holiday to be transformed: "how can anyone speak of celebration and joy—joy at the bloodied corpses of the children of Iran?" Tehran religious scholars announced that the birthday would be observed "this year with no decorative lights or exchange of congratulations." The security police later reported that few stores put up lights, and that the day "was not observed in the same way as in previous years."[26]

The Islamists managed to generate protests in at least ten cities at the end of July, forty days after the non-fatal fortieth-day strike of June 17. They achieved this by observing seventh-day mourning ceremonies for Shaykh Ahmad Kafi, an oppositionist whose death in a car crash on July 20 was widely attributed to the security police. Mourners in a large funeral procession in Mashhad raised anti-regime slogans and clashed with police, who fired into the crowd, killing forty, according to the opposition. Several days of violence ensued, with protesters attacking buildings and soldiers. Rumors in Mashhad told of troops storming the Imam Reza tomb complex—the holiest Shi'i site in Iran—and killing sixteen religious scholars "in revenge." (Khomeini claimed only that a seminary had been stormed and religious students "beaten almost to death.") Observance of the seventh day of mourning, like observance of the fortieth, was transformed into a political act in 1978, but on a much smaller scale.[27]

Islamists similarly transformed the heightened piety of Ramadan, beginning on August 6, into political mobilization. Ramadan, a month of fasting from sunrise to sunset, was traditionally associated with spiritual and bodily purification—one Iranian likened it to running a motorcycle without gasoline to clean out the engine. Another Iranian, the son of a religious scholar, called it "a lazy season in our country": "It is really a big holiday for many. School attendance is not carefully measured. Shop keepers understand why their workers come in late." In 1978, Khomeini indicated that "this year, the holy month is a model . . . for revenge against the injustices of the regime." The month's activism began slowly; U.S. intelligence officials characterized the first days of Ramadan as "somewhat calmer" than the previous week.[28]

The first major protests of Ramadan were local in nature. In Isfahan, the return of Ayatollah Jalaluddin Taheri from internal exile in late July triggered large-scale celebrations and demonstrations. Taheri resumed the anti-government themes that had gotten him exiled months earlier and was re-arrested on August 1. His followers then staged a sit-in at the home of Isfahan's other leading religious scholar, Ayatollah Hossein Khademi, who was far less militant than Taheri. The previous month Khademi had asked participants at a sit-in to leave his house; this time he allowed them to stay, but instructed the Isfahan bazaar merchants to end their strike, which they did. Small groups of radicals engaged in daily brick-throwing attacks on banks, theaters, and the Shah Abbas Hotel, raising tensions in the city, then organized larger and larger demonstrations, tens of thousands strong. The regime responded with force on August 10, killing dozens of protesters, according to the opposition, and clearing out the sit-in at Khademi's house. The unrest was serious enough for the regime to declare martial law and a night-time curfew in Isfahan. Tanks and troop carriers were stationed at all major intersections in the city, and residents worried that the soldiers brought to the city were "butchers" from a minority group who would kill a person for a dollar.[29]

In Shiraz, too, local events sparked major protests. On August 10, a small demonstration poured out of the New Mosque. Police and the military surrounded the area, forced the protesters back inside, and attacked them with gunfire and tear gas. "Three days later Ayatollah [Baha'uddin] Mahallati announced a day of public mourning because

89 people had been killed," one protester recalled. (Other opposition-ists estimated 150 or more killed.) "On that day too there were a lot of soldiers in the square [between the New Mosque and the Shah Cheragh shrine] so there wouldn't be another demonstration." Facing this show of force and fearing further bloodshed if demonstrations continued, the religious leaders of Shiraz called a general strike instead.[30]

These tragedies triggered sympathy protests in six cities around Iran, and there were further casualties in Behbehan and Shahsevar. Kho-meini issued his usual vehement denunciation: "The shah apparently said in an interview that he blocked from publication, 'If I have to leave, I'll raze Iran to the ground before going,' and his recent crimes show that he is busy implementing this plan."[31]

Despite the appearance of an active movement, the Islamists were having difficulty capitalizing on the atrocities that the regime repeat-edly offered as tinder. One problem was their inability to bring the Ramadan protests to Tehran. Late in the evening of August 12, more than two dozen religious leaders of Tehran were meeting at the home of Hojjat al-Islam 'Ali-Asghar Morvarid to plan a response to the most recent killings when police stormed the house, threw them in a truck, and jailed them overnight. A half-dozen other preachers were arrested in the following days for rallying their congregations with fiery eve-ning sermons, and eight mosques were tear-gassed. This crackdown was enough to keep the Tehran religious leaders from issuing opposi-tional pronouncements, much less staging large protests.[32]

A second problem was getting beyond the radicals' core supporters in building the massive movement that Khomeini saw as necessary to topple the shah. Protests plateaued for four months at around ten thousand participants in each major city—excepting Isfahan, where protests had peaked at nearly fifty thousand just before martial law was declared; and excepting also Tehran, which had mobilized only small protests of several thousand people. These numbers represented an al-most fully mobilized "mosque network," as described in the last chap-ter. But the adult population of Iran was more than fifteen million, and limited protests seemed to be having a limited impact.

A massive atrocity two weeks later helped to kick protests into high gear. In Abadan, hundreds were burned to death in a movie theater—

the doors were locked from the outside, and the fire department was slow to respond. Many Iranians immediately blamed the government —some shouted "Burn the shah!"—and a week of mourning protests rocked the city. Around Iran, protests increased in pace and size, with eleven cities placed under martial law by the end of August. Demonstrations reached twenty thousand or more in Mashhad and fifty thousand in Qom—by the government's count![33]

But the government's counting system had changed. On August 26, the regime appointed a new prime minister thought to be more acceptable to the Islamists. Combining repression with concession, as usual, the regime proceeded to scrap the recently introduced imperial calendar and return to the solar Muslim calendar that had been used for fifty years. Casinos were ordered shut. Press freedoms were announced, and from this moment we begin to see a marked change in press reporting of the revolutionary movement. Previously, newspapers would give crowd estimates around one-tenth of the estimates claimed by the opposition; now the difference was about one to two. Previously, newspapers used words like "hooligans" and "anti-national elements" to describe protesters; now, these words disappeared and newspaper accounts began to note that some protests were "peaceful" and "orderly."

Perhaps most significant, the regime permitted large religious demonstrations to be scheduled for September 4, on the occasion of 'Eid-e Fetr, the holiday at the end of Ramadan that marks the finish of a month of daylight fasting. Official permission meant two things for the revolutionary movement. First, it meant that violent repression was less certain than for previous protests, so that supporters beyond the hard core might consider it safe enough to participate. Second, if the soft core was expected to participate, the event might get big enough to generate feelings of safety in numbers, attracting even further participants.

The Islamists tricked the liberal opposition into arranging the venue for the largest demonstration held that day, at a field in the north of Tehran. They implied that this would be nothing more than a larger-scale version of previous years' celebrations at this site. On this understanding, the liberals—political activists from the Tehran bazaar—negotiated official permission. In exchange for permission they promised not to conduct an illegal march. Fourteen thousand people, according to the security police, showed up for the ceremony in a field on a hill in northern Tehran, carrying pictures of Khomeini and large banners. But the Islamists had no intention of limiting themselves to the traditional prayers. At the end of the ceremony, the ranking religious scholar announced disingenuously, "Our program has ended here, and the cloaked marshals will show you to the gate. [Please] cooperate with them." Outside the field, by prior arrangement, the crowd was joined by groups from smaller prayer meetings and set off on a well-organized march to the center of the city. Hundreds of young people on motorbikes cleared the route for the marchers—200,000 according to the newspapers, 400,000–500,000 by the opposition's count. The bazaari organizers hurried along, trying to disperse the crowd and reminding people that they were not supposed to be demonstrating, but to no effect.[34]

As the marchers poured downhill from Qaytariyeh to the center of Tehran, they passed soldiers posted in high-visibility locations, some in armored cars. The military had orders not to intervene, though protesters could not count on their passivity. Two French reporters described a scene that was apparently repeated throughout the day:

> Two trucks full of soldiers, with a machine-gun battery, are at their posts. The procession, which has grown, it appears, roars and dances in the sun: "Soldier, my brother, why do you shoot your brothers?" A spray of flowers falls on the machine-gun barrel, the crowd touches the tarpaulins and the poles on the trucks. Emboldened, it shakes the hands of the soldiers, kisses them, covers them with bouquets. In a whirlwind of shouts, the first guns have been conquered, the soldiers are in a state of shock, bewildered. Some of them cry, their machine-guns henceforth useless. The officers of the convoy speak up: "We belong to the people, but we are in the service, do not commit any violence, we do not want to shoot."[35]

Around the country, 'Eid-e Fetr was the occasion for large-scale demonstrations, pushing the movement beyond the hard core of Islamists. One woman, an architect and secularist, said she attended in her tennis clothes. A leading liberal, caught up in the spirit of the moment, told reporters, "I was in the middle of the crowd. In front of me, behind me, to my side, wherever I looked I saw people in this great wave as drops in the sea, and I too was in the sea of this immeasurable gathering of the people of Iran. There was no 'I' there, we were nothing but 'We.'"[36]

The Islamists' transformation of 'Eid-e Fetr—like their transformation of Ramadan and 15 Sha'ban and seventh- and fortieth-day mourning—marked a significant departure from the rituals of the past. The novel use of religious ceremonies helped to revitalize the revolutionary movement during the summer of 1978, as its leaders recognized. Islamists in Shiraz creatively mixed Shi'i traditions by calling for "'Ashura in Ramadan"—'Ashura, the commemoration of the death of Imam Husayn, is observed four months after Ramadan. Khomeini noted that "the 'Eid-e Fetr this year was an 'Eid of epic movement." The revolutionary movement seemed to be aware that it was shaping Iranian culture as much as the culture was shaping it.[37]

Three days after 'Eid-e Fetr, on September 7, the Islamists scheduled a second prayer rally at Qaytariyeh, to be followed by another march downhill to the center of Tehran. The occasion was the seventh day of mourning for protesters killed in a small clash on September 1. The organizers wanted to pick up the pace of the protest movement, and they had announced the September 7 protest during the 'Eid-e Fetr demonstrations of September 4. The event was almost canceled on September 6, however, when religious leaders met to discuss the potential danger. An observer summarized the objections:

1. News has arrived from "above" that "we are going to make [General Gholam-Reza] Oveissi prime minister." [That is, the shah was planning to install a military government.]
2. On the shah's orders, the decision and command for a killing has been issued.
3. The mayor's ultimatum.
4. Difficulties of leading a crowd that might reach four million people.
5. SAVAK had announced, "Even if you try to march from four points [in the city], we will prevent you."

After hours of discussion, the militants succeeded in keeping their more cautious colleagues from canceling the protest. The account of the meeting continues: "It was decided that if the crowd marched with no danger, or little danger, the religious scholars would cooperate, as they did. If the demonstration had been broken up and dispersed, the government would have killed people without a fuss. A number of people were convinced that there would be no killing, for various reasons, among them the presence of the prime minister of Japan in Tehran." (Keeping up appearances, the shah hosted several foreign leaders in spring and summer 1978.) The militants' conviction proved accurate. Police tried to disperse the crowd in Tehran with tear gas, and when that effort failed they retreated and allowed the protests to continue. The military had issued an order the previous evening for troops not to carry firearms, according to the transcript of a cabinet meeting, so that hotheaded soldiers would not trigger a bloodbath. The top Islamist leaders of Tehran monitored the situation and joined in when it appeared safe, taking a taxicab to the head of the march.[38]

Over the course of the day, the numbers of protesters grew—the opposition's claims of four million in Tehran is outlandish, but even the government estimated that the crowd was larger than the hundreds of thousands on 'Eid-e Fetr, three days earlier. The atmosphere of the demonstration was quite different as well, much more militant and somber. French writers reported: "Fear circulates like a shudder from one demonstrator to another. This time, no flowers."[39]

The September 7 demonstration popularized a new slogan calling for the establishment of an "Islamic Republic." This demand may also have appeared in the resolution—written by Khomeini himself, some said—that was read and approved by acclaim at the march's end in Shahyad Square (renamed Freedom Square by the revolutionaries).[40]

This concept of an Islamic Republic was not a traditional demand. It was a novelty invented by Ruhollah Khomeini less than a decade before and constituted Khomeini's major contribution to Shi'i political theory. Its defining characteristic—what made it "Islamic"—was the entrusting of ultimate governmental responsibility to a single religious scholar, who "will possess the same authority as the Most Noble Messenger (upon whom be peace and blessings) in the administration of society, and it will be the duty of all people to obey him." This is not to say that Khomeini's "rulership of the jurist" emerged from thin air. Shi'i scholars had for centuries debated the role of the religious scholar vis-à-vis political power, and Khomeini's major work of political philosophy—a series of lectures in 1970, transcribed and published as the book *Islamic Government*—was "not very different in content from the customary formulation," according to a scholar who has studied the long history of such treatises.[41]

Where it differed, however, was in two significant particulars. First, Khomeini insisted on the deposition of the monarchy. Earlier Iranian Islamists, by contrast, had been willing to grant the monarch an ongoing role, under clerical supervision. Shaykh Fazlollah Nuri (died 1909) and Ayatollah Abu'l-Qasem Kashani (died 1962), for example—heroes of Khomeini's Islamic Republic—helped put shahs back in power in 1908 and 1953, respectively. Khomeini would have none of this: "The form of government was thoroughly perverted by being transformed into a monarchy, like those of the kings of Iran, the emperors of Rome, and the pharaohs of Egypt." He wanted a republic.[42]

Second, Khomeini insisted on concentrating ultimate Islamic authority in a single individual. This represented a significant break from Shi'i scholarly tradition, in which a half-dozen or more top-ranked religious scholars served as multiple "sources of imitation" for the faithful, who were free to choose among them for guidance. Before 1979, there had only been rare instances—in the late eighteenth century, the mid-nineteenth century, and the 1950s—in which a single scholar was deemed so much more erudite than his peers that one could speak of a single Shi'i "source of imitation." And these instances emerged by chance, not by design, as in Khomeini's political theory. Ironically, Khomeini himself suffered under the last sole "source of imitation," in the 1950s. Ayatollah Hossein Borujerdi disapproved of Khomeini's activism and had him placed under virtual house arrest, allowed out only to teach his classes. "There was no coming and going in the imam's house," a supporter recalled. "His relations with everyone were cut off." After Borujerdi's death in the early 1960s, there was some discussion among Islamic reformers about the downside of such centralization of religious authority. But Khomeini drew the opposite conclusion: centralized authority would be useful and justified, if it were in the right hands.[43]

The novel title of imam completed this shift in Shi'i authority. Not only did Khomeini's followers consider him the rightful ruler of Iran, but they also associated him, if only by analogy, with the divinely in-spired imams of a millennium earlier. Some Iranians took the analogy literally and considered Khomeini to have superhuman powers.[44] A writer from Karaj, for example, heard his mother tell the following story:

> When Khomeini was being taken into exile, along the way he told the driver, "Stop so I can pray." The driver paid no attention. A few steps farther the car broke down. *Aqa* [Khomeini's informal title, meaning "Sir," used be-fore he became known as Imam] got out, read his prayers, and when he was finished with his prayers the car, which wouldn't start no matter what the driver did, started, and they continued on their journey.[45]

An electrician avowed that Khomeini knew "the science of the hid-den." In early fall 1978, and then again in January 1979, the legend cir-culated in Iran that Khomeini's face had been, could be, or would be seen on the moon. Sources hostile to the revolution reported the leg-end as evidence of the simple-mindedness of certain uneducated Irani-ans, whereas Khomeini and his followers denounced the legend as gov-ernment misinformation designed to make the opposition look silly. "That's superstition. Don't believe it," said Ayatollah Sadeq Ruhani upon his release from house arrest in the last weeks of the Pahlavi re-gime.[46]

The transformation of religious authority was not completed, how-ever, until after the Islamic Republic had been installed, and in some sense not even then. Khomeini's directives were never obeyed unani-mously, even by Iranians who considered themselves devout Shi'i Mus-lims. After Khomeini came to power, for example, he ordered Iranians to turn in the weapons that had been dispersed from the armories in the final days of the revolution—but many weapons were not returned. Among those who kept their guns were hard-line members of neigh-borhood committees, who had taken over the maintenance of public order in the wake of the collapse of the Pahlavi state, and who were re-luctant to give up this power, even to Khomeini's new state.[47]

Before the fall of the shah, disobedience to Khomeini's directives was widespread. Khomeini had long called on Iranians to oppose the Pahlavi regime, as shown in the following speech in 1977: "All Muslims have a duty to learn [religious] science, and also to act, to struggle against oppression with all their might." He continued to make such appeals through summer 1978: "This is a true son of Islam, the true Muslim: when he comes out of prison, he clenches his fist and resumes his struggle. If a Muslim shows no concern for the affairs of his fellow Muslims, he is not a Muslim . . ."; "Today, with the nation having risen up and found its good and true path, silence and the order to keep silent are contrary to the sublime interests of Islam and an offense against the Ja'fari Shi'i path." This theme was taken up in some demonstrations, with the slogan, "The silence of each Muslim is an insult to the Qur'an." Yet only a small fraction of the Iranian population heeded Khomeini's calls for activism before and during the summer of 1978, and even fewer Iranians heeded his calls for martyrdom and self-sacrifice. There are various reports of rising religiosity in Iran in the 1970s, including increases in the number of private prayer meetings, mystical groups, religious neighborhood associations, pilgrimages, mosque-building, shrine donations, and the sales of religious publications. Rising religiosity did not, apparently, increase attendance at mosque prayers, which was said to be at an all-time low. Nor did religiosity translate into acceptance of Khomeini's authority until the second half of 1978.[48]

Shi'i activists have no regard for their personal safety and consider martyrdom in the cause of Islam to be an honor. Just ask Esma'il, a seminary student at the time of the Iranian Revolution: "If a high-ranking cleric gave me the order, I'd have to go and die. Dying would be a sign of my morality. If he ordered me to go, say, all the way to the White House in America, I'd have to . . . If I didn't go, I wouldn't be a Muslim." D. K., an Islamist activist in Tehran, recalled the arrest, torture, and death of some of his friends during the revolutionary movement. When asked if he was afraid, he responded, "No, we knew that if we died, it was in the path of God." Ahmad, another activist in Tehran, described distributing illegal oppositional cassettes and pronouncements in Tehran: "if [security forces] had come in and killed us, we would have been martyrs."[49]

This language of martyrdom was an integral part of the revolutionary discourse in Iran. Khomeini touched on the theme frequently, calling on his followers to imitate the great martyrs of Islam who fought on knowing that they would die, in particular Imam Husayn, who

> taught us how to struggle against all the tyrants of history, showed us how the clenched fists of those who seek freedom, desire independence, and proclaim the truth may triumph over tanks, machine guns, and the armies of Satan, how the word of truth may obliterate falsehood. The leader of the Muslims taught us that if a tyrant rules despotically over the Muslims in any age, we must rise up against him and denounce him, however unequal our forces may be, and that if we see the very existence of Islam in danger, we must sacrifice ourselves and be prepared to shed our blood.[50]

As a radical religious scholar in Tehran noted in a mosque speech in late March 1978: "No movement is born without martyrs."[51]

The imagery of martyrdom was woven into many of the events of the Iranian Revolution. The anthropologist Michael M. J. Fischer has called this the "Karbala paradigm": protesters' repeated identification with Imam Husayn and his followers, who were ready to sacrifice themselves at the hands of Yazid, the despotic usurper of the late seventh century, at the battle of Karbala, in today's Iraq. "Iran has become Karbala; every day people are murdered," one group of demonstrators chanted. On several occasions, cadres of protesters wore white shrouds signifying their readiness for martyrdom.[52]

The most militant Islamists were willing to engage the regime with violence, against overwhelming odds. In Qom they filled a taxi with rocks before demonstrations so they would have ample ammunition to toss at the police. In Yazd they hid "cold" weapons like knives and clubs—as opposed to firearms—along the route of demonstrations. Two small groups—one in Tehran and Tabriz, a second in Qom— stashed weapons in preparation for guerrilla warfare. Seyyed 'Ali Andarzgu, a former seminary student with training in Palestinian military camps in Lebanon, planned to assassinate the shah with pistols and explosives smuggled into the palace inside a set of dumbbells, but was killed in August 1978 before the plan could be carried out. The same month, a group in Tehran bombed a restaurant catering to foreigners. It claimed credit for the seventy dead and wounded in a pronouncement beginning "In the name of God, the Destroyer of the Oppressors" and quoting "Imam Khomeini": "Let us struggle against the interests of the Americans, even if this means annihilating them."[53]

This revolutionary violence fits with the long-standing Western view that Muslims, especially Shi'i Muslims, care little for human life, including their own. Voltaire, for example, in his play *Fanaticism, or Muhammad the Prophet* (1741), painted a picture of Muslim troops "drunk on the poisons of error and zeal, sustaining the illusion of false miracles, spreading fanaticism and sedition." In the nineteenth century, a leading Orientalist assured his French audience that Islam involves "eternal war, war that shall not cease until the last son of Ismail dies miserably, or is banished in terror to the depths of the desert. Islam is the complete negation of Europe; Islam is fanaticism." Two centuries later, in 1945, a leading Orientalist wrote of "the aversion of the Muslims from the thought-processes of rationalism." The U.S. Central Intelligence Agency entitled one analysis in 1984 "The Shia Urge toward Martyrdom."[54]

Western popular images of Islamic movements continue to play on this theme. "The veneration of martyrs and the ceaseless fight to wrest land and control from a dominant or threatening culture are constants stretching back almost to the seventh-century genesis of Islam, the youngest of the universal religions," writes a Canadian newsweekly. "From its inception, first within Arabia and then against all unbelievers, Islam has been unthinkable without its mandate for violence, war, terror—in a word, jihad," writes a foreign policy aide for a U.S. senator. The image of the martyr appears as well in some contemporary academic analyses. "Many of them [Muslims] indeed believe that the reward for dying as a martyr for the faith is so immediate and direct that such death is not something to be avoided," writes one political scientist. Understanding these movements, according to a criminologist, requires us to "comprehend the Islamic militants' willingness to martyrdom."[55]

Yet this emphasis on martyrdom as an explanation for Islamic activism—on the part of both the Islamists and hostile Western observers—is a red herring. For one thing, Muslims have no monopoly on the idea of sacrificing for a cause, religious or otherwise. Studies of the U.S. military in World War II, for example, found some American soldiers—drafted from the most individualistic society in the modern world—eager to engage in battle, despite the risks. (They lost this eagerness after facing battle.) For another, the Iranian Revolution suffered remarkably few casualties. The South African anti-apartheid movement, for example, used far more violence than the Iranians—killing hundreds of suspected traitors to the cause with "necklaces" of burning tires, for example—and produced more than 7,000 revolutionary martyrs. In Iran, the Martyr Foundation, established after the revolution to compensate the survivors of fallen revolutionaries, could identify only 744 martyrs in Tehran, where the majority of the casualties were supposed to have occurred. The coroner's office and Tehran's main cemetery, Behesht-e Zahra, counted 895 and 768 martyrs, respectively. These may be undercounts, but even if multiplied many times over they do not match the image of vast masses standing up to machine-gun fire. According to two eyewitnesses, daily protests at the Behesht-e Zahra cemetery late in the revolutionary period sometimes lacked actual martyrs to demonstrate around; protesters had to take up the bodies of people who had died of accidents or illness.[56]

Moreover, the language of martyrdom did not necessarily match behavior in the Iranian Revolution. Shortly after professing their willingness to die for the cause, D. K. and Ahmad described running away from security forces during actual protests in which they had participated. Ahmad dove into the gutter when soldiers opened fire on a sit-in; he and his friends planned protest events by saying, "You do this, you do that, and then we all run away." D. K. explained that young people took part in dangerous demonstrations, not old people, because youngsters could run away from soldiers, climb over walls, and so on: "An old man, he runs one hundred meters and [pants, as though out of breath]. The soldier is going to catch him and pow—he's dead." In other words, demonstrators weren't supposed to die; they were supposed to get away.

Even for committed activists such as these who placed themselves in harm's way, martyrdom was a last resort. Perhaps they wished to reserve their martyrdom for a more opportune moment, when the sacrifice would be most efficacious. Yet such a moment never came. The revolution ended and with it, opportunities for revolutionary martyrdom. (Of course, selection bias is at work here, since the activists who succeeded in martyring themselves are no longer available for interviews.)

The vast majority of Iranians were less committed to revolution and even less willing to be martyred than Ahmad and D. K. For example, Karim, a peasant who migrated to Tehran, chided his fellow demonstrators when they ran away from gunfire and hid in a fruit shop: "I shouted, 'Why are you hiding? Come back here, don't be afraid, we are going to demonstrate even if they kill us! We didn't come here to hide.'" Among the Iranians I interviewed, those who joined the revolutionary movement late or participated only part-time were most likely to express survival concerns. Even these less committed protesters embraced the language of martyrdom. A shopkeeper from Shiraz, for example, said he participated in demonstrations only when the crowds were large: "It wasn't just one, two, or a thousand people." Yet he also described himself as "fanatic" *(ta'asob),* with apparently positive connotations, and said he considered Khomeini's pronouncements an "order": "If I didn't accept it, that would have been *haram* [religiously forbidden] . . . It was like jihad: if you do not go to the front, even your wife is *haram.*"[57]

Not all revolutionary leaders encouraged martyrdom, either. In Shiraz, a man from a nearby village recalled:

Mr. [Ayatollah] Mahallati had said in the mosque, "Young men, please, I beg of you, don't expose yourselves needlessly to machine gun fire. Whenever there is shooting, don't go towards it. Don't go and get killed. Run away. Run away. Whenever you see that conditions aren't good to demonstrate, don't demonstrate. The government wants to kill you. If you go and get killed, what good does it do? Don't go and get killed."

The villager added his own view:

It depends on the situation. You have to anticipate what will happen. You have to use intelligence. When the soldiers have orders to shoot and you are empty-handed, it's stupidity to say, "Go and face the machine guns." The time to say, "Go and face the machine guns" is when you have a machine gun in your hands.[58]

In my interviews with participants in the revolution, I continually heard that "Iranians know no fear." Yet this comment was often, paradoxically, accompanied by accounts of how the respondent had experienced tremendous fear. For example, Moste'ar was twenty-five years old at the time of the revolution, unemployed, the son of an oil worker in Ahwaz, in southwestern Iran. After claiming that Iranians knew no fear, he described a demonstration he had attended:

> "They came and broke up the demonstration. With batons."
>
> "Were you afraid?"
>
> "Were we afraid? Yes. We fled."
>
> "But you knew before you went to the speech that there might be shooting, didn't you?"
>
> "No . . . There was a plan that at a certain hour people would do something [listen to an oppositional speech]. There was nothing—it was all very ordinary—it wasn't extraordinary. We didn't know . . ."[59]

Moste'ar, whom I interviewed in a small crafts shop where friends of his were painting Persian miniatures and engraving bronze bowls, seemed embarrassed to admit his lack of heroism. At a time of great importance, he had not lived up to his image of the brave Iranian. Or perhaps he wished to justify his later dissatisfaction with the post-revolutionary regime by making himself appear less than fervent during the revolution. What is clear is that he was a young man with a difficult life in confusing times, interested in protesting against dictatorship along with his friends, but not so interested that he sought martyrdom.

———

On Thursday, September 8, after demanding an Islamic government, protest organizers announced that their program was finished. But militants in the crowd—it's not clear who—spread the word to gather the next morning, Friday, September 8, in Zhaleh Square in the east of Tehran. No religious ceremony was cited, no memorial services—the movement had progressed beyond the need for symbolic excuses for protest. At a meeting that evening, Khomeini's followers decided to endorse the next day's protest, over the objections of more cautious liberals.[60]

Early on the morning of September 8, however, the regime declared martial law in Tehran and other cities. The news was announced on the radio at 6 A.M. It's not clear how many potential protesters heard the news and stayed home. Several thousand people filled Zhaleh Square by 8 A.M., a small fraction of the large crowds of the previous day. Word went around the crowd that a soldier had killed himself rather than face the protesters, boosting their fortitude. "It is unconscionable that a soldier has killed himself for my sake, and I haven't been killed for his," one protester recalled feeling. According to a French eyewitness, the reporter Yves-Guy Bergès, the crowd faced a line of soldiers wearing gas masks. Tear gas dispersed the crowd, but protesters regrouped. Ayatollah Yahya Nuri, who headed a nearby religious institution, came and spoke with one of the military officers, then told the crowd to sit down in the street. Another volley of tear gas, followed by machine-gun fire in the air, dispersed the crowd a second time. Again the protesters regrouped, following two men and a woman who walked toward the soldiers, unarmed, stopping at a distance of ten meters. The reporter continued:

> 9:15 A.M. From the other end of the square, a cannonade of gunfire. I leap to the ground, barely have time to reach the right-hand sidewalk when the soldiers in the front ranks open fire on us point blank without stopping. There is panic. Pushed, swept along, I am hurled to the ground, losing a camera, squeezed by those who had the same idea, while the hail of bullets—automatic weapons perhaps?—passes over our heads. This lasts only 30 seconds, seeming as many minutes. Against the crowd with no weapons, with no defenses, it is easy game. They aim to frighten them, dissuade them, have to hit hard. Once as a lesson. This is not a fight; this is a massacre. A firing squad at its work.[61]

Crowds still streaming toward Zhaleh Square heard the gunfire and saw people running in the opposite direction. "Going further would take the heart of a lion," wrote a leftist who was late for the event because he couldn't find a parking space. "There is no point in going with empty hands to face armed soldiers," another protester told his brother, who wanted to rush forward. "It is pointless to waste our lives." These Iranians avoided martyrdom.[62]

The crackdown continued all day and into the evening, a conscript in Tehran recalled:

> Shots could still be heard at five in the afternoon as soldiers and conscripts in the [Farah Abad] base were ordered to assemble. Then, one of the chief officers at Farah Abad, Colonel Beglu, told those present "what you have just witnessed should not terrify you or raise doubts as to the objectives of the army. This type of response by the military was necessary in order to defend the monarchy and the country against the communists and enemies of the regime." He continued, "It is because of the action by the army that we now have peace and security throughout the city." Ironically, as he was making these assertions, this writer could hear loud outbursts of gunfire and see flashes made by tracer bullets in the background.[63]

Estimates of casualties on this day, which came to be known as "Black Friday," range from fewer than one hundred to many thousands. The post-revolutionary Martyr Foundation could identify only seventy-nine dead, while the coroner's office counted eighty-two and Tehran's main cemetery, Behesht-e Zahra, registered only forty.[64]

The massacre did not shake U.S. support for the shah. The ambassador took the line, contrary to eyewitness accounts, that "troops were attacked by a stone-throwing, club-wielding crowd." Two days later, President Jimmy Carter took time from the Egyptian-Israeli peace talks at Camp David to telephone the shah and reiterate his support in such difficult times; the president immediately issued a press release to that effect. Oddly, the shah later claimed not to have received such a call. There is nearly contemporaneous evidence, though, that he did. A month and a half later, a U.S. defense official visited Tehran, met with the shah and Iranian military leaders, and reported to Carter, "your telephone call to the Shah in September and your statements at your October 10 press conference were frequently mentioned, and that another such call might be appropriate."[65]

Whatever the number killed, they were part of a demonstration of perhaps five thousand people, a tiny fraction of the demonstrations of one and four days earlier. Where were the other ninety-five thousand or more protesters of the previous day?

Mahmud, for one, survived the Black Friday protest because of a picnic. He was thirty years old at the time, a car mechanic in Shemiran, in northern Tehran. He attended a number of protests, including the Thursday demonstrations. At the end of the Thursday event, everybody was talking about the follow-up the next morning. But Friday being the weekend—the Islamic "Sabbath"—Mahmud had planned to take his children for a picnic in the hills just outside town. It was an easy decision, he recalled, laughing at the memory of his good fortune, shaking his head with wonderment and perhaps a bit of survivor's guilt. The demands of politics could wait, even the demands of religious leaders. Although he described himself as religious, he was not "blindly religious."[66]

Mahmud's picnic is significant in that it suggests devout Shi'i Muslims could place personal life over communal duties, recreation over devotion, and survival over martyrdom. This behavior violates cultural explanations for the Iranian Revolution, specifically the urge toward martyrdom and the unquestioning obedience to religious leaders. A family outing is a cultural phenomenon too, and Mahmud's preference suggests that in the conflict between cultural priorities, religion didn't always carry the day, even among the devout, even in times of mobilization. For the vast majority of Iranians, as for Mahmud, Shi'ism and martyrdom were not enough to risk their lives for.

CHAPTER 5

General Strike: Economic Explanations

FALL 1978

The Black Friday massacre pushed the revolution indoors. No large demonstrations were held for more than two months. Instead, Iranians turned to less dangerous forms of protest: strikes. In the month after September 8, wildcat strikes spread across the country, beginning with the Tehran oil refinery on September 9. Strikes were not unknown in Pahlavi Iran: one review of leftist periodicals counted twenty-seven strikes in 1973, twenty-seven in 1974, fifteen in 1975, eighteen in 1976, and twenty-seven in 1977. During the first eight months of 1978, another leftist source counted fifteen strikes, then fifteen in September, and forty-five in October. In the first week of October 1978, alone, *Kayhan International* reported thirty-six distinct strikes. At one factory that struck that week, workers quickly won concessions from the Ministry of Labor, whose practice it was to intervene in labor disputes and enforce a settlement on all parties, while arresting the strike leaders. Then the workers heard that "at some other factories, workers had succeeded in winning more demands than before, and this had a great influence on the remaining workers." The factory went back on strike to demand subsidized housing. These workers, like the liberal oppositionists discussed in Chapter 2, responded to the opening of political opportunities just as Tocquevillean theory would expect.[1]

By the first week of November, virtually the entire country had stopped work, including journalists at *Kayhan International* and the country's other newspapers, which shut down for two months. The national airline and railroad were on strike. Customs officials and power grid workers were on strike intermittently. The banks were open some days and striking others, so that "twelve of the most senior executives were obliged to carry out the most menial but essential functions to keep the country's banking system in operation . . . The stranglehold on international trade was so complete that for a while the central bank was forced to stop issuing Treasury bills to raise money for the Government because the ink for certification was held up on the quayside."[2]

The most important strike occurred in the oil fields that supplied the regime's financial lifeblood. Oil workers walked off the job in late October, dropping Iranian oil exports from more than five million barrels a day to under two million barrels in two weeks' time. Workers went on strike without a clear set of demands in mind, but in order to participate in the groundswell of opposition that other sectors of the economy had already begun to build. "We had to define our aims," a leader of the oil industry staff employees recalled, and this process took up much of the strike committee's time: "Everyone had a few demands in mind, but all of them had to be put together and presented to the company in a list." The list ultimately developed by the strikers was, to say the least, ambitious:

> End martial law, full solidarity and cooperation with the striking teachers, and unconditional release of all political prisoners. Our economic demands included Iranianization of the oil industry, all communications to be in the Persian language, and for all foreign employees to leave the country . . . The second economic demand was for an end to discrimination against women staff employees and workers. The third demand called for implementation of a law recently passed by both houses of parliament dealing with the housing of oil workers and staff employees. Another demand was for revision of the regulations governing retirement of staff employees. Our final demand was for support to the demands of the production workers. The production workers had raised a demand not included in the list presented by the oil industry staff employees. It was for the dissolution of SAVAK [the security police].[3]

Khomeini had called for strikes in the days after Black Friday: "From now on, it is time for all of us to close our businesses, not forever but for the short time it will take to overthrow the ruling oppressors! Do not hurry to re-open shops and factories." But Khomeini did not, apparently, foresee an extended general strike: "Nobody will die of hunger from several days of striking shops and businesses, in submission to God." He also called for a one-day memorial strike on September 14, suggesting that he wished—as in June—to avoid the bloodshed of public demonstrations. A foreign reporter noted that even the mosques were empty in the week after Black Friday, as the religious leaders "have decided, at least for the moment, to cool it." A group of religious scholars in Tehran congratulated the oil industry strikers in mid-September but made no call for others to follow their example. A month later, in mid-October, Khomeini made passing reference to "all the strikes and protests across Iran." It was yet another month, though, before Khomeini began to talk of an extended general strike: "It is up to the noble nation of Iran to give full support to the workers and officials of the oil company and other state institutions and offices when they are on strike." Perhaps Khomeini had other concerns on his mind during this period. During the weeks that the strike was building, he was placed under house arrest in Iraq, then expelled from the country, refused entry to Kuwait, and forced to move to France. Iraq's government had cut a deal with the shah and had no more need for its resident Iranian opposition.[4]

––––––––––

Khomeini denied that the revolution was spurred by economic causes: "We have not made the revolution for cheap melons, we have made it for Islam." Indeed, the Islamist movement made a point of distinguishing itself from materialist explanations, which it associated with atheistic Marxism. "Look," said a student at a protest in which demonstrators were breaking liquor-shop and bank windows, "this is not a people that is hungry, it's a spiritual revolution. Look at the people breaking [windows]. They are breaking everything. They're not keeping anything for themselves."[5] But in his calls to action Khomeini also made a point of remarking on the poverty Iranians suffered, as a sign of the spiritual corruption of the regime and its Western supporters:

> Ignore the northern sections of Tehran where they have put things in order; go take a look at the south of the city—go look at those pits, those holes in the ground where people live, dwellings you reach by going down about a

hundred steps into the ground; homes people have built out of rush matting or clay so their poor children can have somewhere to live . . . Is our country poor? Our country has an ocean of oil. It has iron; it has precious metals. Iran is a rich country. But those so-called friends of humanity [the Western powers] have appointed their agent to rule this country in order to prevent the poor from benefiting from its riches.[6]

Whereas Khomeini cited religious causes but used a discourse of economic grievance, Islamic leftists in Iran did the opposite. These groups—whose role is described further in Chapter 7—cited economic causes for the revolution but used an Islamic discourse. Class conflict was to be transcended by Islamic unity, the vanguard party was likened to Islamic prophethood, and class struggle was termed religious struggle (jihad).[7]

Outside Iran, those who attribute Islamist activism to economic distress have tended to be those who are most hostile to this activism. An Egyptian governor battling Islamist dissidents, for example, said in the early 1990s, "Religion is used as a banner by the terrorists to exploit those suffering from poverty and unemployment, to exploit those living in filth or those who cannot get their children into schools. The violent clashes that took place in Imbaba [a slum in Cairo] were the least that should have happened, given the living conditions we found there. Actually, there probably should have been more violence." Unsympathetic academic observers have made similar points. Olivier Roy has written, "The masses who follow the Islamists . . . live precariously from menial jobs or remain unemployed in immigrant ghettos, with the frustration inherent in an unattainable consumerist world." And Bernard Lewis: "Westernization made the gap between rich and poor both greater and more visible," and "such disparities did much to provoke and exacerbate the alienation and anger that destroyed the head of state in Egypt [Anwar Sadat, assassinated by Islamists in 1981], and the entire regime in Iran."[8]

International development agencies in rich countries frequently make their funding appeals in a similar language, arguing that alleviating Third World poverty will reduce political unrest, as in a presentation to the U.S. Congress in 1985: "U.S. security interests are . . . often closely linked to the internal political, economic and social health of individual countries and regions in the developing world."[9] The overlap between hostility and economic reasoning is not universal, however. Some Western leftists, for example, attributed the Iranian Revolution to economic causes while expressing a certain sympathy for it; and some hostile observers have denied that economics had anything to do with the revolution.

There is no doubt that Iran was economically distressed in the 1970s. The agricultural sector, for example, could not keep up with the rising demand for food. Land reform, part of the "White Revolution" proclaimed by the shah in the early 1960s, was intended to stimulate productivity while at the same time democratizing landownership. At least that was its stated goal—a number of observers have argued convincingly that its real intent was to bring the power of the state into the countryside, less than a half-century after the state had gained even nominal military control over the hinterlands. As large landholdings, including some Crown lands, were broken up and distributed among the peasants, the state assumed the distribution of resources, including credit, fertilizer, and irrigated water, with most of these channeled toward large agribusinesses that had the right connections. Only 37 percent of farmers in one study, and 15 percent in another, received credit from the state-run rural cooperatives. Yet larger and more mechanized farms were hardly more productive, per hectare, than the small landholdings producing for subsistence.[10]

Overall, agricultural output increased robustly in the 1960s and 1970s, as more land was put into cultivation. But this was not enough. Once self-sufficient, at least in the major crops, Iran became increasingly unable to meet its rising demand for food. A study conducted province by province in 1972–1973 found that 44 percent of the Iranian population was undernourished, with 23 percent receiving less than 90 percent of their minimum daily calories. In 1970, agronomists projected that Iran would encounter production deficits for the rest of the decade in half a dozen major agricultural products, including wheat, sugar, and milk. The state subsidized massive food imports, including the world's most expensive livestock, which were flown to the country in airplane cargo holds because Iran could not divert enough grain to raise cattle itself.[11]

Meanwhile, millions of peasants and landless farm laborers migrated to giant slums in the cities. Apparently, this too was one of the intentions of land reform, as the shah indicated when the U.S. ambassador suggested a rural electrification plan: "Mr. Ambassador, don't you understand? I don't want those villages to survive. I want them to disappear. We can buy the food cheaper than they can produce it. I need the people from those villages in our industrial labor force. They must come into the cities and work in industry. Then we can send all those Afghans, and Pakistanis, and Koreans back home." The number of Iranians living in cities rose continually, from 23 percent of the population in 1941 to 31 percent in 1956, 38–39 percent in 1966, and 43–47 percent in the 1970s. Some urban migrants lived in squalor in shantytowns that sprouted around cities' edges, and a few occupied cave-like pits dug into Tehran city dumps, as mentioned by Khomeini and documented by social scientists—though such households constituted less than 1 percent of all squatters in Tehran, and squatters constituted only 1 percent of all migrants to Tehran. Underemployment was common, as many urban migrants eked out a living selling chewing gum and other trifles from makeshift stands on the streets. A 1972 survey of 481 male heads of household in Tehran squatter settlements found 15 percent unemployed and 56 percent holding unskilled jobs, such as peddler and "keeper of domesticated animals." Non-squatting migrants to Tehran fared somewhat better, according to a 1977 survey.[12]

Oil wealth appears to have increased inequality. According to periodic surveys of household consumption expenditures conducted by the Bank Markazi Iran (the central bank) and the Plan and Budget Organization, the nation's indicators of urban and rural inequality grew ever larger in the 1970s. Subjective impressions of inequality also intensified: the slums of southern Tehran, for example, contrasted sharply with the tree-lined boulevards of the wealthier northern neighborhoods. The 'Own-'Ali slum in Tabriz sat only a short distance from a military base, where the poor could see the multi-million-dollar warplanes recently purchased by the government as part of its military shopping spree ($1.9 billion in 1970 to $7.6 billion in 1977). "Two kilometres away from our area you can see blocks of luxury flats built for the families of army and air force personnel," a resident told a visitor in late 1978. "We do not expect to have those kinds of flats, but we want at least to have water, electricity and work."[13]

Did this economic distress cause the revolution? A straightforward approach is to ask the people who made the revolution. A group of young workers at the industrial zone of Qazvin, for example, were interviewed half a year after the fall of the shah:

Interviewer: Yes, but for what reason did you participate in the revolution, contribute to it?

Jalil: You know, we are all Muslims and our revolution is an Islamic revolution. We can't participate in this revolution at all for our personal interests. Just as the imam didn't make the revolution for his personal interest, but only for his religion, we didn't make the revolution for material reasons . . .

Interviewer: For what reason did you participate in the demonstrations?

Faramarz: Because, our revolution being Islamic, we knew that things would get better, especially for the class of the disinherited . . . That's why I went as much as possible . . . So, I was a worker myself and I got paid 22 tomans [about three dollars]. In fact, my salary has increased somewhat . . . It's not bad. The working class is currently relatively good. And it will improve [further] . . .

Interviewer: But you yourself, individually, how did you get involved in the revolution? . . . For what reason?

Eskandar: It was last September. Here is the reason: when I learned that people were killing our brothers one after another, I let other people know . . .

Interviewer: So, you say that the motivation that stimulated you to demonstration was really the blood?

Eskandar: It was really the blood, the casualties. And I didn't get involved for a religious reason.[14]

These three workers offered different reasons for their own participation in the revolution: Jalil emphasized religious motivations, Faramarz economic motivations, and Eskandar the effects of repression. To make an economic argument out of this varied evidence, we would have to maintain that Faramarz's response was more "typical" of Iranians in general; or that Jalil and Eskandar were unwilling for whatever reason to admit to economic motivations; or that Jalil and Eskandar were unaware of their "real" (economic) motivations. It makes more sense, however, to conclude that motivations for participating in the revolution were varied—in the words of an Iranian woman, speaking to a North American anthropologist: "If you ask a thousand Iranians about the revolution, you will get a thousand different stories and explanations, and each is correct in its own way."[15]

Further evidence for the variety of motivations comes from the demands made by strikers in the fall of 1978. The sociologist Asef Bayat has analyzed the demands made by 105 groups of strikers during this period. He found that the earlier strikes—before October 1978—focused primarily on economic demands. As the movement deepened, however, strikes shifted to what Bayat categorizes as "political" demands: industrial power—the right to change managers, control over profit-sharing plans, and the like—and governmental change, including the lifting of martial law and the abolition of the monarchy. By November, more than 80 percent of all demands were political. Are we to privilege the earlier economic demands as indicative of the "real" causes and downplay later ones as indirect expressions of underlying economic discontent? Or should we downplay the earlier demands as the timid mark of a repressive era and privilege later political demands as the newly permissible expression of strikers' "real" grievances? This issue fuels the academic debate over whether to interpret the wave of strikes in Iran as a working-class revolt, with most leftist analyses arguing the affirmative. Again, the logical conclusion is that strikes had a variety of goals, including economic ones, and that these goals changed over time.[16]

Another approach to economic causation is to avoid individual consciousness or particular strike demands and look instead at patterns of correlation. Was Iran faring worse economically than other countries? No. In comparison with other Islamic countries, Iran was not nearly the most economically distressed. Let us take data from 1977, since the 1978 data are affected by the strikes and other revolutionary protests.

In 1977, Iran's gross domestic product (GDP) per capita—the most widely used indicator of national wealth—was 60 percent larger than in Turkey, three times larger than in Egypt, five times larger than in Indonesia and Pakistan, and more than seven times larger than in Bangladesh. Income inequality, as measured by the Gini coefficient, was just as high in Turkey as in Iran in the 1970s. Food consumption—daily calories per capita—was 8 percent greater than in Turkey, 14 percent greater than in Egypt, 38 percent greater than in Indonesia and Pakistan, and 73 percent greater than in Bangladesh. Approximately 17 million Iranians did not have access to clean drinking water, compared with 38 million in Bangladesh, 53 million in Pakistan, and 125 million in Indonesia. In the decade before the Iranian Revolution, 38 percent of the rural population lived below the poverty line, compared with 43 percent in Pakistan, 47 percent in Indonesia, and 83 percent in Bangladesh. Iran was not the richest country in the world, but it was by no means the poorest.[17]

If poverty caused revolution, we should have seen massive uprisings elsewhere in the Islamic world as well. Yet, as of this writing, Iran remains the only country in which an Islamist movement came to power through revolution. Military action has brought Islamists to power in Afghanistan, Pakistan, Sudan, and elsewhere; Islamists have won national elections in Algeria, Turkey, and arguably Indonesia. But the mass mobilization that toppled the monarchy in Iran remains unparalleled in the Islamic world. Even in countries like Egypt, where militant Islamists have offered a clear break with the regime, poverty has not driven large majorities of Muslims to join in.

Perhaps, some analysts argue, it is not poverty that generates revolution but rather a taste of wealth. As income rises, it can boost popular expectations: "It is a singular fact," wrote Alexis de Tocqueville of the French Revolution, "that this steadily increasing prosperity, far from tranquilizing the population, everywhere promoted a spirit of unrest. The general public became more and more hostile to every ancient institution, more and more discontented; indeed, it was increasingly obvious that the nation was heading for a revolution." If the economy then turns sour, the disappointment is much greater than if people had been left in poverty all along. The contemporary social-scientific term is "relative deprivation," as distinct from absolute deprivation, but many observers of Iran dusted off and quoted an earlier approach, Crane Brinton's schematic outline of the stages of revolution, which was first published in the 1930s. They argued that the Iranian Revolution was "an almost textbook case," fitting "the classic pattern, outlined by Crane Brinton," of "a considerable period of economic growth followed by a shorter, sharp period of economic contraction and decline," generating "frustrated aspirations."[18]

The chief evidence for this approach is the oil boom of 1973–1974.

On December 23, 1973, Shah Mohammad Reza Pahlavi presided over a press conference at his Niavaran Palace in Tehran. Foreign journalists and local dignitaries filled the ornate room. The shah announced that the OPEC ministers then meeting in the capital of Iran had come to a decision on oil prices. As of the following week, the posted price of Persian Gulf crude oil would rise from $5.11 a barrel to $11.65 a barrel, an increase of 128 percent. He himself had proposed the doubling, the shah said. He wanted to link oil prices to the prices of alternative fuels, such as shale and coal. He wanted to wean the industrial world from its dependence on oil. And, of course, he wanted the extra income. "The industrial world will have to realize that the era of their terrific progress and even more terrific income and wealth based on cheap oil is finished," he said. At the same time, he noted, "We don't want to hurt at all the industrialized world. We will be one of them soon."[19]

The shah intended to use Iran's oil revenues, now hugely augmented at a single stroke, to transform his country into one of the world's great industrial powers. He planned a race against the clock to create a self-sustaining industrial economy before the country's oil reserves ran dry. That deadline lay uncomfortably near. Iran's economic planners forecast a slowdown in oil exports around the mid-1980s. The glory days of massive revenues were not expected to last much more than a decade.[20]

This horizon dictated the frenzied pace of the industrialization campaign. "Our barrel of oil will be exhausted in thirty years, and with this same barrel of oil we have to provide our country with everything it needs to become an industrially advanced, self-sufficient nation. We simply have no time to lose," said the shah. "In 10 years' time we shall be what you [Germans] are today, you, the French or the British." Oil made all things seem possible.[21]

Initially, it looked as though the Iranian economy might perform the miracles promised by the shah. Iran's oil revenue quadrupled from 1973 to 1974, and its government revenue tripled during the same period. Industrial exports grew by more than 50 percent that year, and the economy as a whole—gross domestic product, corrected for inflation—grew by more than 11 percent, placing Iran among the highest-growth countries in the world.[22]

Then chaos ensued. The economy overheated, creating double-digit inflation and overwhelming the country's infrastructure. Bottlenecks developed throughout the production process. Embezzled wealth spilled from the system's every pore. Even with the strong showing in 1974, the economy grew not much faster in the four years after 1973 than in the half-dozen years preceding, and neither did industrial exports, on which the shah had planned to base his post-oil economy.[23]

The problem was "absorptive capacity," which the shah's planners had identified as a concern at a three-day cabinet meeting in Gajareh, near Tehran, in July 1974. Although the shah dismissed their concerns, the country was unable to handle a boom of such magnitude. Metalworks increased their production but could not provide enough material for the new factories. Manufacturing itself remained outmoded and dangerous. A shortage of cement temporarily slowed construction. The power grid could not provide enough energy: in the Iranian year 1355 (1976–1977), one factory suffered 760 power cuts. In November 1976, power shortages prompted an Imperial Commission to hold televised hearings on the problem. In the summer of 1977, power outages shut 180 factories and affected production at 700 others. Transportation delays resulted in the wastage of 30 percent of Iran's produce, the agriculture minister estimated in spring 1977. Imported material and machinery, as well as consumer goods, were stuck at Iran's borders for months, waiting to be processed through overloaded shipyards on the Persian Gulf and customs houses at the Turkish border.[24] The Tehran correspondent for the *Financial Times* of London reported:

At Khorramshahr, the principal port, over 200 ships were waiting to unload their cargoes by mid-1975: ships were having to wait 160 days and more before entering harbour. At one point more than 1 million tons of goods were being kept in ships' holds awaiting the opportunity to unload . . . Once the offloading of goods was speeded up, many goods lay around unwarehoused. At Khorramshahr 12,000 tons were being unloaded per day but only 9,000 tons were being removed per day. At the most congested point, in September/October 1975, there were over 1 million tons of goods piled up on the jetties and around the port.

The report continued: there weren't enough vehicles to transport the goods, so the government bought several thousand trucks. Now there weren't enough truck drivers, so the government tried to import foreign drivers. Three years later "rows of trucks, neatly parked at Bandar Abbas," were still waiting for use.[25]

As with all things in Pahlavi Iran, connections helped: for example, a former supplies manager at the National Iranian Oil Company who used the company's port facilities for his new firm "thereby was able to bypass many of the delay problems encountered by others using southern ports." Corruption was not just a deplorable sideshow in Pahlavi Iran; it was a cornerstone of the Iranian economy, the solid link between political power and economic power. The state was intimately involved in virtually every facet of the Iranian economy, despite the shah's hatred of communism and belief in the free market. Increased oil wealth merely exaggerated this involvement. On a mundane level, consider the plight of a poor migrant to Tehran, as related by the political scientist Farhad Kazemi: "Hamid started selling fruit from a box in front of the [squatter] settlement. In a few days, the local police officer asked Hamid for regular extortion payments. Since Hamid could not pay the fee, he was taken to the police station and charged with obstructing traffic."[26]

According to an Iranian industrialist, "It is impossible to do business without bribing someone." A European consulting firm alerted Western businesses interested in the Iranian market that "graft is pervasive and deeply embedded" in both state and private transactions. Such practices were so entrenched that the Iranian prime minister, fearing that anti-corruption regulations would be laughed at, abandoned attempts at reform, keeping his file of incriminating documents secret. Even "clean" types such as Abol Hasan Ebtehaj, who had made enemies as head of the Plan and Budget Organization in the 1950s when he campaigned against corruption, operated in this environment. In 1977, Ebtehaj wanted to sell his shares in the Iranians' Bank, which he had founded. The Central Bank of Iran objected that the purchaser would gain a majority interest. Ebtehaj went to the prime minister, pointed out that many private banks had single majority owners, and got him to force the Central Bank to drop its objection. Then the Tehran Stock Exchange complained that the sale price was too high. Again Ebtehaj turned to his friends, with the result that the shah himself ordered the stock exchange to accept the deal. No bribes were paid, and Ebtehaj may have been in the right. But the use of state connections for economic causes was so commonplace that no impropriety attached to the process. Ebtehaj himself told this story with no apparent embarrassment.[27]

The shah appeared to be genuinely shocked when a German reporter attested to widespread corruption in 1978:

Reporter: Who informs you about the bribery in Iran?

Shah: I have lots of advisers and every time that a case of bribery arises, members of the Imperial Commission brief me on that.

Reporter: But it does not seem as though the Imperial Commission has been very useful in this respect, since I have lived for two years in Iran and seen that bribery is inherent in society. No matter which government department you go to, unless you bribe the officials nobody will do anything for you. Did you know about this?

Shah: I have heard quite a lot about it but I still don't think you could generalize.

Reporter: I can, Your Majesty. In all the government departments that I have been to, they all ask for bribes, without exception.

Shah: I hope this is not true.

Reporter: Unfortunately it is, Your Majesty. Allow me to tell you that if junior government officials in your country are not bribed they will not be able to live decently.

Shah: Are you really forced to bribe them?

Reporter: Yes, every day.

Shah: Are you telling me that you even bribed civil servants?

> *Reporter:* When the dustman did not empty my bin until I bribed him, of course I had to. Believe me, Your Majesty, every Iranian knows what I am telling you.

> *Shah:* We must talk to people about this. Perhaps the salaries are low, but I don't think that salaries in this country are too bad after all.[28]

The influx of petro-dollars also swamped the capital market and launched a frenzy of land speculation. The Tehran Stock Exchange took off, with share transactions increasing twentyfold in three years. Billions of dollars were transferred overseas—$2 billion in 1975 alone—and many more remained in Iran to fuel increased consumption. Speculation drove up the price of land, especially in the swanky neighborhoods of northern Tehran, dragging up land values everywhere. (As the revolution was building, a former secret-police general asked the current head of SAVAK what his agency had been doing all these years for the revolution to take them by surprise: "General," replied the head of SAVAK, "we have been doing real estate.")[29]

At the top end of the scale, an expatriate in the Iranian capital wrote in early 1978, "the cheapest apartment costs at least US$500 a month [average annual income was just over US$2,000] and a small bungalow in the cooler northern foothills of Teheran more than US$2,500." At the other end of the socioeconomic scale, urban migration raised the demand for housing in the poorer neighborhoods. The official statistics on rent showed slow and relatively modest increases, from 10 percent in 1974 to 23 percent in 1977, but an academic study found that rents in Tehran had increased 30–40 percent annually from 1971 to 1977; by the end of this period rents were eight to ten times higher than they had been a decade before. Forty percent of all lodgings in Tehran were over-occupied, according to this study, and 31 percent of all families lived in a single room. A young military officer making $180 per month paid $200 a month for a "modest" apartment in Tehran in 1974, and nearly five times as much by 1978.[30]

The shah's grand strategy for Iran was failing. A decade or two of oil exports, even at the new prices, could not build a viable industrial economy. The Hudson Institute warned in 1974 that "Iran, in the final decade of this century, could prove to be no more than a half-completed industrial edifice, with the trappings of power and international influence and none of the substance." Some Iranian planners apparently knew this as well. The shah was going to lose his race against the clock—even if revolution had not intervened.[31]

This pattern of dashed expectations was not unique to Iran. All petroleum-exporting countries experienced similar booms and busts. Even an industrialized and wealthy country like Holland, whose North Sea natural gas reserves financed a boom in the 1970s, suffered economic dislocations and industrial stagnation as a result. This phenomenon, known in the economics literature as the "Dutch disease," seems to operate without regard to demographic context, previous economic performance, or political administration. It hit populous Nigeria and tiny Gabon; agricultural economies like Indonesia and industrial economies like Norway; longtime exporters like Venezuela and recent arrivals like Mexico, which had pledged to learn from the mistakes of the forerunners.[32]

Debate continues on the mechanisms of the Dutch disease, but several elements appear to be central. First, the "booming sector" tends to draw capital and labor away from other sectors of the economy. Second, reliance on oil makes the economy vulnerable to the fluctuations of a single export market. Third, the boom creates popular pressure for the state to spend the windfall on social services, extending the operations of the state beyond its abilities. Fourth, oil-sector linkages and increased state spending generate inflation, which nullifies much of the gains in real terms.[33]

An apparently random assortment of countries, selected by geological formations to be possessors of hydrocarbon reserves, suffered similar problems as a result of oil booms. The political effects of such problems diverged widely, however. In Iran, revolution ensued, while in other oil-exporting countries there was little or no popular protest. For purposes of comparison with Iran, I have selected five oil exporters in roughly similar socioeconomic positions: Algeria, Indonesia, Iraq, Nigeria, and Venezuela. All these countries had populations of more than twelve million in the 1970s and relatively high population densities, which set them apart from the smaller rentier states such as Saudi Arabia and Libya. All had exported oil for enough years to feel the 1973–

1974 price hike sharply, unlike, say, Egypt and Mexico. All were Third World countries, unlike industrialized exporters such as the Soviet Union and the North Sea nations. Of course, there were differences among these cases: Venezuela had a democracy; Algeria had recently fought a violent war of independence; and so on.

Despite these differences, all five countries encountered many of the macroeconomic dislocations discussed in the previous section on Iran, and in the Dutch disease literature. Government revenues doubled or tripled in all these countries in 1974, except for Indonesia, where, because of massive short-term debts, government revenue rose "only" 80 percent. This vast windfall translated into increased state expenditures, both in real terms and as a percentage of gross domestic product. In Iran, Nigeria, and Venezuela, this percentage jumped by one-half in a year, representing a massive economic shift. Only in Algeria, which gave international agencies an incomplete series of data, did this percentage decrease. GDP leaped ahead in 1974 in all five comparison countries. As in Iran, however, real increases in GDP, taking inflation into account, were significantly lower. Of the five countries reporting real GDP, none had a real growth rate higher in 1974 than in the preceding year (Nigeria's April-to-April reporting period, however, put some of the oil price hikes into the 1973 data). In keeping with Dutch disease models, the consumer price index rose in all five countries. Indonesia and Nigeria saw inflation rise to more than 30 percent in some years, higher than Iran's inflation; all comparison countries reached double-digit inflation at least once.[34]

According to a variety of economic measures, Iran fell in the middle of this pack. Agricultural production grew more slowly in the 1970s than in the 1960s in all comparison countries—though not in Iran. Manufacturing production, which benefited from large state investment, grew faster in the 1970s than in the 1960s—again, Iran performed better than most of the comparison countries. Other indicators, such as urbanization, literacy, school enrollment, gross national product per capita, industrialization, and daily calorie intake, also show Iran in the middle of the range. Over the period 1967–1977, annual economic growth, adjusted for inflation, was higher in Nigeria (averaging 12.5 percent growth a year), Iraq (5.4 percent), and Indonesia (5.3 percent) than in Iran (5.2 percent), Algeria (4.9 percent), and Venezuela (1.0 percent). The pre-revolutionary Iranian economy, as mismanaged and corrupt as it was, compared favorably in some respects with the economies of similar countries.[35]

But Iran was not, by many measures, the best economic performer in the group, so it is difficult to attribute the revolution to economic success, either. One economic explanation for the Iranian Revolution holds that the expansion of the economy generated new social groups that sought a political voice commensurate with their important economic role. The historian Ervand Abrahamian is one of the most eloquent spokespersons for this explanation: "the revolution came because the shah modernized on the socioeconomic level and thus expanded the ranks of the modern middle class and the industrial working class, but failed to modernize on another level—the political level."[36] But this explanation would lead us to expect revolutions in other high-growth autocracies as well—revolutions that did not take place.

Turning from statistical to institutional analyses, we find that in all the comparison countries, oil revenues had a similar impact on relations between state and society. If Third World states in general have a tendency to be "over-developed," windfall revenues exaggerated the tendency. Case studies on all the comparison countries note this development. State dominance in these countries skewed the economy in the direction of high-tech showcase projects and away from local and traditional production: Algeria, for example, began to face food shortages; the "petro-naira syndrome" in Nigeria—the naira being Nigeria's currency—eviscerated the manufacturing sector. Only in Indonesia, where much of the oil revenue was lost through loan repayments, did agricultural production improve in the 1980s. An econometric study has found a correlation in these three countries between higher oil revenues and agricultural decline.[37]

In the rush to industrialize, the oil-rich states tried to subsidize everybody involved, to the detriment of productivity: they sought to meet the workers' wage demands, the owners' profit demands, and the consumers' price demands.[38] Venezuela, for instance, wanted to keep powdered milk affordable but needed to keep the industry profitable so that capital would not flee to the more lucrative oil sector. Comfortably subsidized and shielded from cheaper European competition, production remained inefficient. Inevitably, the producers asked for further price increases:

> The state wishes to maintain its social policy [of affordable milk] but it considers that the milk producers' demands are excessive. It does not wish to reward inefficiency so it allows the importation of powdered milk from French, Danish and Dutch companies. The price of milk now drops dramatically, to half the price of nationally produced milk, and the national dairy industry decides not to produce powdered milk. This happens with all foods subject to price control and consequently Venezuela imported more than 800 million dollars worth of beans, corn, peas, yams, turnips, milk, oil, chickens, eggs and even sugar last year. As a result of cuts in production Venezuela has changed over a few years from being a country which exported 22 thousand tons of sugar annually to being a country which imports more than 400 thousand tons.[39]

Subsidies streamed from the state through corruption as much as through policy.[40] Chinua Achebe, the Nigerian author, reports "that as much as 60 percent of the wealth of this nation is regularly consumed by corruption." His account of Nigeria fits all the comparison countries, as well as Iran:

> The countless billions that a generous Providence poured into our national coffers in the last ten years (1972–1982) would have been enough to launch this nation into the middle-rank of developed nations and transform the lives of our poor and needy. But what have we done with it? Stolen and salted away by people in power and their accomplices. Squandered in uncontrolled importation of all kinds of useless consumer merchandise from every corner of the globe. Embezzled through inflated contracts to an increasing army of party loyalists who have neither the desire nor the competence to execute their contracts. Consumed in the escalating salaries of a grossly overstaffed and unproductive public service. And so on ad infinitum.[41]

Juan Pablo Pérez Alfonso of Venezuela, one of the founders of OPEC, foresaw as much in 1976:

You think we are lucky. I don't think so. We are dying of indigestion . . . I call petroleum "the devil's excrement." It brings trouble. Look around you. Look at this *locura*—waste, corruption, consumption, our public services falling apart . . . And debt, debt we shall have for years. We are putting our grandchildren into debt.[42]

Inequality grew in several of these countries.[43]

This sad economic scene was punctuated with episodes of political mishandling. The Algerian state, for example, forcibly relocated more than a million urban slum dwellers back to their rural hometowns in the 1980s. The Iraqi government hurled itself into two costly wars. Indonesian and Nigerian leaders stood for election, at least, but only retained office through fraud. Only in Venezuela were elections free, and there the ruling party managed to hold on to the presidency only once in five elections after 1973. These states, arrogant with oil wealth in the 1970s and desperate with oil debt in the 1980s, missed few opportunities to damage their own credibility.[44]

Yet during the 1970s and 1980s, years of two oil booms and busts, revolution did not ensue. Not one of these comparison countries generated a national protest movement that seriously threatened the state. The Iraqi Kurdish and Shi'i uprisings of 1990 were easily handled, despite the weakness of a state devastated by the combined military and economic might of the industrialized world. The Ondo State rebellion in Nigeria in 1983 did not spread to the whole country, nor did the Tatsine riots of the early 1980s. University and journalistic criticism in Indonesia was quieted in early 1978, despite the verbal support of several senior military officials, and the regime survived another twenty years. Scattered Venezuelan protests in the late 1970s and late 1980s never coalesced into an organized movement. Algerian food riots and wildcat strikes in 1988 contributed to an electoral opposition movement in 1991, but the military canceled the elections. A revolutionary movement ensued but was contained, though with horrible brutality. None of these protests collected the kind of mass support that the Iranian religious demonstrations received in mid-1978.

In sum, all these comparison countries suffered serious economic dislocation and increased state dominance as a result of the oil boom. All had plenty of reasons to want to overthrow the state. Yet among the populous oil-exporting nations, only Iran had a revolution in the two decades following the oil boom and bust.

―――――――

Iran's boom and bust was not appreciably worse than that of other countries that escaped revolution, nor was it decisively worse in 1978 than in 1975, when little oppositional activity emerged.

Before delving into the statistical evidence, we should note that these figures are not wholly reliable. Unlike many other developing countries, Iran has long suffered an overabundance of statistics. A British consul noted in 1848: "It seldom happens in Persia that two statistical accounts on one subject, even when derived from official sources, are found to correspond." A century later, an economic adviser from the United States discovered the same phenomenon: "there is no dearth of 'statistics.' Indeed, one can get statistical data on almost every conceivable item of economic interest. This data may be published or may be freely offered verbally by a government department head. About the only certainty, however, is that figures on the same subject from different knowledgeable, even official, sources will be conflicting."[45]

The advent of computers did not change this situation. Various state agencies kept differing sets of figures, and some sources were not consistent from year to year, as categories shifted and earlier data were revised without explanation. Moreover, there is cause for concern about political manipulation of economic and social statistics. As one report put it, authorities, "unwilling to reform the condition of life in Iran, kept reforming the data." For these reasons, the statistics that follow should be treated with skepticism.[46]

For example, let us examine data on Iran's economic growth in the fifteen years before the revolution. Two sources report annual figures on real GDP per capita, based on numbers published by the Central Bank of Iran: Ahmad Jazayeri's book *Economic Adjustment in Oil-Based Economies* and the annual statistical yearbook of the International Monetary Fund (IMF). Both sources use the Central Bank's reporting period of March 21 to March 20, the Iranian solar calendar. Yet annual GDP growth differs between the two sources by up to 10 percentage points.

Still, the two sources agree on one thing: economic growth was stronger and more consistent in the decade before the oil price hikes than in the several years after. From 1965–1966 to 1973–1974, Iran did not dip under 5 percent growth by either measure; in the next four years, it only rose above this level once, in 1976–1977. At first glance, then, there is statistical support for an economic explanation of the Iranian Revolution: a disjuncture between the oil boom's heightened expectations and Iran's subsequent macroeconomic performance.

Yet these same economic factors were as visible in 1975 as in 1978. The two sources agree that Iran's economy underwent a major slowdown in 1975–1976, with an economic growth rate near zero (−0.2 in Jazayeri, +0.1 in the IMF yearbook). Only a year after announcing his dreams for a Great Civilization in Iran, to be funded by dramatically increased oil revenues, the shah began in May 1975 to speak of belt-tightening. Ministries were instructed to cut spending, and then instructed to prioritize projects in anticipation of further cuts. In July, a moratorium on new international contracts went into effect, and Iran started to borrow on the world money markets for the first time since the oil boom, as much as $500 million by mid-August. Private investors began to ship their money abroad, $2 billion dollars' worth in 1975. To combat inflation, the government scapegoated retailers, especially in the traditional bazaar sector, imposing strict price controls and accusing certain well-known merchants of profiteering. In the first weeks of the campaign, in July 1975, ten thousand merchants were fined, more than seven thousand arrested, and six hundred shut down. Already in the spring of 1975, U.S. officials noted economic "strains" in Iran, predicted lower growth rates, and worried that a "significant economic, and potentially political, problem centers on the rising expectations that for many can not be fulfilled."[47]

The sources disagree, however, on whether the recession of 1977–1978 was worse than that of 1975–1976. Jazayeri reports that growth rose to 3.2; the IMF reports that it declined to −0.4. Even if we accept the IMF's figures and conclude that Iran's macroeconomic condition was worse in 1977–1978 than in 1975–1976, by what mechanism might a faltering GDP have stimulated revolutionary protest?

One potential mechanism might involve government spending. As the global recession following the 1973 oil price hikes reduced the gov-

ernment's oil revenues, there would be less money available for the regime to buy popular support. Data from the Central Bank of Iran provide provisional support for this hypothesis, showing a slowing rate
of increase in government consumption from 1975–1976 to 1977–
1978. Still, this slowdown was relative, not absolute, as government
consumption continued to increase faster than the rate of population
growth. In addition, the falloff from 1974's growth rate to 1975's
growth rate was steeper than from 1976's to 1977's, suggesting that perceptions of relative deprivation might also have been expected in 1975.
The opposite pattern appears with private consumption, a second possible mechanism. Here the absolute rate of growth is higher in 1977
than in 1975, but the drop-off from the previous year's growth rate is
steeper.[48]

Inflation was another aggravating factor, though in examining this
topic we should keep in mind that Iranian government statistics on inflation were widely considered to be serious underestimates. The Iranian consumer-price scale, reported quarterly according to the Western
calendar, registered unprecedentedly high inflation in early 1977; however, by the time strikes broke out in the fall of 1978, the inflation rate
was back down to familiar levels. Some observers attribute political unrest not to inflation but to its sudden decline, which may have been
due to recession-inducing state policies. Recession did not, however,
appear to generate widespread layoffs. Indeed, employers were facing a
labor shortage during this period and hired workers from Afghanistan,
Pakistan, and elsewhere. Of more than one hundred strikes summarized by one leftist organization in 1978 and early 1979, only a half-
dozen mentioned layoffs among their grievances, and some of these
expulsions seem to have been politically motivated rather than recession related. Moreover, wages did not plummet in this recession. The
quarterly data show an annual cycle throughout the 1970s, with a dramatic wage increase in January–March, a partial rollback in April–June,
a significant increase in July–September, and a small increase in October–December. In early 1978, wages jumped faster than ever previously
recorded—41.1 percent in a single quarter. Half of this increase was
wiped out in the cyclical downswing of the following quarter, but there
is little in these numbers to predict the outbreak of strikes in the fall of
1978.[49]

Annualized inflation and wage figures present a different, but similarly ambiguous, pattern. Iran began running double-digit inflation in 1973–1974, accelerating to 25.1 percent in 1977–1978, according to the Central Bank of Iran. (Figures for the following year are affected by the revolution itself.) Dramatic wage increases more than kept pace with inflation, but the differential eroded after 1975: wages rose by 30 percent more than consumer prices in 1975–1976, 20 percent more in 1976–1977, and only 1 to 7 percentage points more in 1977–1978. (The revolution prevented the collection of comparable statistics for late 1978 and early 1979.) Daily calorie intake, as reported by the United Nations Food and Agriculture Organization, continued to rise during this period, but it did not match the 8 percent increase of 1975. At this macro level, hunger was being alleviated in Iran and wages were rising even above inflation, but more slowly than in previous years.[50]

Iran's macroeconomic conditions, then, were a mess on the eve of the strikes of fall 1978, and there is considerable evidence of the boom-and-bust pattern that is said to generate feelings of relative deprivation—but conditions were not clearly worse than in the recession of 1975–1976, by many measures. Yet compared with 1978, there was very little oppositional political activity in 1975–1976. One of the few incidents of that period occurred in June 1975, when students held a three-day sit-in at a seminary in Qom. Military commandos stormed the building, beat and arrested the students, and shut down the seminary. Khomeini condemned the regime's violence and spoke of forty-five dead. But oppositional pamphlets from the pre-revolutionary era and post-revolutionary Iranian histories—both of which had a great interest in recognizing and honoring protests against the monarchy—reported almost no public response to this provocation, aside from several small student demonstrations, one at a university television station in Tehran, one in Tabriz, and two at a seminary in Mashhad. If recessions generated protest, surely we would expect more of an echo than this.[51]

A final comparison juxtaposes different economic groups within Iran. There is no clear correlation between a group's economic trajectory and its participation in revolutionary activism. I will give four brief examples: villagers, poor urban migrants, bazaaris, and university students.

The countryside—despite its impoverishment—did not, by and large, participate in the revolution. Late in 1978, villagers with connections to urban centers brought the revolution to their hometowns, but "basically [villagers] were apolitical," according to the social scientist Eric Hooglund, who lived near Shiraz at the time. This apolitical attitude survived the agricultural sector's decade and a half of decline. It also survived the entry of the shah's "White Revolution" programs into rural society, which might have focused discontent on the state. It even survived the efforts of the Islamists, who sent seminary students and other activists to mobilize the countryside throughout 1978. According to an activist villager, most rural Iranians stayed out of politics for "fear of insecurity"—the lawlessness and banditry of the era before state control.[52]

Nor were the poorest urban migrants particularly active in the revolution, before the final days. Only 10 percent of the civilian casualties registered with the Martyr Foundation in Tehran had rural origins, less than half the rate of rural migrants in Tehran at large. In one incident in fall 1978, workers at a construction site in Tehran—most construction workers were recent migrants—laughed as protesters fleeing security forces ran into a dead-end alley, and refused to allow the protesters to take refuge on the construction site. Poor residents of Tehran's southern districts resented activists for "causing trouble and bringing difficulties down on their heads," a radical religious leader in this neighborhood recalled. Activists blamed the apolitical attitudes of recent migrants working at a steel plant in Isfahan for the failure of a strike in fall 1978. A leftist in Tabriz blamed workers' peasant-like attitudes for their slowness to join the revolutionary movement: "They want to move from being 'Hassan *khar*' (Hassan the donkey) to 'Hassan *agha*' (Mr. Hassan). These workers want to become owners."[53]

As late as December 1978, when the country was in open revolt, a film crew found that "many people [in a Tabriz shantytown] did not dare to come out and talk in front of the camera." One Tehran shantydweller told a reporter that he "had no time for demonstrations against the Shah," and another said, "We have heard about the demonstrations, but we don't take part; to demonstrate you have to have a full stomach."[54] Farhad Kazemi, a political scientist studying the shantytowns of Tehran during the revolution, concluded that even within the poorest social strata, the neediest were least likely to be politically active:

> In contrast to the nonsquatting migrant poor and the second-generation migrants, mobilization of the squatters was not as effective. Groups of squatters banded together to defend their homes and prevent forceful removals, but they were not as actively involved in political protests and demonstrations. Their preoccupation with the immense problems of day-to-day survival was far too great to permit sustained antiregime activities.[55]

Janet Bauer, an anthropologist conducting fieldwork in the poor districts of Tehran at the same time, also concluded that "up through the end of 1978, relatively few women (or men) from the lowest income neighborhoods of Tehran were actively participating in street events." A young woman from a poor neighborhood in southern Tehran confirmed this observation for Bauer: "I agree that the middle classes and political members [presumably, members of political groups] were quicker to participate in revolutionary events" than poor people. It was only very late in the movement "that people in our neighborhood began to attend demonstrations and rallies." In the final days of the revolution, some poor migrants could be seen protesting in the cold winter weather, wearing "little clothes, or . . . very old and torn clothes," according to a middle-class revolutionary, and commenting on the spaciousness of the government buildings they occupied: "Look!" one poor man said after entering an arms storehouse. "Even this bloody cement room in which they keep their rubbish is a palace compared to my little *kharabeh* [broken-down building], where ten people live."[56]

By contrast, one of the economic sectors that took up the protest movement earliest and most actively fared reasonably well in the 1970s, while facing ongoing challenges to its economic position. This was the bazaar sector, Iran's traditional system of manufacturing and commerce. By many accounts, the bazaar was enjoying an economic boom. One traditional shopping area in Tehran, for instance, added forty shopping alleys in the 1960s and 1970s. In the mid-1970s, the bazaar controlled two-thirds of domestic wholesale trade, one-third of imports, and one-fifth of the credit market. In addition, bazaaris and their sons were increasingly crossing over into the "modern" sectors of the economy. Numerous industrialists had their origins in the bazaar, and modern educations were opening new career paths for the younger generation. "I have no cause for complaint [in terms of economic performance]," a carpet merchant from the Tehran bazaar told an academic in November 1978.[57]

This is not to deny that bazaaris, like other segments of Iranian society, had numerous grievances against the state, including economic ones. Bazaaris had little access to government credit, whose interest ceiling was lower than inflation, generating billions of dollars in subsidies to companies with royal connections. The monarchy's urban planning showed little respect for traditional markets, as new avenues cut through the bazaar in several provincial capitals, destroying the bazaar in two cities. In addition, the bazaar was targeted in the government's July 1975 price-control campaign, when thousands of meagerly trained inspectors were sent into the nation's bazaars to root out "profiteering." "It was like China during the Cultural Revolution," one merchant recalled in 1978. Yet in 1975, these grievances and provocations were not sufficient to push the bazaar into open protest. This shift occurred only in early 1978, after the religious scholars had begun to mobilize in Qom. "After years of silence, a fire has once again been found in the ashes of the bazaar," one revolutionary religious scholar reported in mid-January 1978.[58]

A further contrast is provided by university students, who had been consistently active in oppositional politics since the 1960s. The British ambassador Anthony Parsons says he noted this fact in conversations with the shah:

> "I've been in America at the worst time of the Kent State riots and all that kind of thing" [the ambassador told the shah]. "I've seen our universities in Britain. I've served in places like Egypt where there's always university turbulence." And I said, "I can tell you, your Majesty, that I have never seen anything nearly as bad as the atmosphere on every single university campus in your country" . . . There was an atmosphere of sullenness, of alienation, of discontent . . . You could say that you could cut the atmosphere with a blunt knife. I was very, very struck by this.[59]

Only violent repression kept the opposition from using the universities as a stronghold. In the late 1960s, an American Peace Corps teacher stumbled upon one of countless incidents: "I happened to witness a shock force of National Police invade Tehran University during a student strike. The troops clubbed viciously and indiscriminately, keeping at it after blood was bubbling on the faces of young women as well as young men."[60] Still, the students could never be perfectly suppressed, as one activist at Tabriz University recalled:

> You realize that outside of the universities, there was practically no political movement. That is, the strangulation and surveillance which had been introduced, which the regime had introduced in all official spheres, was very heavy . . . The only place it couldn't completely control was the university, since the university was principally a place of gatherings . . . SAVAK couldn't send an agent to follow every student whenever they went to see their teacher.[61]

This university activism was undertaken by students who enjoyed promising economic prospects. They were the fortunate few who had survived rigorous entry examinations, and in doing so won a valuable ticket to upward mobility. Oppositional activism did not necessarily disqualify these students from cashing in on their education after graduation, as some of the highest-ranking officials in the government were former oppositionists. The shah is reputed to have told a foreign visitor not to worry about youthful subversives in Iran: "We know just who those young men are and will be offering them high-level jobs as appropriate." In other industrializing countries with large university sectors, such as Egypt, the unemployment and underemployment of university graduates was an important factor generating Islamist activism. In Iran, however, the state had the financial resources to hire huge numbers of university graduates, even if they were not technically needed for the operations of government. As a result, half or fewer of Iran's eight hundred thousand civil servants were thought to "have any utility," according to a U.S. diplomat. Abolhassan Bani-Sadr, the postrevolutionary president of Iran, estimated that state bureaucrats performed only seventy-one minutes of work per day. Civil servants did not earn much, and their wages may not have kept pace with inflation, but a good part of the day was free for second careers, which government officials engaged in as a matter of course. One foreign adviser to the Iranian government admitted to the widespread presence of state officials in industrial enterprises but defended it as necessary, given that Iranian investors were reluctant to risk their capital in industrial ventures and government officials "were guaranteed their regular income anyway." Around the globe, the number of college graduates seems to be associated statistically with the downfall of dictatorships—but this is independent of economic explanations.[62]

Thus a relatively rosy economic picture awaited university students, who were among the most active social groups in the revolutionary movement; the bazaaris, prosperous but under threat, were also central to the revolution. The two least prosperous groups considered here, villagers and urban migrants, were considerably less active. If there is an economic argument to be made from this comparison, it is that poverty dampens oppositional activity—confirming the consensus held by social-movement theorists studying North American and European movements.[63]

If we were observing Iran in early 1978, economic data would probably not have led us to predict that a revolution would soon occur. Iran was faring no worse than many other Islamic countries, than other populous oil exporters, or than its own previous recession of 1975. The social groups suffering the most economically were politically quiescent.

Indeed, the economy looked ready for a rebound in early 1978. On March 6, for example, the *Quarterly Economic Review of Iran,* an independent periodical published in London, sounded fairly optimistic about Iran's economic prospects: "It is probable that progress will be brisk but not breakneck as in the past. In real terms the economy should move forward at some 10 per cent during 1978, with industry once again setting the pace." Two months later, this review began to sound far more pessimistic: "Displeasure with the regime will continue to arise from economic causes. There cannot be expected to be immediate cures for some of the economic ills of the country, including the ravages of inflation, the stumbling rate of economic growth, maldistribution of income, and shortages of goods and foodstuffs." But this drastic loss of confidence was not accompanied by statistics or other information that would suggest a shift in economic conditions since the previous, promising forecast. What had changed was the emergence of an unexpected protest movement, which cast a new light on economic issues that observers had previously downplayed, leading economic causes to be identified retroactively.[64]

CHAPTER 6

Failure of the Fist: Military Explanations

WINTER 1978–1979

With strikes cascading around the country and state revenues threatened by the oil workers' walkout, the situation came to a head in early November 1978. Students inside Tehran University—like many academic institutions in the Third World, Iran's premier university was fenced in—clashed with security forces at the campus's main gate as they tried to march outside. Some students were killed, perhaps three, or perhaps, as rumor had it, thousands. The next day, November 5, students rampaged out of the campus and through the center of Tehran, sacking and burning dozens of buildings, including one at the British embassy compound. Witnesses likened the scene to a war zone, and the extent of the destruction led many to speculate that elements within the government had let it happen, or even organized the frenzy, to shock the shah into decisive action. Another view is that the rioters surprised and overwhelmed the security forces stationed in central Tehran, who retreated to form a perimeter and later moved to retake control.[1]

In any case, the shah reacted with a crackdown, dismissing his civilian prime minister and appointing a military government. The military flooded Tehran with armored vehicles and deterred street protests around the country. "It should be recalled that violence in [the] provinces had reached [a] level of 42 or more cities on a single day just prior to Nov[ember] 5," U.S. diplomats wrote two weeks later. "It has now been reduced to only a handful of provincial cities on any given day." The military also moved to clamp down on the press, which had been reporting protests with an increasingly sympathetic tone since early September. According to the U.S. embassy: "[The] Army last night set up guard at National Iranian Radio and Television (NIRT), and today's broadcasts included voices different from those usually heard. [The] NIRT director has resigned. Only [the] *Rastakhiz* [ruling-party] newspaper appeared this morning." Several leading oppositionists were arrested, including two who were picked up by the martial law administrator himself moments before they were scheduled to appear at a press conference. Perhaps most important for the regime, the military forced the oil strikers back to work, bringing oil production back up to near-normal levels. Strike representatives were rounded up and told, "If you don't start work again, you will be killed."[2]

The shah leavened the crackdown with conciliatory measures. In announcing the military government on television, he also expressed his sympathy with certain aspects of the revolutionary movement, seemed to apologize for the regime's repressiveness, and promised to transform his regime into a constitutional monarchy. He later told a confidant that he read the script on the air without reviewing it first:[3]

> Dear Iranian Nation. In the atmosphere of political openness that has been gradually established in the last two years, you, the nation of Iran, have stood up against oppression and corruption. I cannot but approve of the revolution of the nation of Iran, as the king of Iran and as an individual Iranian. Unfortunately, alongside the Iranian Revolution, others have plotted to take advantage of your sentiments and anger, and have engaged in riots, anarchy, and revolts. The wave of strikes, many of which have been legal, has also changed in nature recently, so as to paralyze the wheels of this country's economy and the daily life of the people, and even to cut off the flow of oil, on which the life of this country depends . . .
>
> I am aware that in the name of preventing riots and anarchy, there is the possibility that the mistakes of the past, pressure and strangulation, may be repeated. I am aware that it is possible that some people may feel that in the name of the national interest and the progress of the country, the implementation of pressure raises the fear that the unholy alliance of material pressure and political pressure will be repeated. But I, as your king, who has pledged to protect the country's territorial integrity, national unity, and Twelver Shi'i religion, once again repeat my pledge before the nation of Iran. I promise that the mistakes of the past, the lawlessness and oppression and corruption, will not be repeated, and that [past] mistakes will also be redressed. I promise that after the establishment of order and calm, a national

government will be appointed as soon as possible in order to establish basic freedoms and organize free elections, so that the constitution earned with the blood of the Constitutional Revolution [of 1906] will come into force. I have heard the message of your revolution, nation of Iran . . .[4]

One viewer wrote that he found the shah's "whine" to be "laughable and ludicrous": "Either he is trying to give the people an ultimatum, or he is truly contrite and disillusioned, but it doesn't matter anymore." A liberal oppositionist in Tehran had an even stronger impression. When he heard that a military government was to be installed, he sought shelter at the house of a friend, a former cabinet minister. According to the former cabinet minister, they sat together and watched the shah's speech on television. "After the speech, [the oppositionist] turned to me and said: 'The shah has lost his nerve; he can do nothing.' Then he called his wife to let her know that he would be home for dinner."[5]

The shah's speech is sometimes taken as evidence that the regime's crackdown was either weak or self-contradictory. Indeed, some observers argue that the shah's entire response to the challenge of revolutionary protest was ineffectively "vacillating" or "inconsistent," or even "hamletic." The combination of concession and repression is said to have encouraged protesters while providing them with new reasons to protest. This incompetence may be attributed to the shah's illness—though it was a secret at the time, the shah knew he was dying of cancer, and medication made him depressed and listless. It may also be due to long-standing personality traits. In crises of the 1950s and 1960s, too, the shah was indecisive and reluctant, according to Gholam R. Afkhami, who interviewed generals and politicians involved in these episodes. Incompetence may also have resulted from turnover in the court. Several of the shah's closest advisers had recently died, and palace personnel were reportedly fired wholesale in the summer of 1978. Whatever the cause, Pahlavi's incapacity arguably paralyzed the state, which had been constructed to rely entirely on the person of the shah. The monarch took a personal interest in the most picayune governmental matters, discouraged initiative by frequently overruling and dismissing officials, and refused to allow officials to cooperate, for fear of regicidal conspiracies. The shah was careful to meet with each of his top aides and generals individually. In the absence of a fully functioning shah, the system could not function. As sound as this reasoning may seem, it misses the logic behind the shah's response to the revolutionary upheaval.[6]

Surely the regime could have engaged in far worse repression than it did. The shah frequently told foreign emissaries that he was unwilling to massacre his subjects in order to save his throne: "The instructions I gave were always the same: 'Do the impossible to avoid bloodshed.'" Various military officials have corroborated this claim. During the course of 1978, a martial law commander allegedly proposed to bomb Qom. An air force general supposedly offered to kill a hundred thousand protesters to quell the disturbances. A SAVAK general regaled a guest from the Central Intelligence Agency "with some fairly bloodthirsty details of how he could have put an end to the demonstrations within a week if only the Shah had given him free rein." The head of a neighboring country suggested the execution of seven hundred mollas. The martial law authorities offered to imprison a thousand opposition leaders on a remote island, perhaps in imitation of South Africa's infamous Robbins Island prison. The shah vetoed all these plans.[7]

Yet the refusal to authorize slaughter does not necessarily indicate lack of will or state paralysis. Less extreme measures were vigorously pursued. Throughout the fall of 1978, security forces routinely broke up protests at gunpoint. Generally they shot into the air, but not always. As an American photographer reported in December:

> Troops meant business—instead of starting out by shooting in the air they were leveling their guns and shooting right at the demonstrators. They spotted me and chased me—they opened fire right at me three times. I had to throw myself under a car twice. Shopkeepers were opening their shutters to let demonstrators inside and office workers were shouting warnings from high windows where they spotted troops moving in.[8]

Another report comes from a U.S. diplomat who visited Qazvin:

> One group of demonstrators was fired upon by soldiers as they emerged from [the] bazaar and reportedly suffered 32 dead. (Comment: Emboff [Embassy Officer] observed many bullet holes in walls and doors at that point, ranging from knee height to well above head level . . .).[9]

In late January, still, on the eve of the government's collapse, a U.S. journalist reported:

The troops then took over the center of the square and began firing at the demonstrators on the avenues leading into it. One soldier kneeled down in a sharpshooter's position and took careful aim before firing and hitting a demonstrator. Some officers were seen giving obvious approval to firing soldiers. Others told the soldiers to cease fire—but only after they had each expended a full magazine . . . A doctor in a blood-stained gown in the emergency room of Daroosh Hospital said: "Most of the wounds we have been treating here were in the stomach and chest. The soldiers were shooting to kill."[10]

Protester fatalities escalated. According to one collection of "martyrs of the revolution," 35 demonstrators died in the first eight months of 1978, 33 in Shahrivar (August–September) and 18 in Mehr (September–October), when the revolution turned to strikes instead of street protests. When the military regime was installed, the number of deaths jumped to 45 in Aban (October-November), then 85 in Azar (November–December), 137 in Dey (December–January), and 179 in Bahman (January–February). In addition, the regime arrested virtually every prominent oppositionist in the country at least once, including several hundred in one sweep in April. The military occupied key economic and governmental institutions. Military officials began to draw up plans for a possible coup d'état. All this for a regime that—despite its pretensions—was not overly efficient in the best of times: Iran's intelligence service was hardly more than a glorified police force, according to the head of the French secret service; Tehran had no sewage system and limited postal delivery service; industry sputtered along with frequent power shortages; and tax collection was so inefficient that this task was turned over on key occasions to ruling party activists. The flurry of state actions in response to the revolutionary movement hardly represented paralysis.[11]

Moreover, it is unclear whether a more one-sided policy—either reform or crackdown—would have been more effective in stifling protest. Such a conclusion goes against the counsel of numerous royal advisers. In ancient India, Kautiliya instructed kings on how to deal with revolts: "make use of conciliation, gifts, dissension and force." In eleventh-century Persia, Nezam ol-Molk urged caliphs to imitate the mercy and liberality of Harun ar-Rashid, but also the deviousness and repression of Nushirwan. In sixteenth-century Italy, Niccolò Machiavelli advised princes to gain both the fear of the people and the love of the people, combining punishment and reward, cruelty and clemency. In the twentieth century, the U.S. State Department analyst W. Howard Wriggins theorized about the strategic mix between rewarding the faithful and intimidating the opposition.[12]

The shah tried to implement just such a combination of the carrot and stick as he faced rising protest in 1978. Several times throughout the year, he cracked down on protesters but at the same time offered concessions and promised future reforms:[13]

- In mid-May, soldiers opened fire on demonstrators marching out of a central mosque in Tehran, but the shah announced that liberalization would continue. In a divisive top-level meeting, the shah overruled the hard-liners in his government and ordered troops to be removed from the seminary city of Qom. Within weeks, the prime minister announced a ban on pornographic films, clearly a gesture toward religious oppositionists, and the infamous director of the security police was demoted to ambassador to Pakistan.[14]
- In early August, the shah announced that free elections would be held the following year; but demonstrations in Shiraz and elsewhere were suppressed harshly, and Isfahan was placed under martial law.
- In late August, the government placed eleven cities under martial law but appointed a new prime minister, Jaʿfar Sharif-Emami, thought to be more acceptable to the religious opposition than his predecessor. Sharif-Emami immediately offered a series of concessions, abolishing the recently introduced imperial calendar in favor of the traditional Islamic calendar, closing casinos, and announcing freedom of the press. "Warning!" Khomeini wrote. These concessions are "a plot to fool the nation and break the Islamic movement."[15]

The shah's actions in early November followed the same pattern: he appointed a military government but struck a public note of contrition and repeated promises of future elections and reforms.

There was a clear logic to this approach. The government sent protesters a mixed message, but one with an underlying consistency: stop protesting and you'll get concessions; continue protesting and you'll get killed. The combination of crackdowns with promises of future reforms was intended to defuse the short-term situation while reaffirming the long-term commitment to liberalization.

To call this strategy "vacillating" or "weak"—as opposed to "coherent" and "subtle"—suggests that some other strategy would have been more effective. The alternative most commonly proposed is consistent repression, untainted by any hint of concessions. Such a policy has indeed worked for many dictators: for instance, in Tienanmen Square, Beijing, China, in June 1989. But repression is "a two-edged weapon": it may enrage protesters to further activism; it may offer new grievances to a populace on the edge of revolt; it may escalate minor demands into major ones; and so on. Repression backfired, for instance, in Timisoara, Romania, just six months after it worked in Beijing. Simply put, there is no generic optimal strategy for state response to protest. Repression sometimes works and sometimes backfires; the same is true for concessions.[16]

The problem for the shah was that Iranians had stopped obeying. The sociologist Talcott Parsons has created an analogy that fits the situation perfectly. Coercion, he suggests, is like the reserves of a bank. So long as the demands on it are limited, the reserves can be meted out effectively. When there is a run on the bank, however, the reserves are quickly overwhelmed. No matter how great the shah's reserves of coercion may have been, no state can repress all of the people all of the time.[17]

In Iran in the fall of 1978 there were literally too many protesters to arrest. A SAVAK report in September noted that 124 religious scholars were currently barred from preaching. Others should be added to the list, the report continued, but the security police lacked the resources to enforce any more bans. In Bandar 'Abbas, in the south of Iran, a Ministry of Culture building was looted—the governor said that "he had no guards to spare and had his hands full all around the town." In a crisis meeting on January 15, 1979—the transcript of which has been published as a book—Iran's military commanders discussed plans for arresting 100,000 oppositionists. A survey of facilities, one general reported, showed room for only about 5,000 detainees. Prisoners were reportedly being released to make room for new arrestees.[18]

In the face of such massive opposition, the security forces had to use their resources selectively. One strategy was to try to make do without the cooperation of the citizenry. The generals identified crucial administrative and economic units around the country and moved to take them under military control. This attempt failed. Perhaps military operations are better at occupying sites than at running them:

- *News.* When the military stationed censors at two major newspapers in Tehran in October, for example, the journalists and other staffers simply refused to work, and other newspapers shut down in sympathy. In January, the military threatened to force state television to air pro-shah military material. Television officials warned that employees would see the program, assume that the network was in the hands of the military, and not show up for work.[19]

- *Electricity.* Electrical workers in major cities started systematic blackouts in December for two hours every evening, timed to disrupt the state-run evening news program and to give cover of darkness to demonstrators violating the 8 P.M. military curfew. The military's plans for taking over the electrical stations were hampered by lack of personnel, as all stations had to be taken at the same moment for the plan to succeed.[20]

- *Oil.* In the oil refineries in the south, responsible for exports that funded the operations of the state, the military sent in its own personnel to replace striking workers. One of the workers describes the result: "They brought in 200 technicians from the navy. These are trained technicians who are usually sent abroad for education. They got one of the pumping stations operating for a while but got rattled when they realized that they did not know the direction of the oil flow in the lines. That, of course, is a very alarming situation, since a fire can result from doing the wrong thing. Finally, our people went in to help them shut down the equipment and get out of the area."[21]

The security forces' attempts to run these key sectors by themselves came to naught. A second strategy, therefore, was to focus their coercive power on these areas. The oil worker's account continues:

> The authorities finally realized that we were the only people who can operate the oil industry in Iran. And that is why they went with troops to the homes of workers in Aghajari and Gachsarran [two small oil fields] to pull workers out of their houses and take them to the plants, where they forced them to work . . .
>
> Despite all our tactics, many of our mates had been forced back to work and production had gone up considerably. At this point, we decided to go back to work along with other workers and prepare for a new strike. We did not consider ourselves defeated, since it was obvious that there was a continuing movement of the entire Iranian people.
>
> What was happening was that one group would retreat one day, and the next day would resume the struggle in different form and propel it forward.[22]

Several weeks later, the oil workers again walked off the job. This dynamic was common throughout the country. Industries would strike, return to work when forced to, then go back on strike as soon as possible. According to an activist in one striking metal plant, for example, "Martial law soldiers poured into here. They took some of the workers away in their cars. The rest of the workers said nothing and got back to work . . . We shut down this plant later on when the situation was getting tense." Iran Air struck in early October, again in early November for almost two weeks, in early December for a week, in late December for a week, and again in January 1979. Telecommunications workers struck at the end of September, the beginning of November, and the end of December, while staging slowdowns and partial stoppages in between. Banks were closed intermittently beginning in early October. Customs officials held up imports at the Turkish border for many weeks, then relaxed their strike on January 19 when they heard that the army was about to take over.[23]

Even when workers were forced to stay at their posts, strikes elsewhere often kept them idle. The oil strikes led to periodic shortages of fuel in many major industries. The customs strikes led to shortages of other materials. For instance, in the banking industry, treasury bills could not be issued for lack of printing ink. Local banks could not disburse cash because strikes and slowdowns at the Central Bank limited the distribution of money. Industries closed down because the shortage of money meant they couldn't meet their payrolls.[24]

The security forces could not coerce all people at all times, and when coercion lessened at any given site, the opposition would return to its protest activities. The shah began to realize the limitations of force: "You can't crack down on one block and make the people on the next block behave," he noted in an interview in October 1978. That is perhaps the most succinct description possible of the overdrawing of the reserves of coercion.[25]

Unable to run the country by itself, or to force the country back to work, the Iranian military began to consider its own future. The opposition directed intense and repeated entreaties to military personnel, urging them to desert. For instance, Khomeini pleaded: "Proud soldiers who are ready to sacrifice yourself for your country and homeland, arise! Suffer slavery and humiliation no longer! Renew your bonds with the beloved people and refuse to go on slaughtering your children and brothers for the sake of the whims of this family of bandits!"[26] Military leaders feared that soldiers might start to listen. Already in 1977, they were worried enough about Islamist influences that they closed prayer rooms on military bases. During demonstrations, protesters handed flowers to soldiers—some generals worried that they were poisoned—and chanted slogans such as: "Brother soldier, why do you kill your brothers?" and "The army is part of the nation." One religious scholar in Tehran ran an operation to process deserters: low-ranking soldiers were given civilian clothes to change into, while high-ranking officers were sent back to their posts to collect information. On several occasions, protesters attacked military personnel and even military bases.[27]

The effectiveness of such pressure on the military is unclear. Even in January 1979, as the shah was about to leave Iran, desertions remained relatively low, a thousand a day or fewer among several hundred thousand troops, Chief of Staff 'Abbas Gharabaghi later estimated. This rate would not have affected the military's capability for several months.

But authorized leaves were increasing dramatically, as soldiers requested furloughs and early retirement, ostensibly to check on their families and property after riots and other disturbances. In a meeting of military commanders on January 23, Gharabaghi estimated that the armed forces were only at 55 percent of their strength, though the tone of his comments suggests that this number may have been picked more for effect than for accuracy. Small incidents of mutiny began to multiply, as did evidence of disaffection among the troops. The U.S. embassy reported concerns about the military's cohesion: "Base security has been tightened on more than one base or unit area, apparently because of indications of decreasing loyalty among junior personnel as well as concern that deserters may attempt to return in uniform to seize arms."[28]

Each military operation exposed the troops to fraternization and further appeals from protesters. Dissident officers therefore encouraged more deployment of soldiers in the streets, while loyalists such as the head of the ground forces proposed keeping the soldiers away from nefarious influences: "We should round up the units and send them someplace where [the demonstrators] won't have any contact with the soldiers. Because yesterday they came and put a flower in the end of a rifle barrel, and another on the [military] car . . . The soldiers' morale just disappears." On several occasions, eyewitnesses reported that large throngs of protesters had persuaded soldiers to give up their arms, throw off their uniforms, and join the demonstration.[29]

During the largest demonstrations, military commanders kept their troops well away from the march routes, guarding "key" sites and neighborhoods. On a few occasions they ordered the military back to barracks, twice directly as a result of defections. But hundreds of thousands of troops could not be held in their barracks for long, an Iranian soldier commented in one of my interviews. A number of soldiers, even officers, slipped out and joined protests—out of uniform, of course, for the uniform could have attracted dangerous attention both from the protesters and from the security forces.[30]

Thus the military was in serious danger of disintegrating, and each use of force increased this danger. If the mosque network was an institution built during the course of the revolution, the military was the opposite: a powerful institution that became less and less valuable as the revolution proceeded. "It is useless to fight," the prime minister, General Gholam-Reza Azhari, told a supporter. "It is now too late, and hour by hour the rioters are taking over." General Gholam-ʿAli Oveissi, the military commander of Tehran, gave the order during Tasuʿa and ʿAshura to "take care, so far as possible, to minimize casualties and give no further excuse to the destructive oppositional elements on these sensitive days." Iranian military commanders struggled to keep the military intact and gave up trying to use soldiers to govern the country. They had been trained to fear Soviet incursions, and they saw the collapse of the Iranian military as a certain invitation to aggression. In Mashhad at the height of the unrest, one commander opined that the military was unable to defend the nearby border with the Soviet Union: "The important border now is our own garrison." In early February 1979, when whole units of troops began to demonstrate, in uniform, for Khomeini, disintegration was imminent.[31]

At the same time, each instance of coercion sparked further protest. On an individual level, Iranians I interviewed commonly explained their turn to activism as the result of the massacre of protesters or some other act of repression that had hit close to home. A bank official from Tehran, for example, attributed his anger to the shooting of his brother: "It was this way for everyone. If my brother, or my friend, or my child was shot, I would get angry and pour out into the streets." "When two people were martyred, fear left us," said a devout high school student from Isfahan. A group of oil workers in Abadan singled out one tragedy in their city: "We realized then just how far the regime could go in its ferocity."[32] Responses such as these suggest that repression, not vacillation, hardened the attitudes of the populace and led to the broadening of the protest movement. The anthropologist Mary Hegland, who observed the revolution from a village near Shiraz, reported that this process was called *az khod gozashteh* or *az jan gozashteh* (literally, "abandoning oneself" or "abandoning life"):

> People felt this emotion and gained this attitude through hearing about or participating in events in which government forces treated people with violence and injustice . . . Villagers reported to me their horror, fury, and frustration upon hearing about such events, as well as their resolve that they

would never rest until the shah and the government that did such inhuman things to their fellow Iranians no longer existed. Hearing about the death of a friend or relative could also cause such emotions, as could learning about a previously unknown martyr, about what kind of person he or she was and the circumstances of his or her death.[33]

Back in January 1978 protesters had chanted, "We have abandoned life. With our blood we have written, 'Death or Khomeini.'" The concept came to be taken up as a part of the self-conception of the Islamist movement and was even a subject of jokes: in one, a group of demonstrators in Rasht, stereotyped as cowards, continue to chant "We have abandoned life" as security forces arrive, but change the object of their devotion from Khomeini to the shah.[34]

Repression was such a mobilizing force that the opposition circulated a hoax audio cassette, along with other opposition cassettes, on which an indistinct voice resembling the shah's was heard giving his generals formal orders to shoot demonstrators in the streets. Presumably the opposition felt that listeners would be more outraged than intimidated by the cassette—a calculation that suggests something was very amiss with the shah's carrot-and-stick strategy.[35]

Indeed, after each atrocity the revolution lurched forward. In late August, after the immolation of several hundred moviegoers in a locked theater in Abadan, protests mushroomed from several thousand to hundreds of thousands. In early September, when dozens (rumors said thousands) of peaceful demonstrators were gunned down in Tehran's Zhaleh Square, wildcat strikes spread across the country. In November, when the shah installed a military government, the opposition denounced it as illegal and began planning for huge confrontations in December, which coincided with the Shi'i holy month of Muharram.

In the month of Muharram in the year 680, Imam Husayn died in battle against the usurper Yazid in the desert of Karbala, Iraq. The martyrdom of Husayn—grandson of the Prophet Muhammad and one of the twelve holy imams of Twelver Shi'i Islam—forms the focus of Tasu'a and 'Ashura, arguably the most important days of the Shi'i calendar. In 1978, these commemorations fell on December 10 and 11. Traditionally, Husayn's martyrdom was observed with preaching, passion plays, and mourning processions. "It is no secret to the royal court or to the Shi'ites that the rituals surrounding the Muharram season are full of latent revolutionary expressions," the anthropologist George Braswell noted in 1975, but these potential political implications were generally left latent. The Islamist opposition sought to transform the events into vote-with-your-feet referendums on the monarchy.[36]

A handful of Islamist hard-liners channeled the heightened passion of Muharram, beginning on December 2, into confrontations with the security forces. Consistent with Western images of Muslim activists, these youths dressed in white shrouds signifying their readiness for martyrdom and headed out into the streets after dark, violating martial-law curfews and bans on public assembly. According to some opposition accounts, the casualties on these first days of Muharram were greater than those of Black Friday. Some activists allegedly poured red dye into the gutters of Tehran to heighten the impression of massive casualties.[37] An American Muslim working in Isfahan recorded his experience of December 3:

> Last evening, while at my house, located in northeastern Isfahan, I heard loud chanting, which was muffled by the distance and the walls. It was about 8 P.M., the time that curfew goes into effect in Isfahan. I checked at the upstairs window, overlooking the street, and I could hear that there was a large demonstration occurring, at the corner of Sadredin and Souroush St[reet]s., some 2 miles away. Simultaneously, another large demonstration was taking place directly to the north of our house. Within a short period of time, I could hear the sound of rifle fire, followed by loud chants of "*Allah u Akbar*" (God is Great), repeated three times, after each volley of rifle fire, signifying, according to a Moslem friend, that a demonstrator had fallen, "in the cause of Allah." This pattern of events continued for about 90 minutes and there were numerous volleys, followed by the loud repetitious chant, as if at a football stadium.
>
> At about this time, my attention was quickly diverted and my heart started pounding. I tensed up. On the next street behind my house, some 100 yards away, a large splinter group of demonstrators had formed. Their chanting of "*Allah u Akbar*" and "*Javid Khomeini*" (Long Live Khomeini) made me both tense and nervous. Our *jube* dog (gutter dog), Aziza, began barking loudly and running in circles around the courtyard. My wife, Fatiha, was standing in the bedroom doorway, shaking. My heart was pounding and my ears throbbing with the roar of the chants. I picked up my knife and wooden spear, cursed Jimmy Carter and prepared to defend

my home. At about this time, I could hear my neighbors joining in with the chanting demonstrators. The demonstrators kept their distance, perhaps because they didn't know that foreigners were living there or perhaps the neighbors' chanting kept them away.

At approximately 10 P.M., a new sound reached my ears. I could hear the wailing and crying of Moslem women, from a house, located at the end of our *kuche* (alley). I looked out the window, the moonlight cast a strange yellow glow across the Iranian landscape. All was silent now, except for the mourning cries, which punctuated the semi-darkness. And the usual smell of grass, trees and earth was replaced by the stench of gunpowder, fires and death.[38]

Yet relatively few Iranians participated in these confrontational events. Others showed their support for the revolutionary movement in a more cautious manner, shouting slogans from the safety and anonymity of their houses. In Shiraz: "After dark everyone in the city it seemed was out in their garden or on their roof chanting and yelling." In the northern town of Shahrak: "the young, then the whole village with the help of a cleric, went up onto their roofs on the first day of Muharram and the following days to cry *'Allah akbar'* for hours in the cold and the snow."[39] In Tehran:

We go up to the rooftop terrace. People are shouting in unison, *"Allah akbar"* (God is greatest). Hassan shouts, "That's a joke! They really mean 'Death to the shah.' We should call a shah a shah." And he howls at the top of his voice, *"Marg bar shah"* (Death to the shah), while Shabnam begs him to be more discreet and rejoin the collective, anonymous *Allah akbar*'s.[40]

If Tasu'a and 'Ashura were to constitute an effective referendum on the monarchy, as the Islamists planned, then the prudent masses would have to join in, not just the vanguard cadre. Khomeini's initial plans sounded frighteningly bloody: "We must rise up against [the shah] and denounce him, however unequal our forces may be," and "if we see the very existence of Islam in danger, we must sacrifice ourselves and be prepared to shed our blood." But the Revolutionary Council that Khomeini had recently appointed to run the revolution from Tehran downplayed the rhetoric of confrontation in order to attract a larger crowd. Ayatollah Mohammad Beheshti, the leader of this group, met with Khomeini in France and told him, "In Iran, an issue is being raised repeatedly, even by eminent people that we've had discussions with, connected with this problem of the struggle, its dimensions, and the linking of struggle with martyrdom . . . Some of the religious scholars we've been speaking with . . . are saying, 'You're inviting the people to a slaughterhouse.'" To reassure potential participants that the event would be peaceful, protest organizers issued a pronouncement promising to stick to a prescribed route, shout approved slogans, and wave a limited set of placards, and "not to allow sabotage such as arson, attacks on houses and shops, thievery, and the like"—language that echoed the government's characterization of the opposition—"which often present an excuse for the opportunistic regime to intervene." The Islamists agreed not to shout "Death to the shah" and recruited thousands of marshals to keep order along the route. Furthermore, the Revolutionary Council allowed liberal oppositionists to broker an agreement with the military government, which announced two days before the events that it would permit the processions on Tasuʿa and ʿAshura so long as these remained orderly.[41]

Up to the last minute, though, it was unclear whether the government agreed in good faith, or whether hard-liners might use the occasion as an excuse for yet another violent crackdown. Ayatollah Mahmud Taleqani and the National Front leader Karim Sanjabi, who were slated to head the processions, both received warnings from apparently well-intentioned insiders that violent plots were afoot, either by security forces or by leftists. Rumors of plots were rife, and stories circulated that hundreds of thousands of people were buying shrouds in preparation for martyrdom. The state-run radio reported that 130,000 cars left Tehran in the days preceding Tasuʿa.[42] "Whenever two or three people got together, they would start a discussion. Words, views, advice all differed from top to bottom. It was unclear what would happen," the author Mahmud Golabdareh'i wrote:

My mother is afraid. My father is asleep. My brother made a telephone call and [afterward] told my mother: "Tell the kids not to leave the house tomorrow. They're going to kill everyone tomorrow, like on September 8. They're going to shoot from above, from rooftops and helicopters." My mother started crying. Now he picks up the phone again and dials. He says, "Come and hear for yourself," and puts the receiver in my hand. I say "Hello," then "Yes, I see," then "Goodbye." Now I'm terrified. Everybody has gone to sleep. I can't sleep.[43]

Ayatollah Baha'uddin Mahallati in Shiraz warned on the eve of the demonstrations, "Maybe we'll be killed tomorrow. We're facing guns, rifles and tanks. Whoever is afraid shouldn't come." Islamists organized medical personnel to be on call in case of casualties in Isfahan and Tehran. A young engineer in Tehran wrote out his will before heading out for the demonstration. A woman in Shiraz recalled, "When I went to the 'Ashura march I didn't know if there would be soldiers shooting at us or not, or perhaps we might be bombed from the air. But I didn't care. I had given up on my own life." Mostafa Askari, a villager working in Shiraz, admitted, "I was afraid. The truth is that I was afraid. It's different from going to a demonstration in Washington. In your Washington there aren't machine guns. Here, there are machine guns!"[44]

──────────

It is almost unheard of for a revolution to involve as much as 1 percent of a country's population. The French Revolution of 1789, the Russian Revolution of 1917, perhaps the Romanian Revolution of 1989—these may have passed the 1 percent mark. Yet in Iran, more than 10 percent of the country marched in anti-shah demonstrations on December 10 and 11, 1978. Photographs of these events showed massive avenues filled for miles, not just in Tehran but throughout Iran. So many people marched, according to the French reporters Paul Balta and Claudine Rulleau in Tehran, that "there is no one at the windows to watch the processions pass." The British ambassador Anthony Parsons, looking out his office window—apparently unseen by Balta and Rulleau—said the processions took all morning to pass by: "The street is wide but it was filled from pavement to pavement and from top to bottom as far as the eye could see for a period of three or four hours. And it was only one of the many feeder roads to the main procession route." Foreign journalists estimated the crowd in Tehran at 500,000 to 1 million strong on December 10, and 500,000 to more than 1 million the next day. Opposition publications estimated 2 to 4 million in Tehran on the 11th, plus 700,000 to 1 million each in Isfahan and Mashhad, 500,000 to 700,000 in Tabriz, 400,000 in Rasht, 300,000 in Ahwaz, 250,000 to 300,000 in Shiraz, 200,000 to 300,000 in Abadan, 200,000 in Qom, 150,000 in Khorramshahr, more than 100,000 in Arak and Kermanshah, and tens of thousands in each of a dozen more cities—a total of 6 to 9 million. Even discounting for exaggeration, these figures may represent the largest protest event in history.[45]

Despite the fears of bloodshed, the demonstrations were almost entirely peaceful. Marchers wore expressions "of exhilarated astonishment, as if they can't believe no one is stopping them." The government's permissions and the Islamists' promises held. In keeping those promises, the Islamists transformed Tasu'a and 'Ashura, just as they had transformed other Islamic rituals during the year of revolution. One devout bazaari in Shiraz complained that the fuel shortages the Iranians were experiencing were a just punishment for these sacrilegious transformations.[46] Deemphasizing mourning in favor of activism, the Islamists changed Husayn from a victim to a revolutionary figure:

> In years preceding the revolution, participants in the mourning rituals of 'Ashura had struck their chests and beat their backs with chains while chanting mourning couplets and crying in unison, "Husain, Husain, Husain." In contrast, during the revolutionary processions of 'Ashura 1978, marchers raised their fists to beat the air, marking the rhythm of the phrase *Marg bar shah.* (Down with the shah.)[47]

Traditionally, religious leaders stimulated passions through public narration *(rowzeh-khan)* and reenactment *(ta'ziyeh)* of Husayn's martyrdom, under the wary eye of the police. As the revolution proceeded, the authorities were apparently horrified by the possibility of "hundreds of *ta'ziyeh* performances involving millions of persons being brought to an emotional pitch in a highly moving religious spectacle." In December 1978, by contrast, procession organizers sought to *restrain* passions. French journalists reported, "In fact, while several times the crowd starts shouting 'Death to the shah!', the marshals, ten thousand strong, quickly intervene to obtain silence."[48] On one road in the north of Tehran, for example, a seminary student acting as a marshal tried to dissuade marchers from chanting "Death to this Pahlavi monarchy," according to a leftist writer:

> Suddenly a young seminary student, disturbed and agitated, jumps onto a minibus and grabs a microphone to his lips: "Quiet, quiet, quiet!" he yells. All at once silence falls on the plaza and everyone shuts up. The student's voice shakes. Emotion grips his throat. He is afraid. But the calm does not stick, and behind me I hear him say: "Pay no attention to slogans from outside. They are not with us. People, don't listen!" He is yelling frantically.[49]

Only in Isfahan did the Islamists fail to maintain order. According to an oppositional account, "Groups with red hats"—by implication, leftists—"attacked statues and pulled them down, and a group attacked the SAVAK offices. Shooting started from inside the building. A large number were injured, and ten people killed. Widespread arson got under way in Chahar Bagh Avenue: cinemas, shops, banks were burned. At the end of the evening, a military government was announced to put a stop to the disorder. Shooting could be heard all night."[50]

The peaceful passing of Tasu'a in most cities reduced fears a bit for the next day's 'Ashura processions. An engineer in Tehran, for example, told a reporter, "Yesterday (Sunday) I was the only person in my family to participate. Today, the whole family is demonstrating. They saw that the army did not interfere." The marshals' control over slogans was somewhat laxer on 'Ashura, as well. In Tabriz, where the military governor had forced religious leaders to limit themselves to traditional chants, a small group of Islamists violated the agreement and chanted revolutionary slogans.[51] In Tehran:

> Normally the procession, like the previous day's, would abstain from all slogans against the king. But the cry breaks out, *Marg bar shah* [Death to the king]. "No," protests a *mollah* [religious scholar], "we must shout only religious slogans." Later, this force, this density in motion, shouts out "Death to the shah." . . . "Death to the American dog," "Shah on the Americans' leash," "Shah the traitor." A linguistic polyphony embellishes on the same theme, the Persian language, rich with resources, repeats incessantly, with different forms and rhythms, "Shah, we will kill you."[52]

Yet fears of state repression continued more or less unabated until the last moments of the monarchy. Khomeini's Revolutionary Council in Tehran took no minutes, made no recordings, and generated no written documents until two weeks after the victory of the revolution, out of fear of state repression. In December, Iranians worried that hundreds of American agents were being smuggled into the country to squelch the revolutionary movement. The same month, a journalist wondered, "has the time come to put order into this chaotic situation? The answer is not clear." In late January, rumors flew of an impending coup d'état. In early February 1979, just a few days before the regime fell, a newspaper columnist noted: "In Tehran, conversations are limited to this: how will the revolution, which has gone half-way, deal with the fundamental power of the government? Will [the government] resign? Will there be a fight? And how far would fighting go?" Fear did not prevent protest in Iran, just as it did not prevent civil rights activism in the United States. But it was a real factor that had to be counterbalanced by other factors—in particular, as the next chapter argues, by the growing sense of viability.[53]

CHAPTER 7

A Viable Movement: Anti-Explanation

WINTER 1978–1979

How did the protesters overcome their fear of state repression? Mostafa Askari, quoted earlier on the peril of demonstrating in a country that used machine guns for crowd control, explained his participation in the Tasuʿa march in Shiraz: "I hadn't been in a demonstration before. This was my first one . . . I hadn't planned on coming to take part in the demonstration. I had just planned to come and watch . . . Because I hadn't slept for two nights, I planned to go home to sleep that day. I was going to watch the crowds a bit and then go home to bed. I just wanted to see what was going on. But when I came and saw so many people, I suddenly decided to join in."[1]

That same day, demonstrators in Tehran told reporters, "We are three million strong . . . They cannot—it is impossible—they cannot massacre us."[2]

Similar testimony from numerous other protesters in the last months of the revolution suggests that they were impressed by the number of their fellow demonstrators, and that they felt this number accorded them a certain safety, even if the government did attempt a crackdown. This theme of safety in numbers came up frequently in my interviews with participants in the revolution:

An army conscript from Tehran: The more people, the less fear.

An unemployed former conscript from Tehran: I saw in the streets the crowds getting bigger and bigger . . . I saw my friend in the street shouting, "Death to the shah," and my fear left me.

A telephone company official from Tehran: When everyone was in the streets, huge crowds, I'd go. I didn't go if there was going to be danger and shooting.

A truck driver from Tehran: Everyone was participating, so I participated too . . . SAVAK could only catch one or two people, not everyone.

A shopowner from Shiraz: It wasn't just one, two, or a thousand people.

A government official from Gombad: There were lots of people there. If it had been just one person . . .

A shopowner from Tehran: When everyone is shutting down [their shops], the rest shut down too.

A high school student from Lorestan: When the people were of a piece, I participated.

An auto mechanic from Tehran: It was not an individual decision. Everyone was united. When everyone is united, one person cannot stay separate.[3]

Other researchers have discovered similar sentiments:

Interviewer: So how come you became engaged, all of a sudden?

Faramarz, a factory worker in Qazvin: Because in the month of Shahrivar [August–September], the people spontaneously erupted into the streets and gave up so many martyrs. Primarily because the people demonstrated in the streets and there were martyrs, because this revolution had become an entirely official fact. The people, from that point on, knew that this revolution would be victorious, 100 percent.

Interviewer: You were sure of victory?

Faramarz: Yes, I was sure of it, 100 percent, because 99 percent of Iranians were participating in the revolution.

Interviewer: How did you come to take part in the demonstrations?

Hasan K., an elderly peasant who recently migrated to Tehran: . . . During the revolution, I saw people throw themselves into the streets and, one month later, the streets were full. Nobody could have imagined that this would happen.

Anonymous demonstrator: A sort of fear was in our being, above all in public services. But after the demonstrations and events of September 8, people

realized that there wasn't anything to it, and people expressed their inside on the outside . . . no longer fearing their hierarchical superiors or
subordinates, [no longer fearing] high or low. Fear had left them. [From
this moment] the demonstrations got bigger and bigger.

A worker at a cement factory near Isfahan: When I was certain that the people
were not for the shah, I spoke up.

An author from Karaj: People slowly realized that either they shouldn't come
into the streets, or, if they did, they must all be single-minded and single-
voiced.[4]

Some of these voices were apologetic, as though admitting to a lack of
heroism. Others distanced themselves from the tragic turns that the
revolution later took. Others were proud of the country's unanimity in
protest and of their own participation.

But such recollections cannot be easily dismissed as after-the-fact ra-
tionalizations, as they are confirmed by evidence from the period of
the revolution itself. As noted in Chapter 2, Khomeini's decision to mobilize against the shah in late 1977 appears to have resulted from his
perception that mourning protests for his son Mostafa indicated that
the nation was ready to act. Before he had heard of these protests,
Khomeini spoke about "the few people who we've seen stir and speak
out." Eleven days later, he exulted that "all are awakened." A Mashhad
activist worried in early 1978 that "we can't just strike by ourselves." A
year later, U.S. diplomats in Tehran noted during a strike day:

Most shops have closed during [the] morning . . . as shopkeepers evaluated
[the] local situation: no one wants to have the only open shop on the
block . . . Everyone knew of Khomeini's appeal [to strike], yet [the] vast majority came to work, they decided to stay or return based on what neighbors
were doing.[5]

The expectation of future protest, as much as protest itself, changed
people's thinking about the stability of the current regime:

A university professor from Tehran: A year before, I heard news about demonstrations, but I didn't feel that it was something very important. That is, I
thought, well, something is happening, but I didn't think that it would
bring about a basic change in my country. Later, in September, 1978, at

the start of school, when we began classes, everything had changed. All of a sudden, the feeling arose that things weren't that way anymore.

A foreign businessman in Tehran: A sober, loyalist Iranian who witnessed the famous Thursday (7 September) march said his confidence in the future of the existing order had been shattered by that one sight of such mass passion and discontent: he couldn't see how it could be appeased or permanently held down by the military.

A royal adviser in Tehran: In 1978, especially from the summer on, it was clear that this was a year unlike any other.

A lawyer from Tehran, describing his neighbors' decision to participate in the Tasuʻa demonstration: I had the sense that the bourgeois had come to see what was happening, without much conviction, to eventually, one day, be able to say, "I was there," and not to be looked upon badly by certain devout neighbors. The future was up in the air, better get on board.

An Iranian bishop in Isfahan: A few months earlier you could not have said one word against the Shah, and now his statue, and that of his father, was being toppled, and seemingly no one could do anything about it.[6]

As Iranians faced a future that was "up in the air," some hedged their bets in case the revolution succeeded. At a demonstration in September, marchers took up the cry "The shah is finished," which may have been a bit premature but was undoubtedly sincere. Protesters felt that success was within reach.[7]

"Iranians are like sheep," an expatriate once told me, explaining that Iranians tend to follow the crowd behind a demagogue. Were you like a sheep during the revolution? I asked. No, he said, he knew what was going on and didn't get too involved.

This elitist strain has long competed with populism and conspiracy theories in Iranian self-understandings. During the Constitutional Revolution of 1906, for example, some pro-democracy elites made fun of uneducated people who were said to have no real understanding of the concept of constitutionalism: "In the beginning of constitutional government in Iran, a large crowd gathered in front of the English embassy shouting, 'We want constitutionalism! Constitutionalism, constitutionalism!' By the second or third time, they imagined that constitutionalism was some kind of food! At that moment somebody shouted, 'I've been waiting for two days and I haven't gotten even a single piece of constitutionalism.'"[8]

Orientalist foreigners shared this disparaging opinion of Iranian popular ignorance. The U.S. ambassador, arriving in Iran just after the Constitutional Revolution, believed stories of ignorance to be essentially true, even though he admitted that particular examples were fabricated:

> On my arrival at Enzeli [an Iranian port on the Caspian Sea] I was told the following story by the Mehmandar, my official host: A few days before, a man in that city had been called to account by the authorities for insulting a woman in the street, and in defence he had appealed to the new Constitution. He asked to be informed as to what was meant by "freedom of speech" if he could not tell a person what he thought of him. Many similar stories are current, with or without foundation, and they serve to show how much is understood by the people of the real significance of a Constitution, for which no Persian word existed and one had to be invented.[9]

This elitism was not reserved solely for "Orientals" but was directed toward European and North American masses as well. During the late nineteenth and early twentieth centuries, as non-elites began to organize powerful movements in the West, many elite observers were highly critical of what they saw as sheep-like political behavior. A number of influential social psychologists wrote on this topic almost simultaneously in the 1890s, generating disputes over priority of discovery.[10] Scipio Sighele, for example, based his analysis of "criminal crowds" on the "law" of hypnotic suggestibility, then extended the metaphor to all assemblies, including elected representatives:

> Once formed, Parliament functions again and always in accordance with the laws of collective psychology. And the intellectual level of those who compose it, already quite humble, descends still further as a consequence of the law that we have enunciated. Offices, meetings, commissions, small parliaments within the large, multiply the probabilities of mediocre results and

unpleasant surprises . . . The [parliamentary] Chamber is in sum, from the psychological point of view, nothing but a woman, and often a hysterical woman at that.[11]

Gabriel Tarde argued in 1892 that crowds descend the "ladder of social evolution," defining "crowds" as any organized assembly, including parliaments. The most famous social psychologist to address the subject, Gustave Le Bon, plagiarized and popularized the ideas of his predecessors in 1895, including the analogy with hypnosis, the equation of popular political participation with female inferiority and the barbaric crowd, and even the ladder image (Le Bon wrote that "by the mere fact that he forms part of an organised crowd, a man descends several rungs on the ladder of civilisation").[12]

Derogatory views of crowd behavior continued in the twentieth century. The most prominent example in North America came from Herbert Blumer, who, despite being very sympathetic to progressive movements and purportedly the only white person Malcolm X ever trusted, nonetheless likened crowds to cattle. He argued that "an individual loses ordinary critical understanding and self-control as he enters into rapport with other crowd members and becomes infused by the collective excitement which dominates them." In Europe, the most famous work on collective behavior, Elias Canetti's book *Crowds and Power,* summoned up images of crowds that spread like fire, like water, like wind—a series of naturalistic metaphors that reduced participants to inanimate objects. (As Hannah Arendt has noted, such metaphors may also be adopted by participants themselves when shocked by the transformations they have experienced.)[13]

In the second half of the twentieth century, and especially after 1960s radicals began their long march through academia, the study of protest came to view such dehumanizing treatment of activists as unacceptably reactionary. In 1957, for example, Ralph H. Turner and Lewis M. Killian objected to the notion that collective behavior is inherently irrational and contested the animal-herd analogy. In the second edition of their textbook on the subject, largely rewritten in light of the tumult of the late 1960s, Turner and Killian go even further, repeatedly rejecting pejorative definitions of collective behavior. The "collective-behavior" school was reformed, but it was not saved. The study of protest is now conducted far more often under the rubric of "social movements" than of "collective behavior." The two fields share a single caucus in the American Sociological Association, but the marriage has been a barren one—in John D. McCarthy's striking metaphor—with the social-movement specialists paying little attention to the dwindling band of collective-behavior specialists.[14]

As a result, the sociology of social movements is in danger of losing the great insight of the collective-behavior school: that potential protesters are keenly affected by their perceptions of other potential protesters. We need not characterize this process as hypnotic suggestion, rabid contagion, or unstoppable fire or flood; we can just as easily characterize potential participants as rational actors calculating the costs and prospects of protest. We need not focus on displays of disorganized effervescence; we can find similar processes in highly organized, long-term movements. This chapter presents evidence of such behavior during the Iranian Revolution.

The view that people decide to protest based in large part on their expectation that others will protest as well has survived in the interdisciplinary social-scientific field of "collective action" (not to be confused with the older field of "collective behavior"). Specifically, the literature on "critical mass" phenomena predicts that—as with molecules that generate nuclear explosions when they are surrounded by enough other fissile molecules—people's decisions to engage in collective action depend on expectations that sufficient numbers of like-minded collaborators will also contribute. But critical mass theorists reject the inanimate implications of the naturalistic metaphor. Instead, they assume that people are generally rational, that is, that they "somehow attempt to weigh costs and benefits," in the words of the sociologists Gerald Marwell and Pamela Oliver. Only when perceived benefits outweigh perceived costs, in this view, will people participate in collective action, including social movements.[15]

The original impetus of the collective-action perspective, ironically, was to argue that rational actors would *not* collaborate unless they were promised "selective incentives" that would be withheld from non-participants. The economist Mancur Olson suggested in his book *The Logic of Collective Action* (1965) that it made more sense *not* to contribute to a cause than to contribute, if non-participants (later labeled "free-riders") would benefit from others' doing the job. Why bother participating in a revolution, for example, if you would benefit just the same by letting other people go to the trouble? If everybody calculated this way, of course, no collective action would ever take place.[16]

Critical mass theorists turned this argument on its head. What if people *want* to engage in collective action but only let themselves do so when it looks safe and seems likely to succeed? In addition to the costs of protesting, such as arrest or injury or simply wasting one's time, there may be benefits too, such as being on the winning side of the contest, receiving positive feedback from one's peers, and being true to one's political beliefs. Mancur Olson, reflecting on the overthrow of Communism in Eastern Europe a quarter-century after his initial contribution to the debate, even allowed that the "drama of sudden and awesome political change" might attract some protesters. The political scientist Mark Irving Lichbach has usefully catalogued dozens of ways in which "free-rider" problems can be overcome. If people have "private preferences" for protest, or "hidden transcripts" of resentment, they may be waiting for the right moment to act on them, when the movement reaches a "threshold" with which they are comfortable. The distribution of these thresholds makes all the difference, as the economist Thomas Schelling has spelled out in dizzying permutations.[17]

There is a crucial distinction between "free-rider" and "critical mass" models of protest: as a protest movement attracts increasing numbers of participants, gaining momentum and looking as though it may actually succeed, the free-rider model expects the remaining non-participants to be *less likely* to join in (why bother if the movement is going to win without their having to lift a finger?). The critical mass model expects the remaining non-participants to be *more likely* to join in (they will have greater safety in numbers and a chance to make history by doing what they consider to be the right thing).

When it comes to routine political contests, such as democratic elections, the evidence for either of these effects is limited and contradictory. In non-routine situations such as the Iranian Revolution, by contrast, the evidence lies overwhelmingly on the side of the critical mass position and against the free-rider position. Similar evidence has emerged—with greater precision than can be established for the Iranian case, using survey methods and rigorous sampling procedures—

for a Dutch union movement in the 1970s, a West German anti-nuclear movement in the 1980s, and the East German revolution of 1989. People who expected large numbers of protesters were more likely to engage in protest themselves than were those who expected few people to participate.[18]

These studies may raise hopes that we can predict the emergence and extent of protest activity through surveys. Ask three questions and tabulate the results: (1) Do you support protest (on a given subject)? (2) Would you get involved if the protest were of a certain size? (3) Do you expect the protest to get that big? Critical mass models are generally explicit in treating answers to these questions as constant and exogenous.

The problem with this approach is that each person's answers to these three questions may vary drastically over the course of a protest movement. In Iran in 1977, only heroes, fools, and provocateurs would have told a surveyer that they supported revolution against the shah, that they knew of a threshold past which they would participate in such a revolution, and that they expected protests to pass that threshold. The vast majority of Iranians would surely have declined to answer at all, out of fear of the regime's security forces. But this is not simply a case of "hidden preferences" that later came out of hiding. Preferences changed. Mehdi Bazargan, the liberal oppositionist, did not support revolution in 1977; in early September 1978, he argued, "I don't believe that religious scholars can run a government." Then in October 1978 he changed his position. A leftist woman underwent a catharsis at a major demonstration, when she came to realize that "Islam is a great religion, because it makes all things possible." A man in Tehran described the conversion of his wife to Islamist activism—"a woman who up to a year ago had no truck with such things, whose biggest problem was clothes, which were sent to her from London along with various items of cosmetics." Periods of unrest may be high-torque environments for preferences.[19]

These people could not have predicted their own personal transformations, and they could not have foreseen the conditions under which such transformations would occur. Even Khomeini did not appear to think in September 1977 that he would live to see a revolution: "When humans get old and senility overtakes them, all of their faculties grow weak," he apologized. Before the whole country seemed to be rising up against the regime, it would have been meaningless to ask Iranians, "What would you do if it looked like the whole country was rising up against the regime?" Think about such a question in your own time and country—can you give a meaningful answer? I can't. Even though I study revolutions, I can't imagine living through one myself, in my own country. I am not one of those rare people—mainly professional revolutionaries and bigwigs with exit strategies, I would guess—who give much thought to such strange and remote possibilities. And even if I try to give it some thought, I could not possibly summon up all the permutations that might seem of supreme importance if the revolution were actually taking place—the particularities of the leaders' ideologies, the positions each of my relatives would take, the reliability of the friend who might whisper to me, "Everybody is going to be there."

With forms of protest more routine than revolution, such predictions are less difficult. I might be able to list issues for which I would join a march on the Mall in Washington, D.C., and the minimum number of marchers that would make it worth my while. I can envision a petition on a variety of subjects, and the number of signers (even some particular individuals) I would want to sign with me. I know what these experiences feel like, and I am fairly confident that the parameters will remain constant for the foreseeable future. With these actions I am unlikely, for example, to be arrested or beaten or shot. There are causes for which I am willing to risk imprisonment and injury, but it is difficult to specify the conditions under which I would do so.

Even with routine situations, however, people are not particularly good at predicting their future behaviors—a considerable literature in the field of psychology has established this repeatedly.[20] The less routine the situation, the harder it is to visualize. The harder it is to visualize, the more difficult it is to predict how one would act. And if individuals can't predict their own behavior, then our survey strategy won't work. We might be able to predict the routine, but for breaches of the routine, we'd get too many respondents saying, "I don't know" or "It depends." I imagine that's what I would say.

Yet people conduct such surveys all the time. Not just social scientists—everybody. People are constantly asking family members, friends, acquaintances, and strangers: "What's going on? What are you planning to do? What if . . . ?" And the greater the break from the routine, the more important these surveys become to us. In extraordinary situations, we really need to know what others are planning to do so that we can figure out what to do ourselves. One of the most common themes to arise in my interviews with people who lived through the Iranian Revolution was the politicization of everyday conversations. People stopped talking about topics that had come to seem frivolous and instead spoke obsessively about politics. As the stakes got higher, Iranians broke out of their usual social circles and sampled opinions more widely, striking up conversations at every possible opportunity. In November, as rumors of impending armed uprisings circulated around the country, the security police reported that "everyone is asking everyone what is going to happen."[21] People sought out conversations with strangers they met on the street, on the bus, at work—a strategy for overcoming the biased sample of one's own social circle. "Whenever two or three people got together, they would start a discussion," Mahmud Golabdareh'i wrote. "Words, views, advice all differed from top to bottom. It was unclear what would happen." Under conditions of confusion, people work harder than ever to make sense of the world around them, to generate retroactive predictions for how things could have turned out the way they did and prospective predictions about where things seem to be heading.

The study of social movements has thus embarked on one of the greatest quests in social science: to discover the pattern in conditions of confusion, and therefore the rules underlying behavior that defies the rules. But the experience of confusion undermines social scientists' retroactive predictions about such episodes. If protesters decide to participate in large part based on their expectations of how many others will participate, and these expectations and decisions are confused and constantly in flux, then there is no solid ground for an outsider to stand on.

———

The Pahlavi regime is sometimes said to have lost "legitimacy," as though this were an explanation for the shah's fall. It is unclear what evidence might be offered for such a view, or how to distinguish legitimacy from grudging acquiescence. Is the United States due for a revolution, since polls show that a majority of the population doesn't trust the government, agrees that the "government is run by a few big interests looking out for themselves," and feels that "public officials don't care what people like me think"? The missing ingredient here is the perception of a "viable" alternative.[22]

People evaluate the "legitimacy" of a regime on a relative scale, not an absolute scale. To take the example of economic performance: it's not that a regime delivers or fails to deliver a particular level of growth, but that a different regime would have done "better"—a counterfactual whose attractiveness rises and falls independent of the current regime's actual economic performance. "Better" could mean any number of things, including more growth, or a different distribution of economic gains, or non-economic factors that people come to consider more important than growth. The Iranian recession of 1975 generated little public protest, for example, even though it was by many measures sharper than the recession of 1977–1978. What 1975 lacked—what the United States continues to lack—is the perception of a viable alternative to the existing regime. Khomeini and his followers began to gain viability only in 1977–1978.

A viable alternative is a movement that seems to have a realistic chance of success. Each of the key terms in this definition is subject to the vagaries of popular perceptions: what gets labeled a "movement," what would constitute "success," what counts as a "realistic chance," even what we mean by "seems." The point is not for some social scientist to look back, after the fact, and declare a movement to have been viable. The point is that people make such judgments in real time, during moments of confusion, and that these judgments can be self-fulfilling. If few people consider a movement viable and thus do not waste their time supporting it, then the movement languishes. If enough people call a movement viable and join in as a result, then the movement might be seen as strong. The "critical mass" occurs when the self-fulfilling processes start to work in favor of a movement.

The critical mass moment began in Iran in late 1977, when Khomeini's followers started to mobilize against the shah. These activists numbered perhaps a few hundred in total, in a country with a population of more than thirty million. They were a minority even in the seminaries of Qom, where their numbers were strongest. Yet their willingness to protest even in such small numbers—marching on Qom's Fayziyeh Seminary in December 1977, for example, and trying to force the authorities to reopen it—established their reputation. They could be counted on to continue their activism, unless Khomeini told them to stop—and the recent escalation of his denunciations of the regime sent a signal that he would not soon curb his followers.

This small cadre of revolutionaries spent the next several months trying to mobilize the mosque network, beginning with visits to the leading seminarians in Qom in January 1978. Previously non-revolutionary religious students and scholars, seeking to avoid an open rift in the seminaries and apparently convinced that the cadre was not going to let up its pressure, drifted into support of the movement. By mid-1978, they had succeeded in commandeering portions of the network, and in doing so built the activist cadre into several thousand in most cities of Iran.

In late summer 1978, the movement became "viable" in the minds of many Iranians outside the revolutionary circle. According to one observer, "All of a sudden, the feeling arose that things weren't that way anymore," that protest might actually "bring about a basic change in my country." With much of the religious establishment more or less on board, the movement could be expected to generate large numbers of protesters. Such expectations were self-fulfilling, boosting protest participation from the low tens of thousands to more than one hundred thousand.

In the fall of 1978, Iranians considered the movement to have such tremendous popular support that those who still opposed it became reluctant to voice their concerns publicly. Even military leaders planning a crackdown worried that perceptions of the movement's popularity would undermine soldiers' discipline. Although the movement would not take power officially for several months, victory may be dated to mid-November 1978, when the shah played his last card by installing a military government. This move did not dislodge popular perceptions of the inevitability of the revolution, and these perceptions made Iran ungovernable. Iranians continued to fear the repressive capacity of the state, but they participated in strikes and demonstrations by the millions. Only two weeks earlier, as described at the beginning of this book, some Iranians had considered the revolution unthinkable.

This is the story, then, of a viable movement. It did not have to turn out this way. Khomeini might not have mobilized his followers. The vanguard might have failed to commandeer the mosque network. The mosque network might not have been large enough to convince ordinary Iranians that its movement was viable. The appearance of viability might have disappeared as quickly as it had emerged.

Viability does not explain why the movement turned out as it did. Rather, viability is non-predictive. Its focus on the variability and confusion of protest runs counter to the project of retroactive prediction. In this sense, it is not an explanation but an anti-explanation. Instead of seeking recurrent patterns in social life, anti-explanation explores the unforeseen moments when patterns are twisted or broken off. Instead of emphasizing routine behavior, it emphasizes "deviant" cases and statistical "outliers." Focus on the fringe reminds us that the whole fabric of social life—all the behaviors and institutions that we take for granted, that seem unchangeable—may be vulnerable to unraveling, that the fabric survives only through our collective expectation that it will survive.

What is left when we part from retroactive prediction? Understanding.[23] Sifting through evidence of other minds, trying to perceive what others perceive, is difficult enough when you live with them. Attempting this feat across the hurdles of time and culture is even more challenging. Listening to Iranians talk about their experiences of the revolution, I was acutely aware of the distance between my life and theirs. While I was in grade school, they lived under a brutal dictatorship. While I was in high school, they made a massive revolution. While I was in college, they survived a horrible war. My life paled in comparison and I was jealous of their drama, even as they envied my privilege. But through these conversations, and through my readings, I tried to understand what it felt like to live through the Iranian Revolution. I took it as a mark of my progress to hear a well-educated Iranian tell me, "Iranians are like sheep," and to know that he was wrong, that he had not attempted to understand the experiences of his compatriots. I am no romantic believer in the human ability to meld with other minds, but I believe that partial knowledge is possible, subject to the same epistemological conventions regarding evidence in other cognitive endeavors.

_____

To the extent that one can generalize about a "national culture," Iranian society in the Pahlavi era lacked solidarity outside the family, and sometimes within the family as well. A tradition of personality boundaries in Iran placed great emphasis on the separation between one's inner and outer self, with the pure inside shielded from the outside world by formality and distance. Boundaries are reflected and reinforced, for instance, in the conventions of the Persian language and in the traditional architecture of high-walled courtyards, where one's inner circle of friends and family is clearly delineated from the outside. As one of my respondents phrased it, "In Islam, you are not free in the street, outside the walls. You are free inside the walls, where it is comfortable and open."[24]

Social change, economic turbulence, and political repression no doubt contributed to the lack of solidarity. In the 1930s, an Iranian author worried that

> trust . . . has completely disappeared from Iran. The minister does not trust his deputies; the deputies do not trust their employees; the petitioners do not trust the counsel; the counsel does not trust the judge; the wife does not trust her husband, nor the brother his sister, nor even the father his son; and all of them are quite right.[25]

"My daily hope," said a government employee in the 1970s, "is that I am not being robbed by my friends and colleagues or those with whom I come into contact, and that at the end of the day I am ahead in the roulette game of bribery." SAVAK, the security police, actively encouraged this sense of mistrust. As far away as Lawrence, Kansas, Iranian students worried that "even your brother might be a SAVAK agent, and if he is, it is his duty to report on you." A satirical newspaper broached the topic with a cartoon in which a student says he has to turn his professor in to the authorities "because if I don't report you, he [pointing to another student] will report me!"[26] Two anthropologists have recorded another example:

A much enjoyed joke under the Pahlavi regime was this version of the first night [after death]. "Who is your God?" [ask the angels]. "His Majesty, the Shahanshah!" "What is your religion?" "The White Revolution [the shah's ideology]." "What is your holy book?" "His Majesty's book, *The White Revolution.*" The angels raise their clubs to beat the infidel. God stops them and asks the deceased, "What is the matter with you?" The man replies, "Sorry, God. I thought these two might be SAVAK agents."[27]

Iranians who spoke up in protest were often assumed to be provocateurs. Security police agents, friends told an American academic, were "the only people who would dare lead a demonstration."[28] An activist in one factory recalled soon after the revolution:

In earlier times, we were rather suspicious of each other. For instance, I was suspicious of this friend of mine, Mr Kamali, because of something which happened to him: [he was arrested] and got just two months [in jail]! Considering the way things were at the time, we thought he should have been given more than two months. I and another comrade decided to test him, to see whether or not he was a SAVAK agent.[29]

In the context of such distrust, it was remarkable that Iranians were able to cooperate in collective protest against the shah. Iranians noted this at the time. In fact, they were amazed at the euphoric feelings of solidarity that emerged as people made history together. For example, a woman in Shiraz recalled her participation in the ʿAshura march: "When I thought of myself I was but a drop in the sea. I felt smaller and smaller. Sometimes I felt lost among all of those voices. I was very proud of my nationality. On this day I was so proud."[30] Mostafa Askari felt the solidarity at the Muharram marches in Shiraz:

And then the unity and cooperation which I had always thought would never happen. The attitude of the marchers towards each other was very good. On Tasuʿa I got a nosebleed. My nose suddenly started bleeding. And then everybody wanted to help me. One person gave me a handkerchief. Another gave me a Kleenex. Someone asked, "What happened?" Another said, "Let's get an ambulance." "Hey, it's just a nosebleed," I said. "I'm all right." People gathered around me. Finally they realized that it was nothing serious. This is the way it was. Everyone wanted to help everyone else.[31]

"Solidarity is the most important thing that the revolution has created," Tehran University law professor Nasser Katouzian wrote in the last days of the Pahlavi era. "If, in the past, people lost their patience over the scarcity of various kinds of fruits, now they stay in cold homes, tolerate scarcities of heating oil and gasoline, electricity blackouts, and do not complain when they wait in long lines."[32] A Tehran newspaper commented in January 1979:

> People who used to confront each other with hostility, whose conversations rarely went beyond the price of eggs and meat, or traffic jams . . . now, because of their common struggle, have become kinder to each other and treat each other with generosity . . . Not many people have to wait in the street in cold weather for taxis, because private cars are volunteering their services to them, and few fights are being witnessed.[33]

A liberal oppositionist recalled:

> I don't know how to explain how unity was found among the people—in the bazaar the differences of opinion were many, there were many differences of opinion, some of them almost coming close to hostility sometimes, between the wealthy and non-wealthy, boss and subordinate, higher and lower, and so on. And it was the same way in the rest of the society too. But in the end, such unity was found that it was really indescribable.[34]

As the humorist Hadi Khorsandi put it: "I was tolerating the presence of people whom I had hated all my life. Why? The first reason was that I could see that people who had hated me all their lives were smiling at me and were tolerating my presence."[35]

The pull of solidarity suddenly drew people into street protests. A young seminary student in Tabriz, tired and hungry from a morning of demonstrating, came home to eat, but had barely sat down when he heard slogans being chanted outside. "It's cowardly for me to stay at home while they are shouting slogans." He went out and was killed by security forces.[36] Similar examples can be found in other movements, for example, a teenage Romanian girl during the revolution of 1989: "I feel like a coward sitting here while my friends are there . . . I'm afraid, but I feel I must go." "You feel ashamed if you just go by" a demonstration, said a Palestinian teenager during the intifada uprising. "You are suffering, it's in your heart, inside you. You have to participate."[37]

The Islamists attributed solidarity to ideological consensus. "Our success," Khomeini said at the airport when he returned to Iran on January 31, 1979, "is the result of the unity of all the people in this country. They all follow one word, 'Islam,' and even the religious minorities are united with Islam." Several months earlier, in response to a French reporter's question, "How do you explain that the Iranian people take to the streets following your appeals?" Khomeini answered, "It is because the people consider us to be the servants of Islam and of the country. It is because we explore the problems which arise in the depths of the nation; it is because we give voice to the aspirations of the people."[38]

Yet the sudden pull of solidarity drew a variety of groups into the anti-shah movement, not all of whom shared the Islamists' aspirations for an Islamic Republic. Intellectuals sought intellectual freedoms. Merchants sought freedom of commerce. Leftists sought social justice. Workers sought raises and other benefits. Even a drug counter-culture got in the act, establishing a small Hippi-Abad (Hippie-Town) in a northern Tehran park. The Iranian Revolution was hardly a monolithic movement. Grievances of all sorts suddenly found their voice in late summer 1978, when it appeared that the Islamists were creating a viable opposition movement.[39]

For these groups, Khomeini's authority stemmed not so much from his religious scholarship or aspirations as from his position as leader of a viable movement. The "power of negative thinking," in the sociologist James Jasper's phrase, brought diverse interests under a single anti-shah umbrella. As one intellectual put it, "I hate Khomeini, but if anyone says anything bad about him I get angry. Why, you ask? Because I hate the Shah even more." A bank employee in Tehran said that he was not a Khomeini supporter, "But right now he is the best hope to get rid of the current leeches of society . . . for now I support him."[40] A foreign reporter in the southern city of Ahwaz noted:

> Although it is clear that the Shah's principal critic, the Ayatollah Khomeini, is highly revered here, interviews with a dozen workers revealed that their support for the exiled Moslem leader is motivated more by his opposition to the Shah than by religious dictates. A worker for the Water and Power Authority said the Ayatollah "has brought the eyes of the world on our problem here and made them see that the Shah is a puppet of the foreigners who are stealing our money."[41]

A variety of movements emerged once the Islamists made revolution viable, and each came under pressure to conform to the "unity" that Khomeini was proclaiming. Let us look briefly at four such movements: liberals, leftists, students, and feminists.

Liberals were highly sensitive to the opportunities granted by the regime for opposition activity. They had begun to speak out publicly for reform in 1977 when the shah allowed such opposition to be voiced. In late 1977, when the shah clamped down again after his cordial meetings with Carter, liberals muted their protests. In the summer of 1978, when the shah made a few concessions and promised to hold free elections, liberals were elated and rushed to take advantage of the new freedoms. Yet during the fall of 1978, they began to sense that state opportunities were no longer defining the bounds of opposition activity. Rather, the Islamists were now defining what could and could not be spoken. This sense crystallized for some on September 4, when liberal bazaar oppositionists tried in vain to disperse a massive crowd of demonstrators by reminding people that they were not supposed to be protesting. "Under current conditions, we former organizers have lost the leadership of activism," Mehdi Bazargan noted a few days later. For other liberals, the shift came in October, when "we realized that [the movement] was now out of our hands." When the shah appeared ready to hold a referendum on the form of government, the liberal opposition met and decided that they needed to consult with Khomeini before proceeding. Within two weeks in late October and early November, the liberal leaders Bazargan and Karim Sanjabi traveled to Paris, visited with Khomeini, and came away chastened. Both abandoned independent plans and hewed publicly to the Islamist line.[42]

In private, the liberal opposition grumbled that the revolutionary movement was too strong to oppose. In early November, the U.S. embassy reported that one leading liberal "privately accused Khomeini of irresponsibility and said he 'acts like a false god.' But we have no sign he or any other oppositionist dares to attack Khomeini publicly." In early December, a U.S. diplomat asked a moderate Iranian religious scholar if he and other clerics would approve a constitutional settlement to the crisis and go against Khomeini. The cleric, "perhaps not wanting his followers to understand, replied in broken English, 'That would be dangerous and very difficult.'"[43]

By the end of 1978, when the shah was casting about for a prime minister, a series of liberal oppositionists turned down the position. Several months earlier they would have considered the appointment a dream come true—now they considered it futile. One liberal told Gholam-Reza Sadiqi, a colleague who had been offered the prime ministry, "We are now in a situation where we can't stop the wave." "Dr. Sadiqi, you would be like a drop of pure water that fell into a sewer of filth, into a swamp. It's a waste," another colleague told him.[44] When Sadiqi turned down the post, the shah asked another oppositionist, Shahpour Bakhtiar. Two fellow liberals cornered him and expressed their concerns:

> It was early in the morning. Dr. Bakhtiar was in the lavatory shaving. We closed the door behind us and went into the lavatory, both of us. We strongly, strongly urged him, "Don't do this. You will become a scapegoat. This popular movement will come and pass right by you." Because we had seen the situation from up close, that anyone who did this, anyone who accepted [the shah's offer] was clearly not going to be accepted by the people now, no matter how right he was . . . We insisted that this was how the religious leaders were, that Khomeini won't allow it.[45]

Ironically, even as the liberals were feeling powerless to resist the Islamists, the U.S. embassy was crediting them with having organized the huge ʿAshura demonstration in Tehran:

> [The] mass Tehran rally [of December 11] was nearly entirely political with mere lip service to religion. It was [an] impressive display of [the] mass organizational skills of [the Iranian] National Front (INF) and surprised most observers . . . Marches were run by INF, not Khomeini. According to three different sources, [the] program was drafted by [an] INF committee, and both programs and marches across Iran bear much stronger INF imprint than religious input.[46]

It is unclear who the diplomats' three sources were, but they must have been putting a brave face on an event in which they had played only a token role. The National Front had very few members and little internal solidarity, its leaders were in jail when the December plans were initially drawn up, and its supporters expected only a small fraction of the numbers that participated. Contrary to the U.S. diplomats' account, many of the slogans at the demonstration were religious—one study counted 31 percent of slogans on the topic of Islamic revolution and an Islamic republic, plus 16 percent in honor of Khomeini; another study counted 30 percent on Islamic themes, plus 20 percent for Khomeini. The liberal opposition participated as a barely tolerated junior partner to the Islamists, who had incorporated them into the plans only as a sop toward the slogan of solidarity, according to one of the Islamist organizers assigned to cooperate with the liberals. Indeed, posters picturing Mohammad Mossadeq, the nationalist prime minister in the early 1950s and hero of the liberal opposition, were scarcely allowed during the demonstrations. Another small liberal opposition group agreed to merge its own demonstration in honor of International Human Rights Day (December 10) with the ʿAshura protest but was upset to find that it was given only a parenthetical mention in the joint "statement of unity."[47]

It is worth mentioning, in light of its mistaken analysis, that the U.S. embassy had few Persian-speaking diplomats and no direct contact with the Islamist opposition until near the end of the revolutionary movement, after an additional Persian-speaking foreign service officer was transferred back to Iran. In December 1978, the CIA station chief in Tehran pleaded with his bosses for more Persian-speaking agents; but the CIA apparently understood, as the legitimate diplomats did not, that "the National Front has neither the independent mass following nor any significant ability to mobilize and orchestrate demonstrations."[48]

The liberals were rewarded when the revolution succeeded. Khomeini appointed Mehdi Bazargan provisional prime minister, and he in turn filled his cabinet with other leading liberals. Within months, however, Khomeini withdrew his delegation of authority, and the liberals were frozen out once again. They resigned from office and were subsequently forced out of post-revolutionary electoral politics.[49]

Leftist opposition groups, by contrast with the liberals, were not highly attuned to openings in the opportunity structure of the state. Their greatest mobilization of the 1970s came in the first half of the decade, when the shah's rule seemed fully intact. As a result of this mobilization, the two primary leftist groups were both in crisis as the Islamist movement took off in 1978, having suffered severe state repression and ideological factionalization over the previous several years. The People's Strugglers of Iran *(Mojahedin-e Khalq-e Iran)* was in the middle of an internal debate over whether to continue armed struggle, and the group's own publications report few actions in 1978 and a "relative silence" as the number of actions decreased after June 1978. The Iranian People's Sacrificing Guerrillas *(Cherik'ha-ye Feda'i-ye Khalq-e Iran),* according to one of the group's leaders, "disintegrated and disappeared" after "the blows of 1976," "set itself principally to protecting itself," and engaged only in "scattered actions" to show that it still existed. Only a few dozen members remained at large. Ideologically, the group decided that objective conditions for revolution didn't exist, and as the Islamists' movement escalated, the organization claimed credit for relatively few actions—one in summer 1977, two in early 1978, and five in the summer of 1978, according to the group's pronouncements. At the end of the year, with membership presumably growing, the organization picked up its pace, claiming credit for a half-dozen actions in December 1978 and a dozen in January 1979. A third leftist group, the communist Masses Party *(Hezb-e Tudeh),* had virtually no organized presence inside Iran at this time, according to its own accounts, the testimony of a Soviet agent in Tehran, and the judgment of the U.S. Central Intelligence Agency.[50]

As the revolutionary movement proceeded, leftists became far more active, not just operating in their own name but also contributing to Islamist mobilizations. "I felt we needed a revolution," a village teacher told an anthropologist just after the revolution, "so to get people to join me, I talked in religious terms." Leftists were apparently active in the office of Ayatollah Taleqani after he was released from prison in fall 1978. Taleqani was in ill health but had reluctantly opened his home in Tehran to revolutionaries, who used it as an organizing center. Leftists also played an important role in supporting the mutiny at a Tehran air force base that finally brought down the regime in February 1979. The People's Sacrificers had by coincidence scheduled a demonstration on February 10 to celebrate the anniversary of a 1971 guerrilla attack. The mutiny had begun the previous evening, and the leftists abandoned the celebration to march en masse to the air force base, where they joined thousands of neighborhood residents in fighting off the Imperial Guards' attempts to retake the base.[51]

As leftists became more active in the movement, the Islamists saw them as an increasing threat. As early as the fall of 1978, Islamist demonstrators were clashing with leftist demonstrators. A Khomeini militant, Mehdi 'Eraqi, noted in early January that leftists "have made great strides" and "may be dangerous for us," according to a SAVAK wiretap. In mid-January, Khomeini appointed a committee to rein in the nation's strikes, some of them run by leftists who "let it be known that full-scale production can resume only when they say so, Ayatollah Khomeini's wishes notwithstanding, and that anyone who attempts to thwart them will do so at his own risk." At the same time, Khomeini warned his followers about "those who deviate and oppose Islam," a reiteration of his long-standing condemnation of leftist groups: "The nation must recognize that every deviation and every slogan that opposes the path of the nation plays into the hands of the agents of the [soon-to-be] deposed shah and his allies." On January 19, 1979, leftists participating in a mass demonstration were blocked from reading a resolution; other protesters shouted them down with the chant, "The only party is the party of God [hezbollah]." The following day, Islamists harassed leftist demonstrators in Tehran, shouting "Traitors!" and "Communists!" The next day, Islamists demonstrated at the Kayhan newspaper offices and demanded the same amount of space given to "leftists." The Islamists also worked to curb the leftists' influence in the oil industry of southern Iran. Khomeini appointed a delegation charged with bringing the oil strike to heel, with the short-term goal of restoring domestic fuel supplies in the winter months. The strikers resisted, sensing an infringement on their autonomy, and it took many weeks for a deal to be struck.[52]

After the Islamists came to power, clashes between leftists and Islamists deepened to the point where leftist groups resorted to terrorist bombings, and the Islamists resorted to arrest, torture, and executions. By 1982, organized leftism was virtually eliminated in Iran. Already on the eve of the revolution, some leftists feared such a scenario. On the day before the shah's regime fell, one author wrote in a left-leaning Tehran newspaper warning the mollas—a not particularly respectful term for religious scholars—that the people didn't revolt just to replace one dictatorship with another.[53]

The organized left never claimed more than a few thousand members. But the disorganized left was far larger, centered among Iran's 172,000 university students and 2 million high school students. As noted earlier, schools had long been hotbeds of activism, and this continued through the revolutionary period. A chronology of university protests, listing 86 events from January 1978 through the fall of the monarchy in February 1979, testifies to the ongoing activism at Iran's campuses. Students constituted 172 of the 742 "martyrs" registered in Tehran, 148 of them high school students. Students were prominent not just in Iran but in other late-twentieth-century revolutions as well, earning the sociologist Misagh Parsa's label of "relentless revolutionaries." More often than not, though, student activism failed to topple governments. The student unrest of 1968, for example, crested shy of revolution in France, Mexico, the United States, and elsewhere, despite the intensity of the protests. The path from student activism to full-fledged revolution required broader popular participation than students could mobilize among themselves.[54]

In Iran, too, student oppositionists had little success generating popular support, with the sole exception of Amol, a small city in northern Iran where students led a brief takeover of administrative functions in late October. Elsewhere, student activism was geared largely to the takeover of schools. In October 1978, student unrest kept most schools from beginning the fall semester, culminating in a Week of Solidarity that shut down education nationwide. Students succeeded in taking control of the most prominent institution of higher education in Iran, Tehran University. Armored personnel carriers were stationed outside the campus, while inside, students had free rein to demonstrate, post signs and banners, and talk revolution. The troops made no effort to prohibit entrance or exit, and the government allowed numerous student activists to return to Iran from exile. But on the one occasion when students marched out of the university, on November 5, few outsiders joined their protest. The event spurred the regime to institute a military-led government, but it did not generate a wave of follow-up protests.[55]

The rhythm of the revolution was set by clerical revolutionaries rather than by students. Students joined in clerical-led protests but not vice versa. The tenor was set in late 1977, when a group of university students traveled from Tehran to Qom to offer their support for fortieth-day memorials for Mostafa Khomeini. Hojjat al-Islam Sadeq Khalkhali—later the harshest of the Islamic Republic's revolutionary judges—rebuffed them, saying, "We have our own plan." The clerics largely commandeered the universities in late 1978, just as they had commandeered the mosque network earlier in the year. Although independent student groups continued to exist in this period, religious leaders in Tehran, Isfahan, and elsewhere established their own student organizations "to implement our views," as Ayatollah Mohammad Beheshti told a colleague in December. The process was completed in mid-January 1979, when radical religious scholars from across Iran encamped in the University of Tehran to await Khomeini's return to the country. This space, freed from state intervention by student activism, was transformed into a seat of clerical power. Indeed, after the revolution, the clerics tightened their grip on the universities by purging them of diverse voices, instituting ideological requirements for student admission, and establishing the nation's chief Friday prayer ceremonies on Tehran University's soccer field.[56]

The religious radicals were able to commandeer the universities in part because many students had become increasingly devout over the previous decade; indeed, university scholars estimated that 65–70 percent of students supported the Islamists. A leading symbol and catalyst of this shift was the leftist sociologist 'Ali Shari'ati, who combined Sorbonne socialism with Islamist nativism. Iranian university students thronged to his public appearances, when he was permitted to speak publicly. They devoured his writings, samizdat editions of which were read quickly and then urgently passed along to a friend.

Although Shari'ati helped to bridge leftism and Islamism, his version of Islam was distinct from that of Iran's clerical radicals. Shari'ati was resoundingly critical of seminary-trained religious scholars who "have transformed [Islam] into its present static form," and he called on lay Iranian intellectuals to rescue Islam from the hands of "reactionaries." Nonetheless, Shari'ati had a devoted following among the seminary students of Qom, in addition to his popularity among lay students. Ayatollah Morteza Motahhari, one of Khomeini's chief followers, viewed Shari'ati as a competitor whose popularity among the devout made him dangerous, but Khomeini resisted Motahhari's entreaties to condemn him. When Shari'ati died suddenly in exile in 1977, students in Shiraz demonstrated with huzzahs for both Shari'ati and Khomeini. At the same time, Motahhari and other religious scholars issued pronouncements vilifying him. Yet during the course of the revolution, some of Khomeini's most militant followers praised Shari'ati as a "responsible scholar and great struggler," and Khomeini himself appealed to Shari'ati's memory in an attempt to avoid differences with student activists: "How well he analyzed our forces, our Islamic forces, and made everybody aware of one another. He flayed all sides for the differences between the *minbar* [pulpit], the *mihrab* [altar], the university, and so on—and these differences still exist." In this way, the clerical revolutionaries appropriated Shari'ati, as they did the student movement in general, for their own purposes.[57]

—————

The Iranian Revolution was thoroughly gendered. That is to say, major planks of the Islamists' platform addressed the position of women, primarily through critiques of the sexual looseness and humiliation that the Pahlavi deveiling campaign had supposedly generated over the previous forty years.[58]

Thus far I have not discussed gender in any detail. In part this gap is due to my difficulty in interviewing women about their experiences of the revolution. Iranian women, especially the conservative ones, would not speak with a strange man asking them for an interview, and in couples men generally answered for their wives. Others researching Iran have reported similar difficulties pursuing interviews across gender lines. Moreover, it is not clear to me that there were systematic differences between women and men when it came to deciding to engage in protest. Few men or women protested in large numbers before late summer 1978; both men and women showed up en masse in winter 1978–1979 to show their support for the revolutionary movement.[59]

Paradoxically—to Western eyes—women from conservative households found that Islamist activism offered them significant autonomy and freedom of movement. Khomeini encouraged women to participate in revolutionary protests: "A nation whose respected women demonstrate in modest garb [hejab] to express their disgust with the shah's regime—such a nation will be victorious." For some women, this participation was their first foray into politics. "Before, women didn't do this," a village woman said, describing her involvement in demonstrations. Islamist leaders directed many of their appeals specifically to women, and on at least one occasion they addressed feminist concerns: "Some women fear that an Islamic government would prevent them from working in schools and offices and important careers," Hojjat al-Islam ʿAbdolkarim Hashemi-Nezhad said at a speech in Mashhad in late fall 1978. "No, such a thing does not exist in Islam. If there is an Islamic government, all women will work in partnership with men." Several days after Khomeini's return to Iran, a top aide suggested that women be barred from attending his group audiences. Khomeini refused to bar them, saying, "I threw the shah out with these women, there's no problem with their coming."[60]

Organized feminism had thrown its hat in with the Pahlavi regime in the 1950s. Yet as the revolution proceeded in 1978, feminists turned against the regime. Some came to rue their reliance on the state when the shah, as a sop to the Islamists, dropped the cabinet position on Women's Affairs. "This sudden and premature demise raises the question in the mind of all reasonable people: would an honorable organization based on the support of the women intellectuals of Iran suddenly have been lost and buried by a change of breeze?" a women's magazine asked. "A house of paper is slave to any wind." Members of the Women's Organization of Iran, the parastatal agency associated with the cabinet position, marched in demonstrations and voiced their support for the opposition. "It was a real movement and we couldn't help but think the best of him [Khomeini]," one of these women recalled.[61]

Like the leftists, feminists came to be considered a threat by the Islamists. The area in which feminists posed the clearest challenge during the revolutionary movement was in women's clothing. Islamists in Iran and elsewhere emphasized the sacred duty of modest garb *(hejab),* which for women they interpreted as covering the hair, neck, torso, and limbs. Islamists in Iran, unlike Afghanistan and some Arab countries, did not insist that women cover the face or hands. Some Iranian women adopted the *chador*—literally "tent," a large semi-circular cloth held over the head and draped around the body—as a sign of their renewed piety. Others adopted this and other forms of *hejab* as a symbolic statement of their opposition to the monarchy, which as part of its "modernizing" program had banned *hejab* from many public spaces.[62]

Feminists who resisted this symbolic association with the Islamists were made increasingly uncomfortable at oppositional events. At the 'Eid-e Fetr demonstration in early September, one woman marched in tennis clothes. Several months later this would have been unimaginable, and not just because of the cold Tehran winter. Rumors circulated that women who didn't wear proper *hejab* would have acid thrown at them. At a large march in January 1979, a woman protesting without *hejab* was attacked and beaten. Simply occupying public space without *hejab* made one subject to censure, as one woman found when Islamists shouted angrily at her as she waited for a taxi in Tehran. "What kind of behavior is this for freedom seekers?" she asked.[63]

When the Islamists came to power, they institutionalized *hejab,* and the feminist movement was soon suppressed, only to reemerge some years later in an Islamist guise.[64]

The strength of the revolutionary movement drew a diverse crowd into its tow. Even Iranian Jews demonstrated against the shah when they recognized which way the wind was blowing, despite the monarchy's patronage of the community and Khomeini's outspoken suspicions of it ("From the very beginning, the historical movement of Islam has had to contend with the Jews . . . down to the present").[65]

At its margins, the desire to join the revolutionary movement shaded into fear of persecution for nonparticipation. "I could not go to [the] office against the will of my employees," said the managing director of a state agency that was on strike. "Besides, anything could happen to me." On a few occasions, people who tried to work during a strike were threatened or kicked out of the workplace.[66] The owner of a tiny shop in central Tehran had a similar concern: "He explained candidly that he had put a photograph of the Ayatollah [Khomeini], whom he said he respected, in his store window because he feared it would be smashed otherwise. 'Most of the people want an Islamic Republic,' he said wearily. 'And I want anything that most of the people want.'"[67]

Shops that opened during strikes were sometimes attacked; in Yazd, Ayatollah Mohammad Saduqi sent several dozen youths to attack two shops that had violated a general strike in late March 1978, according to an admiring post-revolutionary account. An architect's office in Tehran received a bomb threat for remaining open at the height of the revolutionary unrest. A column in a Tehran newspaper that allowed telephone callers to dictate brief comments on current events recorded a half-dozen instances of intimidation over a one-month period in early 1979. "Why am I threatened when I want to open my shop? How am I supposed to support my family?" one man called in to say.[68] Another shopowner reported:

> Sunday around 11 in the morning, several people came to the door of my shop and others' and said, "Close your store until the order to re-open is announced." I explained to them that my income is dependent on this shop, and I won't have enough to support my family, and secondly, I'm not doing anything wrong. But they said, "Either close up or say your prayers for your shop."[69]

Others called in to complain that small groups of youths were roaming the streets and forcing people to support pro-revolutionary symbols:

> Ask the youths who demonstrate so eagerly for freedom why they block people's cars and demand that people honk their horns, turn on their lights, shout slogans, or stick approved placards in their windshield.

> How can people who say their children were tortured and killed just for their ideas threaten others on the basis of their ideas?[70]

This persecution should not be overestimated, despite some foreign observers' emphasis on "threats and harassment of the moderates by the well-organized Khomeini fanatics," "fear of retaliation for not clos-

ing [shops on strike days]," and the like. The Iranian Revolution exhib-
ited remarkably little retribution against backsliders, especially when
compared with the revolutionary violence reported in South Africa,
Palestine, the Sikh independence movement in India, and elsewhere.
As expected, interview respondents who supported the revolution told
me that there had been little violence or pressure. But even those who
said they later came to oppose the revolution denied that they had
been pressured into participating. If I hadn't gone to a demonstration,
a student from Borujerd said, people "wouldn't have said anything, but
it would have looked bad." "My friends didn't talk to me for two
months," said a young man from Tehran whose parents made him stop
participating in the protest movement, but that was the extent of it.
"Many people didn't participate," a shopowner from Mashhad told me.
"But if I had spoken out against [the revolution], they would have
killed me or"—he made a chopping attack on his arm. Perhaps so few
such attacks occurred because so few Iranians spoke out against the revolution.[71]

In mid-November 1978, when the shah realized that the military crackdown was not working, he began to search for an oppositionist to take
over the reins of government. At this stage he retained some hope of
remaining a constitutional monarch and commander of the armed
forces. In his inimitable fashion, he had prominent liberal oppositionists arrested, then ordered officials to sound them out about the pre-
miership in jail. The liberals said it was too late for compromises. By
mid-December the shah wanted only to be allowed to stay in Iran;
again he was turned down. In late December, he agreed to leave the
country temporarily; still he was turned down. Finally, in the last days
of 1978, one oppositionist accepted his terms. Shahpour Bakhtiar was
appointed prime minister and was promptly expelled from the oppositional movement.[72]

The shah left Iran on January 16, 1979, placing his monarchy in the
hands of a regency council. Huge crowds celebrated in the streets. Cars
honked, strangers hugged, statues toppled—and the shah's appointees
remained in office. Khomeini did not return to Iran for two weeks, and

the trappings of government were not transferred to him for almost two weeks after that.

The brief delay was due to the difficulty of ensuring Khomeini's survival. The military could easily have shot down Khomeini's plane as he returned to Iran, or shelled the grade school where he took up temporary residence upon his return. These acts would have resulted in massive anti-military sentiment, and the shah's military commanders did not want to incur the people's wrath—they were hunkered down trying to protect military institutions. If Khomeini had made a move to take power by force, though, it would only have taken a few hard-line officers to kill him.

There were plenty of examples of state violence, in addition to the repression experienced by protesters. On November 20, one unit in Shiraz fired into a crowded mosque; on December 12, a unit in Isfahan staged a violent pro-shah demonstration; on December 14, a unit cooperated with thugs in attacking a hospital in Mashhad; on December 27, a unit in Tehran shot at a peaceful funeral procession; on January 17, a unit in Ahwaz commandeered several tanks and went on a rampage. State violence led the opposition to organize collective defenses. Already in the spring of 1978, Islamists in Isfahan had set up "defense groups" to resist government-sponsored attacks on demonstrators. In October, protesters in the small northern city of Amol set up street patrols and banned police from the streets after a series of violent incidents. They arrested suspected security officials and took effective control of the city until the army moved in two days later.[73]

As the state retreated from its everyday duties, the Islamists developed shadow state institutions. In Hamadan, at the end of November, religious leaders organized a group of night watchmen that evolved into a full system of local governance. In January, as police answered calls for help by saying, "Go ask Khomeini," Islamists created "Islamic police forces" around the country to perform basic duties—deterring crime, directing traffic—that were no longer being performed by the state. Neighborhood councils also organized food distribution during the general strike and then branched out into pharmaceuticals, fuel, and winter clothing.[74]

Yet Khomeini and his followers refrained from mobilizing paramilitary institutions. Before the revolution some Islamists had received military training with the Palestinian Liberation Organization, and underground cells were being organized in Qom and elsewhere. But Khomeini had refused to authorize armed struggle early in 1978, after the Qom massacre. And when activists raised the chant for more militant confrontation with the Pahlavi regime in early 1979—"Khomeini, Khomeini, give us arms" and "Machine guns, machine guns, the answer to all"—Khomeini continued to hold them back. His envoy to the tiny Islamist guerrilla groups that had recently formed—Mehdi 'Eraqi, an exponent of violence himself, who had served a dozen years in prison for his role in assassinating an Iranian prime minister in the 1960s—offered little encouragement and few resources to these groups.[75]

In the fall, Hojjat al-Islam Akbar Hashemi-Rafsanjani, a militant Islamist serving a long prison sentence, who later became president of the Islamic Republic, debated with fellow inmates who called for jihad: "If we do such a thing, it will give the regime an excuse to suppress the political movement." Unlike in 1963, Rafsanjani continued, "you can see now that the people have matured, and are not retreating in the face of all this cruelty, crudeness, and killing." Ayatollah Asadollah Madani, the militant religious leader of Hamadan, flatly rejected a proposal for armed uprising in November, according to a SAVAK report. Many religious leaders signed a proclamation in early January 1979 calling on people to remain calm and not to provoke the security forces. Even Mohammad Montazeri, a gun-toting militant known as "Ayatollah Ringo," spoke out against armed action in January 1979, urging people not to confront the military and arguing that such tactics had failed in the past, whereas peaceful protest was now succeeding. Just days before the shah's regime fell, Khomeini told reporters at a Tehran press conference that he was still not calling for an armed jihad just yet: "In the current state of things, we will do the maximum to maintain calm and resolve problems peacefully. But if Mr. [prime minister Shahpour] Bakhtiar, who depends on the United States and Great Britain, appeals to Israeli troops to resist, then we will proclaim jihad." According to SAVAK wiretaps, Khomeini privately told armed followers to hold off on attacks they had planned.[76]

The reluctance to engage in armed struggle reflected Khomeini's patience, not a lack of confidence. In October 1978, Mehdi Bazargan met with Khomeini and was baffled by his calm assurance. In November, the U.S. Central Intelligence Agency reported that "Khomeini seems supremely confident that he has unleashed the forces that will destroy the Shah." In December a visitor asked Khomeini, "Do you think our present course is wise? What will happen if the army keeps on slaughtering people? Will people sooner or later not get tired and discouraged?" Khomeini "responded quite simply that it is our duty to struggle in this fashion and the result is with Allah."[77]

Thus, beginning in mid-November, the Islamists and the military faced each other in a sort of stalemate, neither side eager to break the deadlock by force. Khomeini's authority had not dislodged the military, and the military's power had not broken the general strike. In mirror fashion, the Islamist and military leaders tried to hold back hardliners in each camp seeking armed confrontation.

The most eager hard-liner on the military side was American. General Robert E. Huyser entered Iran secretly, without a visa—by his own account—in early January 1979. President Carter had assigned him to rally Iranian military commanders and help them prepare for a lastresort coup d'état. For months, the Carter administration had supported the use of force in Iran. After the "Black Friday" massacre in September, Carter called the shah to reiterate this support. When the shah installed a military government on November 6, American officials voiced their full support. U.S. National Security Adviser Zbigniew Brzezinski had telephoned the shah several days earlier to encourage him to be firm. Riot-control equipment, blocked for months on human-rights grounds, was shipped to Iran. As late as December 28, 1978, the White House sent its ambassador a firm statement of U.S. support for the shah, rejecting less supportive drafts:[78]

If there is uncertainty either about the underlying orientation of [a civilian] government or its capacity to govern, or if the army is in danger of becoming more fragmented, then the shah should choose without delay a firm military government which would end the disorder, violence and bloodshed . . .

You should tell the shah the above clearly, stating that U.S. support is steady and that it is essential, repeat essential, to terminate the continuing uncertainty.[79]

Huyser met daily with the Iranian high command and tried to cajole them into making plans for a military crackdown, not realizing that such planning had already begun. The problem was not the Iranian generals' inability to work cooperatively, which Huyser complained about repeatedly, but the generals' inability to run the entire nation without the cooperation of the populace. The Iranians, having observed the crackdown in November, realized this, and Huyser did not. As a result, the generals sought to save the military by keeping the troops locked up, and they dragged their feet in response to Huyser's prodding. The hard-liners in Washington were still hoping for a crackdown even after the regime had fallen.[80]

In the middle of the stalemate, the liberal opposition shuttled back and forth between the government, the Americans, and the Islamists, brokering stop-gap negotiations. Liberals negotiated the non-interference of the military in peaceful demonstrations in mid-January, and gained assurances that Khomeini's plane would be allowed to fly safely into Iran. In mid-January 1979, liberals carried messages between Khomeini and Bakhtiar, who had offered to resign as prime minister if Khomeini would then reappoint him. They began to meet with U.S. diplomats and Iranian military leaders in an attempt to prevent a coup. The Islamists were under orders from Khomeini not to have contact with Iranian government officials, with occasional exceptions, according to the memoirs of a Tehran activist. When liberals proposed that Ayatollah Mohammad Beheshti, the leader of Khomeini's secret Revolutionary Council in Tehran, meet with the shah's chief of staff, he played hard to get and finally canceled the meeting at the last minute.[81]

Even Khomeini's return to Iran on February 1 did not upset the balance of power. Khomeini arrived on an Air France plane—presumably it would be harder for the military to shoot down a foreign plane than an Iranian one—and was mobbed by supporters. The select group of invitees who had been allowed into the airport crowded in on him so aggressively that he had to retreat to a back room instead of giving a few remarks, as the organizers had originally intended. Khomeini then left in a motorcade for the main cemetery of Tehran, but the crowd that had come out to see him surged into the street and blocked the route. Part of the motorcade made it back to the airport, where a helicopter took Khomeini to the cemetery. Again the crowd was so thick that marshals had to swing their belts around over their heads to clear a space for the helicopter to land. When Khomeini emerged to give his speech, so many helpful hands reached out to carry him that his turban fell off, revealing an entirely bald head. After giving his speech, Khomeini diverted his helicopter from the Refah School compound, which his followers had selected as his home and headquarters, and flew instead to his older brother's house. For an anxious forty-five minutes, Khomeini's top followers waited at the Refah School and wondered what had happened to him, until his son Ahmad called to say that he was tired and not feeling well and had gone to his brother's house to rest. This dramatic re-entry demonstrated popular enthusiasm for Khomeini, but the shah's appointed caretakers remained in power.[82]

It took an unplanned uprising to break the stalemate. In the absence of mechanisms for transition, Khomeini had simply appointed his own prime minister, Mehdi Bazargan, at a press conference on February 4, but Bakhtiar remained in office. Iran had two governments for a week. On the evening of Friday, February 9, skirmishes broke out on a Tehran air force base between pro-revolutionary military technicians and pro-shah Imperial Guards. According to air force personnel who spoke with reporters the next day, the technicians gathered in salons and dining halls to watch a television re-broadcast of Khomeini's return to Iran. When the picture of Khomeini appeared, they shouted their support:[83]

> One officer came to the hall and told us, "Shut up!" When we paid no attention to him, tanks pointed their guns at us through the windows and the officer threatened to kill us . . . At this very second, Imperial Guard men outside fired at air force men supporting Khomeini and killed one and injured two. The air forcers got angry and mobilized and poured into the streets on the base and demanded the expulsion of the Guards. But the Guards warned them to disperse immediately. At the same time, Guardsmen fired into the crowd outside the base and killed two people. Finally the air forcers went to their dormitories and spent all night drawing up plans for today [Saturday, February 10].[84]

Thousands of civilians rushed to defend the mutineers, but Islamist leaders still hesitated. One religious scholar addressed the crowd around midnight and "said that, in light of the nearness of the curfew, it would be better for the crowd to disperse." The crowd refused. The following morning, Ayatollah Mahmud Taleqani issued a proclamation urging calm: "I strongly request that the person or persons responsible for the night-time attack on the Farah-Abad air force base be identified and turned over for their rightful punishment, and that the people of the nation also control their nerves and refrain from intervention or individual confrontations."[85]

Khomeini was under the weather Saturday morning and not taking visitors (shades of V. I. Lenin, isolated in St. Petersburg on the eve of Russia's October Revolution).[86] In the afternoon, he issued a proclamation warning of a holy war but still hesitating to call for it to begin:

> Although I have not given the order for sacred jihad, and I still wish matters to be settled peacefully, in accordance with the will of the people and legal criteria, I cannot tolerate these barbarous actions [of the loyalist forces], and I issue a solemn warning that if the Imperial Guard does not desist from this fratricidal slaughter and return to its barracks, and if the military authorities fail to prevent these attacks, I will take my final decision, placing my trust in God.[87]

Khomeini never needed to declare a holy war. Iranians were already fighting one. On Saturday morning, February 10, the Imperial Guard returned to the air base but was unable to subdue the insurgents. Three times during the day, tanks rolled toward the base. By now, however, large portions of the population were actively supporting the rebels. On street corners all over Tehran, women and men made Molotov cocktails. Weapons captured from armories and fallen soldiers were distributed to men who could show their military-service cards. Crowds tried to block tanks moving to suppress the uprising. Makeshift barricades did little to slow them, but the tanks were not unstoppable. One column assigned to quell disturbances near the mutinous air base found itself under attack. From roofs and windows on both sides of the avenue, thousands of Molotov cocktails rained down. Two tanks caught fire and the rest were forced to move out. Around the country, crowds prevented military reinforcements from reaching Tehran: troops in Karaj and Hamadan were trapped in their garrisons; a Qazvin battalion was stopped at Karavansara Sangi, 20 kilometers from Tehran; Kermanshah troops were halted at Saveh.[88]

Having defended the mutinous air base, the insurgents went on the offensive. Crowds gathered outside police stations, military garrisons, the electrical office, the television station, and so on. Security forces defended themselves with machine guns and cannons but could not hold out forever.[89]

> The police stations, encircled, bombarded by Molotov cocktails, fall one after the other. The crowd surrounds the one that is near the parliament. Several guerrillas approach it crawling, throwing their incendiary mixtures. The fire takes hold. The policemen surrender or try to flee. The crowd invades the building, sacks it.[90]

Some police officers fled to the north of the city, to a gendarmerie training center, where their tales sowed fear among the gendarmes. Conscripts scrambled over the walls at several bases.[91]

The military retained enough coherence to send out yet another column of tanks early Sunday morning, February 11, to reinforce the besieged guards of the Tehran munitions factory. Yet it, too, fell. Midmorning, the chiefs of staff met and declared the military's "neutrality"—abandoning the shah's caretaker government and allowing the revolutionary forces to take control.[92]

There has been much speculation about secret agreements between military and Islamist leaders, suggesting that the armed forces were delivered to the revolution by a few generals eager to save their necks. Some of the shah's generals, facing execution after the revolution, claimed to have helped the Islamists. Clearly, there was dissent within the military, with some officers reluctant to engage unarmed protesters. But I have found little evidence of a backstage deal. Rather, elite units of the shah's military strove credibly to regain control of Tehran in the last two days of the revolution. On the evening of February 9 and three times on February 10, Imperial Guard tanks made their way, through heavy and hostile crowds, to the rebellious air force base and fought with the insurgents. On February 10, police stations and military bases defended themselves against popular attacks before abandoning their positions. Early on February 11, the tanks rolled again. In two days the military killed hundreds of protesters.[93]

Moreover, the populace continued to expect fierce military action. Early in the evening on February 10, rumors flew of an impending coup d'état.[94] All day long, Tehranis built barricades in the streets, expecting a loyalist crackdown:

> The barricades were everywhere now: usually wretchedly inadequate collections gathered from whatever lay to hand: baulks of timber, the gates of buildings, rocks, cars which had been abandoned by their owners. The Chieftain tanks of the Imperial Guard would ride over such things without noticing them . . . I pointed out to the proud constructors the inadequacy of their work, but they just laughed. There was a wildness in the air, a feeling that nothing mattered.[95]

This wildness sustained a crowd attacking a military installation: "Fear of weapons was gone, fear of shooting, fear of blood, fear of the Guard until recently called Immortal, which had lost its immortality forever in the eyes of the people—this fear was gone. The way people stood up, you would think the Immortals were only setting off firecrackers."[96]

This sense of abandon is difficult to capture in academic prose. But it is central to the understanding of protest movements. In these extraordinary moments, people felt that normal rules of behavior had been suspended. They did not recognize the limits of safety, deference, and routine. The future was suddenly up in the air. Armed primarily with a sense of solidarity, they confronted elite military units, until recently called Immortal. Faced with a population in such a mood, the military prudently withdrew.

CHAPTER 8

Conclusion

And then it was over. Iran's national radio interrupted Maurice Ravel's *Mother Goose Suite* to announce the change of regime. A day and a half of street fighting ended centuries of Iranian monarchy and more than fifty years of Pahlavi rule, which had seemed so secure only months before. The life of the country, and the lives of its residents, became divided in two: before the shah fell and after the shah fell. The process of explaining this split, of retroactively predicting it, began immediately.[1]

I have argued that explanations of the Iranian Revolution are only partially valid. There is evidence that supports each one of them, but there is also evidence that doesn't fit. And the closer we examine the events of the revolution—the closer we listen to the people who made the revolution—the more anomalies we find.[2]

Political explanations argue that we might have seen the revolution coming if we had paid attention to Jimmy Carter's human rights campaign and the shah's liberalization. This approach is partially confirmed by evidence from members of the liberal opposition, who stuck their necks out in response to these developments. Many of the liberals had studied in Europe or North America, and they both watched and responded to international politics. But the explanation weakens with the shah's rapprochement with Carter in November 1977 and his subsequent crackdown. The liberals responded just as attentively to these developments as to the earlier openings, and restrained their activities. The Islamist opposition, by contrast, paid less attention than liberals to international politics, and its activism did not follow the pattern of opening and closing that political explanations propose. Islamist protest emerged only in October 1977, after the death of Mostafa Khomeini. When the shah began to rescind his liberalization in November, the Islamists began to mobilize in a concerted fashion. This mobilization—mistimed, according to a political explanation—was due, it appears, to calculations about popular support, not about political openings. The Islamists felt the time had come for revolt because the Iranian people were "awakened"—that is, their consciousness had been sufficiently raised that they would engage in anti-regime protest. This perception, however, was premature: the vast majority of Iranians were not sufficiently awakened to answer Khomeini's calls to protest in late 1977 and the first half of 1978. But the perception was strong enough to set in motion a chain of events that would draw Iranians into protest a year later.

Organizational explanations suggest that we should not have been surprised by the revolution, given the resources of the mosque network. This approach finds confirmation in the Islamist movement's dependence on religious sites, lines of communication, and relations of religious authority. But such explanations do not account for the difficulties the Islamists had in trying to mobilize the mosque network, which at the outset of the revolution was under the control of non-revolutionary religious leaders. These leaders saw their mandate as protection of the religious institution, and they viewed Islamist activism as an invitation to state repression. For the Islamists to make use of the mosque network, they had to convince or pressure the non-revolutionary leaders to cooperate or step aside. They devoted the first half of 1978 to this task. By the end of summer 1978, they had largely commandeered the mosque network, but this resource was an outcome of mobilization, not a prerequisite.

Cultural explanations argue that the revolution flowed from longstanding practices and positions of Shi'i Islam. This approach can cite the Shi'i idiom of martyrdom adopted by the revolutionary movement, as well as the movement's use of the Shi'i calendar of religious events, such as forty-day mourning ceremonies. But explanations that focus on preexisting religious culture underestimate the fluidity of these traditions. The politicization of forty-day mourning ceremonies was as much a departure from tradition as an expression of it. Moreover, the Islamists transformed other religious traditions as well, including the observance of Ramadan, the ceremonies of Muharram, and the bases of religious authority. The revolutionaries did not draw on culture so much as redraw it.

Economic explanations suggest that the revolution could have been predicted if we had had reliable real-time economic data. Such explanations are confirmed by the hopes generated in the oil boom of 1973–1974, and subsequently undermined by recession. But a series of comparisons offers evidence that doesn't fit: Iran's poverty, and its economic growth, were no more remarkable than its neighbors'; its boom and bust were no more extreme than other oil-exporting countries'; its recession of 1977–1978 was not clearly worse than its recession of 1975, by many measures; and the social groups most affected by boom and bust were not the groups most active in the revolution. Many Iranians cited economic grievances as their reason for participating in the revolution—even Khomeini, who detested materialist explanations, cited such grievances in his appeals—but the distribution of such grievances does not match the distribution of revolutionary protest.

Military explanations propose that the revolution followed inevitably from the weakness of the shah's repressive apparatus. Supporting evidence can be found in the shah's illness and refusal to authorize widespread slaughter. But this approach downplays the extensive repression—the arrests, beatings, shootings, and threats—that the monarchy continued to wield up to its last hours. The shah's military-security complex was not so much weak as overwhelmed. No system of repression is intended to deal with wholesale popular disobedience like that which emerged in Iran in late 1978.

All these explanations, then, face significant anomalies. Among other things, they suffer an inversion of cause and effect. The causal factors that students of social movements are trained to look for tended to be the product of the revolutionary movement and did not pre-date it. Political opportunities emerged for workers in fall 1978, for example, because of the Islamist mobilization of spring and summer 1978; Islamists took control of the mosque network and forged a culture of

166 The Unthinkable Revolution in Iran

revolution during the course of the movement; strikes deepened the country's recession; and the shah's military "broke down" only after it failed to halt months of massive protest.

One response to this situation might be to devise a new explanation of some sort, a novel set of conditions whose presence in Iran in the 1970s might allow us to predict the revolution retroactively. Another approach might be to combine several or all of the explanations in a holistic analysis, like the "combinatorial," "conjunctural," and "contextual" approaches that are becoming common in the study of revolutions and other social movements.[3]

I have chosen a different response. The problem, I contend, is not with these particular explanations but with explanations in general. Any new explanation that I might devise would also, I imagine, face significant anomalies. So rather than swim against this current, perhaps we should embrace it. I propose an anti-explanation that puts anomaly in the foreground.

Anti-explanation means abandoning the project of retroactive prediction in favor of recognizing and reconstructing the lived experience of the moment. For moments of revolution, this experience is dominated by confusion—the anomalies noted in the previous chapters have this in common. They all involve confusion: the Islamists' skepticism about liberalization, the battle for control over the mosque network, the attempt to transform religious traditions, the shaky link between economic distress and political protest, and the calculation of risk and safety during martial law. All these factors point to the instability of the moment and the disruption of routine. The goal of anti-explanation is to understand the variety of responses to confusion.[4]

What are we to do if this subjective evidence differs from the objective explanations that social scientists typically offer? Scholars have offered at least four reasons to privilege social scientists' perspectives over those of their subjects:

1. The attempt to understand subjects' perspectives involves difficult epistemological barriers. Since the nineteenth century, sub-

jectivist philosophers have emphasized the importance of reliving in some way the experience of the people they seek to
understand. But this reliving is a personal act that other scholars
cannot reproduce. As a result, interpretive hypotheses cannot be
confirmed.

2. People's statements about their inner states, especially retrospective statements, may not reflect their actual inner states. Karl
Marx and Friedrich Engels ridiculed historical work that "takes
every epoch at its word and believes that everything it says and
imagines about itself is true": "Whilst in ordinary life every shopkeeper is very well able to distinguish between what somebody
professes to be and what he really is, our historiography has not
yet won this trivial insight." Context affects statements, as do
intentions, narrative tropes, forgetfulness, and any number of
other factors.

3. People may not accurately understand how their own minds
work, or the causes of their own actions, as demonstrated in numerous psychological experiments. In the pithy words of the
great social scientist Pierre Bourdieu, "Social agents do not in-
nately possess a science of what they are and what they do."

4. People may not sufficiently understand those around them. They
have no training in sampling methodologies, so their information may be biased. They have no access to the archives or statistics that shed systematic light on the contexts of their lives.
Certain knowledgeable respondents may have enough information about their social settings to be considered credible "infor-
mants," but even they should be relied upon only when more
systematic data are unavailable.[5]

These are serious challenges for anti-explanation. But the first three
apply just as forcefully to explanations as well. Much of explanation's
seemingly objective evidence is also based on subjects' statements
about their inner states. Surveys elicit statements about opinions and
memories. Unemployment statistics cumulate the statements of people
who claim to be seeking work. Gross domestic product estimates ex-
trapolate from statements about payments made with certain inten-

tions of retail exchange, as distinct from payments made with the intention of gift-giving and wholesaling. One might try to avoid these problems with strictly observational methods, either behaviorist or physiological. But this process involves its own difficulties, which are often overcome in practice by checking against subjects' statements. Lie-detector examinations, for example, became convincing in early tests in large part because they elicited and were corroborated by confessions.[6]

Indeed, explanation imputes inner states, even if it professes to be uninterested in them. Causes affect outcomes through mechanisms. In much of the social sciences, these mechanisms involve human motivation. Explanations for the emergence of democracy, for example—explanations that focus on socioeconomic development, or elite pacts, or other causes—impute particular motivations to members of various social groups: members of this or that group wanted democracy, or tolerated democracy, or objected to democracy. The motivation that is imputed need not be conscious. It could even be autonomic, as in the physiological response of recoiling from extreme heat—though conscious motivation could play a significant role in "deviant" cases of failure to recoil, such as walking intentionally on hot coals.

Regardless of the status of the motivation, disagreement between objectivist and subjectivist approaches, explanation and anti-explanation, resolves into a debate over inner states. For any given episode, which motivation has the greater weight of evidence, direct or indirect, on its side? For Iran, as the previous chapters have shown, the evidence of confusion is so overwhelming as to wash out all attempts at explanation.

One remaining route for objectivist approaches would be to argue that confusion at the conscious level coexists with different, explainable inner states that are not so easily accessible to conscious reflection. Evidence could then be presented for these alternative states, and the reason for their inaccessibility. For example, one could argue that in times of widespread confusion, people fall back on culturally familiar patterns of behavior, even as they attribute their actions to purely personal decisions. Culture might then explain both the actions and the reason for the inaccessibility of the inner state associated with the actions. The sociologist Francesca Polletta offers a compelling example of this phenomenon. During and after the sit-ins for civil rights in the United States in the early 1960s, activists and supporters emplotted the movement, publicly and privately, in terms of spontaneity and unpredictability: "It was like a fever," "This was a surprise (and shock)," "BOOM!—'it' hit with an unawareness that rocked the capital city [Raleigh, North Carolina]." Polletta juxtaposes these accounts with others that described the structural underpinnings of the movement, namely, the prior organizational work that had gone into the sit-ins. The two sets of accounts can be reconciled, Polletta argues, by recognizing the narrative of spontaneity as a powerful statement of identity and recruitment, casting participation in the movement as a result of irresistible, unpredictable, life-altering forces. In this example, structure operates outside of conscious experience—or at least partially outside of it, since the "objective" evidence of prior organization is also based on subjective accounts. For this reason, the subjective experience of unpredictability is discounted in favor of structural explanation—paradoxically, though, it is the structural account that restores agency to the activists, whose subjective accounts deny it.[7]

This objectivist approach works best when structures persist throughout the period under study. The greater the break from routine, the greater the degree of de-institutionalization, the harder it is to argue that people are falling back on an established pattern of behavior without being aware of doing so. Breaches and the resulting confusion draw conscious attention to motivations. To the extent that nonroutine episodes are characterized by confusion, and by increased reflexiveness and intentionality, understanding such moments may undermine explanation.

———

A crucial element in people's responses to confusion is the sense of "viability" discussed in Chapter 7. The concept of viability focuses on potential protesters' estimations of the future actions of other potential protesters. Viability is not the only factor in the experience of protest, and I leave it to others to pursue different aspects of the matter—the emotions of the moment, for example, or the different strategies and tactics that individuals and groups pursue. But in emphasizing viability, I seek to highlight one element for which I have found considerable evidence, both from retrospective interviews and from statements at the time: Iranians were more likely to participate in revolutionary events if they felt that many others would do the same. Moreover, there is evidence that Iranians engaged in intense and continuous, though not necessarily systematic, research to estimate the viability both of the movement as a whole and of the next rumored event. In other words, they worked hard to predict how many people in their city, their neighborhood, or their workplace would show up at the next event, would stay at home, or would go to work. Not everybody came to the same conclusion from this research; indeed, estimations of how many Iranians would participate could vary widely, as could willingness to join the fight on the basis of those estimations.

These estimations cannot be known in advance; nor can the willingness to participate. They shift drastically from moment to moment on the basis of amorphous rumors, heightened emotions, and conflicting senses of duty. These shifts make retroactive prediction impossible. Even the most thorough survey would not have predicted very far into the future—not that thorough surveys are feasible in moments of revolution, or in the dictatorial regimes that seem most prone to revolutions. For this reason, revolutions will remain unpredictable. But people living through an upheaval do not have the luxury of abandoning prediction—their lives, careers, group memberships, and sense of self depend on choosing the proper path through such periods of confusion.

This form of analysis has implications far beyond the particulars of the Iranian Revolution. All social movements aspire to generate confusion, to break with routine to a greater or lesser extent. Even when there are no troops lining the streets and no governments being toppled, social movements challenge people to reconsider their lives and institutions. Reconsideration is necessarily based, at least in part, on an estimation of others' behaviors—Will they go along? How many? Will I be wasting my time and money? Will I look foolish, if they don't?

Even beyond social movements, I would argue, viability offers a window into the whole of social life. The experience of the Iranian Revolution, then—the confusion and risks and obsessive conversations—

offers an approach to the experience of non-revolution in Iran and elsewhere. Given that revolution succeeds by gaining a reputation for viability, might not non-revolutionary social and political structures reproduce themselves in the same way? When institutions and behaviors *don't* change, when social movements *don't* arise, perhaps this reflects estimations of the viability of stasis. I may go along with the status quo because I expect everybody else will too. In other words, we could view "stasis movements" (as oxymoronic as that sounds) as one form of social movement, that is, the attempt to maintain practices as they are. These movements need not be conspicuous—indeed, I would guess, they are mobilized intentionally only when threatened by change.

This approach dovetails with recent trends in social theory which suggest that the reproduction of practices from one moment to the next actually requires work and cannot be taken for granted. This work gains invisibility, and patterns appear to be "structural," through the aura of inevitability. But inevitability is a tissue that can easily tear, and there are movements afoot at all times trying to tear it. So stasis movements remain on guard, warning of social collapse, convincing the next generation, policing the boundaries of the routine, co-opting disruptions that cannot be prevented (capitalism, democracy, technology, and the like), even inaugurating some changes in order to prevent others ("planning").[8]

The shah's regime worked hard to manage change. It cast itself as "revolutionary," labeling the land reforms of the 1960s the "White Revolution" and "the shah and people's revolution." The regime employed the most advanced computers and experts to assist it in "planning," which was intended to meet the goals of economic transformation that the shah had set for the country while blocking political transformations that he refused to countenance. This combination seems hubristic today, but at the time, knowledgeable people found it convincing. One of the shah's North American consultants recounted his optimism:

> About 10 years ago, I was working with the ministry of planning in a Third World country . . . The ministry was staffed by some of the brightest people I have ever met. Most had advanced degrees, including PhDs from top US universities. Many had returned from living abroad, and wanted to share in

the work and excitement of bringing their nation fully into the 20th century. If asked in 1975, I would have said: "This is one of the most successful modelling and long-range planning projects of all time." Our team had ready access to policy makers at the highest level. The minister met with us regularly, and his deputy had an open door to members of our project. In fact we made a three-hour, on-line presentation, sitting at computer terminals with eight members of the cabinet, including the Prime Minister.[9]

That country, the consultant went on to say, was Iran, and the computers failed to model the revolution that swept away the planning and the planners three years later. This failure to anticipate the revolution was not due to a programming error. The regime seemed stable at the time. The shah's longtime security chief later recalled that he and other top officials passed around predictions of disaster in 1977 as a sort of inside joke—"The government seemed stable and such predictions were quite amusing at the time."[10] This appearance of stability was self-fulfilling: if people expected protest to fail, only the courageous or foolhardy would participate. With such small numbers, protest could not fail to fail. So long as revolution remained "unthinkable," it remained undoable. It could come to pass only when large numbers of people began to "think the unthinkable."

About the Sources · Notes · References
Acknowledgments · Index

About the Sources

A close history of the Iranian Revolution has yet to be written. Sufficient source materials are still not available, more than twenty years after the overthrow of the Pahlavi monarchy. Research has instead followed two tracks, the publication of documentary collections and the analysis of these documents.

In the summer of 1978, Khomeini made a point of encouraging documentation of the revolutionary movement:

> For the enlightenment of future generations and the prevention of biased and mistaken accounts, it is necessary that responsible writers turn with careful attention to the precise analysis of the history of this Islamic movement, and record the uprising and demonstrations of the Muslims of Iran in various cities, along with their history and motivation, so that the Islamic themes and the clerical movement may become a model for future societies and generations.[1]

The first wave of documents, accordingly, was published during and just after the revolution. Already in late 1977 or early 1978, a volume called *Shahidi Digar az Ruhaniyat* (Another Martyr from the Clergy)—published by Iranian seminarians in Iraq—documented the mourning for Mostafa Khomeini in fall 1977 through letters from Iran, transcribed speeches, and copies of printed pronouncements. At some point in 1978, a collection of letters and pronouncements covering early 1978, beginning with the Qom protests in January, was published under the title *Dar-bareh-ye Qiyam-e Hamaseh-Afarinan-e Qom va Tabriz* (On the Epic Uprising of Qom and Tabriz). Later that year, or possibly in early 1979, two similar collections appeared: one covering the protests of summer 1978, called *Pareh'i az E'lamiyeh'ha-ye Montashereh dar Iran dar Mah'ha-ye Tir va Mordad 1357* (Selected Pronouncements Published in Iran in the Months of July and August 1978); and the other covering the first three-quarters of 1978, entitled *Asnad va Tasaviri az Mobarezat-e Khalq-e Mosalman-e Iran* (Documents and Pictures from the Struggles of the Muslim People of Iran).

Throughout the revolutionary period, the liberal opposition was publishing its own documentary record, a bimonthly collection called *Zamimeh-ye Khabar-Nameh* (Supplement to The Newsletter), which included all the issues of the generally weekly newsletter called *Khabar-Nameh* (The Newsletter), as well as copies of oppositional pronouncements by liberals, leftists, and Islamists. One of the two most active leftist organizations published a collection of its announcement and position papers in spring 1979, under the title *E'lamiyeh'ha va Bayaniyeh'ha-ye Sazman-e Cherik'ha-ye Feda'i-ye Khalq* (Pronouncements and Announcements of the Organization of the People's Sacrificing Guerrillas).

These samizdat collections are incomplete and appear to have been hastily assembled. Some forgo any kind of organizational scheme, chronological or otherwise. A number of the documents that are reproduced in these collections are barely legible, and many of the documents that are transcribed include typographical errors. In addition, multiple versions of the same document do not entirely agree with one another, suggesting that editorial hands were at work despite the appearance of authenticity. This said, I have not found a case of substantive editing in these collections, but only changes in punctuation, occasional word choices, and the spelling out of abbreviated names and dates.

The great advantage of these early documentary collections, however, is connected to their haphazardness: because they were produced in a hurry, with less time for polish and review, they include a host of documents that do not appear in later, more official collections. Correspondence, for example, offers eyewitness accounts of revolutionary events that were later suppressed: Shaykh Ha'eri's less-than-revolutionary concern that protest "must be peaceful, not in such a way that they will do in the 'Azam Mosque, too, like the Fayziyeh Seminary" appears only in these early collections, several of which published the same anonymous account of the Qom protest of January 1978.[2]

Perhaps the greatest example of the early openness of the documentary record is a master's thesis in sociology at the University of Tehran, filed during the 1982–83 academic year. The author of the thesis, Sohbatollah Amra'i, was an employee in the Martyr Foundation, established in February 1979 to draw up a register of the revolution's "martyrs" and distribute aid to their families. According to the chapter on methodology, Amra'i and others in the foundation accepted applications for four months in Tehran—other offices fielded applications in other regions of Iran—and sifted through them to determine which individuals were truly killed in revolutionary uprisings. Those who died of accidents or natural causes, or were assassinated by revolutionary forces, were excluded from the register. Amra'i then checked his foundation's figures against the records of the Tehran coroner's office and the main Tehran graveyard, Behesht-e Zahra. The numbers were all relatively similar—and relatively low. Around seven hundred to nine hundred Iranians died in Tehran during the year of revolution, not the thousands mentioned in official histories. In an act that dramatically symbolizes the Islamic Republic's attempts to control the historiography of the revolution, the thesis was banned from public view and removed from the University of Tehran library. I was able to see the thesis only when a friend in Iran, who for obvious reasons must remain nameless, smuggled a photocopy to me.

Corresponding to the first wave of documentation is the first wave of analyses of the Iranian Revolution, published in 1979 and the early 1980s. These works came from social scientists and historians who had been studying Iran when the revolution took them by surprise. They generally added "revolution" to the titles of their works and reconstituted their previous research topics as "preludes to revolution." Several strong books and dissertations resulted, a testament to the resourcefulness of scholars forced to engage mid-stream in retroactive prediction. Among the authors were Ervand Abrahamian, who had been studying the Iranian left; Janet Bauer, who had lived among poor women in Tehran; Michael M. J. Fischer, who had conducted an ethnography of the seminaries of Qom; Mary Elaine Hegland, who had done ethnographic work with villagers outside Shiraz; Eric J. Hooglund, who had been working on rural social organization; Farhad Kazemi, who had been interviewing shanty-dwellers in Tehran; Nikki R. Keddie, whose work built on two decades of Iranian historical research; Amin Saikal, who claimed that the revolution only confirmed the author's prediction of regime failure; and Sepehr Zabih, who incorporated an earlier manuscript on "Iran's unique one-party system" that had been almost ready for publication just as the revolution broke out.[3]

The chapters on the revolution itself, in this generation of studies, seem to have been based largely on contemporary news sources. These sources are of course important, but they are also problematic, both for Iranian press accounts and for international media coverage of the Iranian Revolution, whose comprehensiveness and credibility may be called into question. Iranian journalists were heavily censored until late summer 1978, when they reversed position and became cheerleaders for the revolution. The major newspapers'

two-month strike (early November 1978 to early January 1979) left this crucial period covered only by movement papers (*Khabar-Nameh* of the National
Front and *Hambastegi* of the Writers' Guild). When the regular press reap-
peared in early January, its boosterish reports were hardly distinguishable
from the movement papers'. Protesters, referred to as "reactionary" tools of
"foreign hands" a few months earlier, were now "freedom-seekers." Security
forces were now "thugs." One quantitative study reports that the two largest-
circulation dailies in Iran devoted fully a quarter of their stories to interviews,
announcements, and other messages from the opposition during the last five
weeks of the revolution.[4]

The international press, dominated by journalists from the United States,
did not pick up the revolution story until fairly late in 1978. As William A.
Dorman and Mansour Farhang have noted, many of the foreign correspon-
dents when they did arrive tended to be overly deferential to official sources
and unprepared to cover a revolution. Bombarded with conflicting reports on
events—the government spokesmen downplaying and the opposition spokesmen exaggerating the scope and importance of each protest—the foreign journalists were largely unwilling and unable to go out and get eyewitness corroboration. Nonetheless, the media—both Iranian and foreign—do include
numerous tidbits of evidence that help provide a day-to-day picture of the revolutionary movement. One modest example, quoted in several studies of the
revolution, is an interesting story in the *New York Times* describing a poor family in a Tehran shanty-town that "had no time for demonstrations against the
Shah."[5]

A second wave of documentation began by stabilizing the historical record.
A major religious organization published the ten-volume work *Nehzat-e
Ruhaniyun* (The Movement of the Religious Scholars), by ʿAli Davani, himself a
mid-ranking religious scholar who selected and introduced a sequence of documents forming a semi-official account of the revolution (my citations in this
book refer to a second edition published in 1998). Another parastatal institution published the "official" collection of Khomeini's writings and statements,
entitled *Sahifeh-ye Nur* (The Book of Light), in twenty-one volumes. This collection is not entirely reliable when it comes to dating documents—for example, it says improbably that Khomeini responded to the protests of January 9,
1978, on the same day, while contemporaneous accounts place his response
twelve days later.[6] More reliable were collections published independently,
such as *Islam and Revolution,* translated and annotated by Hamid Algar;
Majmuʿehʾi az Maktubat, Sokhanraniʾha, Payamʾha va Fatavi-ye Emam Khomeini

(A Collection of Letters, Speeches, Messages, and Rulings of Imam Khomeini); and its *Zamimeh* (Supplement). Other Islamist leaders were anthologized as well, typically soon after their deaths, including Ayatollahs Mahmud Taleqani and Mohammad Saduqi. Several provincial cities had their own documentary collections, including Seyyed Hasan Nurbakhsh's collection on Isfahan, Ramazan ʿAli Shakeri's collection on Mashhad, and (much later) Muhammad Javad Moradi-Nia's collection on Khomein. In Europe, Wolfgang Behn performed a great service by publishing hundreds of samizdat documents in a microfiche collection entitled *Iranian Opposition to the Shah*.

The Islamists' documentary collections grew more complex and historiographically rich in the mid-1980s with the emergence of a "commemorative" *(yad-nameh)* literature in Iran. Several volumes offered biographical pictures of martyred Islamist leaders, including old interviews with the deceased, documents associated with them, and reflections on their lives by their associates. Several of these volumes focus on specific figures—among them *Shahid Doktor Bahonar* (The Martyr Dr. Bahonar) and *Farzand-e Islam va Qurʾan* (Son of Islam and the Qurʾan—also on Bahonar), and Mostafa Izadi's *Gozari bar Zendegi-ye Faqih ʿAliqadr Ayatollah Montazeri* (Report on the Life of the Great Cleric Ayatollah Montazeri). Others cover a wide range of religious scholars, for example, ʿAli Rabbani Khalkhali's *Shohada-ye Ruhaniyat-e Shiʿa* (Martyrs of the Shiʿi Clergy), Reza Moradi's *Zendegi-Nameh-ye Pishvayan-e Enqelab* (Biographies of the Leaders of the Revolution), and *Pishtazan-e Shahadat* (The Front Ranks of Martyrdom). In the absence of a memoir-writing tradition among Iranian religious scholars—only recently have a few oral history–style memoirs appeared, for example, those by ʿAbdolhossein Dastghayb, Fazlollah Mahallati, and ʿAbbas-ʿAli ʿAmid-Zanjani—these are exceptionally useful sources for historical work on the religious cadres of the revolutionary movement. The material in these collections, however, is almost entirely undocumented, so validity is uncertain. In addition, the presentation can be confusing, to the extent that it is sometimes difficult to distinguish the editors' voice from the subjects'. Nonetheless, the hagiographic intent makes slightly seamy details more credible, for instance, the biography of one young cleric who apparently underwent guerrilla training in Turkey and smuggled guns into Iran—actions that were much rumored at the time and frequently denied.[7] In addition, the use of multiple voices in each volume subverted the mono-vocal canon-formation of the official histories. Here were leaders with specific personalities—despite the unidimensional portraits that hero-worship tends toward—who even disagreed with each other at times.

In the mid-1980s, the Islamists began to take this documentation to its logical next step, instituting a program of oral histories through the Foundation for the History of the Islamic Revolution of Iran. By 1988, the foundation had recorded 180 oral histories and was publishing excerpts in its journal *Yad* (Memory).[8] But this published material was limited to recollections of the 1950s and early 1960s, stopping well before the period of the revolution itself. I have not been able to visit the foundation to study the unpublished material, and no scholar, to my knowledge, has yet used this source for the study of the revolution.

In addition to the Islamists, other groups sought to record their participation in the revolutionary movement. The Liberation Movement of Iran, a moderate opposition group, published an eleven-volume collection of documents under the title *Asnad-e Nehzat-e Azadi-ye Iran* (Documents of the Liberation Movement of Iran). Its leading members, Mehdi Bazargan and Ebrahim Yazdi, published memoirs and documents, as did other political figures such as Abolhassan Bani-Sadr, Mozaffar Baqa'i-Kermani, Houchang Nahavandi, and Karim Sanjabi. On the left, Reza Baraheni and Mahmud Golabdareh'i described their participation in the revolution.

Officials and supporters of the shah's regime, publishing in exile, also recorded their experiences: industrialist Jalal Ahanchian, diplomat Shamsuddin Amir-'Ala'i, cabinet member's wife Azar Aryanpour, Prime Minister Shahpour Bakhtiar (who switched from the opposition at the end of 1978), cultural official Mariam Behnam, social work pioneer Sattareh Farman Farmaian, landowner Manucher Farmanfarmaian, Chief of Staff Abbas Gharabaghi, counterespionage officer Manuchehr Hashemi, cabinet minister Dariush Homayun, diplomats Fereydoun Hoveyda and 'Abdolreza Hushang Mahdavi, royal adviser Ahmad 'Ali Mas'ud-Ansari, UNESCO official Ehsan Naraghi, diplomat Parviz C. Radji, security official Mansur Rafizadeh, court employee Minou Reeves, royal bodyguard 'Ali Shahbazi, and of course Shah Mohammad Reza Pahlavi and his sister Ashraf.

The relative frequency of these memoirs of state elites, most of them writing in the West, highlights the lack of a strong tradition of autobiography among common folk or the educated middle class in Iran.[9] This lack is further highlighted by the abundance of memoirs by foreign observers of the revolution: journalists Paul Balta and Claudine Rulleau, Claire Brière and Pierre Blanchet, Fred Saint-James, and John Simpson; diplomats Anthony Parsons (Britain), William H. Sullivan (United States), and Nazir Ahmad Zakir (Pakistan); United States military envoy Robert E. Huyser; Soviet intelligence agent Vladimir Kuzichkin; and various others who happened to be living in Iran when the revolution broke out, such as Serge Ginger, a French doctor in Tehran; Desmond Harney, a British business official in Tehran; and Charles I. Semkus, an American convert to Islam who wrote technical manuals for the Iranian air force in Isfahan. In addition, a dozen U.S. officials of the period published memoirs discussing the U.S. government's responses to the revolutionary movement in Iran. These responses are also covered in the seventy-seven-volume series of documents, published under the title *Asnad-e Laneh-ye Jasusi* (Documents from the Nest of Spies), that were captured in the U.S. embassy in Tehran by the radical students who took the embassy personnel hostage. The National Security Archive, a non-profit organization in Washington, collected these documents and hundreds more declassified under the Freedom of Information Act, arranged them chronologically with a useful index, and published them on microfiche (now also available by subscription over the Internet) under the title *Iran: The Making of U.S. Policy*. I supplemented this collection by reviewing the *Declassified Document Reference System* from its inception in 1982.

Two other non-profit organizations in the United States embarked on oral history projects: the Harvard Iranian Oral History Program and the Foundation for Iranian Studies' Program of Iranian Oral History in Bethesda, Maryland. Thousands of pages of transcripts in these collections provided a tremendous amount of detail on the revolutionary period, including valuable "insider information" on the liberal opposition and the workings of the state. Both of these collections focused on leading personalities, almost all of them in exile, so the religious groups were under-represented. (An exception was Sa'id Raja'i-Khorasani, a post-revolutionary Iranian ambassador to the United Nations who described his days as an Islamist militant at Tabriz University in the Harvard collection.) In addition, the interviewers tended to be obsequious in the presence of their prominent subjects and did not always challenge evasions and self-serving statements.

A second wave of analyses followed in the late 1980s and early 1990s. The pioneers in this wave were two articles, each of which used the major documentary collections of the first wave and some of the second-wave documentation: Shaul Bakhash's article "Sermons, Revolutionary Pamphleteering and Mobilisation" (1984) and "The State, Classes, and Modes of Mobilization in the Iranian Revolution" (1985), by Ahmad Ashraf and Ali Banuazizi. More than three dozen doctoral dissertations and two dozen books ensued, until the wave petered out around 1994. These works were conceived after the revolution and hence did not have to bend earlier projects to the explanatory service of the revolution. Some of them include interviews with participants and eyewitnesses to the revolution. Yet the available source material was limited.

Some of the limitations have been removed in a third wave of documentation, which has specialized in the publication of Pahlavi-era government documents. The archives from this period are still not open for researchers, so these documents represent a first look into the workings of a state that had its tentacles in every area of social life. Early publications of this sort include an interesting book from 1987, Habibollah Sadiqi's *Mesl-e Barf Ab Khahim Shod* (We Will Melt Like Snow), which transcribes tape-recordings of crisis meetings of the shah's military commanders in January 1979. This source has not, so far as I have found, been verified by the participants, but it seems realistic. In particular, the generals do not appear bloodthirsty or anti-Islamic, as one might expect of a fabricated transcript published in post-revolutionary Iran. According to comments in the transcript, the meetings were recorded on the orders of the shah's chief of staff. A decade later, transcripts were published of security council meetings from August, September, and October 1978: *Ma Gereftar-e Yek Jang-e Vaqe'i Ravani Shodeh-im* (We Are Engaged in a Real Psychological War), on the protests of late summer; *Tasmim-e Shum* (The Ominous Decision), on the Black Friday massacre; and *Aya U Tasmim Darad Bi-Ayad beh Iran* (Is He Deciding to Come to Iran?), on Khomeini's eviction from Iraq.

Another early entry in the document-publishing trend was *Faraz'ha'i az Tarikh-e Enqelab* (High Points of the History of the Revolution), published in 1989, which presented almost one hundred documents from SAVAK archives. It was followed by *SAVAK va Ruhaniyat* (SAVAK and the Religious Scholars), published in 1992, which presented a series of six-month summary reports on the activities of the Islamic opposition to the shah, from 1971 to fall 1978. Both of these volumes offered transcribed texts of the documents, reproducing only a handful of documents by photostat as appendixes.

The wave that followed in the 1990s apparently sought greater credibility by including photostats of almost every document included, alongside the transcribed texts. These transcriptions are quite useful, as some of the documents appear to consist of poor carbon copies with sloppy scribbles in the margins. Major multi-volume series were entitled *Asnad-e Enqelab-e Eslami* (Documents of the Islamic Revolution), published in five volumes in 1990–1996; *Enqelab-e Eslami beh Ravayet-e Asnad-e SAVAK* (The Islamic Revolution According to the Documents of SAVAK), seven volumes of which appeared in 1997–2000; and *Yaran-e Emam beh Ravayet-e Asnad-e SAVAK* (Friends of the Imam According to the Documents of SAVAK), the first twenty-nine volumes of which appeared in 1998–2002. These collections offer an unprecedented window into the revolutionary movement, with real-time reports on protests and protest planning, some based on transcripts of phone taps and bugs. The level of detail is astounding.

Can these collections, published by state and parastatal officials with a considerable stake in the telling of the revolutionary narrative, be trusted? Yes and no. The editors have clearly left out far more documents than they included—the document numbering in some series runs into the tens of thousands, while only a couple thousand reports are included. It is easy to imagine that the documents were not randomly selected, and that some of the missing material would offer a quite different picture from the material that is included. The most obvious bias is the focus on leading members of the Islamist opposition; the activities of leftists and ordinary folk scarcely appear in these works. Liberals appear in some collections, primarily *Asnad-e Laneh-ye Jasusi* and *Faraz'ha'i,* but only in documents intended to embarrass them (for example, by showing their contacts with officials of the U.S. and Pahlavi governments). Even the Islamists' activities are selectively ignored. For example, a contemporaneous account suggested that Ayatollah Mohammad Saduqi tried to disperse a crowd of protesters on the afternoon of March 29, 1978, but this less-than-militant act is omitted from volume 2 of *Yaran-e Emam,* which is devoted to Saduqi. The volume includes reports on Saduqi's activities on March 28 (SAVAK document number H26/3009) and the evening of March 29 (SAVAK document number H26/3034), but none of the intervening documents that might have covered the afternoon of March 29.[10]

That said, the documents that *are* included appear to be genuine. The shah's officials use terms like "trouble-makers" and "fanatics" to describe the religious opposition, and their growing confusion as the revolutionary movement advanced seems entirely plausible. I came across only one document that struck me as a possible forgery: a hand-written document (almost all the others are typed, with hand-written comments and addenda) describing the demonstrations of Tasu'a and 'Ashura in terms that seem implausibly sympathetic to the opposition; it concludes that the peaceful and orderly marches "show the [Iranian] people and the world that it is the government officials who are engaging in destruction, disorder, and arson."[11]

Alongside these documents, the oral history methods launched in the 1980s have been extended recently to cover the revolutionary period. The Center for Documentation of the Islamic Revolution, the parastatal organization that published the four-volume work *Documents of the Islamic Revolution,* has also published three very useful volumes of oral histories on particular revolutionary events, all edited by 'Ali Shirkhani: *Hamaseh-ye 17 Khordad 1354* (The Uprising of June 7, 1975), *Hamaseh-ye 19 Dey-e Qom* (The Qom Uprising of January 9 [1978]), and *Hamaseh-ye 29 Bahman-e Tabriz* (The Tabriz Uprising of February 18 [1978]). These events were crucial to the self-understandings of the Islamist movement in Iran, and they come to life through the testimony of dozens of participants and eyewitnesses. Naturally, there are voices not heard in these collections—voices critical of the uprisings, for example. But the range of voices is greater than any of the other oral history collections thus far published: shopkeepers and low-level seminary figures are included here, as well as clerical elites, whereas other oral history projects have focused almost exclusively on elites. Another parastatal organization, the Office of Literature on the Islamic Revolution, apparently has an Oral History Unit gathering recollections of, for example, eyewitnesses to Black Friday (September 7, 1978), which are quoted in the office's *Ruz-Shomar-e Enqelab-e Eslami* (Chronology of the Islamic Revolution). I have not been able to access this office's files. The journalist ʿEmaduddin Baqi has also published several books on the revolution that include extensive selections from his interviews.

These collections begin to address the great weakness of available sources on the Iranian Revolution: the relative lack of material on the lives of the non-elite. I have tried in this book to pull together all the evidence I could on ordinary Iranians' perceptions of the revolutionary movement. In addition, I tried to interview a representative sample of Iranians about their experiences of the revolution. I was unable to get a visa to do this research in Iran, so I pursued the work in Istanbul, Turkey, in 1989–1990, during a period when many Iranians were visiting for business and tourism (Turkey being one of the few countries to which Iranians could travel without a visa at that time). I conducted semi-structured interviews with eighty-three Iranians age twenty-four and older (that is, age fourteen and older at the time of the revolution) who intended to return to Iran (that is, not expatriates). This sample included Iranians from more diverse backgrounds than can be found among expatriates, but it was not representative of the Iranian population at large—indeed, it was far more urban (over 85 percent, as against 45 percent of the Iranian population), considerably more white-collar (39 percent, as against 11 percent in the Iranian population), and almost entirely male.[12]

Interestingly, of the educated Iranians whom I interviewed—salaried professionals, private and governmental officials, and their high school and college-age children—61 percent (nineteen of thirty-one) named democracy or social democracy as one of the goals of their participation in the Iranian Revolution. Of the rest of the respondents—shopowners, workers, farmers, and their high school and college-age children—only 35 percent (seventeen of forty-nine) listed these goals. Conversely, 55 percent of the educated middle class (seventeen of thirty-one) and 71 percent of the rest (thirty-five of forty-nine) discussed Islamic themes as their goals for participation. (I was unable to determine the social background of three respondents; respondents sometimes gave multiple reasons for participating.) These figures are not, it must be emphasized, the product of a random sampling of the Iranian population, and therefore should be taken as suggestive, not definitive. But what they suggest is that different social groups in Iran may have had different reasons for participating in the anti-shah movement.

In other words, the relative lack of source material on non-elites *matters*. An understanding of the Iranian Revolution based on the experiences of the educated, or religious scholars, or any other elite group, will mislead us if their experiences cannot be generalized to non-elite groups. The third wave of documentation is beginning to offer a much more detailed look at the Iranian Revolution, but a fuller treatment cannot be written until the Iranian government allows a more representative sample of Iranians to enter the historical record. This book's sole prediction is that the emergence of such voices will confirm the confusion and unpredictability that are the focus of the present analysis.

Notes

1. Introduction

1. Central Intelligence Agency, "Iran: Prospects for Stability," October 27, 1978, in National Security Archive, *Iran*, document 1623. Department of State, "Iran Political Assessment," October 18, 1978, in National Security Archive, *Iran*, document 1602. Defense Intelligence Agency, report of September 28, 1978, quoted in United States House of Representatives, *Iran: Evaluation of U.S. Intelligence Performance*, 6.

2. U.S. embassy in Tehran, "Country Team Minutes," September 13, 1978, in National Security Archive, *Iran*, document 1518. John D. Stempel, U.S. embassy memorandum of October 30, 1978, in National Security Archive, *Iran*, document 1630. William H. Sullivan, U.S. embassy memorandum of November 9, 1978, in National Security Archive, *Iran*, document 1711; Sullivan, *Mission to Iran*, 201–203.

3. Brzezinski, *Power and Principle*, 360. Bill, *The Eagle and the Lion*, 246. On "rumor-mongering" see Michael Metrinko, U.S. consul in Tabriz at the time of the revolution, interviewed by William Burr in Washington, D.C., August 29, 1988, Foundation for Iranian Studies, 123–125; interviewed by the author by telephone, November 3, 1999.

4. *Washington Post*, October 28, 1980, A1; Carter, *Keeping Faith*, 446.

5. *Khabar-Nameh*, April 9, 1978, 1.

6. Chehabi, *Iranian Politics*, 240–241; *Asnad-e Nehzat-e Azadi*, vol. 11, 13–17; Bahramian, *Renasans dar Iran*, 97; *Corriere della Sera*, September 30, 1979, 5; *New York Times Magazine*, October 28, 1979, 26; Rubin, *Paved with Good Intentions*, 221–222, 393.

7. Bazargan, *Showra-ye Enqelab*, 21–23; Chehabi, *Iranian Politics*, 242–245.

8. Bazargan, *Enqelab-e Iran*, 57–58.

9. Garfinkel, *Studies in Ethnomethodology*, 11–18. "Attribution theory" in psychology also emphasizes the human need to generate causal explanations for random events, though this field exempts scientists from the observation (Försterling, *Attribution*).

10. Bazargan, *Enqelab-e Iran*, 25. Mooney, "For Your Eyes Only," 39. United States House of Representatives, *Iran: Evaluation of U.S. Intelligence Performance*. Stanley T. Escudero, "What Went Wrong in Iran?", circa June 1979, National Security Archive, *Iran*, document 2629, 12. Henry Kissinger, interviewed in the *Economist*, February 10, 1979, 31.

11. Kurzman, "Can Understanding Undermine Prediction?"

12. Cole, *Colonialism and Revolution in the Middle East*, 10; Keddie, "Can Revolutions Be Predicted?" Censer, "The Not So Inevitable Revolution of 1789"; Goodwin, *No Other Way Out: States and Revolutionary Movements*, 180–213. Markoff, *The Abolition of Feudalism*, 13; and numerous works on political democratization.

13. Respondent 30, interviewed by the author in Istanbul, Turkey, November 6, 1989.

14. *Pishtazan-e Shahadat*, 169.

15. Respondent 11, interviewed by the author in Istanbul, Turkey, October 28, 1989. Donald L. Donham makes a similar point with regard to the Ethiopian Revolution of 1974, in which activists sensed that they were "making local history on a world stage" (Donham, *Marxist Modern*, xv).

16. Maryam Shamlu, former head of the Women's Organization of Iran, interviewed by Mahnaz Afkhami in Washington, D.C., May 1983, Foundation for Iranian Studies, 24.

17. Respondents 15, 16, 32, and 89, interviewed by the author in Istanbul, Turkey, October 31, November 1, November 13, 1989, and February 19, 1990, respectively. For bystanders' reactions see Hegland, "Imam Khomaini's Village," 233–234.

18. Stigler and Becker, "De Gustibus Non Est Disputandum." The stability of preferences is now debated—see, for example, Coleman, *Foundations of Social Theory*, 515–527; Sobel, "Maximization, Stability of Decision, and Actions in Accordance with Reason"—but much empirical work maintains the assumption of stability. The stability of preferences is not to be confused with the well-established psychological phenomenon of "preference reversal," which involves not changes in preferences but inconsistency between different methods of ranking preferences (Tversky, Slovic, and

Kahneman, "The Causes of Preference Reversal"). Arjomand, *The Turban for the Crown,* 109.

19. Respondent 72, interviewed by the author in Istanbul, Turkey, December 13, 1989.

20. Karklins and Petersen, "Decision Calculus of Protestors and Regimes."

2. The Emergence of Protest

1. Jimmy Carter, speech of July 15, 1976, in Carter, *A Government as Good as Its People,* 131–132.

2. M. R. Pahlavi, *Mission for My Country,* 194, 173. M. R. Pahlavi, *Answer to History,* 149. On theories of "readiness" for democracy see Kurzman, "Not Ready for Democracy," 9–10.

3. Baraheni, *Crowned Cannibals;* Amnesty International, "Iran, 1978"; Rejali, *Torture and Modernity,* 70–76; Abrahamian, *Tortured Confessions,* 105–123; Delannoy, *SAVAK,* 15–18; Irfani, *Iran's Islamic Revolution,* 153–160. On embezzlement see Abrahamian, *Iran between Two Revolutions,* 437–438.

4. Alam, *The Shah and I,* 515. Pahlavi, *Answer to History,* 170. Marenches, *The Evil Empire,* 125. Air Force Commander Amir-Hossein Rabi'i quoted in Arjomand, *The Turban for the Crown,* 114. For the survey in Southern California see Hakimfar, "The Downfall of Late King Muhammad Reza Pahlavi." The Isfahan survey consisted of interviews with the families of Iran-Iraq War casualties, according to a sermon by Ayatollah Ahmad Jannati, December 20, 2002, translated by BBC Worldwide Monitoring. On blaming foreigners, see Amuzegar, *The Dynamics of the Iranian Revolution,* 79–96; Daneshvar, *Revolution in Iran,* 94, 126; Moshiri, *The State and Social Revolution in Iran,* 220; and my own interviews.

5. Abrahamian, "The Paranoid Style in Iranian Politics," in *Khomeinism,* 111–131; Ashraf, "The Appeal of Conspiracy Theories to Persians"; Pipes, *The Hidden Hand,* 75–86. Hone and Dickinson, *Persia in Revolution,* 88. Great Britain, *British Documents on the Origins of the War,* vol. 10, pt. 1, 841; Kazemzadeh, *Russia and Britain in Persia,* 639. Ullman, *Anglo-Soviet Relations,* vol. 3, 388. Wilber, *Clandestine Service History: Overthrow of Premier Mossadeq of Iran.*

6. Respondent 51, interviewed by the author in Istanbul, Turkey, November 25, 1989. *Weekly Compilation of Presidential Documents,* January 2, 1978, 1975.

7. Gottlieb, *Do You Believe in Magic?,* 5. Gitlin, *The Sixties,* 424.

8. Perrow, "The Sixties Observed," 196. On the generational shift see Morris

and Herring, "Theory and Research in Social Movements"; Zald, "Looking Backward to Look Forward," 331.

9. Evans, Rueschemeyer, and Skocpol, eds., *Bringing the State Back In*. Skocpol, *States and Social Revolutions*, 14, 66, 117 (emphasis in original). Tocqueville, *The Old Regime and the French Revolution*, 176.

10. McAdam, *Political Process and the Development of Black Insurgency*, 40–41.

11. Skocpol, "Rentier State and Shiʿa Islam in the Iranian Revolution," 267. Ahmad, "Comments on Skocpol," 293. Bashiriyeh, *The State and Revolution in Iran*, 107; see similar references in Kurzman, "Structural Opportunity and Perceived Opportunity," 158. Amuzegar, *The Dynamics of the Iranian Revolution*, 241–243. On area specialists versus theory-builders see Keddie, "Comments on Skocpol," 285.

12. ʿAli-Asghar Hajj-Seyyed-Javadi, interviewed by Zia Sedghi in Paris, France, March 1, 1984, Harvard Iranian Oral History Collection, tape 6, 10–11. On the liberals' lack of organization see Chehabi, *Iranian Politics;* and Siavoshi, *Liberal Nationalism in Iran.*

13. Hajj-Seyyed-Javadi, *Afzal al-Jihad;* Hajj-Seyyed-Javadi said he wrote the letter "some time before the American elections and before anyone had heard of Carter" (Harvard Iranian Oral History Collection, tape 6, 13). ʿAbdul-Karim Lahidji, interviewed by Maryam Shamlu in Paris, France, January 4 and 26, 1985, Foundation for Iranian Studies, 57. Open letter of June 12, 1977, in Hitselberger Collection, Box 4; Siavoshi, *Liberal Nationalism in Iran,* 135. Shapur Bakhtiar, interviewed in Tehran, July 3, 1977, by Graham, *Iran,* 241. Open letter of June 13, 1977, in Philippe, "Voices That Can't Be Ignored," 19–21. U.S. embassy memorandum of July 25, 1977, in National Security Archive, *Iran,* document 1201. Iranian Committee for the Defense of Human Rights, statement of December 10, 1977, in *Asnad-e Nehzat-e Azadi,* vol. 9, pt. 1, 84; on the founding of this organization, see Sanjabi, *Omid'ha va Na-Omidi'ha,* 284; Hajj-Seyyed-Javadi, Harvard Iranian Oral History Collection, tape 6, 16; ʿAbdul-Karim Lahidji, interviewed by Zia Sedghi in Paris, France, March 5, 1984, Harvard Iranian Oral History Collection, tape 4, 4; and Chehabi, *Iranian Politics,* 230–232, who bases his account on interviews with ʿAli-Asghar Hajj-Seyyed-Javadi, ʿAbdul-Karim Lahidji, and Hedayatollah Matin-Daftari in Paris, France, July 1982. On the end of torture, see Rahmatollah Moghadam Maragheh, speaking to a U.S. embassy official in Tehran on April 24, 1978, in National Security Archive, *Iran,* document 1376.

14. Bashiriyeh, *State and Revolution,* 112; Milani, *The Making of Iran's Islamic Revolution,* 111. On the September 1977 meeting see Bazargan, *Enqelab-e Iran,* 26; Pakdaman, "Ta Tabriz," 66; U.S. embassy memorandum of De-

cember 12, 1977, in National Security Archive, *Iran,* document 1253; a later U.S. embassy memorandum, dated May 25, 1978, mistakenly gives the date of the September 1977 meeting as April 1977 (National Security Archive, *Iran,* document 1399; and Ioannides, *America's Iran,* 30). On the October meeting see *Khabar-Nameh,* November–December 1977, 1–7. On the poetry readings see Gholam-Hossein Saʿedi, interviewed by Zia Sedghi in Paris, France, April 5, 1984, Harvard Iranian Oral History Collection, tape 2, 17–19; anonymous letter in *Zamimeh-ye Haqiqat,* January 1978, 1–2.

15. William J. Butler, Richard W. Cottam, Thomas M. Ricks, and Charles W. Naas, testimony of October 26, 1977, in United States House of Representatives, *Human Rights in Iran;* Lahidji, Harvard Iranian Oral History Collection, tape 4, 7. On prison conditions see ʿAmuyi, *Dord-e Zamaneh,* 427–436; Hashemi-Rafsanjani, *Dowran-e Mobarezeh,* vol. 1, 315–316.

16. Cherik'ha-ye Fedaʾiyan-e Khalq-e Iran, *Gozareshati az Mobarezat.* On arrests see Yadallah Sahabi, letter of October 12, 1977, in *Asnad-e Nehzat-e Azadi,* vol. 9, pt. 2, 51–52; Pakdaman, "Ta Tabriz," 67–68; Parsa, *Social Origins,* 207; Hezb-e Tudeh-ye Iran, *Zendeh Bad-e Jonbesh-e Tudeh;* Menashri, "Iran," 465–466; SAVAK six-month summary of religious opposition, September 12, 1977, in *SAVAK va Ruhaniyat,* 190. On Taleqani see *Khabar-Nameh,* November–December 1977, 1, 3; U.S. embassy memoranda of January 26 and February 1, 1978, National Security Archive, *Iran,* documents 1291 and 1296. On torture see Brian Wrobel of Amnesty International, testimony of February 28, 1978, in United States House of Representatives, *Foreign Assistance,* 221; Amnesty International, "Iran, 1978." Lahidji, Harvard Iranian Oral History Collection, tape 4, 3.

17. Carter, *Keeping Faith,* 433; Carter, *First Lady from Plains,* 306.

18. Alfred L. "Roy" Atherton, assistant secretary of state for Near Eastern and South Asian affairs, testimony of June 8, 1977, in United States House of Representatives, *Review of Recent Developments in the Middle East,* 81. Naas, director of the State Department's Office of Iranian Affairs, testimony of October 26, 1977, in United States House of Representatives, *Human Rights in Iran,* 30 and 27. On the shah's visit see Carter, *Public Papers of the Presidents: Jimmy Carter, 1977,* 2028–2029, 2033; White House summary memorandum, November 16, 1977, uncatalogued in the files of the National Security Archive, Washington, D.C.; Carter, *Keeping Faith,* 436–437; see also Carter, "Revolution: A President's Perspective," 219; Patricia M. Derian, letter to Alfred L. "Roy" Atherton, December 5, 1977, in *Declassified Documents Reference System,* document 1993:1420. *New York Times,* November 17, 1977, 3. Pahlavi, *Answer to History,* 152.

19. Among the few analysts to note the crackdown of November 1977 are Foran, *Fragile Resistance,* 378–379; Graham, *Iran,* 212; and Parsa, *Social Origins,* 179. Respondent 3, a student who was inside the hall during the poetry reading, interviewed by the author in Berkeley, California, September 13, 1989; Nategh, "Goft-o-Shenavadi," 12; Lafue-Veron, *Voyage,* 9–10; Union des Étudiants Iraniens en France, *Iran,* 6–7; *Zamimeh-ye Khabar-Nameh,* December 1, 1977, 12. For the quotation on riot police see *Washington Post,* November 22, 1977, A14. Abol Ghassem Lebaschi, an organizer of the event in Karaj, interviewed by Habib Ladjevardi in Paris, France, February 28, 1983, Harvard Iranian Oral History Collection, tape 2, 20–21; Lafue-Veron, *Voyage,* 17–18; Richards, "Carter's Human Rights Policy and the Pahlavi Dictatorship," 97–99; U.S. embassy memorandum of December 12, 1977, in National Security Archive, *Iran,* document 1253; *Zamimeh-ye Khabar-Nameh,* December 1, 1977, 9–11. On the arrest and beating of academics see Lafue-Veron, *Voyage,* 12–14, 19; Pakdaman, "Ta Tabriz," 74–75; Homa Nategh, interviewed by Zia Sedghi in Paris, France, April 1, 1984, Harvard Iranian Oral History Collection, tape 2, 12–16.

20. U.S. embassy memorandum of May 25, 1978, in National Security Archive, *Iran,* document 1399. Movement of the Muslims of Iran, pronouncement of December 1977, in *Asnad-e Nehzat-e Azadi,* vol. 9, pt. 1, 58. U.S. embassy memorandum of February 1, 1978, in National Security Archive, *Iran,* document 1296. Derian to Atherton, December 5, 1977, in *Declassified Documents Reference System,* document 1993:1420.

21. *Zamimeh-ye Khabar-Nameh,* December 1, 1977, to June 1978; *Asnad-e Nehzat-e Azadi,* vol. 9, pts. 1 and 2; Karimi-Hakkak, "Protest and Perish," 212–213. Karim Sanjabi, press-conference statement of January 12, 1978, in *Asnad-e Nehzat-e Azadi,* vol. 9, pt. 2, 95. Mozaffar Baqa'i-Kermani, quoted in SAVAK memorandum of January 25, 1978, in *Faraz'ha'i,* 9. Sanjabi, *Omid'ha va Na-Omidi'ha,* 284. Lahidji, Foundation for Iranian Studies, 64, and Harvard Iranian Oral History Collection, tape 5, 2–4.

22. Ruhollah Khomeini, speech of September 28, 1977, in Khomeini, *Matn-e Sokhanrani,* 5, 15–16; also published in Khomeini, *Majmu'eh'i,* 251, 262–263.

23. On Islamist demonstrations in October 1977 see SAVAK six-month summary of religious opposition, March 14, 1978, in *SAVAK va Ruhaniyat,* 196–197; *Khabar-Nameh,* October–November 1977, 7. On Khomeini's mourning see Haj Ebrahim Dardashti, interviewed in Tehran in 1978 by Taheri, *The Spirit of Allah,* 182, 307. Ruhollah Khomeini, speech of November 1, 1977, in *Shahidi Digar,* 56–57, 52, translated with the help of Ashraf and Banuazizi, "The State," 27; see also the slightly different version in

Zamimeh-ye Khabar-Nameh, January 8, 1978, 23, reprinted in Khomeini, *Zamimeh-ye Majmuʿehʾi,* 39–40, 37. Other sources—Bazargan, *Enqelab-e Iran,* 26, cited in Milani, *The Making of Iran's Islamic Revolution,* 110; and Khomeini, *Sahifeh-ye Nur,* vol. 1, 255, cited in Parsa, *Social Origins,* 209—give different dates for this speech. However, November 1, 1977, is most plausible because of references in the speech to recently received condolences. It may be worth noting that Khomeini also used the term "opportunity" in 1975, in reference not to liberalization but to the outrage generated by the shah's announcement of a single-party state: "May the nation of Islam block these frightening plans with unprecedented resistance from all quarters, before the opportunity disappears" (Ruhollah Khomeini, pronouncement of March 12, 1975, in Davani, *Nehzat-e Ruhaniyun,* vol. 6, 457).

24. Ayatollah Hossein Montazeri, quoted in Rubin, *Paved with Good Intentions,* 195. Jaʿfar Salehi, interviewed in Shirkhani, *Hamaseh-ye 19 Dey,* 116. Mohammad Javad Bahonar, interviewed in Iran in February 1980 by Christos Ioannides, *America's Iran,* 33. Hossein Vafi, interviewed in Shirkhani, *Hamaseh-ye 19 Dey,* 197. Struggling Religious Scholars of Iran, pronouncement of September 16, 1977, in *Asnad-e Enqelab-e Eslami,* vol. 4, 336.

25. Khomeini, "Ayatollah Khomeini's Letter," 107, 109–110; the original Persian version can be found in Davani, *Nehzat-e Ruhaniyun,* vol. 6, 356–361; Khomeini, *Majmuʿehʾi,* 268–271; *Shahidi Digar,* 148–154; and *Zamimeh-ye Khabar-Nameh,* December 1, 1977, 56, 4.

26. Richard W. Cottam, testimony of October 26, 1977, in United States House of Representatives, *Human Rights in Iran,* 10. Pakdaman, "Ta Tabriz," 63. On China see MacFarquhar, *The Hundred Flowers Campaign;* Khomeini never specifically referred to the Chinese experience, so far as I can find. Ruhollah Khomeini, open letter of November 16, 1977, in Davani, *Nehzat-e Ruhaniyun,* vol. 6, 361–364; Khomeini, *Majmuʿehʾi,* 272–277; *Shahidi Digar,* 157–163; and *Zamimeh-ye Khabar-Nameh,* December 1, 1977, 2–3.

27. Moin, *Khomeini,* 180–181, citing Razavi, *Hashemi va Enqelab,* 135 and 192, citing Gruh-e Tahqiq, *Taqvim-e Tarikh-e Enqelab,* 17; Badamchiyan, *Shenakht-e Enqelab-e Eslami,* 144; Taheri, *The Spirit of Allah,* 171. Seyyed Hossein Musavi-Tabrizi, interviewed in Shirkhani, *Hamaseh-ye 19 Dey,* 169–170. On religious scholars in Iran see Mahallati, *Khaterat va Mobarezat,* 92–93; *Laleh'ha-ye ʿEshq-Amuz,* 151.

28. Moghadam, "Iran," 239.

29. Ayatollah Seyyed Hasan Taheri Khorramabadi, interviewed in Shirkhani, *Hamaseh-ye 19 Dey,* 122–123. So far as I can find, only two letters were ever

sent by clerics to an international organization during the Iranian Revolution. One was by a group of expatriates, the Fighting Iranian Clerics Abroad in Najaf, Iraq, who sent an open letter to the United Nations Human Rights Commission in January 1978, printed in *Zamimeh-ye Khabar-Nameh,* February–March 1978, 26–28. The second was by Ayatollah Sadeq Khalkhali, who wrote to Amnesty International in December 1978; Professor Hamid Algar told me that Khalkhali gave him the letter in Paris and asked him to translate and forward it.

30. *Shahidi Digar,* 85; SAVAK memorandum of November 6, 1977, reporting rumors of SAVAK's complicity, in *Enqelab-e Eslami beh Ravayet-e Asnad-e SAVAK,* vol. 1, 72.

31. *Shahidi Digar,* 87–88; Hojjat al-Islam Mohammad Mehdi Akbarzadeh, Hojjat al-Islam 'Abdolkarim 'Abedini, and Mohammad Hasan Zarifian-Yeganeh, then seminary students in Qom, interviewed in Shirkhani, *Hamaseh-ye 19 Dey,* 31–32, 136, 222; SAVAK six-month summary of religious opposition, March 14, 1978, in *SAVAK va Ruhaniyat,* 198. On Kuleini, see Madelung, "al-Kulayni," 362–363; Montazam, *The Life and Times of Ayatollah Khomeini,* 177; Momen, *An Introduction to Shi'i Islam,* 316. On Shiraz, see Dastghayb, *Khaterat,* 35–36, and a SAVAK memorandum of October 30, 1977, in the same book, 96.

32. SAVAK memorandum of October 27, 1977, in *Yaran-e Emam,* vol. 2, 84. Anonymous letter from a religious scholar of Yazd, in *Shahidi Digar,* 122–123. On ceremonies nationwide see *Shahidi Digar,* 97–124, especially 118–119, on Mashhad. Davani, *Nehzat-e Ruhaniyun,* vol. 6, 339, 348. On Tehran, see Hojjat al-Islam Seyyed Zia Mortazavian, then a seminary student, interviewed in Shirkhani, *Hamaseh-ye 19 Dey,* 154.

33. *Shahidi Digar,* 119–121.

34. SAVAK memorandum of October 30, 1977, in *Yaran-e Emam,* vol. 10, 510–511.

35. Mahallati, *Khaterat va Mobarezat,* 91; *Shahidi Digar,* 113; SAVAK memorandum of November 4, 1977, in *Enqelab-e Eslami be Ravayet-e Asnad-e SAVAK,* vol. 1, 52; eyewitness recollection of seminary students Akbarzadeh and 'Abedini, interviewed in Shirkhani, *Hamaseh-ye 19 Dey,* 32 and 141. The first reference to Khomeni as imam that I have found is in an open letter by the Religious Circle of Qom, December 1976, in *Asnad-e Enqelab-e Eslami,* vol. 4, 322; Arjomand ("Traditionalism in Twentieth-Century Iran," 232) reports references as early as 1970.

36. SAVAK six-month summary of religious opposition, March 14, 1978, in *SAVAK va Ruhaniyat,* 202. *Dar-bareh-ye Qiyam,* vol. 1, 138–139. On the clerical hierarchy, see Abdul-Jaber, "The Genesis and Development of

Marja'ism"; Moussavi, "The Establishment of the Position of Marja'iyyat-i Taqlid"; Walbridge, *The Most Learned of the Shi'a.*

37. On raising consciousness see Mohammad Shoja'i, then a seminary student, interviewed in Shirkhani, *Hamaseh-ye 19 Dey*, 84. On rumors see SAVAK memorandum of November 24, 1977, in *Enqelab-e Eslami beh Ravayet-e Asnad-e Savak*, vol. 1, 136. On the use of a microphone see Zarifian-Yeganeh, interviewed in Shirkhani, *Hamaseh-ye 19 Dey*, 228. On tapes see SAVAK memorandum of January 7, 1978, in *Enqelab-e Eslami beh Ravayet-e Asnad-e Savak*, vol. 2, 225; Shoja'i and Hossein Musavi-Tabrizi, interviewed in Shirkhani, *Hamaseh-ye 19 Dey*, 105 and 170. On the fourteen-point resolution, see letter from a student at Qom, printed in *Shahidi Digar*, 253–255; *Zamimeh-ye Khabar-Nameh*, November–December 1977, 36, 20; *Asnad va Tasaviri*, vol. 1, pt. 3, 14; and Davani, *Nehzat-e Ruhaniyun*, vol. 6, 530–531. A slightly different resolution is given in Pakdaman, "Ta Tabriz," 63. The resolution is misdated—conflated with the later protests of January 1978—by 'Abbasi, *Tarikh-e Enqelab-e Eslami*, 724; Abrahamian, "Iran: The Political Challenge," 6; Hezb-e Tudeh-ye Iran, *Javedan Bad Khatereh*, 9–10; and Sreberny-Mohammadi and Mohammadi, *Small Media, Big Revolution*, 139–140. On the mourners' response see Shoja'i, interviewed in Shirkhani, *Hamaseh-ye 19 Dey*, 83.

38. *Shahidi Digar*, 250–252; *Zamimeh-ye Khabar-Nameh*, November–December 1977, 34–36, 20; SAVAK memoranda of early December 1977, in *Enqelab-e Eslami beh Ravayet-e Asnad-e Savak*, vol. 1, 211–212. On the closing of the seminary in 1975, see Kurzman, "The Qum Protests," 287–289. On exiles see SAVAK memoranda of December 1977, in *Yaran-e Emam*, vol. 16, 409–414; SAVAK memorandum, undated, in *Enqelab-e Eslami beh Ravayet-e Asnad-e SAVAK*, vol. 1, 225–226. On Khomein see SAVAK report of December 10, 1977, in Moradi-Nia, *Khomein dar Enqelab*, 230–236 and document 155.

39. Hezb-e Tudeh-ye Iran, *Javedan Bad Khatereh*, 3–4. Parviz Sabeti, memorandum of January 4, 1978, in *Enqelab-e Eslami beh Ravayet-e Asnad-e SAVAK*, vol. 1, 405. On Sabeti see Fardoust, *The Rise and Fall of [the] Pahlavi Dynasty*, 395, 406–409.

40. Hossein Musavi-Tabrizi, interviewed in Shirkhani, *Hamaseh-ye 19 Dey*, 170. Reza Sadeqi, interviewed in Shirkhani, *Hamaseh-ye 19 Dey*, 109.

41. Ruhollah Khomeini, "Islamic Government," lectures of January–February 1970, in Khomeini, *Islam and Revolution*, 126–127.

42. Ibid., 132–133. On propagation activities see U.S. embassy memorandum of February 2, 1978, in National Security Archive, *Iran*, document 1298; Arjomand, *The Turban for the Crown*, 92; Hojjat al-Islam Mohammad Javad

Bahonar's autobiographical account, published both in *Pishtazan-e Shahadat*, 56, and in *Shahid Doktor Bahonar*, 13; Tehranian, "Communication and Revolution," 21; Davani, "Khaterat," 46–56; and Hojjati-Kermani, "'Majaleh'i Bara-ye Howzeh,'" 56–60; Respondent 51, an office worker and member of a small lay propagation group that received proclamations from Khomeini in Iraq and distributed them in Tehran, interviewed by the author in Istanbul, Turkey, November 25, 1989. Ruhollah Khomeini, "Islamic Government," lectures of January–February 1970, in Khomeini, *Islam and Revolution*, 129, 149; Ayatollah Mohammad Beheshti, discussing his activities abroad in *Pishtazan-e Shahadat*, 15; several writings of Ayatollah Morteza Motahhari, quoted in Akhavi, *Religion and Politics*, 123–124, 144; Respondent 15, a former university student and religious activist, interviewed by the author in Istanbul, Turkey, October 31, 1989.

43. Khomeini, "Ayatollah Khomeini's Letter," 106–107, 108.

44. On taping see Zarifian-Yeganeh, interviewed in Shirkhani, *Hamaseh-ye 19 Dey*, 222. *Shahidi Digar*, 256. Mohammad Saduqi, letter of September 7, 1978, in Saduqi, *Majmu'eh-ye Ettela'iyeh'ha*, 87. Ruhani, *Barresi*, 932.

45. Hossein Musavi-Tabrizi, speech of January 9, 1978, in Shirkhani, *Hamaseh-ye 19 Dey*, 268.

3. Mobilization of the Mosque Network

1. *Ettela'at*, January 7, 1978, 7; republished with minor punctuation changes in Shirkhani, *Hamaseh-ye 19 Dey*, 233–236.

2. Shoja'i and Zarifian-Yeganeh, interviewed in Shirkhani, *Hamaseh-ye 19 Dey*, 85, 226. On photocopying see Baqer Sadr and Hasan Musavi-Tabrizi, interviewed in Shirkhani, *Hamaseh-ye 17 Khordad*, 71, 192; and Esma'il (Respondent 65), interviewed by the author in Istanbul, Turkey, December 5, 1989; see also *Enqelab-e Iran beh Ravayet-e Asnad-e SAVAK*, vol. 6, 392. Activist-instructors Hossein Musavi-Tabrizi, Mohammad Mo'men, and Hossein Nuri, interviewed in Shirkhani, *Hamaseh-ye 19 Dey*, 172–173, 186, 191.

3. Seminary student 'Ali, Respondent 7, interviewed by the author in Fort Lee, New Jersey, October 14, 1989. On similar tactics in the past, see Salehi, interviewed in Shirkhani, *Hamaseh-ye 19 Dey*, 115. See the report on the demonstration in *Zamimeh-ye Khabar-Nameh*, March–April 1978, 16–18; this report was later reproduced in *Asnad va Tasaviri*, vol. 1, pt. 3, 26–32; and *Dar-bareh-ye Qiyam*, vol. 1, 39–58; see also Shoja'i, interviewed in Shirkhani, *Hamaseh-ye 19 Dey*, 86–91.

4. On Ha'eri's telephoning colleagues, see Taheri Khorramabadi and Mo'men, interviewed in Shirkhani, *Hamaseh-ye 19 Dey*, 125, 186. For Ha'eri's comments see *Zamimeh-ye Khabar-Nameh*, March–April 1978, 17; in its six-month summary of religious opposition, dated March 14, 1978 (*SAVAK va Ruhaniyat*, 207), SAVAK reported a slightly different wording, but with the same intent: "I am distressed and pained by the contents of the newspapers. My view is that steps must be taken in this matter, but the fear is that if such a matter is spoken here, they will shut this place down like the Fayziyeh Seminary." On waiting for Shari'at-Madari, see seminary students Akbarzadeh and Vafi, interviewed in Shirkhani, *Hamaseh-ye 19 Dey*, 38, 201–203. For Shari'at-Madari's comments see *Zamimeh-ye Khabar-Nameh*, March–April 1978, 16; consistent but somewhat different accounts were given by seminary students Shoja'i, Salehi, 'Abedini, and Vafi, interviewed in Shirkhani, *Hamaseh-ye 19 Dey*, 88, 117, 143, 201–203.

5. For Golpayegani's statement see *Zamimeh-ye Khabar-Nameh*, March–April 1978, 15; similar statement reported by Akbarzadeh, Shoja'i, Salehi, and 'Abedini, interviewed in Shirkhani, *Hamaseh-ye 19 Dey*, 37, 86, 143. On Golpayegani's comments, see Vafi, interviewed in Shirkhani, *Hamaseh-ye 19 Dey*, 200; *Nabard-e Tudeh'ha*, 2. On Najafi-Mar'ashi's comments see Shoja'i, Sadeqi, 'Abedini, Mortazavian, Hossein Musavi-Tabrizi, and Vafi, interviewed in Shirkhani, *Hamaseh-ye 19 Dey*, 88, 110, 144, 152, 174, 204; transcript in Shirkhani, *Hamaseh-ye 19 Dey*, 242. Mo'ini, SAVAK chief in Qom, memoranda of January 8–10, 1978, in *Enqelab-e Eslami beh Ravayet-e Asnad-e SAVAK*, vol. 2, 1–9.

6. Mo'ini, SAVAK memorandum of January 8, 1978, in *Enqelab-e Eslami beh Ravayet-e Asnad-e SAVAK*, vol. 2, 2. Hossein Musavi-Tabrizi and Mo'men, interviewed in Shirkhani, *Hamaseh-ye 19 Dey*, 174–176, 186; Mo'ini, memorandum of January 9, 1978, in *Enqelab-e Eslami beh Ravayet-e Asnad-e SAVAK*, vol. 2, 10.

7. *Zamimeh-ye Khabar-Nameh*, March–April 1978, 19; Mo'ini, memoranda of January 9, 1978, in *Enqelab-e Eslami beh Ravayet-e Asnad-e SAVAK*, vol. 2, 11 and 14. On observing the silence see *Zamimeh-ye Khabar-Nameh*, March–April 1978, 18.

8. *Zamimeh-ye Khabar-Nameh*, March–April 1978, 19–21; Shirkhani, *Hamaseh-ye 19 Dey*; SAVAK memorandum of January 10, 1978, in *Enqelab-e Eslami beh Ravayet-e Asnad-e SAVAK*, vol. 2, 16.

9. Shirkhani, *Hamaseh-ye 19 Dey*, 283–291. U.S. embassy memoranda of January 16 and 26, 1978, in National Security Archive, *Iran*, documents 1282, 1291. On rumors see SAVAK memorandum of January 10, 1978, in *Enqelab-e Eslami beh Ravayet-e Asnad-e SAVAK*, vol. 2, 17; seminary students

Mohammad ʿAli Dast-Afkan and Zarifian-Yeganeh, interviewed in Shir-khani, *Hamaseh-ye 19 Dey*, 74, 226. For opposition estimates see Davani, *Nehzat-e Ruhaniyun*, vol. 7, 48; Khomeini, *Majmuʿehʾi*, 285, 297, 299. The survey in Tehran is reported in Stempel, *Inside the Iranian Revolution*, 91. On the removal of bodies see *Zamimeh-ye Khabar-Nameh*, March–April 1978, 18–21. On the implausibility of silence see Zarifian-Yeganeh, inter-viewed in Shirkhani, *Hamaseh-ye 19 Dey*, 226.

10. U.S. embassy memoranda of January 16, 18, and 26, 1978, in National Se-curity Archive, *Iran*, documents 1282, 1284, 1291. Tehran bazaaris, quoted in *Zamimeh-ye Khabar-Nameh*, February–March 1978, 31.

11. Akhavi, *Religion and Politics in Contemporary Iran*, 208. Somewhat lower fig-ures are reported in *Iran Almanac*, 1975, 395; and Milani, *The Making of Iran's Islamic Revolution*, 18.

12. Classic works on solidarity and resources include McCarthy and Zald, "Re-source Mobilization and Social Movements"; Oberschall, *Social Conflict and Social Movements*; Tilly, *From Mobilization to Revolution*. On African-American churches see McAdam, *Political Process and the Development of Black Insurgency*; Morris, *The Origins of the Civil Rights Movement*. Yet most African-American churches did *not* participate in the civil rights move-ment—see Kurzman, "Organizational Opportunity and Social Movement Mobilization," 31–34.

13. On Shiʿi autonomy see Akhavi, *Religion and Politics in Contemporary Iran*; for a contrasting Sunni case, see Wiktorowicz, *The Management of Islamic Activism*, 140–143, on the barriers to mosque mobilization in Jordan. On post-revolutionary Iran see Momen, *An Introduction to Shiʿi Islam*, 298–299; Zahedi, *The Iranian Revolution Then and Now*, 79–80.

14. Salehi, *Insurgency through Culture and Religion*, 137; see similar statements in Akhavi, *Religion and Politics in Contemporary Iran*, 172; Amjad, *Iran*, 121; Ashraf and Banuazizi, "The State," 27; Burke and Lubeck, "Explaining So-cial Movements in Two Oil-Exporting States," 661; Esposito, *Islam and Pol-itics*, 190–191; Halliday, *Iran*, 19; Hiro, *Iran under the Ayatollahs*, 168; Laqueur, "Why the Shah Fell," 52; Parsa, *Social Origins*, 190, 306; Parsa, *States, Ideologies, and Social Revolutions*, 145; Petras and Morley, "Develop-ment and Revolution," 34; Snow and Marshall, "Cultural Imperialism, So-cial Movements, and the Islamic Revival," 141.

15. Mehdi Bazargan (misspelled as "Barzegan"), interviewed in Gage, "Iran: The Making of a Revolution," 132, 134.

16. Respondent 34, interviewed by the author in Istanbul, Turkey, November 15, 1989.

17. Moradi, interviewed near Isfahan, February 20, 1979, by Boroumand, "Les

Ouvriers, l'Ingénieur et les Militantes Khomeinistes," 63; also in Vieille and Khosrokhavar, *Le Discours Populaire de la Révolution Iranienne,* vol. 2, 7.

18. Braswell, "A Mosaic of Mullahs and Mosques," 102. Respondent 15, interviewed by the author in Istanbul, Turkey, October 31, 1989. 'Amid-Zanjani, *Ravayeti az Enqelab-e Eslami-ye Iran,* 160. On turban-tying see Pliskin, "Camouflage, Conspiracy, and Collaborators," 64; Mossavar-Rahmani, "The Iranian Revolution and Its Theoretical Implications," 228–229; Pliskin heard that incident occurred in Jahrom or Shiraz, while Mossavar-Rahmani heard that it occurred in Qom; I heard this story several times in my interviews as well, with an unspecified location.

19. "L. W. Semakis' Contact List," April 26, 1969, in National Security Archive, *Iran,* document 713. Hashim, interviewed in Mashhad, summer 1978, by Haeri, *Law of Desire,* 159. Religious scholar in Tehran, quoted in Braswell, "A Mosaic of Mullahs and Mosques," 42.

20. *Enqelab-e Eslami beh Ravayet-e Asnad-e SAVAK; Yaran-e Emam.*

21. SAVAK memorandum of November 3, 1975, in *Yaran-e Emam,* vol. 3, 244.

22. Kurzman, "A Dynamic View of Resources," appendixes 1 and 2.

23. Behnam Amini, interviewed by Hegland, "Imam Khomaini's Village," 874; another eyewitness account mentions tear gas thrown into the mosque and beatings just outside (Sayyad-Shirazi, *Khaterat-e Amir-e Shahid,* 86).

24. Motahhari, "The Nature of the Islamic Revolution," 212. Ahmad Khomeini quoted in *Ettela'at,* September 23, 1979, 2; also cited in Parsa, *Social Origins,* 199; and Parsa, *States, Ideologies, and Social Revolutions,* 140. 'Ali-Akbar Hashemi Rafsanjani, sermon of June 25, 1982, in Ram, *Myth and Mobilization,* 42.

25. Allameh Mohammad Taqi Ja'fari-Tabrizi, quoted in SAVAK memorandum of June 10, 1975, in *Yaran-e Emam,* vol. 7, 211–212.

26. Beheshti quoted in SAVAK memorandum of June 25, 1975, in *Yaran-e Emam,* vol. 3, 306. Seyyed 'Ali Akbar Mohtashami, in *Yad,* Winter-Spring 1992–1993, 90–91. "Mr. Qumi," interviewed by Braswell, "A Mosaic of Mullahs and Mosques," 113.

27. Sabahi, *The Literacy Corps in Pahlavi Iran,* 239–240.

28. Tehranian, "Communication and Revolution," 28, 21. Falsafi, *Khaterat,* 425. Braswell, "A Mosaic of Mullahs and Mosques," 132. Said Amir Arjomand, interviewed by the author in Berkeley, California, September 15, 1989. Ayatollah Kazem Shari'at-Madari, quoted in *Los Angeles Times,* December 9, 1978, I:12. On the 1906 constitution see Browne, *The Persian Revolution,* 362–384.

29. Seyyed Mohammad Al-e Teh, quoted in SAVAK memorandum of December 13, 1977, in *Enqelab-e Eslami beh Ravayet-e Asnad-e SAVAK,* vol. 1, 240.

30. Morteza Aba'i, quoted in *Khabar-Nameh,* April 6, 1978, 4.

31. Hossein Khademi, open letter of July 1978, in *Zamimeh-ye Khabar-Nameh,* September–October 1978, 29.

32. On Khomeini's stipends see Fischer, *Iran,* 80–81; SAVAK memorandum of April 18 and 21, 1977, *Yaran-e Emam,* vol. 20, 338–346. On Beheshti see *Pishtazan-e Shahadat,* 16. Seminary activist Esma'il (Respondent 65), interviewed by the author in Istanbul, Turkey, December 11, 1989.

33. "Mr. Khakani," interviewed on January 9, 1974, by Braswell, "A Mosaic of Mullahs and Mosques," 118. On exiles see SAVAK memorandum, undated, in *Enqelab-e Eslami beh Ravayet-e Asnad-e SAVAK,* vol. 1, 225–226; Zarifian-Yeganeh, interviewed in Shirkhani, *Hamaseh-ye 19 Dey,* 229. On Makarem see Hossein Musavi-Tabrizi, interviewed in Shirkhani, *Hamaseh-ye 19 Dey,* 176. On 1978 exiles see *Zamimeh-ye Khabar-Nameh,* July–August 1978, 27–28.

34. 'Abbas Va'ez Tabasi, quoted in SAVAK memorandum of February 27, 1978, in *Yaran-e Emam,* vol. 5, 716.

35. Bakhash, "Sermons, Revolutionary Pamphleteering and Mobilisation."

36. Ruhollah Khomeini, proclamation of October 31, 1971, in Khomeini, *Islam and Revolution,* 206.

37. *Zamimeh-ye Khabar-Nameh,* March–April 1978, 15.

38. *Dar-bareh-ye Qiyam,* vol. 1, 83–89; according to some accounts—Fischer, *Iran,* 194, and the *Washington Post,* January 20, 1978, A31—Shari'at-Madari declared the *government* "non-Islamic" or "un-Islamic," which is a considerably more radical statement than the one reprinted in *Dar-bareh-ye Qiyam,* vol. 1, 86: "I judge *such acts* to be seriously opposed to the law of God and to humanity" (emphasis added).

39. Ruhollah Khomeini, speech of February 19, 1978, in Khomeini, *Islam and Revolution,* 212–213.

40. Kazem Shari'at-Madari, open letter of February 14, 1978, in *Dar-bareh-ye Qiyam,* vol. 1, 88.

41. On the locking of the mosque see SAVAK memorandum of March 14, 1978, in *Faraz'ha'i,* 28–35; Nahavandi, *Iran: Deux Rêves Brisés,* 120–121; Shirkhani, *Hamaseh-ye 29 Bahman.* On radicals' initiating violence see 'Abdolhamid Banabi and Karim Zariye Behruzi, eyewitnesses, interviewed in Shirkhani, *Hamaseh-ye 29 Bahman,* 27 and 42; Hajj Karim Arsalani and Zabihallah Khakpur, Tabriz merchants and eyewitnesses, in *Ruz-Shomar-e Enqelab-e Eslami,* vol. 2, 603–604; Patriotic Muslim Students of Tabriz University, "Report on the Tabriz Uprising," 62–64; Union des Étudiants

Iraniens en France, *Iran,* 11–12; Morad'haseli-Khameneh, *Tabriz dar Khun,* 11; see also SAVAK memorandum of February 19, 1978, in *Enqelab-e Eslami beh Ravayet-e Asnad-e SAVAK,* vol. 3, 28; and Report of the Military High Command's Special Committee to Investigate the Events of February 18, 1978, in the City of Tabriz, dated February 28, 1978, in Shirkhani, *Hamaseh-ye 29 Bahman,* 308. On the first stone cast, see Morad'haseli-Khameneh, *Tabriz dar Khun,* 8–11; Shirkhani, *Hamaseh-ye 29 Bahman,* 149–152; one account has another follower of Khomeini throwing the stone and then ducking when police fired into the crowd (Hasan ʿAbd-Yazdani, interviewed in Shirkhani, *Hamaseh-ye 29 Bahman,* 79). On university protests see Saʿid Rajaʾi-Khorasani, Tabriz University instructor and Islamist activist, interviewed by Zia Sedghi in New York on December 21, 1984, Harvard Iranian Oral History Collection, transcript of tape 1, 21; report of an interagency investigating committee, undated, in *Enqelab-e Eslami beh Ravayet-e Asnad-e SAVAK,* vol. 3, 33. For casualty estimates see *Ruz-Shomar-e Enqelab-e Eslami,* vol. 2, 601; report of an interagency investigating committee, undated, in *Enqelab-e Eslami beh Ravayet-e Asnad-e SAVAK,* vol. 3, 37; Algar, *Roots of the Islamic Revolution,* 103; Federasiyun-e Mohaselin va Daneshjuyan-e Irani dar Faranseh, "The Bloody Uprising of Tabriz," 78. For definitive fatality counts see Shirkhani, *Hamaseh-ye 29 Bahman,* 143–176; *Enqelab-e Eslami beh Ravayet-e Asnad-e SAVAK,* vol. 3, 37, note 1.

42. Kazem Shariʿat-Madari, pronouncement of February 18, 1978, quoted in SAVAK six-month summary of religious opposition, March 14, 1978, in *SAVAK va Ruhaniyat,* 217. Kazem Shariʿat-Madari, pronouncement of March 2, 1978, in Davani, *Nehzat-e Ruhaniyun,* vol. 7, 99. On Shariʿat-Madari's defrocking see Parsa, *Social Origins,* 202.

43. *Zamimeh-ye Khabar-Nameh,* September–October 1978, 28–29; *Pareh'i az Eʿlamiyeh'ha,* 41–54; SAVAK memorandum of August 17, 1978, in *Yaran-e Emam,* vol. 5, 764; Isfahan city official, interviewed by Kraft, "Letter from Iran," 139.

44. On Saduqi and Khomeini see Khalkhali, *Shohada-ye Ruhaniyat,* vol. 2, 577. On Saduqi and the senior scholars of Qom see SAVAK memorandum, undated, in *Yaran-e Emam,* vol. 2, 93. On the protests in Yazd see SAVAK memorandum of March 30, 1978, in *Yaran-e Emam,* vol. 2, 105; Khalkhali, *Shohada-ye Ruhaniyat,* vol. 2, 582; "Do Gozaresh az Qiyam-e Khunin-e Mardom-e Yazd" (Two Reports on the Bloody Uprising of the People of Yazd), undated, in *Dar-bareh-ye Qiyam,* vol. 3, 20, 22–24, 26. At the same time, Saduqi tried to restrain protesters operating independently of his planned events: see "Do Gozaresh," in *Dar-bareh-ye Qiyam,* vol. 3, 21;

Bakhash, "Sermons, Revolutionary Pamphleteering, and Mobilisation," 181–182.

45. Mohammad Saduqi, letter of May 16, 1978, in *Zamimeh-ye Khabar-Nameh,* July–August 1978, 16–17.

46. Mohammad Saduqi, letter of July 4, 1978, in Parsa, *Social Origins,* 204; and *Zamimeh-ye Khabar-Nameh,* September–October 1978, 29.

47. Mohammad Saduqi, telegram of August 2, 1978, in Saduqi, *Majmuʿeh-ye Ettelaʿiyeh'ha,* 68.

48. SAVAK six-month summary of religious opposition, September 30, 1978, in *SAVAK va Ruhaniyat,* 245.

49. Court figure Hedayat Eslaminia, quoted in U.S. embassy memoranda of May 23 and 24, 1978, in National Security Archive, *Iran,* documents 1397 and 1398. SAVAK memorandum of August 6, 1978, in *Yaran-e Emam,* vol. 5, 758. On Shariʿat-Madari's meetings with regime officials see SAVAK memoranda of September 24 and October 8, 1978, in Ruhani, *Shariʿat-Madari dar Dadgah-e Tarikh,* 146–157; this book was part of an official post-revolutionary campaign to discredit Shariʿat-Madari, which led eventually to his house arrest. Shariʿat-Madari had been meeting with an official representative of the shah since April (Masʿud-Ansari, *Man va Khandan-e Pahlavi,* 118–125). On Shariʿat-Madari's lapse into silence see Binder, "Revolution in Iran," 53; also SAVAK six-month summary of religious opposition, September 30, 1978, in *SAVAK va Ruhaniyat,* 277; Masʿud-Ansari, *Man va Khandan-e Pahlavi,* 120–121. On attacks on pro-government scholars see Parsa, *Social Origins,* 201; *New York Times,* January 29, 1979, A4.

50. Lieutenant General Naser Moqadam, head of SAVAK, at meeting of military commanders on August 15, 1978, in *Ma Gereftar-e Yek Jang,* 28. On Hamadan see Khosrokhavar, "Le Comité dans la Révolution Iranienne," 87. On Mashhad see Habib Bahar, member of parliament, quoted in SAVAK memorandum of December 17, 1978, in *Yaran-e Emam,* vol. 5, 838. On Tabriz see unnamed bookkeeper of Kazem Shariʿat-Madari, quoted in Nikbakht and Esmaʿilzadeh, *Zendegi ve Mobarezat-e Shahid Ayatollah Qazi-Tabatabaʼi,* 327. On Isfahan see U.S. Consul David C. McGaffey, two memoranda of December 6, 1978, in National Security Archive, *Iran,* documents 1870 and 1871; Abrahamian (*Iran between Two Revolutions,* 526–527) suggests that Khademi led the revolutionary takeover of governmental functions in Isfahan, but it seems likely that the ninety-year-old Khademi was given only titular leadership. On Khademi as a symbol only, see Mohammad Beheshti, quoted in SAVAK wiretap of December 12, 1978, in *Yaran-e Emam,* vol. 3, 374. Mohammad Beheshti, quoted in SAVAK wiretap of December 15, 1978, in *Yaran-e Emam,* vol. 3, 388.

51. Moaddel, "The Shi'i Ulama and the State in Iran," 542. Kurzman, "A Dynamic View of Resources."

4. Shi'i Appeals

1. SAVAK memoranda in *Enqelab-e Eslami beh Ravayet-e Asnad-e SAVAK,* vol. 3, 1–61; *Ruz-Shomar-e Enqelab-e Eslami,* vol. 2, 601–606, vol. 3, 44–68, vol. 3, 269–314.

2. Mohammad Reza Mahdavi-Kani, quoted in Sick, *All Fall Down,* 40. *Khabar-Nameh,* June 20, 1978, 4. On the mourning of mid-June 1978 see *Ruz-Shomar-e Enqelab-e Eslami,* vol. 3, 509–513.

3. Ruhollah Khomeini, pronouncement of June 10, 1978, in *Zamimeh-ye Khabar-Nameh,* July–August 1978, 74–75. Ruhollah Khomeini, speech of June 5, 1978, in Davani, *Nehzat-e Ruhaniyun,* vol. 7, 157.

4. Kazem Shari'at-Madari, Mohammad-Reza Golpayegani, and Shehabuddin Najafi-Mar'ashi, pronouncement of June 10, 1978, in Davani, *Nehzat-e Ruhaniyun,* vol. 7, 172–173. Kazem Shari'at-Madari, interviewed by Nicholas B. Tatro, Associated Press Wire Service, June 17, 1978.

5. Anonymous pronouncement, undated, in Davani, *Nehzat-e Ruhaniyun,* vol. 7, 126–127; Mohammad-Reza Golpayegani, letters of May 21 to June 7, 1978, in *Asnad-e Enqelab-e Eslami,* vol. 1, 461–471. Secret-police reports in *Ruz-Shomar-e Enqelab-e Eslami,* vol. 3, 294; SAVAK six-month summary of religious opposition, September 30, 1978, in *SAVAK va Ruhaniyat,* 254.

6. Group of religious scholars of Ahwaz, pronouncement of June 15, 1978, in *Asnad-e Enqelab-e Eslami,* vol. 3, 315. Ayatollah 'Abdollah Shirazi, pronouncement of June 11, 1978, in *Asnad-e Enqelab-e Eslami,* vol. 1, 476.

7. Seyyed Mohammad Vahidi, pronouncement of June 11, 1978, in *Asnad-e Enqelab-e Eslami,* vol. 2, 272.

8. Pronouncement of the Religious Scholars of Tehran, undated, in Davani, *Nehzat-e Ruhaniyun,* vol. 7, 163.

9. Pronouncement of the Society of Religious Scholars of Iran, May 31, 1978, in Davani, *Nehzat-e Ruhaniyun,* vol. 7, 164–165. Davani, *Nehzat-e Ruhaniyun,* vol. 7, 166. Mohammad Saduqi, pronouncement of June 14, 1978, in *Asnad-e Enqelab-e Eslami,* vol. 2, 277; Hojjat al-Islam Seyyed 'Abdolhossein Dastghayb, another militant, also supported the strike and its rationale of not giving a "plot or provocation into the hands of the enemy" (SAVAK memorandum of June 15, 1978, in Dastghayb, *Khaterat,* 113). Anonymous street peddler in Qom, interviewed by Nicholas B. Tatro, Associated Press Wire Service, June 17, 1978. On the shah's command see Parviz Raein, Associated Press Wire Service, May 11, 1978;

Newsweek, May 22, 1978, 42; other reports of the incident make no mention of the shah's presence (Hottinger, "Tehran," 29; *Khabar-Nameh,* May 20, 1978, 5). For official denial see *Middle East Economic Digest,* May 19, 1978, 12. SAVAK six-month summary of religious opposition, September 30, 1978, in *SAVAK va Ruhaniyat,* 246.

10. Pronouncement of a group of religious scholars and instructors of the religious circle of Qom, undated, in Davani, *Nehzat-e Ruhaniyun,* vol. 7, 178. See also ʿAbdolrahim Rabbani Shirazi, letter of June 17, 1978, in *Asnad-e Enqelab-e Eslami,* vol. 2, 278–280.

11. *Iran Almanac,* 1975, 395. Muriel Atkin, "Soviet Attitudes toward Shiʿism and Social Protest," 288. John L. Esposito, *Islam and Politics,* 191; see similar arguments in Algar, *The Roots of the Islamic Revolution,* 11; Braswell, "Civil Religion in Contemporary Iran"; Millward, "Theoretical and Practical Grounds for Religious Opposition to Monarchy in Iran"; Moaddel, *Class, Politics, and Ideology in the Iranian Revolution;* and Savory, "The Problem of Sovereignty in an Ithna Ashari ('Twelver') Shiʿi State."

12. Bianu, *Les Religions et . . . La Mort,* 199; Renaerts, *La Mort,* 73; Sande, "Palestinian Martyr Widowhood," 713; Sharif, *Islam in India,* 107.

13. Moaddel, *Class, Politics, and Ideology,* 160.

14. Chelkowski and Dabashi, *Staging a Revolution,* 82.

15. For a bibliography of the event see *Ketabshenasi-ye 15 Khordad.* For differing perspectives see Abrahamian, *Iran between Two Revolutions,* 425–426; Algar, "The Oppositional Role of the Ulama," 245–249; Floor, "The Revolutionary Character of the Iranian Ulama," 512–515; and Tabari, "The Role of the Clergy in Modern Iranian Politics," 66–69. On the death toll see Ayatollah Shehabuddin Marʿashi-Najafi, pronouncement of July 11, 1963, in Davani, *Nehzat-e Ruhaniyun,* vol. 4, 443.

16. Council of United Muslims, undated pronouncement, in Davani, *Nehzat-e Ruhaniyun,* vol. 4, 441–442.

17. On the post-revolutionary period see Azodanloo, "Performative Elements of Shiʿite Ritual and Mass Mobilization"; Good and Good, "Ritual, the State, and the Transformation of Emotional Discourse," 56–60; Ram, *Myth and Mobilization in Revolutionary Iran,* 57–92.

18. Badamchiyan, *Shenakht-e Enqelab-e Eslami,* 145.

19. For a structural approach see Rucht, "The Impact of National Contexts," 189–190. For strategic perspectives see Swidler, "Culture in Action"; Tilly, "Contentious Repertoires"; and Tarrow, *Power in Movement,* 112.

20. See Melucci, *Nomads of the Present,* 30–36, on the construction of new collective identities; and Turner and Killian, *Collective Behavior,* 3rd ed., 7–11, on emergent norms.

21. Combined approaches are proposed by Jasper, *The Art of Moral Protest,* 50–54; Markoff, *The Abolition of Feudalism,* 322–324; Morris and Braine, "Social Movements and Oppositional Consciousness," 24–25; Polletta, "Culture and Its Discontents," 432–438; Pfaff and Yang, "Double-Edged Rituals"; Taylor, "Structure, Culture and Action," 135–148. On framing see Benford and Snow, "Framing Processes and Social Movements."

22. Algar, "The Oppositional Role of the Ulama."

23. Society of Religious Scholars of Rafsanjan, undated pronouncement, in *Pareh'i az E'lamiyeh'ha,* 15. For other protests in July 1978 see *Enqelab-e Eslami beh Ravayet-e Asnad-e SAVAK,* vol. 7.

24. *Kayhan International,* August 6, 1978, 1.

25. Ruhollah Khomeini, pronouncement of July 27, 1978, in Davani, *Nehzat-e Ruhaniyun,* vol. 7, 198. For the liberals' public position see *Khabar-Nameh,* August 11, 1978, 1. Bazargan's comments are paraphrased in a U.S. embassy memorandum of July 18, 1978, in National Security Archive, *Iran,* document 1442. Liberals interviewed in June–July 1978 by Keddie, *Roots of Revolution,* 248. On liberal activism see Manuchehr Hezarkhani, interviewed by Zia Sedghi in Paris, France, June 1, 1984, Harvard Iranian Oral History Collection, tape 2, 4–5; Lahidji, Harvard Iranian Oral History Collection, tape 4, 11–13; U.S. embassy memorandum of July 18, 1978, in National Security Archive, *Iran,* document 1422. Mohammad Tavakoli, quoted in U.S. embassy memorandum of August 21, 1978, in National Security Archive, *Iran,* document 1480.

26. Ruhollah Khomeini, pronouncement of July 4, 1978, in *Khabar-Nameh,* July 11, 1978, 3. Society of Religious Scholars of Tehran, undated pronouncement, in *Khabar-Nameh,* July 21, 1978, 9. SAVAK six-month summary of religious opposition, September 30, 1978, in *SAVAK va Ruhaniyat,* 259–260.

27. *Kayhan International,* July 30–August 1, 1978. 'Ali Tehrani, open letter of July 24, 1978, in *Khabar-Nameh,* August–September 1978, 30. Hitselberger, "Letter," 118. Ruhollah Khomeini, pronouncement of July 27, 1978, in Davani, *Nehzat-e Ruhaniyun,* vol. 7, 197.

28. Workers in Bizhan, paraphrased in Goodell, *The Elementary Structures of Political Life,* 295. Anonymous son of a religious scholar, quoted in Braswell, *To Ride a Magic Carpet,* 90–91. Ruhollah Khomeini, pronouncement of July 27, 1978, in Davani, *Nehzat-e Ruhaniyun,* vol. 7, 198. U.S. Defense Intelligence Agency report of August 16, 1978, in National Security Archive, *Iran,* document 1472.

29. On Khademi see Struggling Muslim Students of Isfahan, undated pronouncement, in *Pareh'i az E'lamiyeh'ha,* 52. *Khabar-Nameh,* August 11,

1978, 4; August 16, 1978, 2. On radicals' activities see Semkus, *The Fall of Iran*, vol. 1, 41–46; Ashraf and Banuazizi, "The State," 9. Casualty estimate: *Khabar-Nameh*, August 16, 1978, 2–3. On the end of the sit-in see Isfahan city official, interviewed by Kraft, "Letter from Iran," 139; *Khabar-Nameh*, August 16, 1978, 2–3; Guilds of Isfahan, undated proclamation in *Pareh'i az E'lamiyeh'ha*, 43–45; other accounts state that the refuge-seekers were already leaving peacefully when they were attacked (proclamations of Struggling People of Isfahan and Struggling Muslim Students of Isfahan, in *Pareh'i az E'lamiyeh'ha*, 41 and 52). On martial law see *Kayhan International*, August 12, 1978; Hitselberger, "Letter," 119–120; Seyyed Hasan Nurbakhsh, *Yadvareh-ye Nehzat-e Eslami*, vol. 1, 142. On "butchers" see Hickman, *Ravaged and Reborn*, 7.

30. A photograph of the demonstration at the New Mosque can be found in *Asnad va Tasaviri*, vol. 1, pt. 1, 91; for descriptions see *Khabar-Nameh*, August 16, 1978, 2–3; Muslim People of Shiraz, pronouncement of August 15, 1978, in *Pareh'i az E'lamiyeh'ha*, 63. Amini, interviewed by Hegland, "Imam Khomaini's Village," 874; the date is given as June 5, 1978, but numerous other sources record this event as taking place on the fifth of Ramadan (August 10, 1978). Eighteen religious scholars of Shiraz, pronouncement of August 11, 1978, in Davani, *Nehzat-e Ruhaniyun*, vol. 7, 207–208.

31. *Khabar-Nameh*, August 16, 1978, 3; August 21, 1978, 1, 6; Movement of the Muslims of Behbehan, undated pronouncement, and anonymous pronouncement of August 15, 1978, in *Pareh'i az E'lamiyeh'ha*, 67–72. Ruhollah Khomeini, pronouncement of August 12, 1978, in Davani, *Nehzat-e Ruhaniyun*, vol. 7, 209.

32. *Khabar-Nameh*, August 16, 1978, 3–4; August 21, 1978, 4–6; Davani, *Nehzat-e Ruhaniyun*, vol. 7, 263–266. The next joint pronouncement from Tehran religious scholars came after the Abadan fire in late August; see Davani, *Nehzat-e Ruhaniyun*, vol. 7, 219–221.

33. *Washington Post*, August 26, 1978, A1; Moss's allegation in "The Campaign to Destabilize Iran," 9—that a Communist newspaper started the rumor of government complicity in early September—can be dismissed as Cold War propaganda. For the week of mourning protests, see *Shah's Inferno*. For the number and size of demonstrations see *Kayhan International*, September 2, 1978; a SAVAK memorandum, undated, estimated the Mashhad crowd at forty thousand (*Yaran-e Emam*, vol. 5, 771).

34. Lebaschi, Harvard Iranian Oral History Collection, tape 3, 4. On the use of the site in previous years, see Hajj Masha'llah Rahimi, interviewed in Tehran on March 4, 2000, by Sharifpur, *Masjed va Enqelab-e Eslami*, 260. SAVAK memorandum of September 4, 1978, in *Yaran-e Emam*, vol. 15, 656.

Pictures and banners can be found in the photographs published in the appendix to Davani, *Nehzat-e Ruhaniyun,* vol. 8. On the demonstration see *Kayhan International,* September 5, 1978; Lebaschi, Harvard Iranian Oral History Collection, tape 3, 5; "A Report on the Great Demonstrations of 'Eid-e Fetr," undated, in *Asnad va Tasaviri,* vol. 1, pt. 1, 141; Parsa, *Social Origins,* 211, has, I think, misinterpreted this source to suggest that the march was spontaneous.

35. Brière and Blanchet, *Iran,* 45–46.

36. Anonymous woman, interviewed by Shirin Sami'i in Paris, France, November 15, 1983, Foundation for Iranian Studies, 15. Sanjabi, *Omid'ha va Na-Omidi'ha,* 305.

37. The Muslims of Shiraz, pronouncement of August 12, 1978, in *Asnad va Tasaviri,* vol. 1, pt. 1, 87–89. Ruhollah Khomeini, pronouncement of September 6, 1978, in Davani, *Nehzat-e Ruhaniyun,* vol. 8, 281.

38. "Report on Thursday [September 6, 1978], the Second Great Islamic Demonstration in Iran," anonymous letter, undated, in *Asnad va Tasaviri,* vol. 1, pt. 1, 158. On foreign leaders' visits see Menashri, *Iran,* 46, 50. On the demonstration see "Report on Thursday," in *Asnad va Tasaviri,* vol. 1, pt. 1, 158; Brière and Blanchet, *Iran,* 47; Raein, Associated Press Wire Service, September 7, 1978; anonymous eyewitness report in *Setareh-ye Sorkh,* October 1978, 1. National police chief Samad Samadianpur in a cabinet meeting on September 7, 1978, transcribed in *Tasmim-e Shum,* 18. On the taxi ride see Mahallati, *Khaterat va Mobarezat,* 94.

39. "Report on Thursday," in *Asnad va Tasaviri,* vol. 1, pt. 1, 160. Minister for Executive Affairs Manuchehr Azmun in a cabinet meeting on September 7, 1978, transcribed in *Tasmim-e Shum,* 26. Brière and Blanchet, *Iran,* 47.

40. Behrang, *Iran,* 47; Chehabi, *Iranian Politics,* 236; Hiro, *Iran under the Ayatollahs,* 76; Menashri, "Iran," 490; Nikazmerad, "A Chronological Survey," 333–334; Raein, Associated Press Wire Service, September 7, 1978; the slogan was apparently pioneered at the demonstration of September 4 (Parsa, *States, Ideologies, and Social Revolutions,* 143). On Khomeini's authorship of the slogan see *Setareh-ye Sorkh,* October 1978, 3. On the crowd's approval see Mahallati, *Khaterat va Mobarezat,* 95, which does not describe the resolution; 'Ali Davani (*Nehzat-e Ruhaniyun,* vol. 8, 281) does not even mention a resolution on this day, and I have yet to find a copy of one.

41. Ruhollah Khomeini, "Islamic Government," lectures of January–February 1970, in Khomeini, *Islam and Revolution,* 62. Sachedina, *The Just Ruler,* 228; for a different perspective see Calder, "Accommodation and Revolution."

42. Ruhollah Khomeini, "Islamic Government," lectures of January–February 1970, in Khomeini, *Islam and Revolution,* 48.

43. On the sole sources of imitation in earlier periods see Akhavi, "Con-

tending Discourses," 236; Algar, "The Oppositional Role of the Ulama," 243; Arjomand, "Ideological Revolution in Shi'ism," 184–185; Fischer, *Iran,* 275, note 11; Moussavi, "The Establishment of the Position of Marja'iyyat-i Taqlid," 44–46. For Borujerdi's limits on Khomeini see Davani, "Khaterat," 49; the Islamic Republic has since rehabilitated Borujerdi; a recent collection of oral histories suggests that Khomeini and Borujerdi were allies in opposition to the regime—Farati, *Tarikh-e Shafahi-ye Enqelab-e Eslami,* 9–13. On reform discussions see Tabataba'i et al., *Bahsi Dar-Bareh-ye Marja'iyat,* one chapter of which has been translated as Motahhari, "The Fundamental Problem in the Clerical Establishment"; Lambton, "A Reconsideration"; Akhavi, *Religion and Politics in Contemporary Iran,* 117–129.

44. Brumberg, *Reinventing Khomeini,* 39–54 and 92–97.

45. Golabdareh'i, *Lahzeh'ha,* 52.

46. Asghar, an electrician, interviewed in Tehran, February 1980, by Vieille and Khosrokhavar, *Le Discours Populaire de la Révolution Iranienne,* vol. 2, 253. For reports of the legend see Bahrampour, *To See and See Again,* 101–102; Farman Farmaian, *Daughter of Persia,* 312; Harney, *The Priest and the King,* 157; Milani, *Tales of Two Cities,* 189; Pliskin, "Camouflage, Conspiracy, and Collaborators," 74; Robert R. Reid, Associated Press Wire Service, February 2, 1979. For differing perspectives on the legend see Arjomand, *The Turban for the Crown,* 101; Delannoy and Pichard, *Khomeiny,* 134; Taheri, *The Spirit of Allah,* 238–239; Sreberny-Mohammadi and Mohammadi, *Small Media, Big Revolution,* 132. Ayatollah Sadeq Ruhani quoted in *Ayandegan,* January 14, 1979, 1.

47. Davani, *Nehzat-e Ruhaniyun,* vol. 10, 281; Bakhash, *The Reign of the Ayatollahs,* 56–59.

48. Ruhollah Khomeini, speech of September 28, 1977, in Khomeini, *Matn-e Sokhanrani,* 14. Ruhollah Khomeini, speech of February 19, 1978, in Khomeini, *Islam and Revolution,* 221. Ruhollah Khomeini, pronouncement of July 27, 1978, in Davani, *Nehzat-e Ruhaniyun,* vol. 7, 198. For the slogan on silence see Abbas, *La Révolution Confisquée,* caption to picture 11; Golabdareh'i, *Lahzeh'ha,* 14. On rising religiosity see Braswell, "A Mosaic of Mullahs and Mosques," 121; Bayat, "Mahmud Taleqani and the Iranian Revolution," 68; Arjomand, "Traditionalism in Twentieth Century Iran," 214–217; *Iran Almanac,* 1977, 394; Sreberny-Mohammadi and Mohammadi, *Small Media, Big Revolution,* 88. On mosque attendance see Parsa, *States, Ideologies, and Social Revolutions,* 137; Sadri and Sadri, "The Mantle of the Prophet: A Critical Postscript," 145.

49. Esma'il (Respondent 65), interviewed by the author in Istanbul, Turkey,

December 5, 1989. D. K. (Respondent 15), interviewed by the author in Istanbul, Turkey, October 31, 1989. Ahmad (Respondent 16), interviewed by the author in Istanbul, Turkey, November 8, 1989.

50. Ruhollah Khomeini, proclamation of November 23, 1978, in Khomeini, *Islam and Revolution,* 242.

51. Hojjat al-Islam Akbar Hamidzadeh, in *Khabar-Nameh,* April 6, 1978, 25.

52. Fischer, *Iran,* 13–27, 170–180, 213–216; on the various strands of the Karbala imagery, see Aghaie, "The Karbala Narrative." For the chant see "Report on Thursday," in *Asnad va Tasaviri,* vol. 1, pt. 1, 159; Kippenberg, "Jeder Tag 'Ashura, Jedes Grab Kerbala"; Pinault, *Horse of Karbala.* On shrouds see Ed Blanche, Associated Press Wire Service, December 2, 1978; Philip Dopoulos, Associated Press Wire Service, December 3, 1978; *Los Angeles Times,* December 4, 1978, I:1.

53. Hossein Musavi-Tabrizi, interviewed in Shirkhani, *Hamaseh-ye 19 Dey,* 178. Mohammad Beheshti, interviewed in Khalkhali, *Shohada-ye Ruhaniyat,* vol. 2, 583. On stashes of weapons see Khalkhali, *Shohada-ye Ruhaniyat,* vol. 2, 101, 147. On Andarzgu see *Jomhuri-ye Eslami,* July 31, 1979, in Davani, *Nehzat-e Ruhaniyun,* vol. 7, 231–232; SAVAK documents in *Yaran-e Emam,* vol. 8. On the restaurant bombing see Group of the Unitarian Line, "military pronouncement #1" of August 13, 1978, in *Zamimeh-e Khabar-Nameh,* September–October 1978, 37.

54. Voltaire, "Le Fanatisme, ou Mahomet le Prophète," 108. Renan, "De la Part des Peuples Sémitiques," 333. H. A. R. Gibb, quoted in Said, *Orientalism,* 106. U.S. Central Intelligence Agency, "The Shia Urge toward Martyrdom," December 13, 1984, in *Declassified Documents Reference System,* document 1988:1303.

55. *Maclean's,* April 1, 1985, 22–25. Jatras, "The Muslim Advance and American Collaboration," 16. Ben-Dor, "The Uniqueness of Islamic Fundamentalism," 247. Kushner, "Suicide Bombers," 329.

56. Stouffer et al., *The American Soldier,* vol. 2, 45. *Truth and Reconciliation Commission of South Africa Report,* vol. 2, 389; vol. 3, 9. For Iranian casualty statistics see Amra'i, "Barresi-ye Moqe'iyat-e Ejtema'i-ye Shohada," 156–166. On false martyrs see Charles W. Naas, U.S. diplomat in Tehran during the revolution, interviewed on April 23, 2000, by Daugherty, *In the Shadow of the Ayatollah,* 233; Mossavar-Rahmani, "The Iranian Revolution and Its Theoretical Implications," 270–271.

57. Karim, interviewed by Khosrokhavar, "Les Paysans Dépaysannés," 176. Respondent 52, interviewed by the author in Istanbul, Turkey, November 27, 1989.

58. Mostafa Askari, interviewed in Hegland, "Imam Khomaini's Village," 879.

59. Moste'ar (Respondent 9), interviewed by the author in Istanbul, Turkey, October 23, 1989.

60. Lebaschi, Harvard Iranian Oral History Collection, tape 3, 7–8; "Report on Friday, September 9 [sic]," anonymous letter, undated, in *Asnad va Tasaviri,* vol. 1, pt. 1, 161; Akbar Askari, an eyewitness, interviewed in December 1983 by Bayat, *Street Politics,* 180. On the endorsement by Khomeini's followers see Stempel, *Inside the Iranian Revolution,* 116.

61. On martial law see Manuchehr Azmun in a cabinet meeting of September 7, 1978, transcribed in *Tasmim-e Shum,* 91–92. "Report on Friday," in *Asnad va Tasaviri,* vol. 1, pt. 1, 191. Mr. Temiyan, interviewed by Davani, *Nehzat-e Ruhaniyun,* vol. 8, 306–307. *Le Figaro,* September 9–10, 1978, 1 and 10, translated in Nobari, *Iran Erupts,* 200. On Nuri see SAVAK six-month summary of religious opposition, September 30, 1978, in *SAVAK va Ruhaniyat,* 272.

62. *Iranshahr,* October 20, 1978, 4. Sabri-Tabrizi, *Iran,* 252.

63. Mossavar-Rahmani, "The Iranian Revolution and Its Theoretical Implications," 268; see also Kuzichkin, *Inside the KGB,* 241.

64. Amra'i, "Barresi-ye Moqe'iyat-e Ejtema'i-ye Shohada," 159; after the revolution, a coroner claimed that his office buried 555 persons killed on Black Friday (Sar Malek, quoted in *Ruz-Shomar-e Enqelab-e Eslami,* vol. 5, 287). Another report based on Martyr Foundation records counts 88 killed on Black Friday, 64 of them in Zhaleh Square (Baqi, "Amar-e Qorbaniyan-e Enqelab").

65. William H. Sullivan, memorandum of September 14, 1978, in National Security Archive, *Iran,* document 1521. Carter, *Public Papers of the President: Jimmy Carter, 1978,* 1515; U.S. Secretary of State Warren Christopher, memorandum of September 10, 1978, in National Security Archive, *Iran,* document 1508. M. R. Pahlavi, *Answer to History,* 161; Zonis, *Majestic Failure,* 253–254. U.S. defense official quoted in Harold Brown, U.S. secretary of defense, memorandum of October 27, 1978, in *Declassified Documents Reference System,* document 1994:1904.

66. Mahmud (Respondent 30), interviewed by the author in Istanbul, Turkey, November 6, 1989.

5. General Strike

1. Behrang, *Iran,* 272–293. *Workers' News,* no. 2, 1979, 4–8. *Chand E'lamiyeh,* 12. On the spread of strikes in fall 1978 see Bayat, *Workers and Revolution in Iran,* 98.

2. Assersohn, *The Biggest Deal,* 25.

3. Incomplete daily data on oil exports from U.S. embassy memoranda, October 1978–January 1979, published in *Asnad-e Laneh-ye Jasusi,* vol. 66; occasional data from *Oil and Gas Journal,* various issues, October 1978–February 1979; weekly averages from *Time,* January 8, 1979, 26; monthly averages from Fesharaki, *Revolution and Energy Policy in Iran,* 42. Iranian Oil Worker, "How We Organized Strike," 60, 61.

4. Ruhollah Khomeini, pronouncement of September 11, 1978, in Davani, *Nehzat-e Ruhaniyun,* vol. 8, 328. Ruhollah Khomeini, pronouncement of September 12, 1978, in Davani, *Nehzat-e Ruhaniyun,* vol. 8, 330. *Los Angeles Times,* September 16, 1978, I:6. Pronouncement signed by more than one hundred religious scholars of Tehran, September 17, 1978, in *Asnad-e Enqelab-e Eslami,* vol. 3, 385–386. For passing reference to the strikes, see Ruhollah Khomeini, pronouncement of October 12, 1978, in Davani, *Nehzat-e Ruhaniyun,* vol. 8, 378. Ruhollah Khomeini, pronouncement of November 15, 1978, in Davani, *Nehzat-e Ruhaniyun,* vol. 8, 400. On Khomeini's expulsion see Davani, *Nehzat-e Ruhaniyun,* vol. 8, 341–366; *Asnad-e Enqelab-e Eslami,* vol. 1, 521–533, vol. 2, 372—385, vol. 3, 387–410, vol. 4, 571–577, vol. 5, 232–237; *Aya U Taṣmim Darad;* Amir-ʿAlaʾi, *Dar Rah-e Enqelab,* 122; Abolhassan Bani-Sadr, interviewed by Zia Sedghi in Paris, France, May 21, 1984, Harvard Iranian Oral History Collection, tape 5, 5–7.

5. Ruhollah Khomeini, quoted in Bayat, *Workers and Revolution in Iran,* 48. On Islamist opposition to materialism see Mutahhari [Motahhari], *Fundamentals of Islamic Thought,* 100–102; Badamchiyan, *Shenakht-e Enqelab-e Eslami,* 67–70. Student quoted in Brière and Blanchet, *Iran,* 80.

6. Ruhollah Khomeini, speech of February 19, 1978, in Khomeini, *Islam and Revolution,* 223–224.

7. Radjavi, *La Révolution Iranienne et les Moudjahédines,* 109–117.

8. *New York Times,* November 29, 1994, A4. Roy, *The Failure of Political Islam,* 3–4. Lewis, "Islamic Revolution," 50.

9. Nossiter, *The Global Struggle for More,* 115.

10. On the expansion of state power see Farazmand, *The State, Bureaucracy, and Revolution in Modern Iran;* Goodell, *The Elementary Structures of Political Life;* Hooglund, *Land and Revolution in Iran.* How many landholdings were distributed is the subject of a debate that I am not qualified to adjudicate: Najmabadi (*Land Reform and Social Change in Iran,* 99–100) argues that exemptions, especially for mechanized farms, allowed more than half of all land to remain in the hands of the landlords; Majd and Nowshirvani ("Land Reform in Iran Revisited," 451) argue that only 5 percent of all land was retained by landlords. On state distribution of resources see

Najmabadi, *Land Reform and Social Change in Iran,* 151; Karshenas, *Oil, State and Industrialization in Iran,* 151–152. For statistics on credit see Naghizadeh, *The Role of Farmer's Self-Determination,* 272, 277–278. On productivity see Najmabadi, *Land Reform and Social Change in Iran,* 121, 123, 158; Bergmann and Khademadam, *The Impacts of Large-Scale Farms on Development in Iran,* 124; Majd, "The Political Economy of Land Reform in Iran," 73.

11. On rising output see Amid, *Agriculture, Poverty and Reform in Iran,* 125; Majd, "The Oil Boom and Agricultural Development"; Majd, "The Political Economy of Land Reform in Iran"; Majd and Nowshirvani, "Land Reform in Iran Revisited." On rising demand see Bharier, *Economic Development in Iran,* 133. Katouzian, *The Political Economy of Modern Iran,* 271–272, citing a province-by-province study by Hossein ʿAzimi. For agricultural forecasts see Looney, *The Economic Development of Iran,* 15–16, citing work by Allen LeBaron. On imported livestock see Graham, *Iran,* 116–117; Weinbaum, "Agricultural Policy," 446.

12. Shah quoted in Sullivan, *Obbligato,* 266. For urbanization statistics see Bharier, "The Growth of Towns and Villages in Iran," 55; Bank Markazi Iran, *Annual Report and Balance Sheet,* 1355 (1976–1977), 160; 1356 (1977–1978), 162; 1358 (1979–1980), 161. Increased urbanization was due partly to natural population growth, not migration, and partly to redefinitions of "urban" that included previously "rural" towns (Hourcade, "Migrations Intérieures et Changement Social en Iran"; Kohli, *Current Trends and Patterns of Urbanization in Iran,* 11; Majd, "On the Relationship between Land Reform and Rural-Urban Migration in Iran"). On cave-dwellers see Kazemi, *Poverty and Revolution in Iran,* 55. Squatters numbered around four thousand households (Kazemi, *Poverty and Revolution in Iran,* 49; Danesh, *Rural Exodus and Squatter Settlements,* 145) in the mid-1970s, in a city with two million migrants (from both urban and rural sources) (Plan and Budget Organization, *National Census of Population and Housing, November 1976,* vol. 3, 5). On underemployment see Elkan, "Employment, Education, Training and Skilled Labor in Iran," 176; Scoville, "The Labor Market in Pre-Revolutionary Iran," 151. For the 1972 survey, see Kazemi, *Poverty and Revolution in Iran,* 53–54; reported somewhat differently in Kamali, *Revolutionary Iran,* 176–177. For the 1977 survey, see Kazemi, *Poverty and Revolution in Iran,* 56; Danesh, *Rural Exodus and Squatter Settlements,* 129–136.

13. Danesh, *Rural Exodus and Squatter Settlements,* 75; Pesaran and Gahvary, "Growth and Income Distribution in Iran," 237–238; Jabbari, "Economic Factors in Iran's Revolution," 174; Karshenas, *Oil, State and Industrialization in Iran,* 200; the figures vary in each source, but within each source,

the trend of increase is apparent. For subjective impressions of inequality see Kazemi, *Poverty and Revolution in Iran,* 47–48; Bahrambeygui, *Tehran,* 50; Marvin Zonis, testimony of July 23, 1973, in U.S. House of Representatives, *New Perspectives,* 104. United States Arms Control and Disarmament Agency, *World Military Expenditures and Arms Transfers, 1968–1977,* 46. Hassan, resident of 'Own-'Ali slum, interviewed in Tabriz on January 16, 1979, by Sabri-Tabrizi, *Iran,* 266–267.

14. Interviewed in Qazvin, October 1979, by Vieille and Khosrokhavar, *Le Discours Populaire de la Révolution Iranienne,* vol. 2, 140, 143, and 156. For the exchange rate see International Monetary Fund, *International Financial Statistics Yearbook,* 1980, 227.

15. Suheilah, interviewed in Bauer, "Ma'ssoum's Tale," 522.

16. Bayat, *Workers and Revolution in Iran,* 86–87. For the working-class–revolt approach see Abrahamian, *Iran between Two Revolutions,* 517–518; Ashraf and Banuazizi, "The State," 33–34; Bayat, *Workers and Revolution in Iran,* chapter 6; Marshall, *Revolution and Counter-Revolution in Iran;* Petras and Morley, "Development and Revolution." For opposing approaches see Arjomand, *The Turban for the Crown,* 107–108; McDaniel, *Autocracy, Modernization, and Revolution,* 137; Mottahedeh, *The Mantle of the Prophet,* 308; Sheikholeslami, "Roots of Contemporary Iranian Politics," 283.

17. For GDP see Penn World Table; Summers and Heston, "The Penn World Table (Mark 5)," 252–255. For Gini coefficients see *World Income Inequality Database* (Version Beta 3). On daily calories and drinking water see World Bank, *World Development Report 1980,* 152–153. On rural poverty see Jazairy, Alamgir, and Panuccio, *The State of World Rural Poverty,* 386–387.

18. Tocqueville, *The Old Regime and the French Revolution,* 175. On relative deprivation see Gurr, *Why Men Rebel;* Davies, "The J-Curve." Brinton, *The Anatomy of Revolution.* For references to Brinton see Sick, *All Fall Down,* 187; Fischer, *Iran,* 189; Keddie, "Iranian Revolutions in Comparative Perspective," 589. Bakhash, *The Reign of the Ayatollahs,* 13.

19. *New York Times,* December 24, 1973, 1, 24; Kapuscinksi, *Shah of Shahs,* 52–53.

20. Amuzegar, *Iran,* 261–262; Vakil, "A Macro-Econometric Projection for Iran," 302; Vakil, "Iran's Basic Macro-Economic Problems," 87–88.

21. Karanjia, *The Mind of a Monarch,* 258. *Washington Post,* February 4, 1974, C5.

22. Bank Markazi Iran, *Annual Report and Balance Sheet,* 1356 (1977–1978), 138, 152. For GDP see Jazayeri, *Economic Adjustment in Oil-Based Economies,* 171; International Monetary Fund, *International Financial Statistics Yearbook,* 1980, 228–229; Penn World Table.

23. Jazayeri, *Economic Adjustment in Oil-Based Economies,* 171; International

Monetary Fund, *International Financial Statistics Yearbook,* 1980, 228–229; Penn World Table. On industrial exports see Bank Markazi Iran, *Annual Report and Balance Sheet,* 1356 (1977–1978), 152.

24. On the Gajareh meeting see Graham, *Iran,* 77–80; Razavi and Vakil, *The Political Economy of Economic Planning in Iran,* 72–75. On metalworks see Bank Markazi Iran, *Bulletin,* 1978, 155. On manufacturing see Bayat, *Workers and Revolution in Iran,* 56–74. On cement see Hirschfield, "Decline and Fall of the Pahlavis," 29; Bank Markazi Iran, *A Comprehensive Report on Construction Activities,* 21; Bank Markazi Iran, *Annual Report and Balance Sheet,* 1354 (1975–1976), 98; Bank Markazi Iran, *Bulletin,* 1st Quarter 1979, 52. On power shortages see Graham, *Iran,* 121, citing *Kayhan International,* July 13, 1977; Afkhami, *The Iranian Revolution,* 85; *Middle East Economic Digest,* June 30, 1978, 11. On transportation see *Wall Street Journal,* April 11, 1977, 1. On border delays see *The Economist,* August 28, 1978, S21.

25. Graham, *Iran,* 87–88.

26. Johnson, *High-Level Manpower in Iran,* 84. Kazemi, *Poverty and Revolution in Iran,* 124.

27. *New York Times,* November 18, 1978, A1. Business International, *Operating in Iran,* 83. On the prime minister see Radji, *In the Service of the Peacock Throne,* 209; Milani, *The Persian Sphinx,* 211–213. On Ebtehaj see Zonis, *The Political Elite of Iran,* 67–68; and Bostock and Jones, *Planning and Power in Iran,* 184.

28. Mohammad Reza Pahlavi, interviewed by Franz Tartarotti and Rolf Winter, *Stern,* August 31, 1978, 105, translated in *Kayhan International,* September 7, 1978, 7.

29. On capital flows see Bank Markazi Iran, *Bulletin,* 1978; Halliday, *Iran,* 165. Anonymous former SAVAK general interviewed on April 11, 1982, by Zonis, *Majestic Failure,* 90.

30. Biniosch, "Letter from Teheran," 58. For average annual income see World Bank, *World Development Report 1980,* 111. For statistics on rent and lodging see International Labour Office, *Year Book of Labour Statistics,* 1978, 591; Vieille, "Transformations des Rapports Sociaux," 27, citing doctoral research by Golam Reza Estifa; see also *Le Monde,* October 3–4, 1976, 4; Halliday, *Iran,* 164, 190; Parsa, *States, Ideologies, and Social Revolutions,* 67. Young military officer: Afrachteh, "Iran," 117.

31. Hudson Institute, quoted in Halliday, *Iran,* 167; see also *Forbes,* July 10, 1978, 68–74, and the comments of the petroleum analyst Walter Levy at a symposium in Persepolis, Iran, in 1975, quoted in Bill, *The Eagle and the Lion,* 217–218. Iranian planners interviewed in September 1976 by Saikal, *The Rise and Fall of the Shah,* 182.

32. Amuzegar, "Oil Wealth: A Very Mixed Blessing"; Gelb and associates, *Oil Windfalls: Blessing or Curse?*

33. Corden and Neary, "Booming Sector and De-Industrialisation in a Small Open Economy"; El Mallakh, Noreng, and Poulson, *Petroleum and Economic Development;* Fardmanesh, "Dutch Disease Economics and the Oil Syndrome"; Gelb and associates, *Oil Windfalls: Blessing or Curse?;* Jazayeri, *Economic Adjustment in Oil-Based Economies;* Scherr, "Agriculture in an Export Boom Economy."

34. International Monetary Fund, *International Financial Statistics Yearbook,* 1980. Pertamina, the Indonesian state oil company, acquired huge short-term debt to avoid cabinet oversight; when capital became scarce in 1974, Pertamina had to spend $1 billion to cover its loans. In 1975, the Indonesian central bank assumed Pertamina's debts (Arndt, *The Indonesian Economy,* 66; Bresnan, *Managing Indonesia,* 165–167, 190).

35. World Bank, *World Development Report 1979,* 128–129, 164–165, 170–171, 126–127, 130–131, and 168–169; Penn World Table.

36. Abrahamian, *Iran between Two Revolutions,* 427; see also Green, "Countermobilization as a Revolutionary Form," 154–156; McDaniel, *Autocracy, Modernization, and Revolution,* 95; Saikal, *The Rise and Fall of the Shah,* 188–191.

37. On the over-developed state see Alavi, "The State in Post-Colonial Societies," 61; Tlemcani and Hansen, "Development and the State in Post-Colonial Algeria"; Schiller, "State Formation in New Order Indonesia"; al-Khalil, *The Republic of Fear;* Joseph, "Class, State, and Prebendal Politics in Nigeria"; Karl, *The Paradox of Plenty* (on Venezuela). For examples see Swearingen, "The Algerian Food Security Crisis"; Graf, *The Nigerian State,* 223; Scherr, "Agriculture in an Export Boom Economy." Econometric study: Fardmanesh, "Dutch Disease Economics and the Oil Syndrome."

38. Eftekhari, "Rente et Dépendence en Algérie," 52–58; Demaine, "Population and Resources," 28 (on Indonesia); Maroun, *L'Économie Pétrolière,* 289–292 (on Iraq); Graf, *The Nigerian State,* 223.

39. Leon, "The Development of Rentist Pauperism," 20.

40. Khong Cho Oon, *The Politics of Oil in Indonesia,* 168; al-Khafaji, "State Incubation of Iraqi Capitalism"; Karl, *The Paradox of Plenty,* chapter 6; Murray, "The 'Deluge' Is Over: Oil Aftershock in Venezuela," 395.

41. Achebe, *The Trouble with Nigeria,* 2–3, 40.

42. Karl, "The Political Economy of Petrodollars," 18.

43. Bentaleb, "Rente et Société Algérienne," 83; Demaine, "Population and Resources," 21 (on Indonesia); Oropeza, *Tutelary Pluralism,* 16 (on Vene-

zuela); data from the *World Income Inequality Database* (Beta 3) show inconsistent trends.

44. Tlemcani and Hansen, "Development and the State in Post-Colonial Algeria," 126; *Far Eastern Economic Review* reporting on Indonesia, January–March 1978; Apter, "Things Fell Apart? Yoruba Responses to the 1983 Elections in Ondo State, Nigeria"; Freedom House, *Freedom in the World 1979*, 246, and *Freedom in the World 1983–1984*, 406.

45. British consul K. E. Abbott, report of 1848, quoted in Issawi, *The Economic History of Iran*, 20. Benedick, *Industrial Finance in Iran*, 256.

46. Parvin and Zamani, "Political Economy of Growth and Destruction," 43.

47. For comparisons with 1975, see Kurzman, "The Qum Protests." For reports on the 1975 recession see *New York Times*, May 28, 1975, *New York Times*, August 13, 1975, 47, and August 5, 1975, 47 and 52; Graham, *Iran*, 93; Halliday, *Iran*, 165. On the price-control campaign see Graham, *Iran*, 94; *Times* (London), August 4, 1975, 5; *New York Times*, August 21, 1975, 51; Parsa, *Social Origins*, 103, citing *Kayhan International*, August 8, 1975. U.S. Central Intelligence Agency, memoranda of April 17 and May 14, 1975, in National Security Archive, *Iran*, documents 948, 957.

48. Jazayeri, *Economic Adjustment in Oil-Based Economies*, 169.

49. On the underestimation of inflation see Ikani, *The Dynamics of Inflation in Iran*, 126; *Quarterly Economic Review: Iran*, 2nd Quarter 1975, 10. See inflation data in International Monetary Fund, *International Financial Statistics*, April 1975, 194–195 (for 1971–1973); April 1978, 182–183 (for 1974–1976); November 1980, 198–199 (for 1977–1978). On the link between recession and protest see Keddie, "Iranian Revolutions in Comparative Perspective," 588; Parsa, *Social Origins*, 84. On labor shortage see Sarraf, *Cry of a Nation*, 7. On strikers' grievances see *Workers' News*, no. 2, 1979, 4–6, 10–11.

50. Bank Markazi Iran, *Annual Report*, 1974, 166 (for 1971–1973); 1976, 74 (1971–1975); 1978, 158 (1972–1977); Jazayeri, *Economic Adjustment in Oil-Based Economies*, 170, reports similar figures from an International Monetary Fund source. For wages see International Monetary Fund, *International Financial Statistics*, April 1977, 186 (for 1971–1972); April 1979, 190 (for 1972–1977). For calorie intake see Food and Agriculture Organization, *Food Balance Sheets*, 1980, 467.

51. Shirkhani, *Hamaseh-ye 17 Khordad 1354; Gozaresh-e Kamel;* Kurzman, "The Qum Protests." Ruhollah Khomeini, pronouncement of July 11, 1975, in *Gozaresh-e Kamel*, 19. *Kayhan-e Hava'i*, June 14, 1975, 1; *New York Times*, June 11, 1975, 10; Baqi, *Jonbesh-e Daneshjuyi-ye Iran*, 223–231; Parsa, *States, Ideologies, and Social Revolutions*, 141; SAVAK six-month summary of religious opposition, September 23, 1975, in *SAVAK va Ruhaniyat*, 128.

52. Hooglund, *Land and Revolution in Iran,* 141; see also Dowlat, Hourcade, and Puech, "Les Paysans et la Révolution Iranienne." On the effect of urban connections see Hegland, "Imam Khomaini's Village," 549–563; Hooglund, *Land and Revolution in Iran,* 143; Hooglund, "Rural Participation in the Revolution," 5–6. On Islamists' efforts see Hossein Fardust, memorandum of February 8, 1978, in *Faraz'ha'i,* 19–20; SAVAK memorandum of January 6, 1979, in *Yaran-e Emam,* vol. 5, 846. Village activist Mohammad Amini, quoted in Hegland, "Imam Khomaini's Village," 645.

53. The idea that poor urban-dwellers were not politically active is contrary to the assessments of Amjad, *Iran,* 121; Kamali, *Revolutionary Iran,* 193; Keddie, *Roots of Revolution,* 246; Khosrokhavar, "Les Paysans Dépaysannés et la Révolution Iranienne," 159–179; and Rahnema and Nomani, *The Secular Miracle,* 15. For casualty statistics see Amra'i, "Barresi-ye Moqe'iyat-e Ejtema'i-ye Shohada," 182. The rate of rural migrants is estimated from Hourcade, "Migrations Intérieures," 65, 68; Kohli, *Current Trends,* 11; Plan and Budget Organization, *National Census,* vol. 3; and Statistical Centre of Iran, *Population Growth Survey,* 102–104. On construction workers see Hakimian, *Labour Transfer and Economic Development,* 157; Golabdareh'i, *Lahzeh'ha,* 41. On Tehran see 'Amid-Zanjani, *Ravayeti az Enqelab-e Eslami-ye Iran,* 168. On Isfahan see Parsa, *Social Origins,* 5. On Tabriz see "Javad," leftist student and factory worker, interviewed in Paris in 1985 by Moghadam, "Industrial Development," 161.

54. Sabri-Tabrizi, *Iran,* 266. *New York Times,* December 4, 1978, A3. *Washington Post,* January 14, 1979, A30.

55. Kazemi, *Poverty and Revolution in Iran,* 95.

56. Bauer, "Poor Women and Social Consciousness in Revolutionary Iran," 160. Ma'ssoum, the daughter of a bus driver in southern Tehran, interviewed in Bauer, "Ma'ssoum's Tale," 529. "Mohammad," interviewed in Kamali, *Revolutionary Iran,* 201. "Gholam," interviewed in Kamali, *Revolutionary Iran,* 201.

57. Tehran bazaari interviewed in 1981 by Ghandchi-Tehrani, "Bazaaris and Clergy," 36. On the proportion of trade conducted by the bazaar, see Graham, *Iran,* 224; Abrahamian, *Iran between Two Revolutions,* 433; *Euromoney,* June 1978, 117. On crossover to the modern sector see Ashraf, "The Bazaar-Mosque Alliance," 563, 569; Bashiriyeh, *State and Revolution in Iran,* 40–41; Graham, *Iran,* 47; Thaiss, "The Bazaar as a Case Study of Religious and Social Change," 196, 198. Carpet merchant from Tehran bazaar quoted by Professor Shaul Bakhash, interviewed by the author in Fairfax, Virginia, October 5, 1989.

58. Salehi-Isfahani, "The Political Economy of Credit Subsidy in Iran," 359–

379. On urban planning see Ashraf, "The Bazaar-Mosque Alliance," 551. For the analogy with China see *Der Spiegel,* December 18, 1978, 114. On the non-economic roots of bazaari discontent, see Denoeux, *Urban Unrest in the Middle East,* 147; for a contrasting view, see Parsa, *Social Origins,* 101–103; and Parsa, *States, Ideologies, and Social Revolutions,* 205. For the ashes metaphor see *Dar-bareh-ye Qiyam,* vol. 1, 138.

59. Anthony Parsons, interviewed by Shusha Assar in South Devon, England, January 30 and March 7, 1985, Foundation for Iranian Studies, 31–32.

60. Rosen and Rosen, *The Destined Hour,* 46.

61. Raja'i-Khorasani, Harvard Iranian Oral History Collection, tape 1, 12, 13. See also Baqi, *Johnbesh-e Daneshjuyi-ye Iran.*

62. Shah quoted in Zonis, *The Political Elite of Iran,* 331–332. On Egypt see Wickham, *Mobilizing Islam.* U.S. diplomat quoted in "Mansur," "The Crisis in Iran," 27. Bani-Sadr, *Sad Maghaleh,* 27. Unnamed foreign official paraphrased in Halliday, *Iran,* 152. Kurzman and Leahey, "Intellectuals and Democratization."

63. Classic works on protesters' need for resources include McCarthy and Zald, "Resource Mobilization and Social Movements"; Oberschall, *Social Conflict and Social Movements;* Tilly, *From Mobilization to Revolution.*

64. *Quarterly Economic Review: Iran,* March 6, 1978, 3, and May 18, 1978, 2.

6. Failure of the Fist

1. *New York Times,* November 6, 1978, 18, reports three killed; Sarraf, *Cry of a Nation,* 9, reports thousands killed. Khalili, *Gam beh Gam,* 73; Parsons, *The Pride and the Fall,* 94; Sullivan, *Mission to Iran,* 177. For speculation that the government organized the riot or let it happen, see Bahramian, *Renasans dar Iran,* 105; Gharabaghi, *Vérités sur la Crise Iranienne,* 53; Golabdareh'i, *Lahzeh'ha,* 35–36; Green, *Revolution in Iran,* 114; Nahavandi, *Iran: Deux Rêves Brisés,* 46; Nahavandi, *Iran: Anatomie d'une Révolution,* 98; Sarraf, *Cry of a Nation,* 9. For the claim that security forces were surprised and overwhelmed, see Green, *Revolution in Iran,* 113. General Hossein Fardust, who as chief of the shah's Special Intelligence Bureau was probably in a position to know, makes no mention in his memoirs of any plot, but his account of the period is not exhaustive (Fardust, *The Rise and Fall of [the] Pahlavi Dynasty,* 490–507).

2. On the military government see Menashri, *Iran,* 59. On armored vehicles see Rosen and Rosen, *The Destined Hour,* 39; Pourkarimi, "Iran and the Collapse of the Monarchy," 145. U.S. embassy memorandum of November 21, 1978, in National Security Archive, *Iran,* document 1784. U.S. embassy

memorandum of November 6, 1978, in National Security Archive, *Iran,* document 1688. On arrests see U.S. embassy memorandum of November 11, 1978, in National Security Archive, *Iran,* document 1720; Bazargan, *Enqelab-e Iran,* 57; Hajj-Seyyed-Javadi, Harvard Iranian Oral History Collection, tape 8, 1–5. On threats to oil workers see *Le Monde,* November 16, 1978, 3, translated in *MERIP Report,* March/April 1979, 18.

3. Mas'ud-Ansari, *Man va Khandan-e Pahlavi,* 129.

4. Khalili, *Gam beh Gam,* 75–76.

5. Ibid., 78. Ex-official of the ministry of justice, interviewed on October 25, 1982, by Mirfakhraei, "The Imperial Iranian Armed Forces and the Revolution of 1978–1979," 442.

6. Abrahamian, *Iran between Two Revolutions,* 518; Keddie, *Roots of Revolution,* 255; Mottahedeh, *The Mantle of the Prophet,* 375; and Siavoshi, *Liberal Nationalism in Iran,* 139, use the term "vacillating." Arjomand, *The Turban for the Crown,* 115; Cottam, "The Imperial Regime of Iran," 18; and Munson, *Islam and Revolution in the Middle East,* 130, call the policies "inconsistent." Mottale, *Iran,* 28, uses the term "hamletic." On the shah's illness see Zonis, *Majestic Failure,* 253–255. On the shah's demeanor see Kraft, "Letter from Iran," 134; Mas'ud-Ansari, *Man va Khandan-e Pahlavi,* 125, 140–145; Nahavandi, *Iran: Deux Rêves Brisés,* 175; Parsons, *The Pride and the Fall,* 71; Sick, *All Fall Down,* 62, 72; Sullivan, *Mission to Iran,* 156, 195, 196, 198; Sullivan, *Obbligato,* 268–269; Zonis, *Majestic Failure,* 253. Afkhami, *The Iranian Revolution,* 94. On new royal advisers see Mas'ud-Ansari, *Man va Khandan-e Pahlavi,* 126; Naraghi, *From Palace to Prison,* v–vii; Shahbazi, *Mohafez-e Shah,* 299. On the shah's style of governance see Arjomand, *The Turban for the Crown,* 114ff., 189ff.; Fatemi, "Leadership by Distrust"; Radji, *In the Service of the Peacock Throne,* 63; Razavi and Vakil, *The Political Economy of Economic Planning in Iran,* 69–70; Zonis, *The Political Elite of Iran,* 96–97, 112; Bill, *The Politics of Iran,* 44; Mohammad Reza Pahlavi, interviewed circa 1975 by Karanjia, *The Mind of a Monarch,* 191; Huyser, *Mission to Tehran,* 27.

7. Marenches, *The Evil Empire,* 130; Parsons, *The Pride and the Fall,* 147; Sullivan, *Mission to Iran,* 167. M. R. Pahlavi, *Answer to History,* 168; see corroboration in Arjomand, *The Turban for the Crown,* 116; Gharabaghi, *Vérités sur la Crise Iranienne,* 120; Hickman, *Ravaged and Reborn,* 4; Zonis, *Majestic Failure,* 93. On proposals for crackdowns see Reeves, *Behind the Peacock Throne,* 188; Mirfakhraei, "The Imperial Iranian Armed Forces and the Revolution of 1978–1979," 443; Copeland, *The Game Player,* 251; Stempel, *Inside the Iranian Revolution,* 280; Mas'ud-Ansari, *Man va Khandan-e Pahlavi,* 130.

8. United Press International, December 28, 1978, quoted in *The Rise,* January 20, 1979, 51.

9. U.S. embassy officer S. T. Escudero, memorandum of January 9, 1979, in National Security Archive, *Iran,* document 2040.

10. *Los Angeles Times,* January 29, 1979, I:8.

11. On martyrs of the revolution see *Laleh'ha-ye Enqelab;* this volume, published by a religious institution, features photographs of "martyrs of the revolution," including name, age, date and place of death, and sometimes occupation; the method of selection is not described. I am indebted to Prof. James A. Bill for directing me to *Laleh'ha-ye Enqelab,* which he too has used as a sampling of revolutionary fatalities (Bill, *The Eagle and the Lion,* 487). On arrests see the unnamed "high ranking security official" interviewed by Milani, *The Persian Sphinx,* 291–292. On coup planning see Iranian government documents, in Yazdi, *Akharin Talash'ha,* 249–299; Copeland, *The Game Player,* 252. On government inefficiency see Marenches, *The Evil Empire,* 121; Balam, *Too Much Too Soon,* 159; Graham, *Iran,* 22; Zakir, *Notes on Iran,* 17; Afkhami, *The Iranian Revolution,* 85; Graham, *Iran,* 120–121; Smith, "Hard Times in the Land of Plenty," 269–271.

12. Kautiliya, *The Kautilîya Arthasâstra,* pt. 2, 414. Nizam al-Mulk, *The Book of Government,* chapters 40 and 44. Machiavelli, *The Prince,* chapters 8 and 17. Wriggins, *The Ruler's Imperative,* 258–263.

13. Abrahamian, *Iran between Two Revolutions,* 508; Bayat, *Workers and Revolution in Iran,* 88; Binder, "Revolution in Iran," 52–53.

14. *Kayhan International,* May 14, 1978, 1. Eslaminia, quoted in U.S. embassy memoranda of May 23 and 24, 1978, in National Security Archive, *Iran,* documents 1397 and 1398.

15. Ruhollah Khomeini, pronouncement of August 28, 1978, in Davani, *Nehzat-e Ruhaniyun,* vol. 7, 254.

16. Thompson, *The Making of the English Working Class,* 129; also Opp and Roehl, "Repression, Micromobilization, and Political Protest"; and Sharp, *The Politics of Nonviolent Action,* 680. On concessions see Huntington, *Political Order in Changing Societies,* 367–368; Oberschall, *Social Conflict and Social Movements,* 75.

17. Parsons, *Sociological Theory and Modern Society,* chapter 9.

18. SAVAK memorandum of early September 1978, in *Yaran-e Emam,* vol. 4, 570–572, and vol. 15, 658–661. Behnam, *Zelzelah,* 208. General Firuzmand at Crisis Meeting of January 15, 1979, in Sadiqi, *Mesl-e Barf,* 71–72. On the plausibility of this transcript, see the essay on source materials in the present book. On the release of prisoners see Rubin, *Paved with Good Intentions,* 205; Pliskin ("Camouflage, Conspiracy, and Collaborators," 61) suggests that this may have been more rumor than fact.

19. Brière and Blanchet, *Iran*, 73–74; Manijeh, interviewed in Tehran, Iran, March 16, 1979, by Quitter, *Im Frühling der Freiheit*, 66–67. On television officials see General Vafa at the Crisis Meeting of January 23, 1979, in Sadiqi, *Mesl-e Barf*, 135.

20. Green, *Revolution in Iran*, 127, 162 (on Tehran); Semkus, *The Fall of Iran*, vol. 2, 387, 394, and 401 (on Isfahan); Soloway, "The Politicization of a Provincial Iranian City," 346 (on Babol Sar). On military plans see U.S. embassy memorandum of December 15, 1978, in National Security Archive, *Iran*, document 1930; Admiral Habibollahi and Generals Khajeh-Nuri and Tufanian at the Crisis Meeting of January 15, 1979, in Sadiqi, *Mesl-e Barf*, 45–46.

21. Iranian Oil Worker, "How We Organized Strike," 63; this report may be exaggerated, as navy personnel operated some oil fields and refineries from early November to early January, according to U.S. embassy memoranda of November 7, November 10, and December 14, 1978, and January 4, 1979, published in *Asnad-e Laneh-ye Jasusi*, vol. 66, 41, 45–46, 85, and 103.

22. Iranian Oil Worker, "How We Organized Strike," 63.

23. Activist metalworker interviewed in Bayat, *Workers and Revolution in Iran*, 85. On Iran Air see Fischer, *Iran*, 200; Nikazmerad, "A Chronological Survey," 337, 338; Radji, *In the Service of the Peacock Throne*, 273; Semkus, *The Fall of Iran*, vol. 2, 428; U.S. embassy memoranda of November 5 and December 27, 1978, in National Security Archive, *Iran*, documents 1685 and 1964; Green, *Revolution in Iran*, 164; *Ayandegan*, January 9, 1979, 4. On telecommunications see Nikazmerad, "A Chronological Survey," 335; U.S. embassy memorandum of November 6, 1978, in National Security Archive, *Iran*, document 1692; Radji, *In the Service of the Peacock Throne*, 293; Mahdavi, *Dar Hashiye-ye Siyasi-ye Khareji*, 276; *Los Angeles Times*, October 27, 1978, II:7; U.S. State Department memorandum of November 22, 1978, in National Security Archive, *Iran*, document 1792; Respondent 48, a telephone company official from Tehran, interviewed by the author in Istanbul, Turkey, November 22, 1989. On banks see Assersohn, *The Biggest Deal*, 24–25; U.S. embassy memorandum of October 1, 1978, in National Security Archive, *Iran*, document 1566; Respondent 59, a bank official interviewed by the author in Istanbul, Turkey, December 3, 1989. On customs see Huyser, *Mission to Tehran*, 157.

24. On fuel see U.S. embassy memorandum of November 16, 1978, in National Security Archive, *Iran*, document 1745. On ink see Assersohn, *The Biggest Deal*, 25. On banks see U.S. embassy memorandum of December 17, 1978, in National Security Archive, *Iran*, document 1934; *New York Times*, December 4, 1978, A1; *Los Angeles Times*, January 19, 1979, I:7. On payrolls see Ahanchian, *Tarh-e Soqut-e Yek Padeshah*, 380–384; U.S. em-

bassy memorandum of January 18, 1979, in National Security Archive, *Iran,* document 2127.

25. Mohammad Reza Pahlavi, interviewed in October 1978 by Kraft, "Letter from Iran," 134.

26. Ruhollah Khomeini, pronouncement of September 6, 1978, in Khomeini, *Islam and Revolution,* 236.

27. Afsharzadeh, a military officer, interviewed in Purbozorg-Vafi, *Madraseh-ye 'Eshq,* 29. On flowers see Baqi, *Tahrir-e Tarikh-e Shafahi,* 386. See slogans in Kamali, *Enqelab,* 404–406; *Farhang-e Sho'ar'ha-ye Enqelab-e Eslami,* 436–450; SAVAK memorandum, undated, in *Faraz'ha'i,* 170–171. On deserters see Afrasiyabi and Dehqan, *Taleqani va Tarikh,* 352. For attacks see Parsa, *Social Origins,* 231–237; photograph of attack on a general in Tehran, *Kayhan,* January 30, 1979, 1; *New York Times,* January 30, 1979, A1; and *Time,* February 12, 1979, 33; SAVAK and military memoranda of October 24 and December 31, 1978, and January 2, 1979, in *Faraz'ha'i,* 189–190, 345–346; minutes of Tehran provincial security council, January 1, 1979, in *Faraz'ha'i,* 304; SAVAK General Nasser Moghadam at the Crisis Meeting of January 29, 1979, in Sadiqi, *Mesl-e Barf,* 226.

28. On desertion and leaves see Gharabaghi, *Vérités sur la Crise Iranienne,* 122; Huyser, *Mission to Tehran,* 83, 160; Zabih, *The Iranian Military,* 33; SAVAK memorandum of January 22, 1979, in *Faraz'ha'i,* 356. On military strength see Gharabaghi at the Crisis Meeting of January 29, 1979, in Sadiqi, *Mesl-e Barf,* 175; also General 'Abdol-'Ali Badreh'i in the same source, 217, and Stempel, *Inside the Iranian Revolution,* 151. Parsa, *Social Origins,* 241–244. For mutinies and disaffection see *Newsweek,* December 11, 1978, 44; *Los Angeles Times,* February 1, 1979, I:10, and February 2, 1979, I:17; SAVAK memorandum of January 22, 1979, in *Faraz'ha'i,* 355–357. U.S. embassy memorandum of December 21, 1978, in National Security Archive, *Iran,* document 1950.

29. Sayyad-Shirazi, *Khaterat-e Amir-e Shahid,* 79. Badreh'i at the Crisis Meeting of January 15, 1979, in Sadiqi, *Mesl-e Barf,* 50. On soldiers' joining demonstrations see Fischer, *Iran,* 208; Simpson, *Behind Iranian Lines,* 33; *Los Angeles Times,* January 29, 1979, I:8.

30. U.S. embassy memorandum of December 10, 1978, in National Security Archive, *Iran,* document 1900; *Ayandegan,* January 20, 1979, 2. On troops being ordered back to barracks, see *Hambastegi,* December 24, 1978, 2; Hiro, *Iran under the Ayatollahs,* 84; Huyser, *Mission to Tehran,* 111; *Los Angeles Times,* December 19, 1978, I:22; Nikazmerad, "A Chronological Survey," 342. Respondent 98, a professional soldier from Tehran, interviewed by the author in Istanbul, Turkey, February 23, 1990. On soldiers' joining

protests see Balta and Rulleau, *L'Iran Insurge,* 59–60; Respondent 94, a conscript from Tehran, interviewed by the author in Istanbul, Turkey, February 21, 1990.

31. General Gholam-Reza Azhari, quoted in Farmanfarmaian, *Blood and Oil,* 448. Generals Oveissi and Khal'atbari, memorandum of December 6, 1978, in *Faraz'ha'i,* 266–267. On fear of Soviet incursion see the statements of various generals at the Crisis Meeting of January 15, 1979, in Sadiqi, *Mesl-e Barf,* 118–121. On Mashhad see *New York Times,* January 4, 1979, A10; see also Reid, Associated Press Wire Service, January 4, 1979. *Kayhan,* February 8, 1979, 1; *Ayandegan,* February 10, 1979, 1.

32. See Bauer, "Demographic Change," 175. Bank official from Tehran, Respondent 59, interviewed by the author in Istanbul, Turkey, December 3, 1989. High school student from Isfahan, Respondent 32, interviewed by the author in Istanbul, Turkey, November 13, 1989. Oil workers in Abadan, in *Le Monde,* November 16, 1978, 1, translated in *MERIP Report,* March–April 1979, 18.

33. Hegland, "Two Images of Husain," 233–234.

34. Shoja'i, interviewed in Shirkhani, *Hamaseh-ye 19 Dey,* 97. 'Ali Tehrani, speech of July 24, 1978, in *Pareh'i az E'lamiyeh'ha,* 26; Shari'atzadeh, *Az Fayziyeh ta Jomhuri-ye Eslami,* 23. For the joke about Rasht see Harney, *The Priest and the King,* 85.

35. Sreberny-Mohammadi and Mohammadi, *Small Media, Big Revolution,* 121.

36. Braswell, "A Mosaic of Mullahs and Mosques," 214, 46, 99–106; Thaiss, "Religious Symbolism and Social Change"; Baktash, "Ta'ziyeh and Its Philosophy," 96.

37. 'Ali-Asghar Hajj-Seyyed-Javadi, open letter of December 7, 1978, in Hajj-Seyyed-Javadi, *Daftar'ha-ye Enqelab,* 326. Daneshvar, *Revolution in Iran,* 111, 210.

38. Semkus, *The Fall of Iran,* vol. 2, 371–372.

39. Shiraz: *MERIP Report,* March–April 1979, 16. Shahrak: Dowlat, Hourcade, and Puech, "Les Paysans et la Révolution Iranienne," 31.

40. Ginger, *Nouvelles Lettres Persanes,* 224.

41. Ruhollah Khomeini, pronouncement of November 23, 1978, in Khomeini, *Islam and Revolution,* 242; the U.S. embassy reported (memorandum of December 1, 1978, in National Security Archive, *Iran,* document 1836) that Khomeini called for demonstrators to wear white, be ready to die for the cause, and let "torrents of blood" be spilled on 'Ashura, but I have been unable to find a statement of Khomeini's that goes this far. Mohammad Beheshti, speech of February 8, 1980, in *Kayhan,* January 13, 1983; quoted in *Yaran-e Emam,* vol. 3, 328. On the Revolutionary Council

see Mohammad Beheshti, in *Jomhuri-ye Eslami,* February 24, 1980, 3; Bazargan, *Showra-ye Enqelab,* 25–26; Hashemi-Rafsanjani, *Dowran-e Mobarezeh,* vol. 1, 361–362. Pronouncement of the religious scholars of Tehran, circa December 8, 1978, in Davani, *Nehzat-e Ruhaniyun,* vol. 9, 42. Badamchiyan, *Shenakht-e Enqelab-e Eslami,* 151. On the agreement with the government see U.S. embassy memorandum of December 8, 1978, in National Security Archive, *Iran,* document 1881; Delannoy (*SAVAK,* 215–216) says that the Islamists negotiated directly with the government, but he gives no source for this information.

42. Afrasiyabi and Dehqan, *Taleqani va Tarikh,* 362; Sanjabi, *Omid'ha va Na-Omidi'ha,* 303; SAVAK memorandum of December 9, 1978, in *Faraz'ha'i,* 269. Green, *Revolution in Iran,* 128. On shrouds see Harney, *The Priest and the King,* 89; military memorandum of December 6, 1978, in *Faraz'ha'i,* 265. On cars see *Los Angeles Times,* December 10, 1978, I:1; Harney, *The Priest and the King,* 113.

43. Golabdareh'i, *Lahzeh'ha,* 54, 58–59.

44. Hegland, "Imam Khomaini's Village," 683. On medical personnel see SAVAK memoranda of December 14 and 18, 1978, in *Yaran-e Emam,* vol. 3, 347 and 379. *Pishtazan-e Enqelab,* 173. Woman in Shiraz, quoted in Hegland, "Islamic Revival," 213. Mostafa Askari interviewed in Hegland, "Imam Khomaini's Village," 879.

45. Balta and Rulleau, *L'Iran Insurge,* 58. Parsons, *The Pride and the Fall,* 110. For opposition estimates see *Hambastegi,* December 12, 1978, 1, 3; and *Khabar-Nameh,* December 12, 1978, 1–4.

46. Bahrampour, *To See and See Again,* 103. Bazaari in Shiraz, quoted in Betteridge, "To Veil or Not to Veil," 127.

47. Hegland, "Two Images of Husain," 232; see also Hegland, "Ritual and Revolution in Iran," 92–94.

48. Braswell, "A Mosaic of Mullahs and Mosques," 99–105; Goodell, *The Elementary Structures of Political Life,* 121–122, 287–294; Good and Good, "Ritual, the State, and the Transformation of Emotional Discourse," 51; Chelkowski, *Ta'ziyeh.* On police monitoring see Braswell, "A Mosaic of Mullahs and Mosques," 214–215. Beeman, "A Full Arena," 366–367; see also a military memorandum of December 6, 1978, in *Faraz'ha'i,* 264–265. Balta and Rulleau, *L'Iran Insurge,* 58.

49. Golabdareh'i, *Lahzeh'ha,* 67.

50. *Hambastegi,* December 12, 1978, 3.

51. *Los Angeles Times,* December 12, 1978, I:1. Hasan Musavi-Tabrizi, interviewed in Shirkhani, *Hamaseh-ye 17 Khordad,* 205.

52. Brière and Blanchet, *Iran,* 105–106.

53. Hashemi-Rafsanjani, *Dowran-e Mobarezeh,* vol. 1, 362. On American agents see Khalili, *Gam beh Gam,* 128. *Khandani'ha,* December 9, 1978, translated by *Joint Publications Research Service,* February 8, 1979, fiche 72787, 17. 'Ali-Asghar Hajj-Seyyed-Javadi, open letter of January 22, 1978, in Hajj-Seyyed-Javadi, *Daftar'ha-ye Enqelab,* 436–450. *Ayandegan,* February 6, 1979, 12. On civil rights activists see Goodwin and Pfaff, "Emotion Work in High-Risk Social Movements."

7. A Viable Movement

1. Askari, interviewed in Hegland, "Imam Khomaini's Village," 879, 877–878.
2. Brière and Blanchet, *Iran,* 105.
3. Army conscript, Respondent 11, interviewed October 26, 1989. Unemployed former conscript, Respondent 46, interviewed November 22, 1989. Telephone official, Respondent 48, interviewed November 22, 1989. Truck driver, Respondent 49, interviewed November 23, 1989. Shopowner from Shiraz, Respondent 52, interviewed November 27, 1989. Government official from Gombad, Respondent 58, interviewed December 1, 1989. Shopowner from Tehran, Respondent 62, interviewed December 4, 1989. High school student from Lorestan, Respondent 67, interviewed December 7, 1989. Auto mechanic, Respondent 77, interviewed December 20, 1989. All interviews conducted in Istanbul, Turkey.
4. Faramarz, interviewed in Qazvin, October 1979, by Vieille and Khosrokhavar, *Le Discours Populaire de la Révolution Iranienne,* vol. 2, 156. Hasan K., interviewed in Tehran, December 1979, by Vieille and Khosrokhavar, *Le Discours Populaire de la Révolution Iranienne,* vol. 2, 248. Anonymous demonstrator, Khosrokhavar, *Anthropologie de la Révolution Iranienne,* 159. Worker at cement factory, Moradi, interviewed near Isfahan, February 20, 1979, by Boroumand, "Les Ouvriers, l'Ingénieur et les Militantes Khomeinistes," 63; also in Vieille and Khosrokhavar, *Le Discours Populaire de la Révolution Iranienne,* vol. 2, 7. Author from Karaj, Golabdareh'i, *Lahzeh'ha,* 53.
5. U.S. embassy memorandum of October 16, 1978, in National Security Archive, *Iran,* document 1594.
6. University professor from Tehran, Maryam Shamlu, former head of the Women's Organization of Iran, interviewed by Mahnaz Afkhami in Washington, D.C., May 1983, Foundation for Iranian Studies, 24. Foreign businessman, Harney, *The Priest and the King,* 34. Royal adviser, Mas'ud-Ansari, *Man va Khandan-e Pahlavi,* 114. Lawyer, Amir, interviewed in Saint-James,

Au Nom de Dieu, 191. Iranian bishop, Dehqani-Tafti, *The Hard Awakening,* 11.

7. Brière and Blanchet, *Iran,* 46.

8. Heravi-Khorasani, *Tarikh-e Peydayesh-e Mashrutiyat-e Iran,* 49.

9. John B. Jackson, U.S. minister in Tehan, to Secretary of State, January 15, 1908, in United States National Archives and Record Administration, Record Group 59, Numerical and Minor Files, M862, Roll 483, Case 5931.

10. Barrows, *Distorting Mirrors,* 137–161; McClelland, *The Crowd and the Mob,* 197; Nye, *The Origins of Crowd Psychology,* 66–67, 71–72.

11. Sighele, "Contre le Parlementarisme," 211, 213.

12. Barrows, *Distorting Mirrors,* 145. Le Bon, *The Crowd,* 52.

13. McPhail, *The Myth of the Madding Crowd,* 1–60. Hochschild, "Memorium for Herbert Blumer," ii. Blumer, "Collective Behavior," 224, 236. Canetti, *Crowds and Power,* 75–90. Arendt, *On Revolution,* 42–43.

14. Turner and Killian, *Collective Behavior,* 1st ed., 16–17, 58; 2nd ed., 3, 9, 12; see also Couch, "Collective Behavior: An Examination of Some Stereotypes"; McPhail, *The Myth of the Madding Crowd,* 61–232. McCarthy, "Foreword," xviii. On radicals' entering academia, see Jacoby, *The Last Intellectuals.*

15. Marwell and Oliver, *The Critical Mass in Collective Action,* 11.

16. Olson, *The Logic of Collective Action.*

17. On the benefits of protesting see Tullock, "The Paradox of Revolution"; Macy, "Learning Theory and the Logic of Critical Mass"; Zolberg, "Moments of Madness," 202–203; Opp, *The Rationality of Political Protest,* 68, in which seventeen of twenty normative, attitudinal, and ideological variables have significant positive effects on protest participation. Olson, "The Logic of Collective Action in Soviet-Type Societies," 18; in the early 1970s, Tullock ("The Paradox of Revolution," 92) also introduced the possibility of the entertainment value of protest participation, but only to belittle the student movements of the period, which he scorned as "pseudo-revolutionary." Lichbach, *The Rebel's Dilemma,* pt. 2. On private preferences see Kuran, *Private Truths, Public Lies,* 17. On hidden transcripts see Scott, *Domination and the Arts of Resistance,* 4–5. On thresholds see Granovetter, "Threshold Models of Collective Behavior"; Granovetter and Soong, "Threshold Models of Diffusion and Collective Behavior." Schelling, "Hockey Helmets, Concealed Weapons, and Daylight Saving."

18. On elections see Mutz, *Impersonal Influence,* 179–196. Klandermans, "Mobilization and Participation," 592–596. Opp, "Community Integration and Incentives for Political Protest." Opp, Voss, and Gern, *Origins of a Spontaneous Revolution,* 196–202. For a historical study of this phenomenon, see Biggs, "Positive Feedback in Collective Mobilization."

19. On Barzargan see Chapter 1 and SAVAK memorandum of September 1978, in *Faraz'ha'i,* 120. Unidentified twenty-seven-year-old leftist woman, interviewed in Tehran, Iran, September 1978, by Bani, *Fatima Statt Farah,* 41; see also Tilgner, *Umbruch im Iran,* 122. On the feeling that "all is possible" see Zolberg, "Moments of Madness," 183. *Ayandegan,* February 8, 1979, 6.

20. Slovic, "The Construction of Preference."

21. SAVAK memorandum of November 27, 1978, in *Faraz'ha'i,* 296.

22. Benard and Khalilzad, *"The Government of God,"* 235; Chubin, "The United States and Iran's Revolution"; Razi, "The Nexus of Legitimacy and Performance." On the United States see Orren, "Fall from Grace: The Public's Loss of Faith in Government," 81–82.

23. For an attempt to theorize understanding in the context of social movements, see Vahabzadeh, *Articulated Experiences.* My approach to understanding, described in Chapter 8, does not limit its applicability to "new" or "anti-hegemonic" movements, as Vahabzadeh's does.

24. Bateson, "'This Figure of Tinsel.'" Beeman, *Language, Status, and Power in Iran.* Shayegan, "The Formative Rhythm of Persian Space." Respondent 31, a devout young shopowner from Tehran, interviewed by the author in Istanbul, Turkey, November 8, 1989. For a cautionary note on cultural generalizations see Banuazizi, "Iranian 'National Character.'"

25. Bill, "The Plasticity of Informal Politics," 145.

26. Plan Organization bureaucrat interviewed by Sarraf, *The Cry of a Nation,* 3. Fischer and Abedi, *Debating Muslims,* 87. Kordi, *An Iranian Odyssey,* 126.

27. Fischer and Abedi, *Debating Muslims,* 491.

28. Richard Cottam, testimony of July 24, 1973, in U.S. House of Representatives, *New Perspectives,* 137; see also Kapuscinski, *Shah of Shahs,* 43–51; Lebaschi, Harvard Iranian Oral History Collection, tape 3, 18, quoted in Parsa, *States, Ideologies, and Social Revolutions,* 207.

29. A strike leader at a tractor plant, interviewed by Bayat, *Workers and Revolution in Iran,* 91.

30. Hegland, "Islamic Revival," 214.

31. Mostafa Askari, interviewed in Hegland, "Imam Khomaini's Village," 882.

32. *Kayhan,* February 6, 1979, translated in Nodjomi, "Dictatorship and Rise of Popular Movement," 166–167.

33. *Ayandegan,* January 10, 1979, translated in Nodjomi, "Dictatorship and Rise of Popular Movement," 165–166.

34. Mohammad Shanehchi, interviewed by Habib Ladjevardi in Paris, France, March 4, 1983, Harvard Iranian Oral History Collection, tape 3, 18.

35. Khorsandi, *The Ayatollah and I,* 106.

36. Hosein Khaz'ali, in Khalkhali, *Shohada-ye Ruhaniyat,* vol. 2, 106; a variant appears in *Zamimeh-e Khabar-Nameh,* July–August 1978, 65.

37. *The Observer* (London), December 31, 1989, 7. *San Francisco Chronicle,* June 27, 1990, Briefing Section, 1.

38. Otto C. Doelling, Associated Press Wire Service, January 31, 1979. Ruhollah Khomeini, interviewed in Najaf, Iraq, September 21, 1978, by French television reporter Maurice Séveno, *Le Monde,* October 17, 1978, 5, translated in Nobari, *Iran Erupts,* 20.

39. On Hippi-Abad see Hourcade, "L'Homme Vertical," 66.

40. Jasper, *The Art of Moral Protest,* 362. A prominent academic and government researcher, interviewed in Tehran, Iran, November 23, 1978, by Green, *Revolution in Iran,* 87. Bank employee S. Jehanfer, interviewed by Sarraf, *The Cry of a Nation,* 16.

41. *New York Times,* November 19, 1978, 20.

42. Mehdi Bazargan, quoted in SAVAK memorandum of September 1978, in *Faraz'ha'i,* 119. Eslam Kazemieh, interviewed by Shirin Sami'i in Paris, France, October 31, 1983, and May 8, 1984, Foundation for Iranian Studies, 32. On the need to consult Khomeini see Bahramian, *Renasans dar Iran,* 109.

43. U.S. embassy memorandum of November 5, 1978, in National Security Archive, *Iran,* document 1685. U.S. embassy memorandum of December 8, 1978, in National Security Archive, *Iran,* document 1882.

44. Ahmad Madani, interviewed by Zia Sedghi in Paris, France, April 2, 1984, Harvard Iranian Oral History Collection, tape 2, 14. Shanehchi, Harvard Iranian Oral History Collection, tape 4, 5–6.

45. Lebaschi, Harvard Iranian Oral History Collection, tape 3, 11.

46. U.S. embassy memorandum of December 13, 1978, in National Security Archive, *Iran,* document 1913; Professor Richard W. Cottam corrected the diplomats several weeks later, in a meeting on January 1, 1979 (U.S. embassy memorandum of January 2, 1979, in National Security Archive, *Iran,* document 2002).

47. On the National Front see Siavoshi, *Liberal Nationalism in Iran,* 152; Sanjabi, *Omid'ha va Na-Omidi'ha,* 303; Shamlu, Foundation for Iranian Studies, 23. On slogans see Bazargan, *Enqelab-e Iran,* 37–38; Milani, *The Making of Iran's Islamic Revolution,* 124. On Islamists see Badamchiyan, *Shenakht-e Enqelab-e Eslami,* 150. On posters see Hajj-Seyyed-Javadi, Harvard Iranian Oral History Collection, tape 5, 11–12; Madani, Harvard Iranian Oral History Collection, tape 3, 2; Sanjabi, *Omid'ha va Na-Omidi'ha,* 304. Lahidji, Harvard Iranian Oral History Collection, tape 5, 5–6.

48. Charles W. Naas, U.S. diplomat in Tehran during the revolution, interviewed on April 23, 2000, by Daugherty, *In the Shadow of the Ayatollah,* 69. Sullivan, *Mission to Iran,* 200, 236. On the CIA see Woodward, *Veil,* 101;

CIA report of December 21, 1978, quoted in Donovan, "National Intelligence and the Iranian Revolution," 158.

49. Menashri, *Iran,* 80.

50. Moghadam, "Socialism or Anti-Imperialism? The Left and Revolution in Iran," 16. On the People's Strugglers see Abrahamian, *The Iranian Mojahedin,* 171; Kian-Thiébault, *Secularization of Iran,* 179; Radjavi, *La Révolution Iranienne et les Moudjahedines,* 160; Behrooz, *Rebels with a Cause,* 73; Mojahedin-e Khalq-e Iran, *Barresi-ye Mohemtarin Tahavolat-e Siyasi,* 11. On the People's Sacrificing Guerrillas see Alireza Mahfoozi, interviewed by Zia Sedghi in Paris, France, April 7, 1984, Harvard Iranian Oral History Collection, tape 1, 8, 16; anonymous Feda'i member, interviewed in New York on June 17 and 23, 1988, by Mirsepassi and Moghadam, "The Left and Political Islam in Iran," 34; Farrokh Negahdar, a Feda'i leader, interviewed by Parsa, *States, Ideologies, and Social Revolutions,* 246; Behrooz, *Rebels with a Cause,* 59, 68; Cherik'ha-ye Feda'i-ye Khalq-e Iran, *Gozareshati az Mobarezat-e Daliraneh-ye Mardom-e Kharej az Mahdudeh;* Cherik'ha-ye Feda'i-ye Khalq-e Iran, *Gerami Bad 19 Bahman;* untitled pronouncement of September 29, 1978, in the collection of the Centre Iranien de Documentation et des Recherches, Paris, France; Cherik'ha-ye Feda'i-ye Khalq-e Iran, *E'lamiyeh'ha va Bayaniyeh'ha.* On the Masses Party see Hezb-e Tudeh-ye Iran, *Zendeh Bad Jonbesh-e Tudeh;* Hezb-e Tudeh-ye Iran, *Javedan Bad Khatereh;* Ekteshafi, *Khaterat-e Sargard-e Havayi Parviz Ekteshafi,* 385–386; Posadas, *The Permanent Process of Revolution in Iran,* 24; Kuzichkin, *Inside the KGB,* 204, 264; U.S. Central Intelligence Agency, "Soviet Involvement in the Iranian Crisis," February 12, 1979, 8–10, in *Declassified Document Reference System,* document 1986:2499.

51. Hegland, "Islamic Revival," 206. Afrasiyabi and Dehqan, *Taleqani va Tarikh,* 339–355. *Ettela'at,* February 10, 1979, 2; Abrahamian, *The Iranian Mojahedin,* 171–172; Behrooz, *Rebels with a Cause,* 68.

52. On clashes see *Ettela'at,* September 16, 1978, 4; Parsa, *States, Ideologies, and Social Revolutions,* 104. Mehdi 'Eraqi, SAVAK memorandum of January 8, 1979, in *Yaran-e Emam,* vol. 12, 389. On Khomeini see Abbas Amir-Entezam, quoted in U.S. embassy memorandum of January 17, 1979, in National Security Archive, *Iran,* document 2116. On leftists see U.S. State Department memorandum of January 20, 1979, in National Security Archive, *Iran,* document 2138. Ruhollah Khomeini, pronouncement of January 17, 1979, in Davani, *Nehzat-e Ruhaniyun,* vol. 9, 132; in October 1976 Khomeini called Muslim leftists "deviationists from the Shi'i religion . . . whom I consider treasonous to the country and Islam and religion" (Khomeini, *Majmu'eh'i,* 249). *Ayandegan,* January 20, 1979, 2. *Los Angeles*

Times, January 21, 1979, I:1. *Kayhan,* January 22, 1979, 1; Sreberny-Mohammadi and Mohammadi, *Small Media, Big Revolution,* 160. On Khomeini's delegation see Bazargan, *Enqelab-e Iran,* 66–67; Hojjat al-Islam Mohammad Javad Bahonar's autobiographical account, published in *Pishtazan-e Shahadat,* 56, and in *Shahid Doktor Bahonar,* 14; Bayat, *Workers and Revolution in Iran,* 95–96; Strike Committee documents in *Asnad-e Nehzat-e Azadi,* vol. 9, pt. 3, 64, 79–132, and in Tilgner, *Umbruch im Iran,* 42–44.

53. *Ayandegan,* February 10, 1979, 8.

54. Enrollment figures from 1977 in UNESCO, *Statistical Yearbook 1980,* 456 and 344. Chronology in *Kaavoshgar,* 1987, number 1, 96–102; 1988, number 2, 67–71; 1989, number 3, 58–67; see also Baqi, *Jonbesh-e Daneshjuyi-ye Iran,* 308–326. On martyrs see Amra'i, "Barresi-ye Moqe'iyat-e Ejtema'i-ye Shohada," 172; university students may have been undercounted in this source—if their families lived outside of Tehran, they may not have been registered as martyrs in the Tehran records to which Amra'i had access, as he notes (p. 23). Parsa, *States, Ideologies, and Social Revolutions,* 94–107.

55. Brière and Blanchet, *Iran,* 75–76; Interior Ministry and SAVAK telegrams, undated, in *Faraz'ha'i,* 205–208. On Tehran University see Kraft, "Letter from Iran," 144. On returning from exile see Matin-Asgari, *Iranian Student Opposition to the Shah,* 161.

56. Zarifian-Yeganeh, interviewed in Shirkhani, *Hamaseh-ye 19 Dey,* 228. On Khalkhali's later career see Bakhash, *The Reign of the Ayatollahs,* 59–63, 110–112. Beheshti quoted in SAVAK memorandum of December 14, 1978, in *Yaran-e Emam,* vol. 3, 362.

57. Parsons, *The Pride and the Fall,* 56; U.S. embassy memorandum of October 30, 1978, in National Security Archive, *Iran,* document 1630. On Shari'ati's popularity see Braswell, "A Mosaic of Mullahs and Mosques," 90–91; Rahnema, *An Islamic Utopian,* 265–266; Ebtekar, *Takeover in Tehran,* 49. Shari'ati, "Where Shall We Begin?" 21. On Shari'ati's popularity in the seminaries see Hossein Musavi-Tabrizi and Vafi, interviewed in Shirkhani, *Hamaseh-ye 19 Dey,* 168, 181, 195; SAVAK report of March 14, 1978, in *SAVAK va Ruhaniyat,* 227; Clerics of the Seminary Circle of Qom, open letters of March 19, 1975, and June 19, 1976, in *Asnad-e Enqelab-e Eslami,* vol. 4, 281 and 320; Mottahedeh, *The Mantle of the Prophet,* 16; Rahnema, *An Islamic Utopian,* 336–337. On Motahhari and Khomeini see Rahnema, *An Islamic Utopian,* 274–275, 354; Motahhari, *Ostad Motahhari va Rowshanfekran,* 34–70; letter of Morteza Motahhari to Ruhollah Khomeini, 1977, in *Asnad-e Enqelab-e Eslami,* vol. 2, 218–225; Morteza Motahhari and Mehdi Bazargan, open letter of December 14, 1977, in *Asnad-e Enqelab-e*

Eslami, vol. 2, 216–217. On Shiraz see SAVAK memorandum of July 28, 1977, in *Yaran-e Emam,* vol. 20, 367. For vilifications of Shariʻati see open letters of September 1977–June 1978, in *Asnad-e Enqelab-e Eslami,* vol. 1, 458, 480–481; vol. 2, 210–211, 214–217, 250. For praise of Shariʻati see Sadeq Khalkhali and ʻAli Tehrani, open letter of June 17, 1978, in *Asnad-e Enqelab-e Eslami,* vol. 2, 274; see also the open letters by the Seminary Circle of Qom, November 1977 and March 1978, in *Asnad-e Enqelab-e Eslami,* vol. 4, 363 and 457. Khomeini speech of October 31, 1978, in Khomeini, *Neda-ye Haqq,* 265; and in *Sahifeh-ye Nur,* vol. 2, 250.

58. Moghadam, "Gender and Revolution."

59. Of the women who did speak in the presence of their husbands, several chided their spouses for not giving enough credit to the Islamists; since further discussion was not possible, I do not know whether they made these comments out of fear of repression by the Islamists, ideological commitment to Islamism, or a desire to set the historical record straight. For similar difficulties see Haeri, *The Law of Desire,* 16–17; Loeffler, *Islam in Practice,* 6.

60. Paidar, *Women and the Political Process in Twentieth-Century Iran,* 218. Ruhollah Khomeini, pronouncement of January 22, 1978, in Davani, *Nehzat-e Ruhaniyun,* vol. 7, 49. Raʻna, village woman quoted in Hegland, "Aliabad Women: Revolution as Religious Activity," 185. SAVAK memorandum of December 3, 1978, in *Yaran-e Emam,* vol. 5, 823. Mahallati, *Khaterat va Mobarezat,* 112.

61. Afkhami, "Iran," 331–332; Sanasarian, *The Women's Rights Movement in Iran,* 80–81. On the cabinet shift see Menashri, *Iran,* 41; Paidar, *Women and the Political Process in Twentieth-Century Iran,* 194; Poya, *Women, Work, and Islamism,* 52–53. *Zan-e Ruz,* October 7, 1978, 7. On Women's Organization members' marching, see Afkhami, "Iran," 335. Anonymous Women's Organization official, quoted in Sanasarian, *The Women's Rights Movement in Iran,* 117; see also Sullivan, *Obbligato,* 270–271.

62. Betteridge, "To Veil or Not to Veil," 110. For *hejab* as a symbolic statement see Azari, "Islam's Appeal to Women in Iran," 67; Betteridge, "To Veil or Not to Veil," 121–123; Khosrokhavar, "Les Femmes et la Révolution Islamique," 88.

63. On rumors of acid see Bauer, "Poor Women and Social Consciousness in Revolutionary Iran," 159. *Ayandegan,* January 22, 1979, 12. Women without *hejab* were sometimes pelted with snowballs or eggs in earlier years—see Baqi, *Jonbesh-e Daneshjuyi-ye Iran,* 248–249; Shahidian, *Women in Iran,* 108.

64. Ziba Mir-Hosseini, *Islam and Gender: The Religious Debate in Contemporary Iran.*

65. Cohler-Esses, "Iranian Jewry's Agent of Influence." Ruhollah Khomeini, "Islamic Government," lectures of January–February 1970, in Khomeini, *Islam and Revolution,* 27.

66. Farazmand, *The State, Bureaucracy, and Revolution in Modern Iran,* 172. Respondent 64, an office worker from Tehran, interviewed by the author in Istanbul, Turkey, December 5, 1989; *New York Times,* November 10, 1978, A11.

67. *New York Times,* February 2, 1979, A9.

68. Respondent 62, a clothing shopowner from Tehran, interviewed by the author in Istanbul, Turkey, December 4, 1989. On Yazd see Khalkhali, *Shohada-ye Ruhaniyat,* vol. 2, 582. On the architect's office see Bahrampour, *To See and See Again,* 115; see also Behnam, *Zelzelah,* 209. The format of the "Words of the People" column in *Ayandegan* was open to abuse, since there was no way to identify callers—several times, the column ran denials from people whose names had been published in previous columns. *Ayandegan,* January 24, 1979, 12.

69. *Ayandegan,* January 31, 1979, 12.

70. *Ayandegan,* January 17, 1979, 12; February 1, 1979, 12.

71. U.S. embassy memorandum of August 17, 1978, in National Security Archive, *Iran,* document 1474; U.S. consul in Shiraz, memorandum of September 23, 1978, in National Security Archive, *Iran,* document 1542. Respondents interviewed by the author in Istanbul, Turkey: student from Borujerd, Respondent 22, interviewed November 5, 1989; young man from Tehran, Respondent 66, interviewed December 7, 1989; shopowner from Mashhad, Respondent 43, interviewed November 20, 1989.

72. Bazargan, *Enqelab-e Iran,* 57–58. Baqi, *Tahrir-e Tarikh-e Shafahi,* 359–360; Sanjabi, *Omid'ha va Na-Omidi'ha,* 308–309; Varjavand, *Yad-nameh-ye Doktor Gholam-Hossein Sadiqi,* 193–221; 'Abdolrahim Borumand, interviewed by Zia Sedghi in Paris, France, June 3, 1985, Harvard Iranian Oral History Collection, transcript of tape 3, 12–13; Borumand also says that the head of SAVAK visited Sanjabi in prison in November, which Sanjabi denies in one interview (Sanjabi, *Omid'ha va Na-Omidi'ha,* 306) and confirms in another (Baqi, *Tahrir-e Tarikh-e Shafahi,* 359).

73. For an overview of state violence see Parsa, *Social Origins,* 226–228. For particular cities see Ja'far Askari, interviewed by Hegland, "Imam Khomaini's Village," 875–876 (on Shiraz); Semkus, *The Fall of Iran,* vol. 2, 410–412, and *New York Times,* December 13, 1978, A1, A11 (on Isfahan); Shakeri, *Enqelab-e Eslami-ye Mardom-e Mashhad,* 109, and U.S. embassy memorandum of December 17, 1978, in National Security Archive, *Iran,* document 1933 (on Mashhad); *Los Angeles Times,* December 28, 1978, I:10 (on Teh-

ran); *New York Times,* January 18, 1979, A1, A15, and *Los Angeles Times,* January 18, 1979, I:1, 14 (on Ahwaz). On collective defenses see Ashraf and Banuazizi, "The State, Classes, and Modes of Mobilization," 15–16; *Kayhan,* January 31, 1979, cited in Nodjomi, "Dictatorship and Rise of Popular Movement," 165. On Isfahan see U.S. embassy memorandum of August 2, 1978, in National Security Archive, *Iran,* document 1460. On Amol see Brière and Blanchet, *Iran,* 75–76; Interior Ministry and SAVAK telegrams, undated, in *Faraz'ha'i,* 205–208.

74. Khosrokhavar, "Le Comité dans la Révolution Iranienne," 88–89; SAVAK memoranda of January 1 and 2, 1979, in *Yaran-e Emam,* vol. 4, 599–600. On police see U.S. embassy memorandum of January 29, 1979, in National Security Archive, *Iran,* document 2192; daily reports on Islamic police forces in the Tehran press, mid-January 1979; Semkus, *The Fall of Iran,* vol. 2, 667 (on Isfahan); Huyser, *Mission to Tehran,* 162–163 (on Qom); U.S. embassy memoranda of January 11 and 14, 1979, in National Security Archive, *Iran,* documents 2061 and 2089 (on several cities); in Shiraz and Isfahan the "Islamic police" retreated after several days, according to a U.S. embassy memorandum of January 21, 1979, in National Security Archive, *Iran,* document 2143. On cooperative stores see *Ayandegan,* January 10, 1979, 12; January 15, 1979, 5, 10.

75. On PLO training see Bakhash, *The Reign of the Ayatollahs,* 63; Hiro, *Iran under the Ayatollahs,* 377; Farsi, *Zavaya-ye Tarik,* 445; Khalkhali, *Shohada-ye Ruhaniyat,* vol. 1, 146. On underground cells see Shoja'i, interviewed in Shirkhani, *Hamaseh-ye 19 Dey,* 87; Gruh-e Tahqiq, *Taqvim-e Tarikh-e Enqelab,* 19–20. SAVAK memorandum of February 18, 1978, in *Yaran-e Emam,* vol. 3, 319. Chants: Balta and Rulleau, *L'Iran Insurge,* 89; *New York Times,* January 29, 1979, A6. SAVAK memoranda on Mehdi 'Eraqi, August 1978–January 1979, in *Yaran-e Emam,* vol. 12. In January 1979, Ayatollah Beheshti denied that the clerical movement had any involvement with recent guerrilla attacks (Bahramian, *Renasans dar Iran,* 123).

76. Hashemi-Rafsanjani, *Dowran-e Mobarezeh,* vol. 1, 300. On Madani see SAVAK memorandum of November 21, 1978, in *Yaran-e Emam,* vol. 4, 592. Various Tehran newspapers, January 8, 1979; U.S. embassy memorandum of January 8, 1979, in National Security Archive, *Iran,* document 2025. Mohammad Montazeri, in *Farzand-e Islam,* vol. 1, 175–176; on Montazeri's nickname see Fischer, *Iran,* 87; Zabih, *The Iranian Military,* 113. Ruhollah Khomeini quoted in *Le Monde,* February 4, 1979, 1; rumors were rife that the monarchy had called upon Israeli troops to commit the worst atrocities of the revolution. SAVAK memorandum of February 8, 1979, in *Yaran-e Emam,* vol. 12, 395–396.

77. CIA memorandum of November 20, 1978, in National Security Archive, *Iran*, document 1778. Unnamed Iranian quoted in Algar, *The Roots of the Islamic Revolution*, 54. I do not believe the statements of Bani-Sadr (*My Turn to Speak*, 1–2), the French-trained social scientist and later president of Iran, that Khomeini "did not think it possible to overthrow the Shah. Two or three times a week I reassured him by telling him that the Shah was going to relinquish power." See also Bani-Sadr's interview with Kamrava, *Revolution in Iran*, 38.

78. Huyser, *Mission to Tehran*, 19, 21, 18. On U.S. support see *New York Times*, November 7, 1978, 14; Brzezinski, *Power and Principle*, 364–365; Carter, *Keeping Faith*, 439; M. R. Pahlavi, *Answer to History*, 165. On riot-control equipment see Rubin, *Paved with Good Intentions*, 225; *Newsweek*, November 20, 1978, 43. On rejection of less supportive drafts see *U.S. News and World Report*, November 20, 1978, 43. Vance, *Hard Choices*, 332–333.

79. U.S. Department of State, memorandum of December 28, 1978, in National Security Archive, *Iran*, document 1972; the message concluded, it should be noted, with the judgment that "it will be impossible [for the shah] to restore his absolute power."

80. Huyser, *Mission to Tehran*, 45–46, 55–56, 61–62. Iranian government documents, in Yazdi, *Akharin Talash'ha*, 249–299; Copeland, *The Game Player*, 252. Huyser, *Mission to Tehran*, 283.

81. On negotiations with the military see Bazargan, *Enqelab-e Iran*, 70; Huyser, *Mission to Tehran*, 151, 199–200, 230; U.S. embassy memoranda of January 19 and 30, 1979, in National Security Archive, *Iran*, documents 2129 and 2201. On negotiations with Bakhtiar see Yazdi, *Akharin Talash'ha*, 137–159; Baqi, *Tahrir-e Tarikh-e Shafahi*, 419–428. On efforts to prevent a coup see Gharabaghi, *Vérités sur la Crise Iranienne*, 179–180; Sullivan, *Mission to Iran*, 244. Tehran activist Mahallati, *Khaterat va Mobarezat*, 95, 108. On Ayatollah Mohammad Beheshti's leadership of the Revolutionary Council see *Jomhuri-ye Eslami*, February 24, 1980, 3. On Beheshti's plans to meet the chief of staff see U.S. embassy memoranda of January 14, 1979 (twice), January 15, and January 30, in National Security Archive, *Iran*, documents 2083, 2087, 2094, 2201; Gharabaghi, *Vérités sur la Crise Iranienne*, 113–115; Huyser, *Mission to Tehran*, 109; Sullivan, *Mission to Iran*, 238; Yazdi, *Akharin Talash'ha*, 185. Huyser's memoir (page 210) suggests that Gharabaghi did meet with Beheshti on January 26; Gharabaghi (page 166) denies ever meeting Beheshti; the U.S. embassy memorandum of January 30 supports Gharabaghi's version: "This is [the] second time that Beheshti has in effect ducked face-to-face meeting with key military leaders." In Oc-

tober 1978, Beheshti also cancelled a meeting with the U.S. ambassador at the last minute (Bahramian, *Renasans dar Iran*, 96).

82. Mahallati, *Khaterat va Mobarezat*, 110. Bill, *The Eagle and the Lion*, photograph of Khomeini's helicopter between 316 and 317; Simpson, *Behind Iranian Lines*, 37. See Abbas, *Iran*, photograph 29, for a picture of Khomeini without his turban. On the diversion of the helicopter see Mahallati, *Khaterat va Mobarezat*, 111.

83. *Ettela'at*, February 10, 1979, 2.

84. *Ayandegan*, February 11, 1979, 2.

85. *Ettela'at*, February 10, 1979, 2.

86. Ibid. On Lenin see Pearson, *The Sealed Train*, 267.

87. Khomeini, *Islam and Revolution*, 261; this source gives a date of February 11, but contemporary accounts place the proclamation on February 10.

88. *Ettela'at*, February 10, 1979, 2; February 11, 1979, 8. In addition to newspaper accounts, see Baraheni, *Dar Enqelab-e Iran*, 123; Farmanfarmaian, *Blood and Oil*, 454; Grogan, *Insurrection in Tehran*, 6; Golabdareh'i, *Lahzeh'ha*, 327–332; Stempel, *Inside the Iranian Revolution*, 178–179; SAVAK memorandum of February 10, 1979, in *Faraz'ha'i*, 371 and 395; Simpson, *Behind Iranian Lines*, 43; Balta and Rulleau, *L'Iran Insurge*, 92; and Gharabaghi, *Vérités sur la Crise Iranienne*, 228. Karaj: Grogan, *Insurrection in Tehran*, 7. Hamadan: Khosrokhavar, "Le Comité dans la Révolution Iranienne," 91–92. Qazvin battalion: Gharabaghi, *Vérités sur la Crise Iranienne*, 224–225. Kermanshah troops: *Ettela'at*, February 11, 1979, 7.

89. *Ettela'at*, February 11, 1979, 7, 8; *Christian Science Monitor*, February 12, 1979, 13; Golabdareh'i, *Lahzeh'ha*, 326; and the vivid (and partly fictionalized) account in Follett, *On Wings of Eagles*, 275.

90. Balta and Rulleau, *L'Iran Insurge*, 92.

91. Gharabaghi, *Vérités sur la Crise Iranienne*, 221. Respondent 98, a soldier from Tehran, interviewed by the author in Istanbul, Turkey, February 23, 1990.

92. *Ettela'at*, February 11, 1979, 8; Simpson, *Behind Iranian Lines*, 43. On the declaration of neutrality see Gharabaghi, *Vérités sur la Crise Iranienne*, 207–249; Fardoust, *The Rise and Fall of [the] Pahlavi Dynasty*, 536–538.

93. Halliday, "The Iranian Revolution," 43, 60; Hirschfeld, "Decline and Fall of the Pahlavis," 133; interviewer Zia Sedghi in the oral history of naval officer Ahmad Madani, interviewed in Paris, France, April 2, 1984, Harvard Iranian Oral History Collection, tape 3, 8. The air force general Amir-Hossein Rabi'i was one of those who claimed to have helped Islamists; see

Ettela'at, April 10, 1979, 5. On officers who were reluctant to engage protesters see Siad-Shirazi, *Khaterat,* 75.

94. *Ettela'at,* February 11, 1979, 8; Stempel, *Inside the Iranian Revolution,* 179–180.

95. Simpson, *Behind Iranian Lines,* 41.

96. Baraheni, *Dar Enqelab-e Iran,* 122.

8. Conclusion

1. Farrokhfal, "Media and Modernity in Pre-Revolutionary Iran." On divided lives see Khosrokhavar, *L'Utopie Sacrifiée,* 191–201.

2. Eric Selbin makes a similar point with regard to the consolidation phase of revolutions (Selbin, *Modern Latin American Revolutions,* 27–31).

3. Holistic: Gouldner, *Against Fragmentation,* 284. Combinatorial: Tilly, "To Explain Political Processes." Conjunctural: Foran, "Theories of Revolution Revisited"; Goldstone, "Comparative Historical Analysis and Knowledge Accumulation in the Study of Revolutions," 80–82. Contextual: Rucht, "The Impact of National Contexts."

4. This section draws on Kurzman, "Can Understanding Undermine Explanation?"

5. Martin, *Verstehen,* 41–69. Marx and Engels, "The German Ideology," 62. Nisbett and Wilson, "Telling More Than We Can Know"; Wegner, *The Illusion of Conscious Will;* Wilson, *Strangers to Ourselves.* Bourdieu, "Understanding," 620.

6. Porter, *Trust in Numbers.* On lie-detector tests see Alder, "To Tell the Truth."

7. Polletta, "'It Was Like a Fever . . .': Narrative and Identity in Social Protest."

8. Giddens, *The Constitution of Society.*

9. Richardson, "Violence and Repression," 651–652.

10. Fardoust, *The Rise and Fall of [the] Pahlavi Dynasty,* 485.

About the Sources

1. Ruhollah Khomeini, pronouncement of July 27, 1978, in Davani, *Nehzat-e Ruhaniyun,* vol. 7, 199.

2. See *Zamimeh-ye Khabar-Nameh,* March–April 1978, 17; *Asnad va Tasaviri,* vol. 1, pt. 3, 28; and, in slightly different form, *Dar-bareh-ye Qiyam,* vol. 1, 44.

3. Saikal, *The Rise and Fall of the Shah,* xi–xii; Zabih, *Iran's Revolutionary Upheaval,* preface.

4. On the shift in terminology see Alidoost-Khaybari, "Religious Revolution-

aries," 442–444; Qasemi, *Nehzat-e Emam Khomeini va Matbu'at,* 118–124. Badii and Atwood, "How the Tehran Press Responded to the 1979 Iranian Revolution."

5. Dorman and Farhang, *The U.S. Press and Iran. New York Times,* December 4, 1978, A3.

6. Khomeini, *Sahifeh-ye Nur,* vol. 2, 1; *Dar-bareh-ye Qiyam,* vol. 1, 22; *Majmu'eh'i az Maktubat,* 284. Shirkhani's *Hamaseh-ye 19 Dey,* which presents myriad documents on the events of January 9, 1978, diplomatically leaves the date off Khomeini's message (p. 295), but none of the memoirs in the volume mentions an immediate response from Khomeini.

7. Khalkhali, *Shohada-ye Ruhaniyat-e Shi'a,* vol. 2, 147.

8. For the number of oral histories see *Yad,* Winter 1989, 40.

9. Hanaway, "Half-Voices," 60–61; Milani, *Tales of Two Cities,* 224–225; Zonis, "Autobiography and Biography," 60–63.

10. Saduqi tried to disperse: "Do Gozaresh," in *Dar-bareh-ye Qiyam,* vol. 3, 21. Documents omitted: *Yaran-e Emam,* vol. 2, 104–105.

11. SAVAK memorandum of December 12, 1978, in *Yaran-e Emam,* vol. 3, 350–355.

12. Urban population: World Bank, *World Development Report 1979,* 165. White-collar: Abrahamian, *Iran between Two Revolutions,* 431–435.

References

Documentary Collections

Asnad-e Enqelab-e Eslami (Documents from the Islamic Revolution). 1990–1996. 5 vols. Tehran: Merkez-e Asnad-e Enqelab-e Eslami.

Asnad-e Laneh-ye Jasusi (Documents from the Nest of Spies). 1980–1991. 77 vols. Tehran: Daneshjuyan-e Mosalman-e Payrow-e Khat-e Emam.

Asnad-e Nehzat-e Azadi: Safahati az Tarikh-e Mo'aser-e Iran (Documents from the Liberation Movement of Iran: Pages from the Contemporary History of Iran). 1982–1984. 11 vols. Tehran: Nehzat-e Azadi-ye Iran.

Asnad va Tasaviri az Mobarezat-e Khalq-e Mosalman-e Iran (Documents and Pictures from the Struggles of the Muslim People of Iran). 1978. Tehran: Abuzar. Reproduced in Behn, *Iranian Opposition to the Shah,* document 10:3.

Aya U Tasmim Darad Bi-Ayad beh Iran: Mozakerat-e Showra-ye Emniyet-e Melli, 9 va 13/7/1357 (Is He Deciding to Come to Iran?: Discussions of the National Security Council, October 1 and 5, 1978). 1997. Tehran: Merkez-e Asnad-e Enqelab-e Eslami.

Behn, Wolfgang. 1984. *Iranian Opposition to the Shah.* Zug, Switzerland: Inter Documentation Company.

Centre Iranien de Documentation et des Recherches (Iranian Center for Documentation and Research). Paris.

Dar-bareh-ye Qiyam-e Hamaseh-Afarinan-e Qom va Tabriz (On the Epic Uprising of Qom and Tabriz). 1978. 3 vols. Tehran: Nehzat-e Azadi-ye Iran.

Davani, 'Ali. [1981] 1998. *Nehzat-e Ruhaniyun-e Iran* (The Movement of the Clerics in Iran). 10 vols. Tehran: Bonyad-e Farhang-e Emam Reza.

Declassified Document Reference System. 1982–1999. Microfiche Collection. Woodbridge, Conn.: Research Publications.

Enqelab-e Eslami beh Ravayet-e Asnad-e SAVAK (The Islamic Revolution According to SAVAK Documents). 1997–2000. 7 vols. Tehran: Sorush and Merkez-e Barresi-ye Asnad-e Tarikhi-ye Vezarat-e Ettela'at.

Faraz'ha'i az Tarikh-e Enqelab beh Ravayet-e Asnad-e SAVAK va Amrika (High Points of the History of the Revolution According to the Documents of SAVAK and America). 1989. Tehran: Ravabet-e 'Omumi-ye Vezarat-e Ettela'at.

Foundation for Iranian Studies, Program of Oral History. 1981 to present. Unpublished transcripts. Bethesda, Md.: Foundation for Iranian Studies.

Harvard Iranian Oral History Collection. 1981 to present. Unpublished transcripts. Cambridge, Mass.: Harvard University Center for Middle Eastern Studies. Some transcripts available at *http://www.fas.harvard.edu/~iohp.*

James F. Hitselberger Collection, Archives of the Hoover Institution on War, Revolution, and Peace. Stanford University.

Khomeini, Ruhollah. 1979. *Neda-ye Haqq: Majmu'eh'i az Payam'ha, Mosahebeh'ha va Sokhanrani'ha-ye Emam Khomeini dar Paris* (The Voice of Truth: A Collection of the Messages, Interviews, and Speeches by Imam Khomeini in Paris). Solon, Ohio: Mimeo of the Muslim Student Societies in America, Europe, and Canada. Tehran: Entesharat-e Qalam.

———. 1981. *Islam and Revolution: Writings and Declarations of Imam Khomeini,* trans. Hamid Algar. Berkeley, Calif.: Mizan Press.

———. 1982. *Majmu'eh'i az Maktubat, Sokhanrani'ha, Payam'ha va Fatavi-ye Emam Khomeini* (A Collection of Letters, Speeches, Messages, and Opinions of Imam Khomeini), ed. M. Dehnavi. Tehran: Entesharat-e Chapkhass.

———. 1982. *Zamimeh-ye Majmu'eh'i az Maktubat, Sokhanrani'ha, Payam'ha va Fatavi-ye Emam Khomeini* (Supplement to a Collection of Letters, Speeches, Messages, and Opinions of Imam Khomeini), ed. M. Dehnavi. Tehran: Entesharat-e Chapkhass.

———. 1983–1990. *Sahifeh-ye Nur: Majmu'eh-ye Rahnamud'ha-ye Emam Khomeini* (The Book of Light: The Collection of Imam Khomeini's Guidance). 21 vols. Tehran: Merkez-e Madarek-e Farhangi-ye Enqelab-e Eslami.

Ma Gereftar-e Yek Jang-e Vaqe'i Ravani Shodeh-im: Mashruh-e Mozakerat-e Farmandehan-e Nazami dar Tarikh'ha-ye 24 va 30/5/1357 (We Are Engaged in a Real Psychological War: Transcript of the Discussions of the Military Commanders on August 15 and 21, 1978). 1997. Tehran: Merkez-e Asnad-e Enqelab-e Eslami.

National Security Archive. 1990. *Iran: The Making of U.S. Policy, 1977–1980,* ed. Eric J. Hooglund. Microfiche collection. Alexandria, Va.: Chadwyck-Healey.

———. Uncatalogued documents on Iran not included in *Iran: The Making of U.S. Policy.* Washington, D.C.

Pareh'i az E'lamiyeh'ha-ye Montashereh dar Iran dar Mah'ha-ye Tir va Mordad 1357 (Selected Pronouncements Published in Iran in the Months of July and August 1978). 1978. Willamette, Ill.: Organization of Iranian Moslem Students. Reproduced in Behn, *Iranian Opposition to the Shah,* document 20:121.

Ruz-Shomar-e Enqelab-e Eslami (Chronology of the Islamic Revolution). 1997–2000. 7 vols. Tehran: Howzeh-ye Honari-ye Daftar-e Adabiyat-e Enqelab-e Eslami.

Sadiqi, Habibollah. 1987. *Mesl-e Barf Ab Khahim Shod: Mozakerat-e "Showra-ye Farmandehan-e Artesh" (Dey-Bahman 1357)* (We Will Melt Like Snow: Discussions of the "Council of the Army Commanders" [January 1979]). 3rd ptg. Tehran: Nashr-e Ney.

Saduqi, Mahmud. 1983. *Majmu'eh-ye Ettela'iyeh'ha-ye Sevvomin Shahid-e Mehrab Hazrat Ayatollah Saduqi* (Collection of Pronouncements of the Third Holy Martyr, the Honorable Ayatollah Saduqi). Tehran: Vezarat-e Ershad-e Eslami.

SAVAK va Ruhaniyat: Buleten'ha-ye Nubeh-ye SAVAK az Tarikh-e 49/12/25 ta 57/ 6/30 (SAVAK and the Religious Scholars: Periodic SAVAK Bulletins from March 16, 1971, to September 19, 1978). 1992. Tehran: Howzeh-ye Honari-ye Sazman-e Tablighat-e Eslami; Daftar-e Adabiyat-e Enqelab-e Eslami; Merkez-e Asnad-e Vezarat-e Ettela'at.

Shahidi Digar az Ruhaniyat (Another Martyr from the Clergy). 1977. Najaf, Iraq: Ruhaniyat-e Mobarez-e Irani, Kharej az Keshvar, Najaf-e Ashraf.

Shirkhani, 'Ali. 1998. *Hamaseh-ye 17 Khordad 1354* (The Uprising of June 7, 1975). Tehran: Entesharat-e Merkez-e Asnad-e Enqelab-e Eslami.

———. 1998. *Hamaseh-ye 19 Dey* (The Uprising of January 9 [1978]). Tehran: Entesharat-e Merkez-e Asnad-e Enqelab-e Eslami.

———. 1999. *Hamaseh-ye 29 Bahman-e Tabriz* (The Tabriz Uprising of February 18 [1978]). Tehran: Entesharat-e Merkez-e Asnad-e Enqelab-e Eslami.

Tasmim-e Shum, Jom'e-ye Khunin: Mashruh-e Mozakerat-e Showra-ye Emniyet-e Melli va Hay'at-e Dowlat dar 16/6/1357 va Mashruh-e Mozakerat-e Showra-ye Emniyet-e Melli dar 18/6/1357 (The Ominous Decision, Bloody Friday: Details of the Discussion of the National Security Council and the Cabinet on September 7, 1978, and Details of the Discussion of the National Security Council on September 9, 1978). 1997. Tehran: Merkez-e Asnad-e Enqelab-e Eslami.

United States National Archives and Record Administration, Record Group 59 (Department of State). College Park, Md.

Yaran-e Emam beh Ravayet-e Asnad-e SAVAK (Friends of the Imam According to the Documents of SAVAK). 1998–2002. 29 vols. Tehran: Merkez-e Barresi-ye Asnad-e Tarikhi-ye Vezarat-e Ettela'at.

Zamimeh-ye Khabar-Nameh (Supplement to the Newsletter). 1977–1978. Tehran: Jebheh-ye Melli-ye Iran.

Periodicals

Associated Press Wire Service, New York, New York

Ayandegan (Future Generations), Tehran, Iran

Business Week, New York, New York

Corriere della Sera (Evening Courier), Milan, Italy

The Economist, London, England

Ettela'at (Information), Tehran, Iran

Euromoney, London, England

Far Eastern Economic Review, Hong Kong

Le Figaro (The Barber), Paris, France

Forbes, New York, New York

Hambastegi (Solidarity), Tehran, Iran

Iran-Emrooz (Iran Today), Mainz, Germany

Iranshahr, London, England

Joint Publications Research Service, Arlington, Virginia

Jomhuri-ye Eslami (Islamic Republic), Tehran, Iran

Kaavoshgar (Explorer, Journal of Iranian University Professors in Exile), New York, New York

Kayhan (The Globe), Tehran, Iran

Kayhan-e Hava'i (The Globe, Airmail Edition), Tehran, Iran

Kayhan International, Tehran, Iran

Khabar-Nameh (The Newsletter), Tehran, Iran

Khandani'ha (Things Worth Reading), Tehran, Iran

Los Angeles Times, Los Angeles, California

Maclean's, Toronto, Canada

MERIP Reports, Washington, D.C.

Middle East Economic Digest, London, England

Le Monde (The World), Paris, France

Newsweek, New York, New York

The New York Times, New York, New York

The New York Times Magazine, New York, New York

The Observer, London, England

Oil and Gas Journal, Tulsa, Oklahoma

Quarterly Economic Review: Iran, London, England

The Rise (Organization of Iranian Moslem Students), Wilmette, Illinois

San Francisco Chronicle, San Francisco, California

Setareh-ye Sorkh (Red Star), [Tehran, Iran?]

Der Spiegel (The Mirror), Hamburg, West Germany

Stern Magazin (Star Magazine), Hamburg, West Germany

Time, New York, New York

The Times, London, England

U.S. News and World Report, New York, New York

The Wall Street Journal, New York, New York

The Washington Post, Washington, D.C.

Weekly Compilation of Presidential Documents, Washington, D.C.

Workers' News (Iranian Students for the Freedom of the Working Class), England

Yad (Memory), Qom, Iran

Zamimeh-ye Haqiqat (Supplement to *The Truth*), [Tehran, Iran?]

Zan-e Ruz (Today's Woman), Tehran, Iran

Books and Essays

Abbas. 1980. *La Révolution Confisquée* (The Confiscated Revolution). Paris: Éditions Clétrat.

'Abbasi, Mohammad. 1980. *Tarikh-e Enqelab-e Eslami* (History of the Islamic Revolution). Tehran: Entesharat-e Sharq.

Abdul-Jaber, Faleh. 2002. "The Genesis and Development of *Marja'ism* versus the State." Pages 61–89 in Faleh Abdul-Jaber, ed., *Ayatollahs, Sufis, and Ideologues: State, Religion, and Social Movements in Iraq.* London: Saqi Books.

Abrahamian, Ervand. 1978. "Iran: The Political Challenge." *MERIP Reports,* no. 69, 3–8.

———. 1982. *Iran between Two Revolutions.* Princeton, N.J.: Princeton University Press.

———. 1989. *The Iranian Mojahedin.* New Haven, Conn.: Yale University Press.

———. 1993. *Khomeinism: Essays on the Islamic Republic.* Berkeley, Calif.: University of California.

———. 1999. *Tortured Confessions: Prisons and Public Recantations in Modern Iran.* Berkeley, Calif.: University of California Press.

Achebe, Chinua. 1983. *The Trouble with Nigeria*. London: Heinemann.

Afkhami, Gholam R. 1985. *The Iranian Revolution: Thanatos on a National Scale*. Washington, D.C.: Middle East Institute.

Afkhami, Mahnaz. 1984. "Iran: A Future in the Past—The 'Prerevolutionary' Women's Movement." Pages 330–337 in Robin Morgan, ed., *Sisterhood Is Global*. Garden City, N.Y.: Anchor Press/Doubleday.

Afrachteh, Kambiz. 1981. "Iran." Pages 90–119 in Mohammed Ayoob, ed., *The Politics of Islamic Reassertion*. London: Croom Helm.

Afrasiyabi, Bahram, and Saʿid Dehqan. 1981. *Taleqani va Tarikh* (Taleqani and History). 2nd ptg. Tehran: Entesharat-e Nilufar.

Aghaie, Kamran. 2001. "The Karbala Narrative: Shiʿi Political Discourse in Modern Iran in the 1960s and 1970s." *Journal of Islamic Studies,* vol. 12, 151–176.

Ahanchian, Jalal. 1982. *Tarh-e Soqut-e Yek Padeshah* (The Plot to Topple a King). Mill Valley, Calif.: Self-published.

Ahmad, Eqbal. 1982. "Comments on Skocpol." *Theory and Society,* vol. 11, 293–300.

Akhavi, Shahrough. 1980. *Religion and Politics in Contemporary Iran: Clergy-State Relations in the Pahlavi Period*. Albany, N.Y.: State University of New York Press.

———. 1996. "Contending Discourses in Shiʿa Law on the Doctrine of *Wilayat al-Faqih* [Rulership of the Jurist]." *Iranian Studies,* vol. 29, 229–268.

Alam, Asadollah. 1991. *The Shah and I: The Confidential Diary of Iran's Royal Court, 1969–1977*. London: I. B. Tauris.

Alavi, Hamza. 1972. "The State in Post-Colonial Societies: Pakistan and Bangladesh." *New Left Review,* no. 74, 59–81.

Alder, Ken. 1988. "To Tell the Truth: The Polygraph Exam and the Marketing of American Expertise." *Historical Reflections,* vol. 24, 487–525.

Algar, Hamid. 1972. "The Oppositional Role of the Ulama in Twentieth-Century Iran." Pages 231–255 in Nikki R. Keddie, ed., *Scholars, Saints, and Sufis*. Berkeley, Calif.: University of California Press.

———. 1983. *The Roots of the Islamic Revolution*. London: The Open Press.

Alidoost-Khaybari, Yadollah. 1981. "Religious Revolutionaries: An Analysis of Religious Groups' Victory in the Iranian Revolution of 1978–79." Ph.D. diss., Department of Sociology, University of Michigan.

ʿAmid-Zanjani, ʿAbbas-ʿAli. 2000. *Ravayeti az Enqelab-e Eslami-ye Iran: Khaterat-e Hojjat al-Islam va al-Moslemin ʿAmid-Zanjani* (A Narrative of the Islamic Revolution of Iran: Memoirs of Hojjat al-Islam ʿAmid-Zanjani). Tehran: Merkez-e Asnad-e Enqelab-e Eslami.

Amir-'Ala'i, Shamsuddin. 1983. *Dar Rah-e Enqelab: Doshvari'ha-ye Mamuriyat-e Man dar Faranseh* (In the Path of the Revolution: The Tribulations of My Posting in France). Tehran: Ketab-Forushi-ye Dehkhoda.

Amjad, Mohammed. 1989. *Iran: From Royal Dictatorship to Theocracy.* New York, N.Y.: Greenwood Press.

Amnesty International. 1980. "Iran, 1978." Fiche 1 in *Amnesty International Country Reports, 1978,* Middle East (H2612). Zug, Switzerland: Inter Documentation Company.

Amra'i, Sohbatollah. 1982. "Barresi-ye Moqe'iyat-e Ejtema'i-ye Shohada-ye Enqelab-e Eslami az Shahrivar 1357 ta Akharin-e Bahman 1357" (Analysis of the Social Background of the Martyrs of the Islamic Revolution from August 1978 to February 1979). M.A. thesis, Department of Sociology, University of Tehran, Iran.

'Amuyi, Muhammad 'Ali. 1998. *Dord-e Zamaneh: Khaterat-e Muhammad 'Ali 'Amuyi, 1320–1357* (On Pain of Death: Memoirs of Muhammad 'Ali 'Amuyi, 1941–1978). Tehran: Entesharat-e Anzan.

Amuzegar, Jahangir. 1977. *Iran: An Economic Profile.* Washington, D.C.: Middle East Institute.

———. 1982. "Oil Wealth: A Very Mixed Blessing." *Foreign Affairs,* vol. 60, 814–835.

———. 1991. *The Dynamics of the Iranian Revolution.* Albany, N.Y.: State University of New York Press.

Apter, Andrew. 1987. "Things Fell Apart? Yoruba Responses to the 1983 Elections in Ondo State, Nigeria." *Journal of Modern African Studies,* vol. 25, 489–503.

Arendt, Hannah. 1965. *On Revolution.* New York, N.Y.: Viking Press.

Arjomand, Said Amir. 1984. "Traditionalism in Twentieth-Century Iran." Pages 195–232 in Said Amir Arjomand, ed., *From Nationalism to Revolutionary Islam.* Albany, N.Y.: State University of New York Press.

———. 1988. "Ideological Revolution in Shi'ism." Pages 178–209 in Said Amir Arjomand, ed., *Authority and Political Culture in Shi'ism.* Albany, N.Y.: State University of New York Press.

———. 1988. *The Turban for the Crown: The Islamic Revolution in Iran.* New York, N.Y.: Oxford University Press.

Arndt, H. W. 1984. *The Indonesian Economy.* Singapore: Chopmen Publishers.

Aryanpour, Azar. 1998. *Behind the Tall Walls: From Palace to Prison.* Danbury, Conn.: Rutledge Books.

Ashraf, Ahmad. 1988. "The Bazaar-Mosque Alliance." *International Journal of Politics, Culture and Society,* vol. 1, 538–567.

———. 1997. "The Appeal of Conspiracy Theories to Persians." Pages 57–88 in William Harris et al., *Challenges to Democracy in the Middle East.* Princeton, N.J.: Markus Wiener Publishers.

Ashraf, Ahmad, and Ali Banuazizi. 1985. "The State, Classes, and Modes of Mobilization in the Iranian Revolution." *State, Culture, and Society,* vol. 1, 3–40.

Assersohn, Roy. 1982. *The Biggest Deal.* London: Methuen.

Atkin, Muriel. 1986. "Soviet Attitudes toward Shi'ism and Social Protest." Pages 275–301 in Juan R. I. Cole and Nikki R. Keddie, eds., *Shi'ism and Social Protest.* New Haven, Conn.: Yale University Press.

Azari, Farah. 1983. "Islam's Appeal to Women in Iran." Pages 1–71 in Farah Azari, ed., *Women of Iran.* London: Ithaca Press.

Azodanloo, Heidar G. 1993. "Performative Elements of Shi'ite Ritual and Mass Mobilization: The Case of Iran." *Critique,* no. 3, 35–54.

Badamchiyan, Asadollah. 1995. *Shenakht-e Enqelab-e Eslami va Risheh'ha-ye An* (Understanding the Islamic Revolution and Its Roots). Tehran: Daneshgah-e Azad-e Eslami.

Badii, Naiim, and L. Erwin Atwood. 1986. "How the Tehran Press Responded to the 1979 Iranian Revolution." *Journalism Quarterly,* vol. 63, 517–523, 536.

Bahrambeygui, H. 1977. *Tehran, Iran: An Urban Analysis.* Tehran: Sahab Books Institute.

Bahramian, Bahram. 2001. *Renasans dar Iran: Rowshangari-ye Zavaya-ye Tarik-e Enqelab-e Bahman 1357* (Renaissance in Iran: An Illumination of the Dark Corners of the Revolution of February 1979). Rockville, Md.: Center for Technology Management.

Bahrampour, Tara. 1999. *To See and See Again: A Life in Iran and America.* New York, N.Y.: Farrar, Straus and Giroux.

Bakhash, Shaul. 1984. "Sermons, Revolutionary Pamphleteering, and Mobilisation." Pages 177–194 in Said Amir Arjomand, ed., *From Nationalism to Revolutionary Islam.* Albany, N.Y.: State University of New York Press.

———. 1990. *The Reign of the Ayatollahs.* Rev. ed. New York, N.Y.: Basic Books.

Bakhtiar, Chapour. 1982. *Ma Fidelité* (My Fidelity). Paris: Albin Michel.

———. 1982. *Si-o-Haft Ruz Pas Az Si-o-Haft Sal* (Thirty-seven Days after Thirty-seven Years). Paris: Entesharat-e Radio-e Iran.

Baktash, Mayel. 1979. "Ta'ziyeh and Its Philosophy." Pages 95–120 in Peter J. Chelkowski, ed., *Ta'ziyeh: Ritual and Drama in Iran.* New York, N.Y.: New York University Press.

Balam, Betty. 1987. *Too Much Too Soon: A Portrait of Iran from 1967 to the Fall of the Shah.* Tallahassee, Fla.: Loiry Publishing House.

Balta, Paul, and Claudine Rulleau. 1979. *L'Iran Insurge* (Iran Rises). Paris: Sindbad.

Bani, Omol. 1980. *Fatima Statt Farah: Erfahrungen einer Frau in der iranischen Revolution* (Fatima in Place of Farah: Experiences of a Woman in the Iranian Revolution). Tübingen: Iva-Verlag.

Bani-Sadr, Abolhassan. 1980. *Sad Maghaleh* (One Hundred Articles). Tehran: Payam-e Azadi.

———. [1989] 1991. *My Turn to Speak: Iran, the Revolution and Secret Deals with the U.S.* Washington, D.C.: Brassey's (U.S.).

Bank Markazi Iran. 1963–1980. *Annual Report and Balance Sheet*. Tehran: Bank Markazi Iran.

———. 1972. *National Income of Iran, 1338–50 (1959–72)*. Tehran: Bank Markazi Iran, Bureau of National Accounts.

———. 1974–1978. *Bulletin*. Tehran: Bank Markazi Iran, Economic Research Department.

———. 1976. *A Comprehensive Report on Construction Activities of the Private Sector in the Urban Areas of Iran During 2534*. Tehran: Bank Markazi Iran, Economic Statistics Department.

Banuazizi, Ali. 1977. "Iranian 'National Character': A Critique of Some Western Perspectives." Pages 210–239 in L. Carl Brown and Norman Itzkowitz, eds., *Psychological Dimensions of Near Eastern Studies*. Princeton, N.J.: The Darwin Press.

Baqaʾi-Kermani, Mozaffar. 1979. *Shenakht-e Haqiqat* (Knowing the Truth). Kerman, Iran: Hezb-e Zahmatkeshan-i Mellat-i Iran.

Baqi, ʿEmaduddin. 1994. *Tahrir-e Tarikh-e Shafahi-e Enqelab-e Eslami-e Iran: Majmuʿeh-ye Barnameh-ye Dastan-e Enqelab az Radio B.B.C.* (Writing the Oral History of the Islamic Revolution of Iran: Collection of the B.B.C. Radio Program, Stories of the Revolution). Tehran: Nashr-e Tafakkor.

———. 1999. *Jonbesh-e Daneshjuyi-ye Iran: Az Aghaz ta Enqelab-e Eslami* (The Student Movement in Iran: From the Beginning to the Islamic Revolution). Tehran: Jameʿeh-ye Iraniyan.

———. 2000. *Faradestan va Forudestan: Khaterat-e Shafahi-ye Enqelab* (Land of Ups and Downs: Oral History of the Revolution). Tehran: Jameʿeh-ye Iraniyan.

———. 2003. "Amar-e Qorbaniyan-e Enqelab" (Statistics of Victims of the Revolution). *Iran-Emrooz* (Iran Today), July 30.

Baraheni, Reza. 1977. *Crowned Cannibals: Writings on Repression in Iran*. New York, N.Y.: Vintage Books.

———. 1979. *Dar Enqelab-e Iran, Cheh Shodeh va Cheh Khahad Shod?* (In the Iranian Revolution, What Happened and What Will Happen?). Tehran: Nashr-e Zaman.

Barrows, Susanna. 1981. *Distorting Mirrors: Visions of the Crowd in Late Nineteenth-Century France*. New Haven, Conn.: Yale University Press.

Bashiriyeh, Hossein. 1984. *State and Revolution in Iran, 1962–1982*. New York, N.Y.: St. Martin's Press.

Bateson, Mary Catherine. 1979. "'This Figure of Tinsel': A Study of Themes of Hypocrisy and Pessimism in Iranian Culture." *Daedalus,* vol. 108, 125–134.

Bauer, Janet. 1981. "Changes in the Behavior and Consciousness of Iranian Women (1963–1978)." Ph.D. diss., Department of Anthropology, Stanford University.

———. 1983. "Poor Women and Social Consciousness in Revolutionary Iran." Pages 141–169 in Guity Nashat, ed., *Women and Revolution in Iran*. Boulder, Colo.: Westview Press.

———. 1985. "Demographic Change, Women and the Family in a Migrant Neighborhood of Tehran." Pages 158–186 in Asghar Fathi, ed., *Women and the Family in Iran*. Leiden: E. J. Brill.

———. 1993. "Ma'ssoum's Tale: The Personal and Political Transformations of a Young Iranian 'Feminist' and Her Ethnographer." *Feminist Studies,* vol. 19, 519–548.

Bayat, Asef. 1987. *Workers and Revolution in Iran*. London: Zed.

———. 1997. *Street Politics: Poor People's Movements in Iran*. New York, N.Y.: Columbia University Press.

Bayat, Mangol. 1987. "Mahmud Taleqani and the Iranian Revolution." Pages 67–94 in Martin Kramer, ed., *Shi'ism, Resistance, and Revolution*. Boulder, Colo.: Westview Press.

Bazargan, Mehdi. 1983. *Showra-ye Enqelab va Dowlat-e Movaqat* (The Revolutionary Council and the Provisional Government). Tehran: Nehzat-e Azadi-ye Iran.

———. 1984. *Enqelab-e Iran dar Do Harekat* (The Iranian Revolution in Two Movements). Tehran: Daftar-e Nehzat-e Azadi-ye Iran.

Beeman, William O. 1981. "A Full Arena: The Development and Meaning of Popular Performance Traditions in Iran." Pages 361–381 in Michael E. Bonine and Nikki R. Keddie, eds., *Modern Iran: The Dialectics of Continuity and Change*. Albany, N.Y.: State University of New York Press.

———. 1986. *Language, Status, and Power in Iran*. Bloomington, Ind.: Indiana University Press.

Behnam, Mariam. 1994. *Zelzelah: A Woman before Her Time*. Dubai: Motivate Publishing.

Behrang. 1979. *Iran: Le Maillon Faible* (Iran: The Weak Link). Paris: François Maspero.

Behrooz, Maziar. 1999. *Rebels with a Cause: The Failure of the Left in Iran*. London: I. B. Tauris.

Benard, Cheryl, and Zalmay Khalilzad. 1984. *"The Government of God": Iran's Islamic Republic*. New York, N.Y.: Columbia University Press.

Ben-Dor, Gabriel. 1997. "The Uniqueness of Islamic Fundamentalism." Pages 239–252 in Bruce Maddy-Weitzman and Efraim Inbar, eds., *Religious Radicalism in the Greater Middle East*. London: Frank Cass.

Benedick, Richard Elliot. 1964. *Industrial Finance in Iran*. Boston, Mass.: Harvard Business School.

Benford, Robert D. 1997. "An Insider's Critique of the Social Movement Framing Perspective." *Sociological Inquiry,* vol. 67, 409–430.

Benford, Robert D., and David A. Snow. 2000. "Framing Processes and Social Movements: An Overview and Assessment." *Annual Review of Sociology,* vol. 26, 611–639.

Bentaleb, Fatima. 1984. "Rente et Société Algérienne" (Rent and Algerian Society). *Peuples Méditerranéens* (Mediterranean Peoples), no. 26, 75–104.

Bergmann, Herbert, and Nasser Khademadam. 1975. *The Impacts of Large-Scale Farms on Development in Iran*. Saarbrücken: Verlag der SSIP-Schriften, Publications of the Research Centre for International Agricultural Development.

Betteridge, Anne H. 1983. "To Veil or Not to Veil." Pages 109–128 in Guity Nashat, ed., *Women and Revolution in Iran*. Boulder, Colo.: Westview Press.

Bharier, Julian. 1971. *Economic Development in Iran, 1900–1970*. London: Oxford University Press.

———. 1972. "The Growth of Towns and Villages in Iran, 1900–1966." *Middle Eastern Studies,* vol. 8, 51–61.

Bianu, Zeno. 1981. *Les Religions et . . . La Mort* (Religions and . . . Death). Paris: Éditions Ramsay.

Biggs, Michael. 2003. "Positive Feedback in Collective Mobilization: The American Strike Wave of 1886." *Theory and Society,* vol. 32, 217–254.

Bill, James A. 1972. *The Politics of Iran: Groups, Classes, and Modernization*. Columbus, Ohio: Charles E. Merrill.

———. 1973. "The Plasticity of Informal Politics: The Case of Iran." *Middle East Journal,* vol. 27, 131–151.

———. 1988. *The Eagle and the Lion: The Tragedy of American-Iranian Relations*. New Haven, Conn.: Yale University Press.

Binder, Leonard. 1979. "Revolution in Iran: Red, White, Blue or Black." *The Bulletin of the Atomic Scientists,* vol. 35, 48–54.

Biniosch, Carol. 1978. "Letter from Teheran." *Far Eastern Economic Review,* March 17, 1978, 58.

Blumer, Herbert. 1939. "Collective Behavior." Pages 219–280 in Robert E.

Park, ed., *An Outline of the Principles of Sociology.* New York, N.Y.: Barnes & Noble.

Boroumand, Ladan. 1979. "Les Ouvriers, l'Ingénieur et les Militantes Khomeinistes: Entretien dans Usine au Lendemain de la Révolution" (The Workers, the Engineer, and the Khomeini Militants: Interview in a Factory in the Wake of the Revolution). *Peuples Méditerranéens* (Mediterranean Peoples), no. 8, 59–76.

Bostock, Frances, and Geoffrey Jones. 1989. *Planning and Power in Iran: Ebtehaj and Economic Development under the Shah.* London: Frank Cass.

Bourdieu, Pierre. [1993] 1999. "Understanding." Pages 607–626 in Pierre Bourdieu et al., *The Weight of the World: Social Suffering in Contemporary Society,* trans. Priscilla Parkhurst Ferguson et al. Cambridge, England: Polity Press.

Braswell, George W., Jr. 1975. "A Mosaic of Mullahs and Mosques: Religion and Politics in Iranian Shi'ah Islam." Ph.D. diss., Department of Anthropology, University of North Carolina at Chapel Hill.

———. 1975. *To Ride a Magic Carpet.* Nashville, Tenn.: Broadman Press.

———. 1979. "Civil Religion in Contemporary Iran." *Journal of Church and State,* vol. 21, 223–246.

Bresnan, John. 1993. *Managing Indonesia: The Modern Political Economy.* New York, N.Y.: Columbia University Press.

Brière, Claire, and Pierre Blanchet. 1979. *L'Iran: La Révolution au Nom de Dieu* (Iran: Revolution in the Name of God). Paris: Seuil.

Brinton, Crane. [1938] 1965. *The Anatomy of Revolution.* Revised and expanded ed. New York, N.Y.: Vintage.

Browne, Edward G. [1910] 1995. *The Persian Revolution, 1905–1909.* Washington, D.C.: Mage Publishers.

Brumberg, Daniel. 2001. *Reinventing Khomeini: The Struggle for Reform in Iran.* Chicago, Ill.: University of Chicago Press.

Brzezinski, Zbigniew. 1983. *Power and Principle: Memoirs of the National Security Advisor, 1977–1981.* New York, N.Y.: Farrar, Straus, Giroux.

Burke, Edmund, III, and Paul Lubeck. 1987. "Explaining Social Movements in Two Oil-Exporting States: Divergent Outcomes in Nigeria and Iran." *Comparative Studies in Society and History,* vol. 29, 643–665.

Business International. 1978. *Operating in Iran: An Economy Coming of Age.* Geneva: Business International Research Report 78–1 (February).

Canetti, Elias. [1960] 1978. *Crowds and Power,* trans. Carol Stewart. New York, N.Y.: Seabury Press.

Calder, Norman. 1982. "Accommodation and Revolution in Imami Shi'i Jurisprudence: Khumayni and the Classical Tradition." *Middle Eastern Studies,* vol. 18, 3–20.

Carter, Jimmy. 1977. *A Government as Good as Its People*. New York, N.Y.: Simon and Schuster.

———. 1978. *Public Papers of the Presidents: Jimmy Carter, 1977*. 2 vols. Washington, D.C.: U.S. Government Printing Office.

———. 1979. *Public Papers of the Presidents: Jimmy Carter, 1978*. 2 vols. Washington, D.C.: U.S. Government Printing Office.

———. 1982. *Keeping Faith: Memoirs of a President*. New York, N.Y.: Bantam Books.

Carter, Rosalyn. 1984. *First Lady from Plains*. Boston, Mass.: Houghton Mifflin.

Censer, Jack R. 1996. "The Not So Inevitable Revolution of 1789." *Consortium on Revolutionary Europe, 1750–1850: Selected Papers,* vol. 1996, 1–17.

Chand E'lamiyeh az Jonbesh-e Kargari-ye Iran (Several Pronouncements from the Workers' Movement of Iran). 1978. London: Ettehadiyeh-ye Daneshjuyan-e Irani dar London.

Chehabi, H. E. 1990. *Iranian Politics and Religious Modernism: The Liberation Movement of Iran under the Shah and Khomeini*. Ithaca, N.Y.: Cornell University Press.

Chelkowski, Peter J., ed. 1979. *Ta'ziyeh: Ritual and Drama in Iran*. New York, N.Y.: New York University Press.

Chelkowski, Peter J., and Hamid Dabashi. 1999. *Staging a Revolution: The Art of Persuasion in the Islamic Republic of Iran*. New York, N.Y.: New York University Press.

Cherik'ha-ye Feda'i-ye Khalq-e Iran (The Iranian People's Sacrificing Guerrillas). Circa 1977. *Gozareshati az Mobarezat-e Daliraneh-ye Mardom-e Kharej az Mahdudeh* (Reports on the People's Valiant Struggles outside the [City] Limits). [Tehran?]: Sazman-e Cherik'ha-ye Feda'i-ye Khalq.

———. Circa 1978. *Gerami Bad 19 Bahman, Salruz-e Aghaz-e Jonbesh-e Maslahaneh-ye Khalq-e Iran* (Cherished Be February 8 [1978], Anniversary of the Beginning of the Armed Movement of the People of Iran). Europe: Confederation of Iranian Students (National Union).

———. 1979. *E'lamiyeh'ha va Bayaniyeh'ha-ye Sazman-e Cherik'ha-ye Feda'i-ye Khalq dar Sal-e 1357* (Pronouncements and Proclamations of the Organization of the People's Sacrificing Guerrillas in the Year 1978–1979). [Tehran?]: Entesharat-e Sazman-e Cherik'ha-ye Feda'i-ye Khalq.

Chubin, Shahram. 1979. "The United States and Iran's Revolution: Local Soil, Foreign Plants." *Foreign Policy,* no. 34, 20–23.

Cohler-Esses, Lawrence. 1999. "Iranian Jewry's Agent of Influence." *New York Jewish Week,* October 8, 1999, 1.

Cole, Juan R. I. 1993. *Colonialism and Revolution in the Middle East: Social and Cultural Origins of Egypt's 'Urabi Movement*. Princeton, N.J.: Princeton University Press.

Coleman, James S. 1990. *Foundations of Social Theory.* Cambridge, Mass.: Harvard University Press.

Copeland, Miles. 1989. *The Game Player: Confessions of the C.I.A.'s Original Political Operative.* London: Aurum Press.

Corden, W. Max, and J. Peter Neary. 1982. "Booming Sector and De-Industrialisation in a Small Open Economy." *Economic Journal,* vol. 92, 825–848.

Cottam, Richard W. 1980. "The Imperial Regime of Iran: Why It Collapsed." Pages 9–24 in *L'Iran d'Hier et de Demain* (Iran of Yesterday and Tomorrow). Quebec: Collection Choix.

Couch, Carl L. 1968. "Collective Behavior: An Examination of Some Stereotypes." *Social Problems,* vol. 15, 310–322.

Danesh, Abol Hassan. 1987. *Rural Exodus and Squatter Settlements in the Third World: Case of Iran.* Lanham, Md.: University Press of America.

Daneshvar, Parviz. 1996. *Revolution in Iran.* New York, N.Y.: St. Martin's Press.

Dastghayb, Seyyed 'Abdolhossein. 1999. *Khaterat-e Hojjat al-Islam Seyyed 'Abdolhossein Dastghayb* (Memoirs of Hojjat al-Islam Seyyed 'Abdolhossein Dastghayb). Tehran: Merkez-e Asnad-e Enqelab-e Eslami.

Daugherty, William J. 2001. *In the Shadow of the Ayatollah: A C.I.A. Hostage in Iran.* Annapolis, Md.: Naval Institute Press.

Davani, 'Ali. 1987. "Khaterat-e Hojjat al-Islam Aqa-ye 'Ali Davani" (Memoirs of Hojjat al-Islam Mr. 'Ali Davani." *Yad* (Memory), no. 8, 46–56.

Davies, James C. 1969. "The J-Curve of Rising and Declining Satisfactions as a Cause of Some Great Revolutions and a Contained Rebellion." Pages 690–730 in Hugh Davis Graham and Ted Robert Gurr, eds., *Violence in America.* New York, N.Y.: Bantam Books.

Dehqani-Tafti, H. B. 1981. *The Hard Awakening.* New York, N.Y.: The Seabury Press.

Delannoy, Christian. 1990. *SAVAK.* Paris: Stock.

Delannoy, Christian, and Jean-Pierre Pichard. 1988. *Khomeiny: La Révolution Trahie* (Khomeini: The Revolution Betrayed). Paris: Carrère.

Demaine, Harvey. 1985. "Population and Resources." Pages 12–42 in Leslie Palmier, ed., *Understanding Indonesia.* Brookfield, Vt.: Gower.

Denoeux, Guilan. 1993. *Urban Unrest in the Middle East: A Comparative Study of Informal Networks in Egypt, Iran, and Lebanon.* Albany, N.Y.: State University of New York Press.

Donham, Donald L. 1999. *Marxist Modern: An Ethnographic History of the Ethiopian Revolution.* Berkeley, Calif.: University of California Press; Oxford, England: J. Currey.

Donovan, Michael. 1997. "National Intelligence and the Iranian Revolution." *Intelligence and National Security,* vol. 12, 143–163.

Dorman, William A., and Mansour Farhang. 1987. *The U.S. Press and Iran: Foreign Policy and the Journalism of Deference*. Berkeley, Calif.: University of California Press.

Dowlat, Manijeh, Bernard Hourcade, and Odile Puech. 1980. "Les Paysans et la Révolution Iranienne" (Peasants and the Iranian Revolution). *Peuples Méditerranéens* (Mediterranean Peoples), no. 10, 19–42.

Ebtekar, Massoumeh, as told to Fred A. Reed. 2000. *Takeover in Tehran: The Inside Story of the 1979 U.S. Embassy Capture*. Vancouver: Talonbooks.

Eftekhari, Nirou, 1984. "Rente et Dépendence en Algérie" (Rente and Dependence in Algeria). *Peuples Méditerranéens* (Mediterranean Peoples), no. 26, 31–74.

Ekteshafi, Parviz. 1998. *Khaterat-e Sargard-e Havayi Parviz Ekteshafi, az Mas'ulin-e Shakhe-ye Havayi-ye Sazman-e Ofiseri-ye Hezb-e Tudeh-ye Iran (1323–1333 va 22 Sal Mohajerat dar Shuravi)* (Memoirs of Air Force Major Parviz Ekteshafi, a Leader of the Air Force Branch of the Officers' Organization of the Masses Party of Iran, 1944–1954, and 22 Years' Exile in the Soviet Union), ed. Hamid Ahmadi. Cologne: Murtazavi.

Elkan, Walter. 1977. "Employment, Education, Training and Skilled Labor in Iran." *Middle East Journal,* vol. 31, 175–187.

Esposito, John L. 1987. *Islam and Politics*. 2nd ed. Syracuse, N.Y.: Syracuse University Press.

Evans, Peter B., Dietrich Rueschemeyer, and Theda Skocpol, eds. 1985. *Bringing the State Back In*. Cambridge, England: Cambridge University Press.

Falsafi, Mohammad-Taqi. 1997. *Khaterat va Mobarezat-e Hojjat al-Islam Falsafi* (Memoirs and Struggles of Hojjat al-Islam Falsafi). Tehran: Merkez-e Asnad-e Enqelab-e Eslami.

Farati, 'Abdolvahhab. 2000. *Tarikh-e Shafahi-ye Enqelab-e Eslami: Az Marja'iyyat-e Emam Khomeini ta Tab'id* (Oral History of the Islamic Revolution: From the Religious Leadership of Imam Khomeini to Exile). Tehran: Merkez-e Asnad-e Enqelab-e Eslami.

Farazmand, Ali. 1989. *The State, Bureaucracy, and Revolution in Modern Iran: Agrarian Reforms and Regime Politics*. New York, N.Y.: Praeger.

Fardmanesh, Mohsen. 1991. "Dutch Disease Economics and the Oil Syndrome: An Empirical Study." *World Development,* vol. 19, 711–717.

Fardoust, Hossein. 1995. *The Rise and Fall of [the] Pahlavi Dynasty*. Tehran: Hadis Publishing House.

Farhang-e Sho'ar'ha-ye Enqelab-e Eslami (Dictionary of Slogans of the Islamic Revolution). 1990. Tehran: Merkez-e Asnad-e Enqelab-e Eslami.

Farman Farmaian, Sattareh, with Dona Munker. 1992. *Daughter of Persia: A*

Woman's Journey from Her Father's Harem through the Islamic Revolution.
New York, N.Y.: Crown Publishers.

Farmanfarmaian, Manucher, and Roxane Farmanfarmaian. 1997. *Blood and Oil: Inside the Shah's Iran.* New York: The Modern Library.

Farrokhfal, Reza. 2001. "Media and Modernity in Pre-Revolutionary Iran." Paper presented at the Annual Meeting of the Center for Iranian Research and Analysis, April 28, Toronto.

Farsi, Jalal al-Din. 1994. *Zavaya-ye Tarik* (Dark Corners). Tehran: Daftar-e Adabiyat-e Enqelab-e Eslami.

Farzand-e Islam va Qur'an (Son of Islam and the Qur'an). 1983. 2 vols. Tehran: Vahed-e Farhangi-ye Bonyad-e Shahid.

Fatemi, Khosrow. 1982. "Leadership by Distrust: The Shah's Modus Operandi." *Middle East Journal,* vol. 36, 48–61.

Federasiyun-e Mohaselin va Daneshjuyan-e Irani dar Faranseh (Federation of Iranian Pupils and University Students in France). 1978. "The Bloody Uprising of Tabriz," trans. S. Azad. *Review of Iranian Political Economics and History* (RIPEH), vol. 2, 75–92.

Fesharaki, Fereidun. 1980. *Revolution and Energy Policy in Iran.* London: The Economist Intelligence Unit.

Fischer, Michael M. J. 1980. *Iran: From Religious Dispute to Revolution.* Cambridge, Mass.: Harvard University Press.

Fischer, Michael M. J., and Mehdi Abedi. 1990. *Debating Muslims: Cultural Dialogues in Postmodernity and Tradition.* Madison, Wis.: University of Wisconsin Press.

Floor, Willem M. 1980. "The Revolutionary Character of the Iranian Ulama: Wishful Thinking or Reality?" *International Journal of Middle East Studies,* vol. 12, 501–524.

Follett, Ken. 1983. *On Wings of Eagles.* New York, N.Y.: William Morrow.

Food and Agriculture Organization. 1980. *Food Balance Sheets.* Rome: Food and Agriculture Organization of the United Nations.

Foran, John. 1993. *Fragile Resistance: Social Transformation in Iran from 1500 to the Revolution.* Boulder, Colo.: Westview Press.

———. 1993. "Theories of Revolution Revisited: Toward a Fourth Generation?" *Sociological Theory,* vol. 11, 1–20.

Försterling, Friedrich. 2001. *Attribution: An Introduction to Theories, Research and Applications.* Philadelphia, Penn.: Taylor & Francis.

Freedom House. 1980. *Freedom in the World 1979,* ed. Raymond D. Gastil. Boston, Mass.: G. K. Hall.

———. 1984. *Freedom in the World 1983–1984,* ed. Raymond D. Gastil. Westport, Conn.: Greenwood Press.

Gage, Nicholas. 1978. "Iran: The Making of a Revolution." *New York Times Magazine*, December 17, 1978, 24–26, 114–115, 132–139.

Garfinkel, Harold. 1967. *Studies in Ethnomethodology.* Englewood Cliffs, N.J.: Prentice-Hall.

Gelb, Alan, and Associates. 1988. *Oil Windfalls: Blessing or Curse?* New York, N.Y.: Oxford University Press for the World Bank.

Ghandchi-Tehrani, Davoud. 1982. "Bazaaris and Clergy: Socio-Economic Origins of Radicalism and Revolution in Iran." Ph.D. diss., Department of Sociology, City University of New York.

Gharabaghi, Abbas. [1984] 1985. *Vérités sur la Crise Iranienne* (Truths about the Iranian Crisis). Paris: La Pensée Universelle.

Giddens, Anthony. 1984. *The Constitution of Society.* Berkeley, Calif.: University of California Press.

Ginger, Serge. 1981. *Nouvelles Lettres Persanes* (New Persian Letters). Paris: Éditions Anthropos.

Gitlin, Todd. 1987. *The Sixties: Years of Hope, Days of Rage.* New York, N.Y.: Bantam Books.

Golabdareh'i, Mahmud. 1986. *Lahzeh'ha* (Moments). 3rd ptg. Tehran: Entesharat-e Kayhan.

Goldstone, Jack A. 2003. "Comparative Historical Analysis and Knowledge Accumulation in the Study of Revolutions." Pages 41–90 in James Mahoney and Dietrich Rueschemeyer, eds., *Comparative Historical Analysis in the Social Sciences.* Cambridge, England: Cambridge University Press.

Good, Mary-Jo Delvecchio, and Byron J. Good. 1988. "Ritual, the State, and the Transformation of Emotional Discourse in Iranian Society." *Culture, Medicine and Psychiatry*, vol. 12, 43–63.

Goodell, Grace E. 1986. *The Elementary Structures of Political Life: Rural Development in Pahlavi Iran.* New York, N.Y.: Oxford University Press.

Goodwin, Jeff. 2001. *No Other Way Out: States and Revolutionary Movements, 1945–1991.* Cambridge, England: Cambridge University Press.

Goodwin, Jeff, and Steven Pfaff. 2001. "Emotion Work in High-Risk Social Movements: Managing Fear in the U.S. and East German Civil Rights Movements." Pages 282–302 in Jeff Goodwin, James M. Jasper, and Francesca Polletta, ed., *Passionate Politics: Emotions and Social Movements.* Chicago, Ill.: University of Chicago Press.

Gottlieb, Annie. 1987. *Do You Believe in Magic? The Second Coming of the Sixties Generation.* New York, N.Y.: Times Books.

Gouldner, Alvin W. 1985. *Against Fragmentation: The Origins of Marxism and the Sociology of Intellectuals.* New York, N.Y.: Oxford University Press.

Gozaresh-e Kamel-e Tazahorat-e 15–17 Khordad '54 (Complete Report on the Demonstrations of June 5–7, 1975). 1976. Springfield, Mo.: Nehzat-e Azadi-ye Iran, Kharej az Keshvar. Reproduced in Behn, *Iranian Opposition to the Shah,* document 20:42.

Graf, William D. 1988. *The Nigerian State: Political Economy, State Class and Political System in the Post-Colonial Era.* London: James Currey; and Portsmouth, N.H.: Heinemann.

Graham, Robert. 1980. *Iran: The Illusion of Power.* Rev. ed. New York, N.Y.: St. Martin's Press.

Granovetter, Mark. 1978. "Threshold Models of Collective Behavior." *American Journal of Sociology,* vol. 83, 1420–1443.

Granovetter, Mark, and Roland Soong. 1983. "Threshold Models of Diffusion and Collective Behavior." *Journal of Mathematical Sociology,* vol. 9, 165–179.

Great Britain. 1936. *British Documents on the Origins of the War, 1898–1914,* ed. G. P. Gooch and Harold Temperley. Vol. 10, pt. 1. London: His Majesty's Stationery Office.

Green, Jerrold. 1982. *Revolution in Iran: The Politics of Counter-Mobilization.* New York, N.Y.: Praeger.

———. 1984. "Countermobilization as a Revolutionary Form." *Comparative Politics,* vol. 16, 153–169.

Grogan, Brian. 1979. *Insurrection in Tehran.* London: The Other Press.

Gruh-e Tahqiq-e Entesharat-e Sorush (Sorush Publishers Research Group). 1991. *Taqvim-e Tarikh-e Enqelab-e Eslami-ye Iran: Khabar'ha va Ruyidad'ha-ye Ruzane, Mordad 1356–Farvardin 1358* (Calendar of the History of the Islamic Revolution of Iran: Daily News and Events, July–August 1977 to March–April 1979). Tehran: Sorush.

Gurr, Ted Robert. 1970. *Why Men Rebel.* Princeton, N.J.: Princeton University Press.

Haeri, Shahla. 1989. *Law of Desire: Temporary Marriage in Shi'i Iran.* Syracuse, N.Y.: Syracuse University Press.

Hajj-Seyyed Javadi, 'Ali-Asghar. 1977. *Afzal al-Jihad* (The Preference for Religious Struggle). 2nd ptg. [Tehran?]: Entesharat-e Modarres. Reproduced in Behn, *Iranian Opposition to the Shah,* document 20:33.

———. 1979. *Daftar'ha-ye Enqelab* (Notebooks of the Revolution). Tehran: Jonbesh Bara-ye Azadi.

Hakimfar, Bahram Bob. 1991. "The Downfall of Late King Mohammad Reza Pahlavi: Views of the Iranian Community in Southern California." Ph.D. diss., U.S. International University.

Hakimian, Hassan. 1988. "Industrialization and the Standard of Living of the

Working Class in Iran, 1960–1979." *Development and Change,* vol. 19, 3–32.

———. 1990. *Labour Transfer and Economic Development: Theoretical Perspectives and Case Studies from Iran.* New York, N.Y.: Harvester Wheatsheaf.

Halliday, Fred. 1979. *Iran: Dictatorship and Development.* Harmondsworth: Penguin Books.

———. 1988. "The Iranian Revolution: Uneven Development and Religious Populism." Pages 31–64 in Fred Halliday and Hamza Alawi, eds., *State and Ideology in the Middle East and Pakistan.* New York, N.Y.: Monthly Review Press.

Hanaway, William. 1990. "Half-Voices: Persian Women's Lives and Letters." Pages 55–63 in Afsaneh Najmabadi, ed., *Women's Autobiographies in Contemporary Iran.* Cambridge, Mass.: Harvard University Press.

Harney, Desmond. 1999. *The Priest and the King: An Eyewitness Account of the Iranian Revolution.* London: I. B. Tauris.

Hashemi, Manuchehr. 1994. *Davari: Sokhani dar Kar-Nameh-ye SAVAK* (Judgment: A Discourse on the Report Card of SAVAK). London: Entesharat-e Ars.

Hashemi-Rafsanjani, Akbar. 1997. *Dowran-e Mobarezeh* (The Era of Mobilization). 2 vols. Tehran: Daftar-e Nashr-e Ma'aref-e Enqelab.

Hegland, Mary Elaine. 1983. "Aliabad Women: Revolution as Religious Activity." Pages 171–194 in Guity Nashat, ed., *Women and Revolution in Iran.* Boulder, Colo.: Westview Press.

———. 1983. "Ritual and Revolution in Iran." *Political Anthropology,* vol. 2, 75–100.

———. 1983. "Two Images of Husain: Accommodation and Revolution in an Iranian Village." Pages 218–235 in Nikki R. Keddie, ed., *Religion and Politics in Iran.* New Haven, Conn.: Yale University Press.

———. 1986. "Imam Khomaini's Village: Recruitment to Revolution." Ph.D. diss., Department of Anthropology, State University of New York at Binghamton.

———. 1987. "Islamic Revival or Political and Cultural Revolution?" Pages 194–219 in Richard T. Antoun and Mary Elaine Hegland, eds., *Religious Resurgence: Contemporary Cases in Islam, Christianity, and Judaism.* Syracuse, N.Y.: Syracuse University Press.

Heravi-Khorasani, Mohammad Hasan. 1953. *Tarikh-e Peydayesh-e Mashrutiyat-e Iran* (History of the Founding of the Iranian Constitutional Revolution). Mashhad, Iran: Sherkat-e Chap-Khaneh-ye Khorasan.

Hezb-e Tudeh-ye Iran. 1977. *Zendeh Bad-e Jonbesh-e Tudeh-ye Aban va Azar Mah 56* (Long Live the Mass Movement of November and December

1977). [Location not indicated]: Entesharat-e Sazman-e Enqelabi-ye Hezb-e Tudeh-ye Iran. Reproduced in Behn, *Iranian Opposition to the Shah,* document 20:166.

———. 1978. *Javedan Bad Khatereh-ye Qiyam-e Khunin-e Tabriz* (Eternal Be the Memory of the Bloody Uprising of Tabriz). [Rome?]: Entesharat-e Sazman-e Enqelabi-ye Hezb-e Tudeh-ye Iran.

Hickman, William F. 1982. *Ravaged and Reborn: The Iranian Army, 1982.* Washington, D.C.: The Brookings Institution.

Hiro, Dilip. 1985. *Iran under the Ayatollahs.* London: Routledge and Kegan Paul.

Hirschfeld, Yair P. 1979. "Decline and Fall of the Pahlavis." *Jerusalem Quarterly,* no. 12, 20–33.

Hitselberger, Jim. 1979. "Letter." *Review of Iranian Political Economy and History* (RIPEH), vol. 3, 117–121.

Hochschild, Arlie Russell. 1987. "Memorium for Herbert Blumer." *Berkeley Journal of Sociology,* vol. 32, i–iii.

Hojjati-Kermani, ʿAli. 1987. "'Majaleh'i Bara-ye Howzeh': Khaterat-e Hojjat al-Islam Aqa-ye ʿAli Hojjati-Kermani" (An Article for the Religious Circle: The Memoirs of Hojjat al-Islam Mr. ʿAli Hojjati-Kermani). *Yad* (Memory), no. 8, 56–60.

Hone, J. M., and Page L. Dickinson. 1910. *Persia in Revolution.* London: T. Fisher Unwin.

Hooglund, Eric J. 1980. "Rural Participation in the Revolution." *MERIP Report,* no. 87, 3–6.

———. 1982. *Land and Revolution in Iran, 1960–1980.* Austin, Tex.: University of Texas Press.

Hottinger, Arnold. 1978. "Tehran, Iran: Portrait of a Troubled City." *Swiss Review of World Affairs,* October, 27, 29.

Hourcade, Bernard. [1987]. "L'Homme Vertical: Un Mythe, une Ville, un Divorce" (Vertical Man: A Myth, a City, a Divorce). *Autrement* (Otherwise), no. 27, Hors-Séries ("Téhéran"), 60–68.

———. 1993. "Migrations Intérieures et Changement Social en Iran" (Internal Migrations and Social Change in Iran). *Méditerranée* (Mediterranean), vol. 50, 63–69.

Hoveyda, Fereydoun. 1980. *The Fall of the Shah,* trans. Roger Liddell. New York, N.Y.: Wyndham Books.

Humayun, Daryush. 1981. *Diruz va Farda* (Yesterday and Tomorrow). United States: [No publisher indicated].

Huntington, Samuel P. 1968. *Political Order in Changing Societies.* New Haven, Conn.: Yale University Press.

Huyser, Robert E. 1986. *Mission to Tehran*. New York, N.Y.: Harper and Row.

Ikani, Azizollah. 1987. *The Dynamics of Inflation in Iran, 1960–1977*. Tilburg, the Netherlands: Tilburg University Press.

International Labour Office (ILO). 1978. *Year Book of Labour Statistics*. Geneva: International Labour Office.

International Monetary Fund. 1975–1980. *International Financial Statistics,* vols. 28–33. English ed. Washington, D.C.: International Monetary Fund.

———. 1980–1981. *International Financial Statistics Yearbook,* vols. 33–34. English ed.. Washington, D.C.: International Monetary Fund.

Ioannides, Christos P. 1984. *America's Iran: Injury and Catharsis*. Lanham, Md.: University Press of America.

Iran: Vagues d'Offensive Populaire dans Plus de 50 Villes (Iran: Waves of Popular Offensive in More than 50 Cities). 1978. Paris: Union des Étudiants Iraniens en France.

Iran Almanac. 1975, 1977. Tehran: Echo of Iran.

Iranian Oil Worker. 1979. "How We Organized [the] Strike That Paralyzed Shah's Regime." *Intercontinental Press,* January 29, 1979, 60–63.

Iranian Students for the Freedom of the Working Class. 1979. *Workers' News,* no. 2. [London?]: Iranian Students for the Freedom of the Working Class—England.

Irfani, Suroosh. 1983. *Iran's Islamic Revolution*. London: Zed Books.

Issawi, Charles, ed. 1971. *The Economic History of Iran, 1800–1914*. Chicago, Ill.: University of Chicago Press.

Izadi, Mostafa. 1983. *Gozari bar Zendegi-ye Faqih 'Aliqadr Ayatollah Montazeri* (Report on the Life of the Great Cleric Ayatollah Montazeri). Tehran: Sorush.

Jabbari, Ahmad. 1981. "Economic Factors in Iran's Revolution: Poverty, Inequality, and Inflation." Pages 163–214 in Ahmad Jabbari and Robert Olson, eds., *Iran: Essays on a Revolution in the Making*. Lexington, Ky.: Mazda Publishers.

Jacoby, Russell. 1987. *The Last Intellectuals: American Culture in the Age of Academe*. New York, N.Y.: Basic Books.

Jasper, James M. 1997. *The Art of Moral Protest: Culture, Biography, and Creativity in Social Movements*. Chicago, Ill.: University of Chicago Press.

Jatras, James George. 1999. "The Muslim Advance and American Collaboration." *Chronicles: A Magazine of American Culture,* February, 14–17.

Jazairy, Idriss, Mohiuddin Alamgir, and Theresa Panuccio. 1992. *The State of World Rural Poverty*. New York, N.Y.: New York University Press, International Fund for Agricultural Development.

Jazayeri, Ahmad. 1988. *Economic Adjustment in Oil-Based Economies*. Aldershot, England: Avebury.

Johnson, Gail Cook. 1980. *High-Level Manpower in Iran: From Hidden Conflict to Crisis*. New York, N.Y.: Praeger.

Joseph, Richard A. 1983. "Class, State, and Prebendal Politics in Nigeria." *Journal of Commonwealth and Comparative Politics*, vol. 21, 21–38.

Kamali, ʿAli. 1979. *Enqelab* (The Revolution). Tehran: Massoud Publishing House.

Kamali, Masoud. 1998. *Revolutionary Iran: Civil Society and State in the Modernization Process*. Aldershot, England: Ashgate.

Kamrava, Mehran. 1990. *Revolution in Iran: The Roots of Turmoil*. London: Routledge.

Kapuscinski, Ryszard. 1985. *Shah of Shahs*, trans. William R. Brand and Katarzyna Mroczkowska-Brand. London: Quartet Books.

Karanjia, R. K. 1977. *The Mind of a Monarch*. London: George Allen and Unwin.

Karimi-Hakkak, Ahmad. 1985. "Protest and Perish: A History of the Writers' Association of Iran." *Iranian Studies*, vol. 18, 189–229.

Karklins, Rasma, and Roger Petersen. 1993. "Decision Calculus of Protestors and Regimes." *Journal of Politics*, vol. 55, 588–615.

Karl, Terry Lynn. 1982. "The Political Economy of Petrodollars: Oil and Democracy in Venezuela." Ph.D. diss., Department of Political Science, Stanford University.

———. 1997. *The Paradox of Plenty: Oil Booms and Petro-States*. Berkeley, Calif.: University of California Press.

Karshenas, Massoud. 1990. *Oil, State and Industrialization in Iran*. Cambridge, England: Cambridge University Press.

Katouzian, Homa. 1981. *The Political Economy of Modern Iran: Despotism and Pseudo-Modernism, 1926–1979*. New York, N.Y.: New York University Press.

Kautiliya. 1972. *The Kautilîya Arthaśastra*, pt. 2, ed. R. P. Kangle. 2nd ed. Bombay: University of Bombay.

Kazemi, Farhad. 1980. *Poverty and Revolution in Iran*. New York, N.Y.: New York University Press.

Kazemzadeh, Firuz. 1968. *Russia and Britain in Persia, 1864–1914*. New Haven, Conn.: Yale University Press.

Keddie, Nikki R. 1981. *Roots of Revolution: An Interpretive History of Modern Iran*. New Haven, Conn.: Yale University Press.

———. 1982. "Comments on Skocpol." *Theory and Society*, vol. 11, 285–292.

————. 1983. "Iranian Revolutions in Comparative Perspective." *American Historical Review,* vol. 88, 579–598.

————. [1992] 1995. "Can Revolutions Be Predicted?" Pages 13–33 in *Iran and the Muslim World: Resistance and Revolution.* New York, N.Y.: New York University Press.

Ketabshenasi-ye 15 Khordad (Bibliography of June 5 [1963]). 1996. Tehran: Merkez-e Asnad-e Enqelab-e Eslami.

al-Khafaji, 'Isam. 1986. "State Incubation of Iraqi Capitalism." *MERIP Middle East Reports,* no. 142, 4–9, 12.

al-Khalil, Samir. 1989. *The Republic of Fear.* Berkeley, Calif.: University of California Press.

Khalili, Akbar. 1981. *Gam beh Gam ba Enqelab* (Step by Step with the Revolution). Tehran: Sorush.

Khalkhali, 'Ali Rabbani. 1982, 1983. *Shohada-ye Ruhaniyat-e Shi'ah dar Yek-sad Saleh-ye Akhir* (Martyrs of the Shi'i Clergy in the Past Century). 2 vols. Qom: Entesharat-e Maktab-al-Hussein.

Khomeini, Ruhollah. 1977. *Matn-e Sokhanrani* (Text of the Speech). Paris: Ruhaniyun-e Mobarez-e Iran. Reproduced in Behn, *Iranian Opposition to the Shah,* document 20:51.

————. 1978. "Ayatollah Khomeini's Letter to the Iranian People, November 12, 1977," trans. Liberation Movement of Iran. *Review of Iranian Political Economy and History* (RIPEH), vol. 2, 105–110.

Khong Cho Oon. 1986. *The Politics of Oil in Indonesia.* Cambridge, England: Cambridge University Press.

Khorsandi, Hadi. 1987. *The Ayatollah and I,* trans. Ehssan Javan. New York, N.Y.: Readers International.

Khosrokhavar, Farhad. 1979. "Le Comité dans la Révolution Iranienne: Cas d'une Ville Moyenne: Hamadan" (The Committee in the Iranian Revolution: The Case of a Mid-Sized City— Hamadan), *Peuples Méditerranéens* (Mediterranean Peoples), no. 9, 85–100.

————. 1993. "Les Femmes et la Révolution Islamique" (Women and the Islamic Revolution). *Projets Féministes* (Feminist Projects), no. 2, 83–102.

————. 1993. *Utopie Sacrifiée: Sociologie de la Révolution Iranienne* (Utopia Sacrificed: Sociology of the Iranian Revolution). Paris: Presses de la Fondation Nationale des Sciences Politiques.

————. 1997. *Anthropologie de la Révolution Iranienne* (Anthropology of the Iranian Revolution). Paris: L'Harmattan.

————. 1999. "Les Paysans Dépaysannés et la Révolution Iranienne" (Uprooted Peasants and the Iranian Revolution). *Cahiers d'Études sur la*

Méditerranée Orientale et le Monde Turco-Iranien (Annals of Studies on the Eastern Mediterranean and the Turco-Iranian World), vol. 27, 159–179.

Kian-Thiébault, Azadeh. 1998. *Secularization of Iran: A Doomed Failure? The New Middle Class and the Making of Modern Iran.* Paris: Peeters.

Kippenberg, Hans. 1981. "Jeder Tag ʿAshura, Jedes Grab Kerbala: Zur Ritualisierung der Strassenkämpfe im Iran" (Every Day ʿAshura, Every Grave Karbala: On the Ritualization of Street Fighting in Iran). Pages 217–256 in Kurt Greussing, ed., *Religion und Politik im Iran* (Religion and Politics in Iran). Frankfurt am Main: Syndikat.

Klandermans, Bert. 1984. "Mobilization and Participation: Social-Psychological Expansions of Resource Mobilization Theory." *American Sociological Review,* vol. 49, 583–600.

Kohli, K. L. 1977. *Current Trends and Patterns of Urbanization in Iran, 1956–76.* Tehran: Statistical Centre of Iran.

Kordi, Gohar. 1991. *An Iranian Odyssey.* London: Serpent's Tail.

Kraft, Joseph. 1978. "Letter from Iran." *New Yorker,* December 18, 1978, 134–168.

Kuran, Timur. 1995. *Private Truths, Public Lies: The Social Consequences of Preference Falsification.* Cambridge, Mass.: Harvard University Press.

Kurzman, Charles. 1994. "A Dynamic View of Resources: Evidence from the Iranian Revolution." *Research in Social Movements, Conflicts and Change,* vol. 17, 53–84.

———. 1996. "Structural Opportunities and Perceived Opportunities in Social-Movement Theory: Evidence from the Iranian Revolution of 1979." *American Sociological Review,* vol. 61, 153–170.

———. 1998. "Not Ready for Democracy: Theoretical and Historical Objections to the Concept of Prerequisites." *Sociological Analysis* (Tirana, Albania), vol. 1, no. 4, 1–12.

———. 1998. "Organizational Opportunity and Social Movement Mobilization: A Comparative Analysis of Four Religious Social Movements." *Mobilization,* vol. 3, 23–49.

———. 2003. "Can Understanding Undermine Explanation? The Confused Experience of Revolution." Unpublished paper.

———. 2003. "The Qum Protests and the Coming of the Iranian Revolution, 1975 and 1978." *Social Science History,* vol. 27, 287–325.

Kurzman, Charles, and Erin Leahey. 2004. "Intellectuals and Democratization, 1905–1912 and 1989–1996." *American Journal of Sociology,* vol. 109.

Kushner, Harvey W. 1996. "Suicide Bombers: Business as Usual." *Studies in Conflict and Terrorism,* vol. 19, 329–337.

Kuzichkin, Vladimir. 1990. *Inside the KGB: My Life in Soviet Espionage,* trans. Thomas B. Beattie. New York, N.Y.: Pantheon Books.

Lafue-Veron, Madeleine. 1978. *Voyage au Pays de la Peur, Iran 1978* (Voyage to the Land of Fear, Iran 1978). Geneva: Comité Suisse de Défense des Prisonniers Politiques Iraniens.

Laleh'ha-ye Enqelab: Yad-nameh-ye Shohada (The Tulips of the Revolution: Commemoration of the Martyrs). Circa 1980. [Tehran?]: Entesharat-e Anjoman-e Khedmat-e Eslami.

Laleh'ha-ye 'Eshq-Amuz (The Love-Inspiring Tulips). 1986. Tehran: Vezarat-e Amuzesh va Poruresh.

Lambton, A. K. S. 1964. "A Reconsideration of the Position of *Marja' al-Taqlid* and the Religious Institution." *Studia Islamica,* vol. 20, 115–135.

Laqueur, Walter. 1979. "Why the Shah Fell." *Commentary,* March, 47–55.

Le Bon, Gustave. [1895] 1995. *The Crowd.* New Brunswick, N.J.: Transaction Publishers.

Leon, Roberto Briceno. 1982. "The Development of Rentist Pauperism: Social Policy and Oil Revenues—Some Negative Aspects in Venezuela." *Critical Social Policy,* vol. 2, 17–23.

Lewis, Bernard. 1988. "Islamic Revolution." *New York Review of Books,* January 21, vol. 34, issue 21–22, 46–50.

Lichbach, Mark Irving. 1995. *The Rebel's Dilemma.* Ann Arbor, Mich.: University of Michigan Press.

Loeffler, Reinhold. 1988. *Islam in Practice: Religious Beliefs in a Persian Village.* Albany, N.Y.: State University of New York Press.

Looney, Robert E. 1973. *The Economic Development of Iran: A Recent Survey with Projections to 1981.* New York, N.Y.: Praeger.

MacFarquhar, Roderick. 1960. *The Hundred Flowers Campaign and the Chinese Intellectuals.* New York, N.Y.: Frederick A. Praeger.

Machiavelli, Niccolò. 1980. *The Prince,* trans. Luigi Ricci, revised by E. R. P. Vincent. New York, N.Y.: New American Library.

Macy, Michael W. 1990. "Learning Theory and the Logic of Critical Mass." *American Sociological Review,* vol. 55, 809–826.

Madelung, Wilferd. 1986. "al-Kulayni, Abu Djafar." Pages 362–363 in C. E. Bosworth et al., eds., *The Encyclopaedia of Islam,* vol. 5. Leiden: Brill.

Mahallati, Fazlollah. 1997. *Khaterat va Mobarezat-e Shahid Mahallati* (Memoirs and Struggles of the Martyr Mahallati). Tehran: Merkez-e Asnad-e Enqelab-e Eslami.

Mahdavi, 'Abdolreza Hushang. 2000. *Dar Hashiye-ye Siyasi-ye Khareji: Az Dowran-e Nehzat-e Melli ta Enqelab (1327–1359)* (On the Margins of Foreign Policy: From the Era of the National Front to the Revolution, 1948–1980). Tehran: Nashr-e Goftar.

Majd, M. G. 1989. "The Oil Boom and Agricultural Development: A Reconsideration of Agricultural Policies in Iran." *Journal of Energy and Development,* vol. 15, 125–140.

———. 1991. "The Political Economy of Land Reform in Iran." *Land Use Policy,* vol. 8, 69–76.

———. 1992. "On the Relationship between Land Reform and Rural-Urban Migration in Iran, 1966–1976." *Middle East Journal,* vol. 46, 440–455.

Majd, M. G., and V. F. Nowshirvani. 1993. "Land Reform in Iran Revisited." *Journal of Peasant Studies,* vol. 20, 442–458.

El Mallakh, Ragaei, Øysten Noreng, and Barry W. Poulson. 1984. *Petroleum and Economic Development: The Cases of Mexico and Norway.* Lexington, Mass.: Lexington Books.

Mansur, Abul Karim (pseudonym). 1979. "The Crisis in Iran: Why the United States Ignored a Quarter Century of Warning." *Armed Forces International Journal,* vol. 116, 26–33.

Marenches, Alexander de. 1988. *The Evil Empire: The Third World War Now,* interviewed by Christine Ockrent, trans. Simon Lee and Jonathan Marks. London: Sidgwick and Jackson.

Markoff, John. 1996. *The Abolition of Feudalism: Peasants, Lords, and Legislators in the French Revolution.* University Park, Penn.: Pennsylvania State University Press.

Maroun, Ibrahim. 1986. *L'Économie Pétrolière pour L'Économie de Guerre Permanente: Étude Socio-économique des Problèmes du Développement en Irak* (Oil Economy for the Economy of Permanent War: Socio-Economic Study of Development Problems in Iraq). Beirut: Publications de l'Université Libanaise, Section des Études Économiques.

Marshall, Phil. 1988. *Revolution and Counter-Revolution in Iran.* London: Bookmark.

Martin, Michael. 2000. *Verstehen: The Uses of Understanding in Social Science.* New Brunswick, N.J.: Transaction Publishers.

Marwell, Gerald, and Pamela Oliver. 1993. *The Critical Mass in Collective Action.* Cambridge, England: Cambridge University Press.

Marx, Karl, and Friedrich Engels. [1846] 1976. "The German Ideology." Pages 19–539 in *Karl Marx, Frederick Engels: Collected Works,* vol. 5. New York, N.Y.: International Publishers.

Mas'ud-Ansari, Ahmad 'Ali. 1991. *Man va Khandan-e Pahlavi* (Me and the Pahlavi Family). Tehran: Nashr-e Elborz.

McAdam, Doug. 1999. *Political Process and the Development of Black Insurgency, 1930–1970*. 2nd ed. Chicago, Ill.: University of Chicago Press.

McCarthy, John D. 1991. "Foreword." Pages xi–xviii in Clark McPhail, *The Myth of the Madding Crowd*. New York, N.Y.: Aldine de Gruyter.

McCarthy, John D., and Mayer N. Zald. 1977. "Resource Mobilization and Social Movements: A Partial Theory." *American Journal of Sociology,* vol. 82, 1212–1241.

McClelland, J. S. 1989. *The Crowd and the Mob: From Plato to Canetti*. London: Unwin Hyman.

McDaniel, Tim. 1990. *Autocracy, Modernization, and Revolution in Russia and Iran*. Princeton, N.J.: Princeton University Press.

McPhail, Clark. 1991. *The Myth of the Madding Crowd*. New York, N.Y.: Aldine de Gruyter.

Melucci, Alberto. 1989. *Nomads of the Present: Social Movements and Individual Needs in Contemporary Society*. Philadelphia, Penn.: Temple University Press.

Menashri, David. 1979. "Iran." Pages 463–512 in Colin Legum, ed., *Middle East Contemporary Survey,* vol. 2, 1977–1978. New York, N.Y.: Holmes and Meier, 1979.

———. 1990. *Iran: A Decade of War and Revolution*. New York, N.Y.: Holmes and Meier.

Milani, Abbas. 1996. *Tales of Two Cities: A Persian Memoir*. Washington, D.C.: Mage.

———. 2001. *The Persian Sphinx: Amir Abbas Hoveyda and the Riddle of the Iranian Revolution*. Washington, D.C.: Mage.

Milani, Mohsen M. 1994. *The Making of Iran's Islamic Revolution: From Monarchy to Islamic Republic*. 2nd ed., Boulder, Colo.: Westview Press.

Millward, William G. 1980. "Theoretical and Practical Grounds for Religious Opposition to Monarchy in Iran." Pages 35–64 in *L'Iran d'Hier et de Demain* (Iran of Yesterday and Tomorrow). Quebec: Collection Choix.

Mirfakhraei, Hooshmand. 1984. "The Imperial Iranian Armed Forces and the Revolution of 1978–1979." Ph.D. diss., Department of Political Science, State University of New York at Buffalo.

Mir-Hosseini, Ziba. 1999. *Islam and Gender: The Religious Debate in Contemporary Iran*. Princeton, N.J.: Princeton University Press.

Mirsepassi, Ali, and Valentine Moghadam. 1991. "The Left and Political Islam in Iran." *Radical History Review,* no. 51, 27–62.

Moaddel, Mansour. 1986. "The Shi'i Ulama and the State in Iran." *Theory and Society,* vol. 15, 519–556.

————. 1993. *Class, Politics, and Ideology in the Iranian Revolution*. New York, N.Y.: Columbia University Press.

Moghadam, Val. 1984. "Iran: Development, Revolution, and the Problem of Analysis." *Review of Iranian Political Economy and History* (RIPEH), vol. 16, 227–240.

————. "Industrial Development, Culture and Working-Class Politics: A Case Study of Tabriz Industrial Workers in the Iranian Revolution." *International Sociology*, vol. 2, 151–175.

————. 1987. "Socialism or Anti-Imperialism? The Left and Revolution in Iran." *New Left Review*, no. 166, 5–28.

————. 1997. "Gender and Revolution." Pages 137–167 in John Foran, ed., *Theorizing Revolutions*. London: Routledge.

Moin, Baqer. 1999. *Khomeini: The Life of the Ayatollah*. London: I. B. Tauris.

Mojahedin-e Khalq-e Iran (The People's Strugglers of Iran). 1979. *Barresi-ye Mohemtarin Tahavolat-e Siyasi az Nimeh-ye Khordad 57 ta Nakhost-Vaziri-ye Bakhtiar* (Analysis of the Most Important Political Developments from the Middle of June 1978 to the Prime Ministership of Bakhtiar). [Tehran?]: Sazman-e Mojahedin-e Khalq-e Iran.

Momen, Moojan. 1985. *An Introduction to Shi'i Islam*. New Haven, Conn.: Yale University Press.

Montazam, Mir Ali Asghar. 1994. *The Life and Times of Ayatollah Khomeini*. London: Anglo-European Publishing Limited.

Mooney, Chris. 2000. "For Your Eyes Only: Now That the Cold War Is Over, It's Once Again Respectable for Scholars to Work for the C.I.A., Should It Be?" *Lingua Franca*, November, 35–43.

Morad'haseli-Khameneh, A'zam. 2001. *Tabriz dar Khun* (Tabriz in Blood). Tehran: Merkez-e Asnad-e Enqelab-e Eslami.

Moradi, Reza. 1984. *Zendegi-Nameh-ye Pishvayan-e Enqelab* (Biographies of the Leaders of the Revolution). 2 vols. Tehran: Entesharat-e Kazemi.

Moradi-Nia, Muhammad Javad. 1998. *Khomein dar Enqelab* (Khomein in the Revolution). Tehran: Mo'aseseh-ye Chap va Nashr-e 'Oruj.

Morris, Aldon D. 1984. *The Origins of the Civil Rights Movement: Black Communities Organizing for Change*. New York, N.Y.: Free Press; London: Collier Macmillan.

Morris, Aldon [D.], and Naomi Braine. 2001. "Social Movements and Oppositional Consciousness." Pages 20–37 in Jane Mansbridge and Aldon Morris, eds., *Oppositional Consciousness: The Subjective Roots of Social Protest*. Chicago, Ill.: University of Chicago.

Morris, Aldon D., and Cedric Herring. 1987. "Theory and Research in Social

Movements: A Critical Review." *Annual Review of Political Science,* vol. 2, 137–198.

Moshiri, Farrokh. 1985. *The State and Social Revolution in Iran.* New York, N.Y.: Peter Lang.

Moss, Robert. 1978. "The Campaign to Destabilize Iran." *Conflict Studies,* no. 101, 3–17.

Mossavar-Rahmani, Shahin. 1987. "The Iranian Revolution and Its Theoretical Implications." Ph.D. diss., Graduate Group in International Relations, University of Pennsylvania.

Motahhari, Morteza [also spelled Motahari, Mutahhari]. 1985. *Fundamentals of Islamic Thought,* trans. R. Campbell. Berkeley, Calif.: Mizan Press.

———. 1985. "The Nature of the Islamic Revolution." Pages 201–219 in Haleh Afshar, ed., *Iran: A Revolution in Turmoil.* Albany, N.Y.: State University of New York Press.

———. 1994. *Ostad Motahhari va Rowshanfekran* (Professor Motahhari and the Intellectuals). 2nd ed. Tehran: Entesharat-e Sadra.

———. [1962] 2001. "The Fundamental Problem in the Clerical Establishment," trans. Farhad Arshad, introduction by Hamid Dabashi. Pages 161–182 in Linda S. Walbridge, ed., *The Most Learned of the Shi'a: The Institution of the Marja' Taqlid.* New York, N.Y.: Oxford University Press.

Mottahedeh, Roy. 1985. *The Mantle of the Prophet: Religion and Politics in Iran.* New York, N.Y.: Simon and Schuster.

Mottale, Morris Mehrdad. 1987. *Iran: The Political Sociology of the Islamic Revolution.* Tel Aviv: Dayan Center for Middle Eastern and African Studies, the Shiloah Institute, Tel Aviv University.

Moussavi, Ahmad Kazemi. 1985. "The Establishment of the Position of Marja'iyyat-i Taqlid in the Twelver-Shi'i Community." *Iranian Studies,* vol. 18, 35–51.

Munson, Henry, Jr. 1988. *Islam and Revolution in the Middle East.* New Haven, Conn.: Yale University Press.

Murray, J. E. (pseudonym). 1983. "The 'Deluge' Is Over: Oil Aftershock in Venezuela." *The Nation,* October 29, 1983, 394–397.

Mutz, Diana C. 1998. *Impersonal Influence: How Perceptions of Mass Collectives Affect Political Attitudes.* Cambridge, England: Cambridge University Press.

Nabard-e Tudeh'ha: Chand Gozaresh az Iran (The Struggle of the Masses: Several Reports from Iran). 1978. Frankfurt am Main: Ettehadiyeh-ye Daneshjuyan-e Irani dar Alman. Reproduced in Behn, *Iranian Opposition to the Shah,* document 20:111.

Naghizadeh, Mohammad. 1984. *The Role of Farmer's Self-Determination, Collective Action and Cooperatives in Agricultural Development: A Case Study of Iran.* Tokyo: Institute for the Study of Languages and Cultures of Asia and Africa.

Nahavandi, Firouzeh. 1988. *Aux Sources de la Révolution Iranienne* (On the Sources of the Iranian Revolution). Paris: L'Harmattan.

Nahavandi, Houchang. 1981. *Iran: Deux Rêves Brisés* (Iran: Two Broken Dreams). Paris: Albin Michel.

———. 1983. *Iran: Anatomie d'une Révolution* (Iran: Anatomy of a Revolution). Paris: S.E.G.E.P.

Najmabadi, Afsaneh. 1987. *Land Reform and Social Change in Iran.* Salt Lake City, Utah: University of Utah Press.

Naraghi, Ehsan. 1994. *From Palace to Prison: Inside the Iranian Revolution,* trans. N. Mobasser. Chicago, Ill.: Ivan R. Dee.

Nategh, Homa. 1982. "Goft-o-Shenavadi ba Rafiq Homa Nategh" (Question and Answer with Comrade Homa Nategh), *Jehan* (The World), January 2, 1982, 2–3, 12–15, 7.

Nikazmerad, Nicholas M. 1980. "A Chronological Survey of the Iranian Revolution." *Iranian Studies,* vol. 13, 327–368.

Nikbakht, Rahim, and Samad Esma'ilzadeh. 2001. *Zendegi ve Mobarezat-e Shahid Ayatollah Qazi-Tabataba'i* (The Life and Struggles of the Martyr, Ayatollah Qazi-Tabataba'i). Tehran: Merkez-e Asnad-e Enqelab-e Eslami.

Nisbett, Richard E., and Timothy D. Wilson. 1977. "Telling More than We Can Know: Verbal Reports on Mental Processes." *Psychological Review,* vol. 84, 231–259.

Nizam al-Mulk. 1960. *The Book of Government, or Rules for Kings (Siyasat-Namih),* trans. Hubert Darke. London: Routledge and Kegan Paul.

Nobari, Ali Reza, ed. 1978. *Iran Erupts.* Stanford, Calif.: Iran-American Documentation Group.

Nodjomi, Mohssen. 1986. "Dictatorship and Rise of Popular Movement: The Case of Iran." Ph.D. diss., Department of Sociology, City University of New York.

Nossiter, Bernard D. 1987. *The Global Struggle for More: Third World Conflicts with Rich Nations.* New York, N.Y.: Harper & Row.

Nurbakhsh, Sayyid Hasan. 1982. *Yad-vareh-ye Nehzat-e Eslami ta 22 Bahman* (Remembrance of the Islamic Movement up to February 11 [1979]), vol. 1. Tehran: Daftar-e Nashr-e Farhangi-ye Eslami.

Nye, Robert A. 1975. *The Origins of Crowd Psychology.* London: SAGE Publications.

Oberschall, Anthony. 1973. *Social Conflict and Social Movements.* Englewood Cliffs, N.J.: Prentice-Hall.

Olson, Mancur. 1965. *The Logic of Collective Action.* Cambridge, Mass.: Harvard University Press.

———. 1990. "The Logic of Collective Action in Soviet-Type Societies." *Journal of Soviet Nationalities,* vol. 1, no. 2, 8–27.

Opp, Karl-Dieter. 1988. "Community Integration and Incentives for Political Protest." *International Social Movement Research,* vol. 1, 83–101.

———. 1989. *The Rationality of Political Protest.* Boulder, Colo.: Westview Press.

Opp, Karl-Dieter, and Wolfgang Roehl. 1990. "Repression, Micromobilization, and Political Protest." *Social Forces,* vol. 69, 521–547.

Opp, Karl-Dieter, Peter Voss, and Christiane Gern, 1995. *Origins of a Spontaneous Revolution: East Germany, 1989.* Ann Arbor, Mich.: University of Michigan Press.

Oropeza, Luis J. 1983. *Tutelary Pluralism: A Critical Approach to Venezuelan Democracy.* Cambridge, Mass.: Harvard Studies in International Affairs.

Orren, Gary. 1997. "Fall from Grace: The Public's Loss of Faith in Government." Pages 77–107 in Joseph S. Nye, Jr., Philip D. Zelikow, and David C. King, eds., *Why People Don't Trust Government.* Cambridge, Mass.: Harvard University Press.

Pahlavi, Ashraf. 1980. *Faces in a Mirror: Memoirs from Exile.* Englewood Cliffs, N.J.: Prentice-Hall.

Pahlavi, Mohammad Reza. 1961. *Mission for My Country.* New York, N.Y.: McGraw-Hill.

———. 1980. *Answer to History.* New York, N.Y.: Stein and Day.

Paidar, Parvin. 1995. *Women and the Political Process in Twentieth-Century Iran.* Cambridge, England: Cambridge University Press.

Pakdaman, Naser. 1986. "Ta Tabriz: Nazari beh Ruyedad'ha-ye Enqelab-e Iran ta 29 Bahman 1356" (To Tabriz: A View of the Events of the Iranian Revolution up to February 18, 1978). *Cheshm-Andaz* (Perspective), no. 1, 61–94.

Parsa, Misagh. 1989. *The Social Origins of the Iranian Revolution.* New Brunswick, N.J.: Rutgers University Press.

———. 2000. *States, Ideologies, and Social Revolutions: A Comparative Analysis of Iran, Nicaragua, and the Philippines.* Cambridge, England: Cambridge University Press.

Parsons, Anthony. 1984. *The Pride and the Fall: Iran, 1974–1979.* London: Jonathan Cape.

Parsons, Talcott. 1967. *Sociological Theory and Modern Society.* New York, N.Y.: Free Press.

Parvin, Manoucher, and Amir N. Zamani. 1979. "Political Economy of Growth and Destruction: A Statistical Interpretation of the Iranian Case." *Iranian Studies,* vol. 12, 43–78.

Patriotic Muslim Students of Tabriz University. 1978. "Report on the Tabriz Uprising," trans. S. Azad. *Review of Iranian Political Economy and History* (RIPEH), vol. 2, 60–74.

Pearson, Michael. 1975. *The Sealed Train.* New York, N.Y.: Putnam.

Penn World Table (Mark 5.6). 1994. Computer-Readable Format. Cambridge, Mass.: National Bureau of Economic Research [distributor].

Perrow, Charles. 1979. "The Sixties Observed." Pages 192–211 in Mayer N. Zald and John D. McCarthy, eds., *The Dynamics of Social Movements: Resource Mobilization, Social Control, and Tactics.* Cambridge, Mass.: Winthrop Publishers.

Pesaran, M. H., and F. Gahvary. 1978. "Growth and Income Distribution in Iran." Pages 231–245 in Richard Stone and William Peterson, eds., *Econometric Contributions to Public Policy.* London: Macmillan.

Petras, James, and Morris H. Morley. 1981. "Development and Revolution: Contradictions in the Advanced Third World Countries—Brazil, South Africa, and Iran." *Studies in Comparative International Development,* vol. 16, 3–43.

Pfaff, Steven, and Guobin Yang. 2001. "Double-Edged Rituals and the Symbolic Resources of Collective Action: Political Commemorations and the Mobilization of Protest in 1989." *Theory and Society,* vol. 30, 539–589.

Philippe, Lucien. 1978. "Voices That Can't Be Ignored." *Index on Censorship,* vol. 7, 15–24.

Pinault, David. 2001. *Horse of Karbala: Muslim Devotional Life in India.* New York, N.Y.: Palgrave.

Pipes, Daniel. 1996. *The Hidden Hand: Middle East Fears of Conspiracy.* New York, N.Y.: St. Martin's Press.

Pishtazan-e Shahadat dar Enqelab-e Sevvom (The Front Ranks of Martyrdom in the Third Revolution). 1981. Qom, Iran: Daftar-e Entesharat-e Eslami.

Plan and Budget Organization. 1980. *National Census of Population and Housing, November 1976,* vol. 3, "Tehran." Tehran: Plan and Budget Organization, Statistical Center of Iran.

Pliskin, Karen L. 1980. "Camouflage, Conspiracy, and Collaborators: Rumors of the Revolution." *Iranian Studies,* vol. 13, 55–81.

Polletta, Francesca. 1997. "Culture and Its Discontents: Recent Theorizing on the Cultural Dimensions of Protest." *Sociological Inquiry,* vol. 67, 431–450.

———. 1998. "'It Was Like a Fever . . .': Narrative and Identity in Social Protest." *Social Problems,* vol. 45, 137–159.

Porter, Theodore M. 1995. *Trust in Numbers: The Pursuit of Objectivity in Science and Public Life.* Princeton, N.J.: Princeton University Press.

Posadas, J. 1980. *The Permanent Process of Revolution in Iran.* London: Scientific, Cultural and Political Editions.

Pourkarimi, Mehdi. 1980. "Iran and the Collapse of the Monarchy." Ph.D. diss., Department of Political Science, Claremont Graduate School.

Poya, Maryam. 1999. *Women, Work, and Islamism: Ideology and Resistance in Iran.* London: Zed Books.

Purbozorg-Vafi, ʿAli-Reza. 2001. *Madraseh-ye ʿEshq: Zendegi-Nameh-ye Sardar-e Rashid-e Eslam Timsar-e Sar-Lashgar-e Seyyed Musa Namjui* (School of Love: Biography of the Brave Commander of Islam, Army General Seyyed Musa Namjui). Tehran: Merkez-e Asnad-e Enqelab-e Eslami.

Qasemi, Tahmures. 2002. *Nehzat-e Emam Khomeini va Matbuʿat: Rezhim-e Shah, 1341–1357* (The Movement of Imam Khomeini and the Press: The Shah's Regime, 1962–1979). Tehran: Merkez-e Asnad-e Enqelab-e Eslami.

Quitter, Christa. 1979. *Im Frühling der Freiheit: Iranisches Tagebuch* (In the Springtime of Freedom: Iranian Diary). Frankfurt am Main: Druckladen.

Radjavi, Kazem. 1983. *La Révolution Iranienne et les Moudjahedines* (The Iranian Revolution and the Strugglers). Paris: Éditions Anthropos.

Radji, Parviz C. 1983. *In the Service of the Peacock Throne: The Diaries of the Shah's Last Ambassador to London.* London: H. Hamilton.

Rafizadeh, Mansur. 1987. *Witness: From the Shah to the Secret Arms Deal: An Insider's Account of U.S. Involvement in Iran.* New York, N.Y.: William Morrow.

Rahnema, Ali. 1998. *An Islamic Utopian: A Political Biography of Ali Shariʿati.* London: I. B. Tauris.

Rahnema, Ali, and Farhad Nomani. 1990. *The Secular Miracle: Religion, Politics and Economic Policy in Iran.* London: Zed Books.

Ram, Haggay. 1994. *Myth and Mobilization in Revolutionary Iran.* Washington, D.C.: American University Press.

Razavi, Hossein, and Firouz Vakil. 1984. *The Political Economy of Economic Planning in Iran, 1971–1983: From Monarchy to Islamic Republic.* Boulder, Colo.: Westview Press.

Razavi, Masʿud. 1997. *Hashemi va Enqelab: Tarikh-e Siyasi-ye Iran az Enqelab ta Jang* ([ʿAli Akbar] Hashemi[-Rasfanjani] and the Revolution: The Political

History of Iran from the Revolution to the War). Tehran: Entesharat-e Hamshahri.

Razi, G. Hossein. 1987. "The Nexus of Legitimacy and Performace: The Lessons of the Iranian Revolution." *Comparative Politics,* vol. 19, 453–469.

Reeves, Minou. 1986. *Behind the Peacock Throne.* London: Sidgwick and Jackson.

Rejali, Darius M. 1994. *Torture and Modernity: Self, Society, and State in Modern Iran.* Boulder, Colo.: Westview Press.

Renaerts, Monique. 1986. *La Mort, Rites et Valeurs dans l'Islam Maghrébin* (Death, Rites, and Values in Maghrebi Islam). Brussels: Université Libre de Bruxelles, Institut de Sociologie, Centre de Sociologie de l'Islam.

Renan, Ernest. [1862] 1947. "De la Part des Peuples Sémitiques dans l'Histoire de la Civilisation" (On the Role of the Semitic Peoples in the History of Civilization). Pages 317–335 in *Oeuvres Complètes de Ernest Renan* (Complete Works of Ernest Renan), vol. 2. Paris: Calmann-Livy.

Richards, Helmut. 1978. "Carter's Human Rights Policy and the Pahlavi Dictatorship." Pages 90–114 in Ali-Reza Nobari, ed., *Iran Erupts.* Stanford, Calif.: Iran-American Documentation Group.

Richardson, John M., Jr. 1987. "Violence and Repression: Neglected Factors in Development Planning." *Futures,* vol. 19, 651–668.

Rosen, Barbara, and Barry Rosen, with George Feifer. 1982. *The Destined Hour: The Hostage Crisis and One Family's Ordeal.* Garden City, N.Y.: Doubleday.

Roy, Olivier. 1994. *The Failure of Political Islam,* trans. Carol Volk. Cambridge, Mass.: Harvard University Press.

Rubin, Barry. 1981. *Paved with Good Intentions: The American Experience and Iran.* New York, N.Y.: Penguin Books.

Rucht, Dieter. 1996. "The Impact of National Contexts on Social Movement Structures: A Cross-Movement and Cross-National Comparison." Pages 185–204 in Doug McAdam, John D. McCarthy, and Mayer N. Zald, eds., *Comparative Perspectives on Social Movements.* Cambridge, England: Cambridge University Press.

Ruhani (Ziyarati), Hamid. 1982. *Barresi va Tahlili az Nehzat-e Emam Khomeini* (Explanation and Analysis of Imam Khomeini's Movement), vol. 1, 11th ed. [Tehran]: Entesharat-e Rah-e Emam.

———. 1982. *Shari'at-Madari dar Dadgah-e Tarikh* (Shari'at-Madari in the Court of History). Qom, Iran: Daftar-e Entesharat-e Eslami.

Sabahi, Farian. 2002. *The Literacy Corps in Pahlavi Iran (1963–1979).* Lugano, Switzerland: Sapiens.

Sabri-Tabrizi, Gholam-Reza. 1989. *Iran: A Child's Story, a Man's Experience.* New York, N.Y.: International Publishers.

Sachedina, Abdulaziz Abdulhussein. 1988. *The Just Ruler (al-Sultan al-ʿAdil) in Shiʿite Islam.* New York, N.Y.: Oxford University Press.

Sadri, Mahmoud, and Ahmad Sadri. 1985. "The Mantle of the Prophet: A Critical Postscript." *State, Culture and Society,* vol. 1, 136–147.

Said, Edward W. [1978] 1979. *Orientalism.* New York, N.Y.: Vintage Books.

Saikal, Amin. 1980. *The Rise and Fall of the Shah.* Princeton, N.J.: Princeton University Press.

Saint-James, Fred. 1983. *Au Nom de Dieu Clément et Miséricordeux* (In the Name of God, Benevolent and Merciful). Paris: Mercure de France.

Salehi, M. M. 1988. *Insurgency through Culture and Religion: The Islamic Revolution of Iran.* New York, N.Y.: Praeger.

Salehi-Isfahani, Djavad. 1989. "The Political Economy of Credit Subsidy in Iran, 1973–1978." *International Journal of Middle East Studies,* vol. 21, 359–379.

Sanasarian, Eliz. 1982. *The Women's Rights Movement in Iran.* New York, N.Y.: Praeger.

Sande, Hans. 1992. "Palestinian Martyr Widowhood: Emotional Needs in Conflict with Role Expectation?" *Social Science and Medicine,* vol. 34, 709–717.

Sanjabi, Karim. 1989. *Omidʾha va Na-omidiʾha: Khaterat-e Siyasi-ye Doktor Karim Sanjabi* (Hopes and Despairs: Political Memoirs of Dr. Karim Sanjabi). London: Jebhe, Entesharat-e Melliyun-e Iran.

Sarraf, Tahmoores. 1990. *Cry of a Nation: The Saga of the Iranian Revolution.* New York, N.Y.: Peter Lang.

Savory, Roger M. 1981. "The Problem of Sovereignty in an Ithna Ashari ('Twelver') Shiʿi State." Pages 129–138 in Michael Curtis, ed., *Religion and Politics in the Middle East.* Boulder, Colo.: Westview Press.

Sayyad-Shirazi, ʿAli. 1999. *Khaterat-e Amir-e Shahid Sepahbod Sayyad-Shirazi* (The Memoirs of the Martyred Commander, Lieutenant General Sayyad-Shirazi). Tehran: Merkez-e Asnad-e Enqelab-e Eslami.

Schelling, Thomas C. 1973. "Hockey Helmets, Concealed Weapons, and Daylight Saving: A Study of Binary Choices with Externalities." *Journal of Conflict Resolution,* vol. 17, 381–428.

Scherr, Sara J. 1989. "Agriculture in an Export Boom Economy: A Comparative Analysis of Policy and Performance in Indonesia, Mexico and Nigeria." *World Development,* vol. 17, 543–560.

Schiller, James William. 1986. "State Formation in New Order Indonesia: The Powerhouse State in Jakarta." Ph.D. diss., Monash University.

Scott, James C. 1990. *Domination and the Arts of Resistance: Hidden Transcripts.* New Haven, Conn.: Yale University Press.

Scoville, James G. 1985. "The Labor Market in Pre-Revolutionary Iran." *Economic Development and Cultural Change,* vol. 34, 143–155.

Selbin, Eric. 1999. *Modern Latin American Revolutions.* 2nd ed. Boulder, Colo.: Westview Press.

Semkus, Charles I. 1980. *The Fall of Iran, 1978–1979.* 2 vols. New York, N.Y.: Copen Press.

Shahbazi, ʿAli. 1998. *Mohafez-e Shah: Khaterat-e ʿAli Shahbazi* (The Shah's Bodyguard: Memoirs of ʿAli Shahbazi). Tehran: Entesharat-e Ahl-e Qalam.

Shahid Doktor Bahonar, Olgu-ye Honar-e Moqavamat (The Martyr Dr. Bahonar, a Model of the Art of Resistance). 1983. Vol. 1. Tehran: Vahid-e Farhangi-ye Bonyad-e Shahid-e Enqelab-e Eslami.

Shahidian, Hammed. 2002. *Women in Iran: Gender Politics in the Islamic Republic.* Westport, Conn.: Greenwood Press.

Shah's Inferno: Abadan, Aug. 19, 1978. 1978. Berkeley, Calif.: Iranian Students Association in the United States.

Shakeri, Ramazan ʿAli. 1980. *Enqelab-e Eslami-ye Mardom-e Mashhad az Aghaz ta Esteqrar-e Jomhuri-ye Eslami* (The Islamic Revolution of the People of Mashhad from the Beginning to the Founding of the Islamic Republic). Mashhad, Iran: Part-e Grafik-e Mashhad.

Shariʿati, ʿAli. [1971] 1986. "Where Shall We Begin?" Page 128 in Farhang Rajaee, ed., *What Is to Be Done.* Houston, Tex.: Institute for Research and Islamic Studies.

Shariʿatzadeh, Mehdi. 1979. *Az Fayziyeh ta Jomhuri-ye Eslami* (From Fayziyeh [Seminary] to the Islamic Republic). Tehran: Merkez-e Entesharat-e Aʿlami.

Sharif, Jaʿfar. [1921] 1975. *Islam in India.* London: Curzon Press.

Sharifpur, Reza. 2001. *Masjed va Enqelab-e Eslami* (The Mosque and the Islamic Revolution). Tehran: Merkez-e Asnad-e Enqelab-e Eslami.

Sharp, Gene. 1973. *The Politics of Nonviolent Action.* Boston, Mass.: Porter Sargent.

Shayegan, Daryush. 1986. "The Formative Rhythm of Persian Space." Pages 9–25 in Mehdi Khansari and Minouch Yavari, *Espace Persan: Architecture Traditionelle en Iran* (Persian Space: Traditional Architecture in Iran). Brussels: Pierre Mardaga.

Sheikholeslami, Ali Reza. 1980–1981. "Roots of Contemporary Iranian Politics." *The Turkish Yearbook of International Relations,* vol. 20, 273–287.

Siad-Shirazi, ʿAli. 1999. *Khaterat-e Amir Shahid Sepahbod Siad-Shirazi* (Memoirs of the Martyred Commander, Lieutenant General Siad-Shirazi). Tehran: Merkez-e Asnad-e Enqelab-e Eslami.

Siavoshi, Sussan. 1990. *Liberal Nationalism in Iran: The Failure of a Movement.* Boulder, Colo.: Westview Press.

Sick, Gary. 1985. *All Fall Down: America's Tragic Encounter with Iran.* New York, N.Y.: Random House.

Sighele, Scipio. 1898. "Contre le Parlementarisme" (Against Parliamentarism). Pages 185–228 in *Psychologie des Sectes* (Psychology of Sects). Paris: V. Giard & E. Brière.

Simpson, John. 1988. *Behind Iranian Lines.* London: Robson Books.

Skocpol, Theda. 1979. *States and Social Revolutions.* Cambridge, England: Cambridge University Press.

———. 1982. "Rentier State and Shiʿa Islam in the Iranian Revolution." *Theory and Society,* vol. 11, 265–283.

Slovic, Paul. 1995. "The Construction of Preference." *American Psychologist,* vol. 50, 364–371.

Smith, Benjamin B. 2002. "Hard Times in the Land of Plenty: Oil Wealth and Opposition in Late Developing States." Ph.D. diss., Department of Political Science, University of Washington.

Snow, David A., and Susan E. Marshall. 1984. "Cultural Imperialism, Social Movements, and the Islamic Revival." *Research in Social Movements, Conflicts, and Change,* vol. 7, 131–152.

Sobel, Jordan Howard. 1990. "Maximization, Stability of Decision, and Actions in Accordance with Reason." *Philosophy of Science,* vol. 57, 60–77.

Soloway, Irving H. 1980. "The Politicization of a Provincial Iranian City." *Conflict,* vol. 2, 333–350.

Sreberny-Mohammadi, Annabelle, and Ali Mohammadi. 1994. *Small Media, Big Revolution: Communication, Culture, and the Iranian Revolution.* Minneapolis, Minn.: University of Minnesota Press.

Statistical Centre of Iran. 1978. *Population Growth Survey of Iran: Final Report, 1973–1976.* Tehran: Plan and Budget Organization.

Stempel, John D. 1981. *Inside the Iranian Revolution.* Bloomington, Ind.: Indiana University Press.

Stigler, George J., and Gary S. Becker. 1977. "De Gustibus Non Est Disputandum." *American Economic Review,* vol. 67, 76–90.

Stouffer, Samuel A., et al. 1949. *The American Soldier,* vol. 2, *Combat and Its Aftermath.* Princeton, N.J.: Princeton University Press.

Sullivan, William H. 1981. *Mission to Iran.* New York, N.Y.: W. W. Norton.

———. 1984. *Obbligato, 1939–1979: Notes on a Foreign Service Career.* New York, N.Y.: W. W. Norton.

Summers, Robert, and Alan Heston. 1991. "The Penn World Table (Mark 5):

An Expanded Set of International Comparisons, 1950–1988." *Quarterly Journal of Economics,* vol. 106, 327–368.

Swearingen, Will. 1990. "The Algerian Food Security Crisis." *Middle East Report,* no. 166, 21–25.

Swidler, Ann. 1986. "Culture in Action: Symbols and Strategies." *American Sociological Review,* vol. 51, 273–286.

Tabari, Azar. 1983. "The Role of the Clergy in Modern Iranian Politics." Pages 47–72 in Nikki R. Keddie, ed., *Religion and Politics in Iran.* New Haven, Conn.: Yale University Press.

Tabataba'i, Mohammad Hossein, et al. 1962. *Bahsi Dar-bareh-ye Marjaʿiyat va Ruhaniyat* (A Discussion of Religious Leadership and Religious Scholars). Tehran: Sherkat-e Sehami-ye Enteshar.

Taheri, Amir. 1986. *The Spirit of Allah: Khomeini and the Islamic Revolution.* Bethesda, Md.: Adler and Adler.

Taleqani, Mahmud. 1979. *Az Azadi ta Shahadat* (From Liberation to Martyrdom). Tehran: Abu Zarr.

Tarrow, Sidney. 1998. *Power in Movement: Social Movements and Contentious Politics*. 2nd ed. Cambridge, England: Cambridge University Press.

Taylor, Michael. 1989. "Structure, Culture and Action in the Explanation of Social Change." *Politics and Society,* vol. 17, 115–162.

Tehranian, Majid. 1980. "Communication and Revolution in Iran: The Passing of a Paradigm." *Iranian Studies,* vol. 13, 5–30.

Thaiss, Gustav. 1971. "The Bazaar as a Case Study of Religious and Social Change." Pages 189–216 in Ehsan Yar-Shater, ed., *Iran Faces the Seventies.* New York, N.Y.: Praeger.

———. 1972. "Religious Symbolism and Social Change: The Drama of Husain." Pages 349–366 in Nikki R. Keddie, ed., *Scholars, Saints, and Sufis.* Berkeley, Calif.: University of California Press.

Thompson, E. P. [1963] 1966. *The Making of the English Working Class.* New York, N.Y.: Anchor Books.

Tilgner, Ulrich, ed. 1979. *Umbruch im Iran: Augenzeugenberichte—Analysen—Dokumente* (Breakdown in Iran: Eyewitness Reports, Analyses, Documents). Hamburg: Rowohlt Taschenbuch Verlag.

Tilly, Charles. 1978. *From Mobilization to Revolution.* Reading, Mass.: Addison-Wesley.

———. 1995. "Contentious Repertoires in Britain, 1758–1834." Pages 15–42 in Mark Traugott, ed., *Repertoires and Cycles of Collective Action.* Durham, N.C.: Duke University Press.

———. 1995. "To Explain Political Processes." *American Journal of Sociology,* vol. 100, 1594–1610.

Tlemcani, Rachid, and William W. Hansen. 1989. "Development and the

State in Post-Colonial Algeria." *Journal of Asian and African Studies,* vol. 24, 114–133.

Tocqueville, Alexis de. [1858] 1955. *The Old Regime and the French Revolution,* trans. Stuart Gilbert. Garden City, N.Y.: Doubleday Anchor.

Truth and Reconciliation Commission of South Africa Report. 1998. Cape Town: The Commission.

Tullock, Gordon. 1971. "The Paradox of Revolution." *Public Choice,* vol. 11, 89–99.

Turner, Ralph H., and Lewis M. Killian. 1957. *Collective Behavior.* Englewood Cliffs, N.J.: Prentice-Hall.

———. 1972. *Collective Behavior.* 2nd ed. Englewood Cliffs, N.J.: Prentice-Hall.

———. 1987. *Collective Behavior.* 3rd ed. Englewood Cliffs, N.J.: Prentice-Hall.

Tversky, Amos, Paul Slovic, and Daniel Kahneman. 1990. "The Causes of Preference Reversal." *American Economic Review,* vol. 80, 204–217.

Ullman, Richard H. 1972. *Anglo-Soviet Relations, 1917–1920,* vol. 3, *The Anglo-Soviet Accord.* Princeton, N.J.: Princeton University Press.

UNESCO. 1980. *Statistical Yearbook 1980.* Paris: United Nations Economic, Social, and Cultural Organisation.

Union des Étudiants Iraniens en France. 1978. *Iran: Vagues d'Offensive Populaire dans Plus de 50 Villes* (Iran: Wave of Popular Offensive in More Than 50 Cities). Paris: Union des Étudiants Iraniens en France. Reproduced in Behn, *Iranian Opposition to the Shah,* document 20:73.

United States Arms Control and Disarmament Agency. 1979. *World Military Expenditures and Arms Transfers, 1968–1977.* Washington, D.C.: United States Arms Control and Disarmament Agency.

United States House of Representatives. 1973. *New Perspectives on the Persian Gulf.* Committee on Foreign Affairs, Subcommittee on the Near East and South Asia, hearings of June 6, July 17, 23, and 24, and November 28, 1973. Washington, D.C.: U.S. Government Printing Office.

———. 1977. *Human Rights in Iran.* Committee on International Relations, Subcommittee on International Organizations, hearing of October 26, 1977. Washington, D.C.: U.S. Government Printing Office.

———. 1977. *Review of Recent Developments in the Middle East.* Committee on International Relations, Subcommittee on Europe and the Middle East, hearing of June 8, 1977. Washington, D.C.: U.S. Government Printing Office.

———. 1978. *Foreign Assistance Legislation for Fiscal Year 1979 (Part 4).* Committee on International Relations, Subcommittee on International Organizations, hearing of February 28, 1978. Washington, D.C.: U.S. Government Printing Office.

———. 1979. *Iran: Evaluation of U.S. Intelligence Performance Prior to November 1978*. Report of the Permanent Select Committee on Intelligence, Subcommittee on Evaluation. Washington, D.C.: U.S. Government Printing Office.

Vahabzadeh, Peyman. 2003. *Articulated Experiences: Toward a Radical Phenomenology of Contemporary Social Movements*. Albany, N.Y.: State University of New York Press.

Vakil, Firouz. 1976. "Iran's Basic Macro-Economic Problems: A Twenty-Year Horizon." Pages 83–104 in Jane W. Jacqz, ed., *Iran: Past, Present and Future*. New York, N.Y.: Aspen Institute for Humanistic Studies.

———. 1976. "A Macro-Econometric Projection for Iran." Pages 291–332 in Khodadad Farmanfarmaian, ed., *The Social Sciences and Problems of Development*. Princeton, N.J.: Princeton University Program in Near Eastern Studies.

Vance, Cyrus. 1983. *Hard Choices: Critical Years in American Foreign Policy.* New York, N.Y.: Simon and Schuster.

Varjavand, Parviz. 1993. *Yad-nameh-ye Doktor Gholam-Hossein Sadiqi* (Commemoration of Dr. Gholam-Hossein Sadiqi). Tehran: Chapakhsh.

Vieille, Paul. 1979. "Transformations des Rapports Sociaux et Révolution en Iran" (Transformations of Social Relations and Revolution in Iran). *Peuples Méditerranéens* (Mediterranean Peoples), no. 8, 25–58.

Vieille, Paul, and Farhad Khosrokhavar. 1990. *Le Discours Populaire de la Révolution Iranienne* (Popular Discourse of the Iranian Revolution). 2 vols. Paris: Contemporanéité.

Voltaire, François Marie Arouet de. [1741] 1877. "Le Fanatisme, ou Mahomet le Prophète: Tragédie en Cinq Actes" (Fanaticism, or Muhammad the Prophet: A Tragedy in Five Acts). Pages 91–167 in *Oeuvres Complètes de Voltaire* (Complete Works of Voltaire), vol. 4. Paris: Garnier Frères.

Walbridge, Linda S., ed. 2001. *The Most Learned of the Shi'a: The Institution of the Marja' Taqlid*. New York, N.Y.: Oxford University Press.

Wegner, Daniel M. 2002. *The Illusion of Conscious Will*. Cambridge, Mass.: MIT Press.

Weinbaum, M. G. 1977. "Agricultural Policy and Development Politics in Iran." *Middle East Journal,* vol. 31, 434–450.

Wickham, Carrie Rosefsky. 2002. *Mobilizing Islam: Religion, Activism and Political Change in Egypt*. New York, N.Y.: Columbia University Press.

Wiktorowicz, Quintan. 2001. *The Management of Islamic Activism: Salafis, the Muslim Brotherhood, and State Power in Jordan*. Albany, N.Y.: State University of New York Press.

Wilber, Donald N. 1969. *Clandestine Service History: Overthrow of Premier Mossadeq of Iran, November 1952–August 1953*. [Langley, Virginia?]: Central Intelligence Agency, CS Historical Paper, no. 208. Published on the *New York Times* website, *http://www.nytimes.com/library/world/mideast/iran-cia-intro.pdf*, June 16, 2000.

Wilson, Timothy D. 2002. *Strangers to Ourselves: Discovering the Adaptive Unconscious*. Cambridge, Mass.: Harvard University Press.

Winch, Peter. 1958. *The Idea of a Social Science*. London: Routledge & Kegan Paul.

Woodward, Bob. 1987. *Veil: The Secret Wars of the C.I.A., 1981–1987*. New York, N.Y.: Simon and Schuster.

World Bank. 1979, 1980. *World Development Report 1979* and *1980*. Washington, D.C.: The World Bank.

World Income Inequality Database. 1999. Version Beta 3. Helsinki: United Nations University, World Institute for Development Economics Research; New York, N.Y.: United Nations Development Programme.

Wriggins, W. Howard. 1969. *The Ruler's Imperative: Strategies for Political Survival in Asia and Africa*. New York, N.Y.: Columbia University Press.

Yazdi, Ebrahim. 1984. *Akharin Talash'ha dar Akharin Ruz'ha* (The Final Efforts in the Final Days). Tehran: Entesharat-e Qalam, 1363.

Zabih, Sepehr. 1979. *Iran's Revolutionary Upheaval*. San Francisco, Calif.: Albany Press.

———. 1988. *The Iranian Military in Revolution and War*. London: Routledge.

Zahedi, Dariush. 2000. *The Iranian Revolution Then and Now*. Boulder, Colo.: Westview Press.

Zakir, Nazir Ahmad. 1988. *Notes on Iran: Aryamehr to Ayatollah*. Karachi, Pakistan: Royal Book Co.

Zald, Mayer N. 1992. "Looking Backward to Look Forward: Reflections on the Past and Future of the Resource Mobilization Research Program." Pages 326–348 in Aldon D. Morris and Carol McClurg Mueller, eds., *Frontiers in Social Movement Theory*. New Haven, Conn.: Yale University Press.

Zolberg, Aristide R. 1971. "Moments of Madness." *Politics and Society,* vol. 2, 183–207.

Zonis, Marvin. 1971. *The Political Elite of Iran*. Princeton, N.J.: Princeton University Press.

———. 1991. "Autobiography and Biography in the Middle East." Pages 60–88 in Martin Kramer, ed., *Middle Eastern Lives: The Practice of Biography and Self-Narrative*. Syracuse, N.Y.: Syracuse University Press.

———. 1991. *Majestic Failure: The Fall of the Shah*. Chicago, Ill.: University of Chicago Press.

Acknowledgments

I thank my interview respondents for their willingness to discuss their lives with an imperfect stranger. I also thank my dissertation committee—Hamid Algar, Victoria Bonnell (chair), Neil Smelser, and Kim Voss—for their support. I am grateful to the institutions that have funded various phases of the research: the National Science Foundation Graduate Fellowships, the University of California at Berkeley, the Phi Beta Kappa Dissertation Award, Georgia State University, and the University of North Carolina at Chapel Hill. Dozens of libraries and archives, including the Foundation for Iranian Studies, the Iranian Oral History Project at Harvard University, the Hoover Institution at Stanford University, and many, many offices of interlibrary borrowing were invaluable to my research. Numerous teachers, friends, and colleagues provided welcome assistance and encouragement, among them Yashar Afshar, Betigül Argun, Said Arjomand, Ahmad Ashraf, Shaul Bakhash, Deborah Barrett, Assef Bayat, James Bill, Jason Brownlee, Peter Chelkowski, Carl Ernst, Michael Fischer, Willem Floor, Jeff Goodwin, Patrick Heller, James Jasper, Bruce Lawrence, Akbar Mahdi, John Markoff, John Martin, Valentine Moghadam, Afsaneh Najmabadi, Margaret Phillips, Jaleh Pirnazar, Ahmad Sadri, Mahmoud Sadri, Wheeler Thackston, Judith Vichniac, Quintan Wiktorowicz, and several persons in Iran who must remain anonymous. As it is said in the Middle East, may my life be sacrificed for your sake.

Index